Modern Secondary Education

MORRIS GALL
Norwalk, Connecticut, Public Schools

WILLIAM V. HICKS
Michigan State University

AMERICAN BOOK COMPANY

NEW YORK

Preface

MODERN SECONDARY EDUCATION is a basic text in the principles and practices of today's secondary school. We attempt to give the comprehensive picture every prospective secondary-school teacher will need, whether he teaches English, physical education, science, or any other subject or combination of subjects.

Secondary education in the United States has undergone tremendous changes during the last decade. If he is to understand the vast education system of which he is to become a part, the prospective teacher needs to see these changes in context, and so we trace the transformation of the American secondary school from a college-preparatory institution to a school for all the children of all the people.

The prospective teacher needs an overall view, a configuration, of the world in which he will be working. This is the subject of Part I, where we discuss the program—the tasks—of the secondary school and its curriculum. Here too we discuss the colleagues with whom the teacher will be working and those other colleagues in the teaching-learning process, the students he will have. Thus, the attempt is made to give a descriptive analysis of the personnel (in the widest sense of that term) and the content, both formal and informal, of the secondary school.

The prospective teacher needs to know, too, how education in the secondary school comes about. Part II takes up methods and process—including kinds of planning, presentation, testing, and evaluation—not only for his own subject but for all subjects.

In both Part I and Part II we hope to instill an awareness of the whole content and method of secondary education which will save the teacher from the provincialism that lessens the value of teaching no matter how otherwise skillful it may be.

No teacher is fully effective unless he knows how to work with the school administration as part of the educational team, and unless he understands the function of the school as an institution in the life of the community. These are the concerns of Part III.

Finally, we take up again the story of secondary education as part of the stream of American life, and we attempt to analyze trends as they project into the future. The objective here is to develop a flexible point of view, to prepare the prospective teacher who has learned to feel at home in the school of today to be equally at home in the school of tomorrow.

The questions "for deliberation and discussion" have been selected from those which the authors have found important in their own secondary teaching and useful and stimulating in the classes they have conducted in colleges and universities. The bibliographies are carefully selective for maximum interest and utility at this stage of the student's development.

The authors have drawn liberally on the research of others, and we wish to acknowledge our indebtedness to them and their publishers for permission to quote from their work. We also wish to express our appreciation to our colleagues in the public schools of Norwalk, Connecticut and in the College of Education at Michigan State University for their encouragement during the writing of this book.

M. G.
W. V. H.

Contents

PART IV: THE FUTURE OF SECONDARY EDUCATION

PART I: THE MODERN SECONDARY SCHOOL

1 The Task of The Modern Secondary School

THE AMERICAN PUBLIC HIGH SCHOOL: A UNIQUE INSTITUTION

The American public high school of the second half of the twentieth century is unique. Nowhere in history is its counterpart to be found. No other society has ever attempted to provide for each child—girl and boy, rich and poor, native and alien, gifted and retarded—a continuing education through the twelfth grade.

In every state this education is not only available but compulsory, though the legal requirements for attendance vary from state to state. In thirty-two states attendance is compulsory for children from seven to sixteen; in seven states from eight to sixteen; and in Ohio from six to eighteen.[1] In 1962–1963, the total school-age population (children ages five through seventeen) was 46,495,585, and there was an actual school enrollment of 45,333,196 or 98.5 percent. The enrollment in grades nine to twelve was 9,785,000 or approximately 84 percent of that group.

---

[1] The State of Oregon even attempted to make attendance in public schools compulsory, but the United States Supreme Court in *Pierce, et al.* v. *Society of Sisters*, 268, U.S. 510 (1925) declared this statute unconstitutional, so that while education is compulsory, attendance in approved private schools, secular or denominational, is permissible.

(Of these, 1,102,500 were enrolled in the non-public secondary schools.)

High-School Enrollment

The number of students attending high school has mounted steadily since 1880 (except during World War II), and the ratio of high-school students to the school-age population of fourteen to seventeen is expected to continue to rise. (See Figure 1 and Tables 1 and 2.)

The decline in high-school enrollment in the 1940's resulted from the decline in the birth rate during the depression of the 1930's and the heavy dropout rate caused by enlistment of high-school boys in the armed services and the expanded employment opportunities of the 1940's. Enrollment has gone up

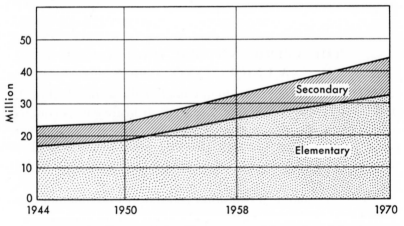

Figure 1. Enrollment in Public Elementary and Secondary Schools: 1944–1970[2]

in the 1950's and 1960's because these factors have been reversed. The current trend indicates that during the next decade the percentage of students in the fourteen to seventeen age group attending school will approximate the almost universal attendance in the elementary school.[3] It is estimated that by 1970 the per-

[2] *Ibid.*, p. 75.
[3] NEA, *Research Bulletin*, 7, No. 3 (October, 1959). See also NEA, *Research Report, Status and Trends: Vital Statistics, Education, and Public Finance* (Washington, D.C.: 1959–R13).

centage of adolescents attending school will be approximately 90 percent (almost 15 million) of the total eligible.[4]

Continuous progress in the elementary school, strengthening of compulsory secondary education, social pressure toward schooling beyond the eighth grade, industry's demands for educated workers, and restrictions on child labor have all combined to increase the percentage of the adolescent population attending secondary school. The increased holding power of the high school can be attributed to the vastly improved program offered by the high schools to make schooling more practical for potential dropouts.[6] Together with the population explosion these

TABLE 1

Enrollment in Elementary and Secondary Schools,
by Level and Control, 1900 to 1970 (In thousands)[5]

School year ended	Public-school enrollment			Private-school enrollment		
	K–8	9–12	Total	K–8	9–12	Total
1900	14,984	519	15,503	1,241	111	1,352
1910	16,899	915	17,814	1,558	117	1,675
1920	19,378	2,200	21,578	1,486	214	1,700
1930	21,279	4,399	25,678	2,310	341	2,651
1940	18,833	6,601	25,434	2,153	458	2,611
1944	17,713	5,554	23,267	2,179	477	2,656
1946	17,678	5,622	23,300	2,373	615	2,988
1948	18,291	5,653	23,944	2,538	629	3,190
1950	19,464	5,752	25,216	2,735	681	3,416
1952	20,770	5,908	26,678	3,177	665	3,842
1954	22,649	6,315	28,964	3,613	756	4,369
1956	24,413	6,901	31,314	3,904	834	4,738
1958	25,801	7,895	33,696	4,319	938	5,257
1960	27,602	8,485	35,087	4,640	1,035	5,675
*1961	28,400	8,900	37,300	4,900	1,100	6,000
*1962	28,700	9,500	38,200	5,100	1,200	6,300
*1963	29,400	10,300	39,700	5,400	1,300	6,700
**1964	30,000	10,300	40,900	5,500	1,400	6,900
**1965	30,500	11,400	41,900	5,600	1,400	7,000
**1966	31,000	11,600	42,600	5,700	1,400	7,100
**1967	31,500	11,800	43,300	5,800	1,500	7,300
**1968	32,000	12,000	44,000	5,800	1,600	7,400
**1969	32,400	12,400	44,800	5,900	1,600	7,500
**1970	32,800	12,800	45,600	6,000	1,600	7,600

* Estimated.
** Projected.
[4] *Ibid.*, p. 25.
[5] U.S. Office of Education publications.
[6] NEA, *Research Bulletin,* p. 77. See also Office of Education, *Survival Rates of Pupils,* 1941 and NEA, *School Retention Rates* (January, 1960).

TABLE 2

Total School Enrollment, and Total and Public-School
Enrollments as Percents of Population 5–17 Years of Age, 1900–1970[7]

School year ended	Total school enrollment (thousands)	Total school enrollment as percent of population 5–17 years	Public-school enrollment as percent of population 5–17 years
1900	16,855	78.3%	72.0%
1910	19,489	79.9	73.0
1920	23,279	83.2	77.1
1930	28,361	89.6	81.2
1940	28,044	94.1	85.4
1946	26,288	92.2	81.7
1948	27,134	93.7	82.7
1950	28,632	93.2	82.1
1952	30,520	91.9	80.4
1954	33,333	92.7	80.5
1956	36,052	93.0	80.8
1958	38,953	93.2	80.6
1960	40,762	92.3	79.5
1961	43,300	95.6	82.4
1962	44,500	95.4	81.9
1965	48,900	98.4	84.3
1970	53,200	98.0	84.0

trends are increasing the numbers in our secondary schools to unprecedented totals.

Although the high-school retention rate is increasing, it is not causing a comparable decrease in the number of high-school dropouts. In April, 1963, the number of fifteen-year-olds was 3.6 million; sixteen-year-olds, 3.5 million; and seventeen-year-olds 2.7 million. If the dropout rate is assumed to be 25 percent, then 700,000 would have dropped out of the seventeen-year-old group, and 900,000 would drop out next year, when this year's sixteen-year-olds turn seventeen. In fact, over a two-year period, the dropout rate would have to decrease by 5 percent to stabilize the number of dropouts. Thus the dropout rate is decreasing slowly, while the numbers in the age groups are increasing rapidly.[8]

[7] Based on U.S. Office of Education and U.S. Department of Commerce, Bureau of the Census data.
[8] NEA, *School Dropouts*, Research Memorandum 1963–10 (April, 1963).

In 1950, 9,650,000 students were enrolled in public schools in grades seven to twelve. We estimate that in 1965 over 15,000,000 will be enrolled in grades seven through twelve, and by 1970 that this figure will increase to over 17,000,000. If, at the same time, the holding power of the secondary schools continues to increase to a point where 80 percent of the sixth grade finishes school instead of 60 percent, the total estimated enrollment could well reach 24,000,000 by 1970 for the upper six years compared to over 12,000,000 today.[9]

DEVELOPMENT OF THE
AMERICAN SECONDARY SCHOOL

School enrollments were not always so heavy. The pioneer, concerned with taming and settling a continent, found little time or need for learning. Hence, for more than two centuries, the traditional schooling of American youth was confined to the three R's. As Dr. Charles R. Keller has observed:

> Since the secondary school during much of our history has really been secondary, the chapter order in Samuel Eliot Morison's *The Puritan Pronaos* is appropriate, and not just the result of his being a Harvard man. A chapter on "The Beginnings of Higher Education" comes first, then a chapter entitled "The Elementary Schools," and finally one on secondary schools under their seventeenth century name, "The Public Grammar Schools."[10]

Colonial Secondary Schools

The need for ministers provided the exception which gave rise to our first colleges and then to preparatory schools, our earliest secondary schools. But since only people of means could afford to educate a son for the ministry, Colonial secondary schooling was reserved to a very small percentage of the population.

The Latin Grammar School of Boston, which began in 1635, and similar institutions in other New England cities, were complemented in the Southern colonies by tutorial schools or private

[9] Stanton Legett, "Tangible and Intangible Controls," *The American Secondary School* (New York: College Entrance Examination Board, 1959), p. 25.
[10] Charles R. Keller, "Origins and History of the Secondary School," in *The American Secondary School*, p. 2.

tutors.[11] Thomas Jefferson, for example, studied under a private tutor and went on to William and Mary College. Benjamin Franklin received only the most rudimentary schooling but entered a vocation (printing) which gave his fertile mind a chance to develop. Whether an education was acquired on the job or in college, formal schooling did not extend beyond the teens. Jefferson was graduated from William and Mary at nineteen, Gouverneur Morris from Kings College at sixteen, John Hancock from Harvard at seventeen, and Ralph Waldo Emerson from Harvard at eighteen.

It was Franklin who first saw the need for a "practical" education which would prepare young men for vocations other than the ministry. He recognized that skilled surveyors, mechanics, farmers, and seamen were a necessity. The Academy, based on a proposal which Franklin drew up in 1743, opened in Philadelphia in 1749. It was financed by private endowment and proved tremendously popular, developing in Franklin's lifetime into the University of Pennsylvania.

In one sense the Academy may be considered the forerunner of our technical high school. Its curriculum emphasized mathematics and science in contrast with the emphasis on humanities in the grammar schools. However, both schools were designed for the few—boys of the upper-middle class. Thus, at the beginning of the nineteenth century barely one child in a hundred received more than a rudimentary formal education.[12]

Beginning of the Public Secondary School

The first public secondary school in America was established by law in Boston in 1821. The Massachusetts education law of 1827 was widely copied and became the major impetus to the establishment of other public secondary schools. The law required every town of five hundred families to provide instruction in American history, algebra, geometry, bookkeeping, and

---

[11] See the description of a private tutorial school in colonial Williamsburg in Elswyth Thane's *Dawn's Early Light* (New York: Duell, Sloan, and Pearce, 1943). The author throws much light on colonial attitudes toward the education of girls.

[12] It was not until 1805, with the establishment of the Free School Society in New York under DeWitt Clinton as president of the board, that the free school system was launched in America.

surveying in addition to the basic elementary subjects. Towns of four thousand families were required to provide instruction in general history, rhetoric, logic, Latin, and Greek.[13]

Secondary education for girls developed simultaneously but separately. (Co-education on the secondary level is largely a twentieth-century phenomenon.) In enrollment, girls' education lagged far behind that for boys, and in curriculum it tended to emphasize the humanities and to neglect science and mathematics. By 1910, however, the percentage of girls in day high schools had exceeded that of boys, and it has remained at 50 percent or more during almost all of the past half-century.[14]

The American High School in the Twentieth Century

Beginning in 1880, high-school enrollments doubled every ten years until 1930. Table 3 shows a steady increase in the ratio of high-school enrollment to population fourteen to seventeen years of age, from 11.4 percent in 1900 to an estimate of about 85 percent in 1965. The projection is that at least 90 percent of our teenagers will be enrolled in secondary schools by 1970.

In addition to the increase in enrollment the number of days in the school year has grown from 144.6 days in 1890 to 178.6 days in 1950.[15] At present there are slightly more than 180 days in the average secondary-school year. The average length of the public-school term increased seven weeks from 1900 to 1954: it was twenty-nine weeks in 1900 and almost thirty-six weeks in 1954. Paralleling the lengthened school year was the rise in school attendance during this time. Attendance increased to almost thirty-two weeks in 1954,[16] from less than twenty weeks out of the year in 1900. In 1964 attendance is thirty-six weeks. At the same time the number of high schools has increased from less than 2,500 in 1890 to more than 30,000 today.[17]

---

[13] Adolphe E. Meyer, *An Educational History of the American People* (New York: McGraw-Hill, 1957), p. 191.

[14] The United States Office of Education report of 1961 indicates that for the first time in the history of its periodic surveys, more men than women were teaching and more boys than girls were enrolled in the secondary schools.

[15] Isaac L. Kandel, *American Education in the Twentieth Century* (Cambridge: Harvard U. Press, 1957), p. 77.

[16] *Status and Trends*, p. 12.

[17] American Association of School Administrators, *The High School in a Changing World* (Washington, D.C.: NEA, 1958), p. 35.

TABLE 3

School and College Enrollments as Percents of
School- and College-Age Populations[18]

School year ended	Percent secondary-school enrollment is of population 14–17 years	Percent higher education enrollment is of population 18–21 years
1900	11.4%	
1910	15.4	
1920	32.3	
1930	51.4	
1940	73.3	
1942	71.1	
1944	63.8	
1946	68.9	22.1%
1947		25.2
1948	71.3	26.3
1949		27.2
1950	76.8	25.5
1951		24.0
1952	77.5	25.0
1953		26.4
1954	80.2	29.0
1955		31.2
1956	84.4	33.5
1957		34.3
1958	87.5	36.0
1959		36.6
1960	86.1	37.5
1961		37.7
1962	90.0	38.9

The vast increase in secondary attendance is attributable to a number of factors. The population trend indicates that there may be more than 240 million people in the United States by 1975. This means that the potential secondary-school population will be over 30 million. The practice of continuous promotion in the elementary school, though somewhat lessened in recent years, assures that almost all elementary-school children will move on to the secondary school. Moreover, state laws have extended compulsory school attendance through adolescence, and child labor laws have helped eliminate the alternative of full-time employment for boys and girls. At present the need for vo-

[18] U.S. Department of Health, Education, and Welfare, Office of Education. *Digest of Educational Statistics,* 1963 edition. Bulletin 1963, No. 43. Washington, D.C.: Government Printing Office, 1963, p. 11 and 59.

TABLE 4

Retention Rates,[a] Ninth Grade Through High-School Graduation, in Public and Nonpublic Schools: 48 States and the District of Columbia, 1928–1932 to 1958–1962[19]

Grade	Number continuing per 1,000 pupils in the ninth grade in:										
	1928–29	1934–35	1944–45	1946–47	1948–49	1950–51	1952–53	1954–55[b]	1956–57[b]	1957–58[b]	1958–59[b]
Ninth[c]	1,000	1,000	1,000	1,000	1,000	1,000	1,000	1,000	1,000	1,000	1,000
Tenth	768	847	892	884	822	889	921	913	924	933	930
Eleventh	627	687	725	748	766	735	818	800	825	831	831
Twelfth	562	601	649	668	648	669	717	713	738	745	744
High-school graduates	495	541	616	626	616	634	673	657	687	692	692
Year of graduation	1932	1938	1948	1950	1952	1954	1956	1958	1960	1961	1962

Source:
U.S. Department of Health, Education, and Welfare, Office of Education. "Statistical Summary of Education, 1955–56." Biennial Survey of Education in the United States: 1954–56. Washington, D.C.: Government Printing Office, 1959. Chapter 1, p. 31.

[a] These retention rates are approximate only. They are based on enrollments in successive grades in successive years in public secondary schools, and are adjusted to include estimates for nonpublic schools.
[b] Calculated by the NEA Research Division.
[c] Ninth grade in 12-grade systems; eighth grade in 11-grade systems.

[19] School Dropouts, p. 3.

TABLE 5
School Enrollment Gains in Sixteen- and
Seventeen-Year-Olds, 1947–1961[20]

| Year | Percent enrolled in school | |
	16 and 17 years old	18 and 19 years old
1947	67.6%	24.3%
1948	71.2	26.9
1949	69.5	25.3
1950	71.3	29.4
1951	75.1	26.3
1952	73.4	28.7
1953	74.7	31.2
1954	78.0	32.4
1955	77.4	31.5
1956	78.4	35.4
1957	80.5	34.9
1958	80.6	37.6
1959	82.9	36.8
1960	82.6	38.4
1961	83.6	38.0

cational training is such that every teen-ager must go to high school. As automation develops this factor will become even more significant since unskilled and low-skilled jobs will practically disappear. Financial aid in the form of state and federal contributions, as well as private assistance, have made secondary-school attendance feasible for more students. Improved high-school methodology and curricula (see Part II) have increased the holding power of the secondary school. Finally, social pressure subtly but effectively requires secondary school attendance as the practice becomes almost universal.

Qualitative Changes in the Secondary-School Student Body

Since 1900, the picture of the secondary school as a college preparatory school has changed gradually. The tremendous influx of immigrants in the years preceding World War I forced communities to provide secondary education for the children of these people as well as for native-born children. Furthermore, the forces described above are so pervasive that the composition of the high-school population has undergone qualitative transformation in the last twenty-five years.

[20] Ibid., p. 3.

The transformation is significant in at least three respects. (1) The average IQ of the high-school student has dropped from about 120 to about 105.[21] This means that many high-school students today have IQ's of 80 or less. In some secondary schools, the *average* is 90 or below. (2) Today the high-school population includes not only upper-middle-class students but also those of the lower class, with substantial numbers of foreign-born, non-English-speaking students. (3) Only half the school student body now has college preparation as its main objective.

THE CHANGING SECONDARY SCHOOL

Although the four-year academic high school developed during the nineteenth century remains the standard today, it is undergoing transformation in all directions. This is most clearly evident in the development of programs to meet the needs of millions of students who are not college-bound. The so-called comprehensive high school, with programs designed for all American youth, is emerging as the pattern of the future.

Patterns of Change

It has been difficult for the rural high school with a graduating class of less than one hundred, and frequently less than fifty, to meet the needs of the new student body, and a pronounced trend toward consolidation in rural areas is in progress.[22] Students often travel by bus to centrally located schools where a more diversified curriculum meets a variety of needs. In suburban areas the comprehensive or community high school is the emerging pattern.

In large cities a trend toward specialization of function in individual high schools has resulted in a remarkable program diversification. In New York City, for example, among the fifty-seven so-called academic high schools, there are such specialized

[21] The concept of the IQ as an indicator of native ability, talent, and competence has been under severe attack. See John Hersey, *Intelligence, Choice, and Consent* (New York: Woodrow Wilson Foundation, 1959). No doubt the IQ is not a complete measure of predictable achievement. If used judiciously, however, it may help give teachers and school officials some indication of what may reasonably be expected of each student at least in the area of academic (intellectual) attainment.

[22] James Bryant Conant, *The American High School Today: A First Report to Interested Citizens* (New York: McGraw-Hill, 1959), p. 40. See also *The Point of Beginning: The Local School District* (Washington, D.C.: NEA, 1958), p. 6.

schools as the High School of Commerce, High School of Music and Art, Bronx High School of Science, and Newtown High School Agricultural Annex. This city's secondary schools are also noted for the growth of vocational high schools. From an enrollment of 171 in one school in 1903, vocational education has grown to over 40,000 students in thirty schools today. These schools have specialized programs in such areas as secretarial and commercial skills, food trades, fashion industries, machine and metal trades, printing, art and design, automotive trades, and aviation mechanics. Most of New York's so-called academic secondary schools offer academic, commercial, and general courses.

The New York pattern is repeated on a smaller scale in other cities where the concentration of population makes it possible to offer specialized programs in some schools and comprehensive programs in others. For example, Salt Lake City has Salt Lake Vocational High School; Detroit, Cass Technical High School; Yonkers, New York, Saunders Trade and Technical High School; and Cincinnati has Central High School which offers programs in ten trades.

Since 1900 there has been significant growth in the number of private and denominational schools and in the number of students they enroll. Private-school enrollment in grades nine and above has increased from 111,000 in 1900 to an estimated 1,443,-000 in 1965. (See Table 1.)

The traditional four-year high school no longer is universal. Many school systems have adopted a 6–3–3 arrangement where the first six grades of the elementary school are followed by a three-year junior high school for grades seven through nine and a three-year senior high school for grades ten through twelve. Others are organized on a 6–2–4 pattern with the junior high school serving grades seven and eight. (The organization and function of the junior high school is discussed in Chapter 3.)

It is interesting to note that a new movement toward schooling beyond the high school is developing. At the turn of the century most high-school graduates went on to college. Gradually, the number who entered college declined, until in 1930 only about 25 percent were college-bound. Since 1930, the percentage of students continuing formal education beyond high school has been increasing steadily. In 1940 it was about 30 percent; in

1960 it rose to 50 percent, and by 1975 it may well be 80 percent or more.

The Diversified High School

In the twentieth century, the American high school has become an institution for the education of the masses, and its function as a college preparatory school has been superseded. However, there seems to be a lag between the traditional college-preparatory program and a program of education more appropriate for those for whom high school is the terminal education. The high-school curriculum, of course, has been made less and less academic in its orientation because it has been modified to meet the needs and capacities of a new student population. The first development was a recognition that the formal education of large number of girls would terminate with a high-school diploma. This prompted the schools to offer a commercial course as an alternative to the academic course. Other vocational and technical courses began to be introduced to meet the needs of non-college-bound youth. Finally, as the academic potential of the average high-school student declined, the schools introduced the general course for which lower standards of academic attainment were acceptable. Other programs were organized to meet the needs of average and below-average students.

Different types of high-school diplomas were developed to conform to the types of courses pursued. Students received academic diplomas, commercial diplomas, and general diplomas. Now high-school diplomas may vary so much that the course of study leading to one diploma has little in common with that for another. In fact, the Conant Report suggests that a permanent copy of the actual high-school courses and grades be issued instead of a diploma. Anyone experienced at reading these reports would have little difficulty in determining at a glance the nature of the program pursued and the quality of work completed by the student.

Most high schools, especially those with a student body of five hundred or more, have introduced a system of "tracking," whereby classes in English, social studies, science, and mathematics are organized homogeneously. Thus the curriculum of a college-bound student in an honor group is very different from that of a general student.

Many high schools have introduced cooperative work-study programs with emphasis on educational and vocational guidance. In the academic and vocational high schools this program is called the cooperative course. (The term "distributive education" is common in retailing programs.) Students hold positions related to school studies in the following areas: accounting, bookkeeping, business machines, clerical practice, retailing, stenography, typewriting, automotive trades, design, dressmaking, food trades, machine shop, millinery, needle trades, hospital aides, and plastic trades. Diploma credit is allowed for satisfactory employment, pupils are supervised on their jobs, and prevailing wages are paid. Several schedules are offered, such as part-time daily, alternate-week, alternate-two-week, and alternate-month. In a few school systems school credit is offered under a supervised farm-cadet program for boys during the summer.

Obviously, the high school is no longer merely a college-preparatory school. Of course, some public schools and most independent preparatory schools gear their programs to college entrance, but for many students in comprehensive or community high schools and in vocational high schools, the twelfth year is the last year of school. It is the year of the senior prom, the senior trip, and graduation. Class officers, the yearbook, senior hats, senior day, and senior buttons are all important, for there will be no college with its fraternities, sororities, proms, and socials.

What then can the high school do for these boys and girls? Since they are going to work, getting married, or going into the armed services, the high school must prepare them for work, help them find jobs, teach them useful skills, and give them insights into the workaday world or into homemaking.

INCREASING RESPONSIBILITIES OF THE HIGH SCHOOL

In recent years the academic and vocational functions of the secondary school have been extended and altered by a multiplicity of new responsibilities. Changes in the student body and the vacuum left by the home, church, and industry have forced the school to assume added civic, social, aesthetic, personal, and moral, as well as intellectual functions.

Today the secondary school is expected to prepare its students to understand and to participate effectively in solving social, political, and economic problems. The public expects the secondary school to prepare girls and boys to meet and get along with the opposite sex, to mate, build a home, raise a family, and function adequately in human relations. The school is expected to help students find a personal philosophy of life, establish goals, and make necessary life adjustments. As a part of its terminal program, it is expected to give students a basis for intellectual pursuits, aesthetic appreciation, and leisure-time activities, and to be concerned with moral and spiritual education as well.

Not satisfied with expecting the secondary school to solve the many problems which no other society is solving for its adolescents, some educators feel that the American secondary school should attempt to solve society's problems, too. Some would have the high school go directly into the community to help make a better world.

In short, the nineteenth-century concept of the secondary school has been radically transformed. The relentless pressures of a student body differing both quantitatively and qualitatively from that of the past, a dedicated professional corps of teachers, and the demands of a society in flux have resulted in a concept of the secondary school which assigns to it the responsibility for meeting every need of the adolescent and many of the needs of society.

PHILOSOPHIES OF EDUCATION

Differences in basic philosophy result in differences in the aims of the secondary school. While there are shadings and overlapping of position, three philosophic positions seem to be sufficiently distinct to warrant description and comparison. These are the *scholastic position,* the *religious-denominational view,* and the *progressive education orientation.*

The Scholastic Position

Spokesmen for this concept of the kind of high school we need not only disagree with other positions but differ among themselves. The following, however, have enough in common to warrant bracketing them together as representatives of the scholastic position: Hutchins, Adler, Bestor, and Rickover.

Those in this school of thought agree that the high school should be predominantly *a place for intellectual training.* They would like to have our schools patterned on those of France, with heavy emphasis on formal academic instruction, homework, memorization, tests, imposed discipline, and rigorous mental training.

Rickover says: "Basic knowledge and mind development are the objectives of a good school; techniques in applying these to the diverse problems which one meets in life are the responsibility of the individual."[23] And Bestor: "The school makes itself ridiculous whenever it undertakes to deal *directly* with real life problems, instead of *indirectly* through the development of generalized intellectual powers."[24] Hutchins states: "The notion of educating a man to live in any particular time or place, to adjust him to any particular environment, is foreign to a true conception of education."[25]

The position of Hutchins, Adler, Barr, and others, is that the "elements in our common human nature" may be best developed by a careful study of the great classics which teach truths that are the same always and everywhere.

The Religious-Denominational View

This view holds that all education must be soundly grounded in religion. It is contended that moral tenets are inherent in the nature of man and of the universe, and that they must be sought through the mediation of religion. Those who hold this view have become increasingly outspoken in recent years in demanding that the public schools undertake to teach moral and spiritual values. They have also been responsible for the rapid increase in the number of religious denominational schools and of movements, such as release-time from public schools for religious instruction, the inclusion of compulsory prayer in public-school programs,[26] and pressure on the federal and state governments to provide buses, textbooks, health serv-

[23] Hyman G. Rickover, *Education and Freedom* (New York: Dutton, 1959), p. 198.
[24] Arthur G. Bestor, *Educational Wastelands: The Retreat From Learning in Our Public Schools* (Urbana: U. of Illinois Press, 1953), p. 63.
[25] Robert M. Hutchins, *The Higher Learning in America* (New Haven: Yale U. Press, 1936), p. 66.
[26] Outlawed by the United States Supreme Court in *Abington* v. *Schempp* and *Murray* v. *Curlett,* June 17, 1963.

ices, scholarships, and finally, schools and teachers for religious-denominational education.[27]

It is interesting to note that Conant, who is in sympathy with some of the tenets of educational conservatives, is vigorously opposed to tax support for religious schools. He argues, "To use taxpayers' money to assist private schools is to suggest that American society use its own hands to destroy itself,"[28] and "If a religious group starts a school in a community, it is difficult for the promoters to avoid showing a derogatory attitude towards the rival public school."[29]

Progressive Education

"Progressive education" is commonly associated with the work of John Dewey, and especially with that of one of his leading followers, William Heard Kilpatrick. Dewey's philosophy was grounded in secularism which taught that intelligence is an instrument by which all our problems—moral, spiritual, and physical—could be solved. He denied the traditional philosophical dualism of mind and body, natural and supernatural, ends and means, structure and function, and so on, holding instead that there was a practical interaction of these elements resulting in unity. The child was to learn by doing, thus uniting the functions of mind and body in a practical educational process.

The implementation of this philosophy under Kilpatrick caused far-reaching changes in educational practice during the twentieth century in many parts of the world, particularly in the United States. The educational focus became the child—his physical, emotional, social well-being, as well as his intellectual development. Children were to learn through organized experiences. They were encouraged to express their wishes and to participate in making decisions which affected them. School and community were to be united. In time, the newer attitudes af-

[27] See *Moral and Spiritual Values in Public Schools* (Washington, D.C.: NEA, 1951); James O'Neill, *Religion and Education Under the Constitution* (New York: Harper, 1949), p. 356; Statement by Catholic Bishops of America on Secularism and Schools, *New York Times*, Nov. 16, 1952; and Henry Ehlers and Gordon C. Lee, *Crucial Issues in Education* (Holt, Rinehart, and Winston, 1959), pp. 118–178.

[28] James B. Conant, *Education and Liberty, The Role of the Schools in Modern Democracy* (Cambridge: Harvard U. Press, 1956), p. 81.

[29] *Ibid.*, p. 45.

fected curriculum and methods, and the intellectual aim became only one of a number of concerns of the school.[30]

Against progressive education the scholastics made the charge of "anti-intellectualism," and the religious-denominationalists applied the epithet "godless."

In succeeding chapters we shall see how these philosophic differences enter into many phases of school practice. There is nevertheless enough agreement among the various positions to make it possible for schools to work miracles in educating over 45 million of our youth in elementary and secondary schools.

AIMS OF SECONDARY EDUCATION

Obviously the school must have objectives if it is to know where it hopes to go, and these objectives should be stated specifically so that the outcomes of the school's work may be evaluated. Of course, a person's philosophy of education will determine the aims he will emphasize and the way he will state them. Hence, the aims or objectives in the following statements should be studied with reference to the philosophic positions discussed above.

In 1918, the Commission on the Reorganization of Secondary Education (an NEA body) issued its report entitled "Cardinal Principles of Secondary Education." The seven cardinal principles were health, command of the fundamental processes (reading, writing, arithmetical computations, the elements of oral and written expression), worthy home-membership, vocation, civic education, worthy use of leisure, and ethical character.[31]

The Educational Policies Commission of the NEA issued *The Purpose of Education in American Democracy* in 1938 listing the objectives of education under four headings: self-realization; human relationships; economic efficiency; and civic responsibility.[32]

The changing character of secondary education was recog-

---

[30] The story of the progressive education movement in the United States is told in detail by Lawrence A. Cremin in *The Transformation of the School* (New York: Knopf, 1961).

[31] *Cardinal Principles of Secondary Education* (Washington, D.C.: Department of the Interior, Bureau of Education, 1918), No. 35, pp. 11–16.

[32] *The Purpose of Education in American Democracy* (Washington, D.C.: NEA, 1938), p. 25.

nized in a 1938 report of the New York State Regents' Inquiry published after a two-year survey of the schools of the state. The spirit of the report is contained in the following quotations:

> Now that all the children are in school, the idea that the school program should be planned from the top down, primarily to meet the needs of the colleges, is wrong. Without neglecting preparation for college, the school program should be planned from the bottom up, fully to meet the needs of youth who will have to live and work in America today and tomorrow without further formal schooling.

> What these boys and girls now need is a broad general education which will give to all alike at least the same minimum essential tools of intercommunication and thinking, the same minimum up-to-date acquaintance with the world in which we live, both natural and social, an appreciation of the culture and standards of our civilization, the beginnings of the ability to work well with others, a common understanding and belief in the democratic process, and the desire to preserve and defend self-government.

> Make general education the central objective of the secondary school program by devoting the greater part of the time up to the end of the twelfth grade to the study of general science, human relations, community life, world history, general mathematics, and the arts—subjects which touch many now-divided academic topics, and which cover matters of direct value and interest to the average American citizen. Present those broad fields of knowledge in the ways in which they are generally encountered in life and work, and not as semester hours for college entrance. . . .

> Recognize that the school has a direct responsibility for character education, not by multiplying rules and disciplines, but by establishing student activities and standards of mankind, and above all, by furnishing inspiring leadership in school. Make understanding and enthusiasm for the democratic part of character education.[33]

A statement concerned specifically with the aims of secondary education was prepared by the division of secondary-school

[33] *Education for American Life* (Albany: 1938), pp. 11, 12, 46–47. Quoted by Harrison C. Thomas, "General Education in the High School," *High Points* (April, 1956), pp. 27–28.

principals of the National Education Association in 1948. It listed ten needs of youth:

1. All youth need to develop salable skills and those understandings and attitudes that make the worker an intelligent and productive participant in economic life. To this end, most youth need supervised work experience as well as education in the skills and knowledge of their occupations.

2. All youth need to develop and maintain good health and physical fitness.

3. All youth need to understand the rights and duties of a citizen of a democratic society, and to be diligent and competent in the performance of their obligations as members of the community and citizens of the state and nation, and of the world.

4. All youth need to understand the significance of the family for the individual and society and the conditions conducive to successful family life.

5. All youth need to know how to purchase and use goods and services intelligently, understanding both the values received by the consumer and the economic consequences of their acts.

6. All youth need to understand the methods of science, the influence of science on human life, and the main scientific facts concerning the nature of the world and of man.

7. All youth need opportunities to develop their capacities to appreciate beauty in literature, art, music, and nature.

8. All youth need to be able to use their leisure time well and to budget it wisely, balancing activities that yield satisfaction to the individual with those that are socially useful.

9. All youth need to develop respect for other persons to grow in their insight into ethical values and principles, and to be able to live and work cooperatively with others.

10. All youth need to grow in their ability to think rationally, to express their thoughts clearly, and to read and listen with understanding.[34]

[34] National Association of Secondary School Principals, *Bulletin* (Washington, D.C.: NEA, 1948), pp. 48–49.

Conant essays a brief statement of secondary-school objectives as follows:

The three main objectives of a comprehensive high school are: first, to provide a general education for all the future citizens; second, to provide good elective programs for those who wish to use their acquired skills immediately on graduation; third, to provide satisfactory programs for those whose vocations will depend on their subsequent education in a college or university.[35]

At the White House Conference on Education in 1955, the following statement of objectives was prepared. While these were the goals accepted for the schools in general, it is obvious that the high school is the division charged with the major role in their fulfillment.

It is the consensus of these groups that the schools should continue to develop:

The fundamental skills of communication—reading, writing, spelling, as well as other elements of effective oral and written expression; the arithmetical skills, including problem solving. While schools are doing the best job in their history in teaching these skills, continuous improvement is desirable and necessary.

Appreciation for our democratic heritage.

Civic rights and responsibilities and knowledge of American institutions.

Respect and appreciation for human values and for the beliefs of others.

Ability to think and evaluate constructively and creatively.

Effective work habits and self-discipline.

Social competency as a contributing member of his family and community.

Ethical behavior based on a sense of moral and spiritual values.

Intellectual curiosity and eagerness for life-long learnings.

Esthetic appreciation and self-expression in the arts.

Physical and mental health.

Wise use of time, including constructive leisure pursuits.

---

[35] Conant, p. 17. For a sharp criticism of the Conant Report see "Another Look at the First Conant Report," by Francis Griffiths in *Bulletin* of the National Association of Secondary School Principals (October, 1960).

Understanding of the physical world and man's relation to it as represented through basic knowledge of the sciences.
An awareness of our relationships with the world community.[36]

These statements of objectives and many others issued during the past half-century show considerable similarity in the concept of the functions of secondary education. In varying degrees, the lists of aims describe a diversity of purposes for the modern secondary school. The academic or intellectual function seldom is emphasized as much as other objectives. It is clear that today's educators believe that the function of the secondary school goes far beyond that of training the mind to undertake the rigorous requirements of a college education.

COMMON GOALS IN EDUCATIONAL PRACTICE

In practice, all the proponents of particular philosophical positions agree that a well-educated person must demonstrate rigorous application of the mind to the facts and ideas of the culture, a sensitivity to our moral and spiritual heritage, and an adaptability to the changing patterns of society. The common goals in secondary education may be summarized as follows:

The Intellectual Aim.   The secondary school is charged with the responsibility of providing each child with an opportunity to acquire the basic tools of communication; to become familiar with the world in which he lives; to gain understanding and appreciation of mathematics, science, the social studies and the humanities; to develop an intellectual curiosity; to achieve a critical, inquiring habit of mind; and to learn good work habits and skills.

The Civic Aim.   The secondary school is expected to help each child understand the social institutions in which he lives; to participate effectively in the political life of the community; to value the democratic way of life and to be at home in it; and to understand the obligations of citizenship and to learn to discharge them on his own level.

The Physical Aim.   The secondary school is expected to give each child an understanding and appreciation of the elements of physical, mental, and emotional health in order to help him

[36] *A Report to the President* (Washington, D.C.: United States Government Printing Office, 1956).

meet the problems of adolescence and to prepare him for a life of physical and emotional well-being.

The Personal Aim.   The secondary school is charged with the responsibility of helping each child find his vocational aptitude and the means toward its development and to establish the beginning of a sound philosophy of life and his place in society.

TRENDS IN SECONDARY EDUCATION

The American secondary school has been undergoing a thorough scrutiny in recent years. Like any other growing institution, many problems have beset the high school, and attempts to solve them have resulted in some marked trends.

The Tendency toward Consolidation.   As the number of secondary school students increases the number of schools does not show a corresponding increase because of a growing tendency toward consolidation. Today there are about 8,000 high schools with student populations of less than two hundred. In the decade ahead it is probable that the number of these schools will decline rapidly.

The Tendency toward Full-time Use of the School Building. Mounting registrations have caused a large number of schools to go on double and triple sessions. In addition, the secondary school building increasingly is being used as a center for evening classes and adult education, a twelve-month school year, summer classes, and even weekend classes.

The Tendency toward Junior High School and Junior College. The high school is tending to become an intermediate school between the junior high school and the community junior college, and as it relinquishes the work of the ninth grade to the junior high school, it is undertaking the work of the thirteenth year with its more able students.

The Tendency toward the Expansion of Private and Denominational Education.   As the high school becomes more and more heterogeneous, more parents are choosing to send their children to private and denominational schools. The rapid growth of Catholic high schools is one example of this trend; another is the development of a private-school system in the South, as a result of the Supreme Court order for integration, and in the North, as a result of the fierce competition for college admission.

Changing Patterns of Instruction.   A tremendous transformation of high-school teaching methods, now in its infancy, lies ahead. Undoubtedly we shall see more special programs for the gifted, the retarded, and the handicapped; the wider use of such teaching aids as television, tape, programmed material, and other devices; greater use of community resources and facilities; and a wider range of educational materials and publications, notably the use of paperback books as texts. Self-instruction, team teaching, flexible scheduling, large and small group instruction, and acceleration are patterns we can already recognize.

Reorganization of Administration.   Increasingly important functions are being assumed by specialized personnel, such as curriculum specialists, guidance counselors, psychologists, and testers.

New Categories of Teaching Personnel.   There is a growing trend toward the recognition of master teachers, who are given special status and salary. There are television teachers, special demonstration teachers, team teachers, and assistant or intern teachers. The secondary school may introduce the general (common learnings) teacher, the equivalent of the common branches teacher in the elementary school.

Professionalization.   The great need for better qualified teachers and specialists has resulted in greater and more rigid licensing (with a view toward higher salaries), professional treatment, and concommitantly a movement toward ridding the profession of incompetents.

Expansion and Improvement of Teacher Preparation Facilities. Universities and colleges preparing teachers have begun to expand their facilities for the preparation of master teachers, for research in education, for the preparation of specialists in guidance, psychological services, special education, audio-visual experts, and curriculum consultants.

Emphasis on Guidance.   The traditional concept of guidance as a function of the classroom teacher is being supplemented by the concept that adequate guidance service requires a staff of specially trained personnel, who will work with a number of students throughout their secondary-school years in personal, vocational, and scholastic guidance. The gifted and the retarded are now given special care, and the trend in this direction will be greatly extended in the years ahead.

Improved Liaison between the Junior High School, the Senior High School, and the Junior or Community College.   Joint planning of programs, orientation of students, and special attention to the individual is a trend which will minimize the effects of the transitions from one school to another.

Experimentation and Research.   Financed by government agencies, private foundations, and universities, greater effort is being made to improve school methods, curricula, and school organization on the basis of data gathered by trained research workers.

Introduction of Humanities Instruction.   A final trend, quite noticeable in secondary education in 1963, is the introduction of humanities into the curriculum. Of course, if art, music, literature, and philosophy are combined for integrated instruction, differently trained teachers will be required. The construction and implementation of a course of study encompassing these areas will also demand a high level of cooperation among faculty members in the high schools.

It is clear that the next quarter-century will see changes in our secondary schools which can be only dimly anticipated today. These are the necessary reflections of a number of forces, including the population explosion, the competition with Russia, the improvements in methods resulting from research and experimentation, the tendency toward lengthening the period of formal schooling for youth, the pressure of mounting tax burdens to support education, the conflict of educational ideologies, and the demands of economic and social forces. In the absence of a crystal ball, we can only attempt to recognize trends and plan to meet exigencies. The future holds unpredictable novelty; the challenge and the opportunity are overwhelming.

FOR DELIBERATION and DISCUSSION

1. The following factors distinguish the elementary school from the high school: teachers teach more than one subject; parents are more directly concerned with the work of the school; comparatively little retention in grades; greater informality in instructional procedures; emphasis on reading, writing, and arithmetic. Which of these tendencies are likely to become more pronounced in the high school in the coming decades? Why?
2. The American secondary school, like other institutions in his-

tory, owes its existence and development to the needs of the time. Discuss this statement, comparing the changing patterns of secondary education with changes in American society. On this basis what changes may we anticipate?

3. Critically analyze the forces mentioned in the chapter as contributing toward the increase in high-school population. Rank them in order of importance. Which, if any, would you challenge? Why? Can you add any not mentioned? Explain.

4. "Let's take a penetrating look at the junior high school, and then let's abolish it." (Benjamin Fine in North American Newspaper Alliance story, April 2, 1961.) Do you agree? Explain.

5. What advantages are attained by having students in the same high school pursue different programs leading to different diplomas? What are the disadvantages? What changes would you introduce if you were in a position of leadership? Why? Would the practice of giving each graduate a plasticoated photostat of his high-school record solve the problem? Explain.

6. In 1932 only 495 of every 1,000 who had entered high school four years earlier were graduated. In 1956 the number was 673 out of every 1,000 who had entered four years earlier. To what do you attribute the increasing retention rates of the high school?

7. Did the eighteenth-century Americans who completed their college education while still in their teens attain distinction because of or in spite of this fact? Should we attempt to revert to this system today? Can we?

8. Examine the trends in secondary education cited in the text. List them in the order of their descending validity. Defend your judgment.

9. The "statements of objectives . . . show surprising consensus in their conception of the function of secondary education." Give evidence to prove or disprove this statement.

FOR ADDITIONAL READING

AMERICAN ASSOCIATION OF SECONDARY SCHOOL PRINCIPALS. *Bulletin.* Issued monthly September to May inclusive. Each issue contains reports of recent research, extensive book reviews, and bibliographical material, and professional information pertaining to secondary education; generally organized around a major topic.

American Secondary School, The. New York: College Entrance Examination Board, 1959. Eight articles grouped under three headings: 1. The diversity of American secondary education, 2. Tangible and intangible controls, and 3. The role of the secondary school. Authoritative, original, and provocative analytical statements. (Copies may be purchased from Educational Testing Service, Princeton, N.J.)

BESTOR, ARTHUR E. *Educational Wastelands—The Retreat From Learning in Our Public Schools.* Urbana: U. of Illinois Press, 1953. Argues that the intellectual level of our high school students is low because professors of education are intellectually inferior.

CONANT, JAMES B. *The American High School Today: A First Report to Interested Citizens.* New York: McGraw-Hill, 1959. With a Carnegie grant Dr. Conant and/or his assistants visited one-hundred and three suburban high schools and report their finding that the comprehensive high school is geared to meet the needs of all American youth, including the talented. Twenty-one specific recommendations.

CREMIN, LAWRENCE A. *The Transformation of the School: Progressivism in American Education* (1876–1957). New York: Knopf, 1961. The most comprehensive and authoritative account of "progressive education" extant.

EDUCATIONAL POLICIES COMMISSION. *An Essay on Quality in Public Education.* Washington, D.C.: NEA, 1959. A concise statement of policy on curriculum, guidance, staff, administration and other school matters.

HERSEY, JOHN. *The Child Buyer.* New York: Knopf, 1960. (Bantam Book Edition, 1961.) A searching examination of the structure and goals of American education and society in the form of a legalistic senatorial investigation of a fantastic sort.

High School in a Changing World, The. Washington, D.C.: American Association of School Administrators, 1958. (Thirty-sixth yearbook.) Discussion of goals, curriculum, experiments and trends in high-school education. Chapters on the junior college, teacher education, student activities, and supervision.

High School We Need, The. Washington, D.C.: Association for Supervision and Curriculum Development, 1959. (Prepared by Kimball Wiles and Franklin Patterson.) A report issued by the twenty-five members of the Commission summarizing "Beliefs about the American High School," "Program of the High School," "Teachers for the American High School," "Basic Beliefs Concerning the Education of Adolescents," and "Selected References." (See also *The Junior High School We Need* prepared for the ASCD by Jean D. Grambs, *et al.*)

KANDEL, ISAAC L. *American Education in the Twentieth Century.* Cambridge: Harvard U. Press, 1957. A thoughtful, informed treatment of many aspects of American education, including statistics of growth, federal aid, the work of the NEA, and educational philosophy by a keen analyst and expert on comparative education. Includes systematic examination of attacks on the high school.

KILPATRICK, WILLIAM H. *Philosophy of Education.* New York: Macmillan, 1951. The philosophy of experimentalism as applied to educational practice. The author examines basic positions in education subjecting tradition and authority to the searching scrutiny of intelligence.

LYND, ALBERT. *Quackery in the Public Schools.* Boston: Little, Brown, 1950. A Massachusetts business man and board of education member insists that "educationists" (professional educators) have made a racket of education and urges parents and taxpayers to take over, hire competent teachers, and see that they teach fundamentals whether the children like it or not.

MACHLUP, FRITZ. *Production and Distribution of Knowledge in the United States.* Princeton: Princeton U. Press, 1962. An original contribution based on good insights with data. Argues in the chapter on education (pp. 51–144) for reducing the years of formal schooling from twelve to ten.

MEYER, ADOLPHE E. *An Educational History of the American People.* New York: McGraw-Hill, 1957. An authentic account of the development of American education from the seventeenth century to the present, written from a sociological point of view.

NEA *Research Bulletin.* Published four times a year in February, March, October, and December by Research Division of NEA. Each issue is full of data, charts, graphs, and information reporting special studies on salaries, working conditions, population, status and trends of classroom teachers, education law and similar matters of current concern.

What Shall the High School Teach? Washington, D.C.: Association for Supervision and Curriculum Development, 1956. "A guidebook for workers in secondary education as they explore, experiment and seek more satisfactory answers to the difficult and baffling problems they face." Combines facts and theory. Excellent discussion of curriculum problems, "general education," what the high schools are teaching, and social context as it influences adolescent development in the high school.

2 The Adolescent

DEVELOPMENT OF THE ADOLESCENT

The typical student enters high school in his fourteenth year and is graduated in his eighteenth. During these four years the youngster undergoes extensive changes in his physical, emotional, sexual, and psychological development. Essentially he is becoming a self. While growth continues throughout life, the rate of growth—physical, emotional, psychological, and spiritual —is especially rapid for most girls and boys during their high-school years. Adolescence is, therefore, a particularly disturbed and disturbing time. The inner forces of change and growth, the process of self-discovery and identification, and the quest for equilibrium produce enormous tensions and present formidable obstacles to adjustment.

Physical Development

Statistically, the girl of thirteen and a half who enters the ninth grade is 5 feet 3½ inches tall and weighs 110 pounds. Four years later she is 5 feet 5½ inches tall and weighs 123 pounds. The boy of thirteen and a half is 5 feet 3 inches tall and weighs 108 pounds. Four years later he is 5 feet 9½ inches tall and weighs 150 pounds.[1]

Between the ages of twelve and fourteen, girls are generally taller and heavier than boys. For the most part the girl of thirteen or fourteen has entered puberty, the average age of me-

[1] Statistics based on compilations made by the Metropolitan Life Insurance Company, *Statistical Bulletin*, 41 (October, 1960): 4.

narche for American girls being thirteen years, seven months. Her interest in the opposite sex is more than casual. During the next four years she will have developed considerable poise, will be at home in the company of boys, and may have engaged in sex play.

The boy is likely to be a year or more behind the girl in development. At thirteen or fourteen, he generally shows little or no interest in girls, but during high school his voice will deepen, he will begin to shave, his sexual potency will awaken, and he will enter early manhood. With few exceptions he will find his sexual outlet in masturbation. He will be ashamed of this and in many cases seriously worried and disturbed about it. According to Kinsey, his sex drives and outlets during these years are actually at their highest.[2]

The maturing of the body and the development of the sex instinct of adolescents constitute the ever-present backdrop against which the high-school drama is enacted. "The principal lessons [of adolescence]," writes Havighurst, "are emotional and social, not intellectual."[3]

Psychological Development

Havighurst's work at the University of Chicago in identifying and describing the learning tasks peculiar to each age has helped us understand the developmental psychology of the adolescent. For the ages from twelve to eighteen he describes the following ten tasks:

1. Achieving new and more mature relations with age mates of both sexes.
2. Achieving a masculine or feminine social role.
3. Accepting one's physique and using the body effectively.
4. Achieving emotional independence of parents and other adults.
5. Achieving assurance of economic independence.
6. Selecting and preparing for an occupation.

[2] Alfred C. Kinsey, et al., Sexual Behavior in the Human Male (Philadelphia: Saunders, 1948), pp. 222–223. See also William Healy, et al., Reconstructing Behavior in Youth (New York: Knopf, 1938), "A boy or girl may carry an enormous load of sexual ideation that is pernicious for his own well being. . . ." p. 43.
[3] Robert J. Havighurst, Developmental Tasks and Education (New York: Longmans Green, 1948), p. 33. Courtesy of David McKay Company, Inc.

7. Preparing for marriage and family life.
8. Developing intellectual skills and concepts necessary for civic competence.
9. Desiring and achieving socially responsible behavior.
10. Acquiring a set of values and an ethical system as a guide to behavior.[4]

The thirty-sixth yearbook (1958) of the American Association of School Administrators quotes Stephen M. Corey, who groups the tasks confronting adolescents into five basic categories:

1. Coming to terms with their own bodies.
2. Learning new relationships to their age mates.
3. Achieving independence from parents.
4. Achieving adult social and economic status.
5. Acquiring self-confidence and a system of values.[5]

While each period of life has its own new tasks and adjustments, there is probably no period that presents a greater challenge to the developing individual than the years from twelve to eighteen. At every function—proms, games, movies, parties, outings, trips, plays, even assemblies—a sensitive observer cannot fail to feel the tension, excitement, and pleasurable anticipation of adolescent boys and girls. These group activities are an essential, if not the primary part of a good high-school program, for the youngster must be given every opportunity to overcome his shyness, to gain self-confidence, to learn the "rules of the game" in meeting the opposite sex.

During the four critical years in high school the childish naïveté of the freshman will develop into the self-consciousness of the sophomore, the eager excitement and self-satisfaction of the junior, and the sophistication and blasé boredom of the senior. This is, of course, a caricature. Nor are the descriptions offered in the preceding pages more than norms. There are wide variations among individuals. Some will have developed to maturity by their fourteenth year; others will not have attained it by their eighteenth. Some will never achieve it, but will remain adolescents all their lives—talking, hoping, dreaming but never doing.

<hr/>

[4] *Ibid.*, pp. 33–71.
[5] *The High School in a Changing World* (Washington, D.C.: American Association of School Administrators, 1958), p. 3.

For many high-school youth the tensions produced by the rapid changes of this period result in problems that are very serious. The developmental tasks they face are crucial; the adequacy and the fullness of the life they will live depends on their successful solution.

PROBLEMS OF ADOLESCENCE

The adolescent often suffers from a pronounced feeling of inferiority, resulting from some physical difference which he sees out of proportion to fact or reality. Large feet or hands may have a determining effect on his outlook; wearing glasses or teeth braces, or having a minor physical defect may have a similar effect. "My inferiority complex is that my nose is pointy," writes one girl.[6] "I have an inferiority feeling about my height," writes another. "At times it doesn't bother me at all. But then someone might come up to me and call me 'shortie' and it starts all over again." "When it comes to dancing," says a boy, "I have two left feet."

Frequently there is the feeling of not being able to meet peers easily and comfortably. "My inferior feeling occurs when I make new acquaintances and I have to start a conversation." "When I am out with my friends I am very cheerful and not at all shy, but as soon as I meet new acquaintances I clam up." "My boy friend comes from a very well-educated family and every time I have to go to his house to eat dinner or for a visit I feel very inferior talking with them." "One of my troubles is getting to know new boys and girls in my classes. I don't know how to go about it. How would you get to know a person in your class when you don't say 'hello' to them? Should you say hello first, and how would you go about making a conversation, and how would you keep it going?" "My inferiority complex is very common among teenagers, I think. It deals with talking alone with a person you've met." "I have trouble making friends. I don't know what to talk about."

The lack of self-confidence is rooted in the fact that youngsters, though they are becoming adults, have not yet learned to meet the standards of adults. As one sensitive senior girl

[6] These and succeeding quotations are from papers written by adolescent girls and boys in English, social studies, and core classes of one of the authors.

wrote, "I must admit, when I think of my future I become a little frightened."

Students, asked to write anonymously on the theme "What I Worry About," disclosed a variety of anxieties. A major source of worry was failure or poor results in school work.[7] Other themes occurred with considerable frequency. One ninth-grade boy was obsessed with a fear of atomic destruction, a common source of worry. Others expressed deep anxiety about their own health and that of members of their family, about religion, race, economic security and similar problems.

In considering the emotional basis of adolescent behavior it is well to remember differences in behavior between individuals and between boys and girls as a group. For example, in a sampling of 2,500 high-school boys and girls of all grades from all parts of the country, Remmers and Radler found that a significantly higher percentage of girls than boys are easily excited, lose their tempers, daydream, are lonely, have a crush on an older person, or are afraid to speak up in class. Among the problems expressed by large numbers of teenagers are: want to gain (or lose) weight, 52 percent; want to improve posture or body build, 37 percent; want to get rid of pimples, 33 percent; seldom have dates, 44 percent; need to develop self-confidence, 36 percent.[8]

An interesting discussion of emotional differences between adolescent boys and girls is presented by Friedenberg. "Boys, for example, seem to me more concerned with their appearance than girls. . . . Boys seem on the whole to be moodier, more intense, more mystical almost."[9] Although Friedenberg concedes that his "observations contradict the stereotype," it is clear that the adolescent is subject to exceptional emotional tensions.

The adolescent has a very highly developed sense of justice, which can be a source of problems for him. This attitude, built slowly from childhood, attains its zenith in the high-school years. The adolescent resents actual or apparent unfairness by a teacher —favoritism, prejudice, unequal treatment, sarcasm directed at

---

[7] See also H. H. Remmers and D. H. Radler, *The American Teenager* (Indianapolis: Bobbs-Merrill, 1957), p. 59.

[8] *Ibid.*, pp. 80–85.

[9] Edgar Z. Friedenberg, *The Vanishing Adolescent* (Boston: Beacon, 1959), pp. 52–56.

a student, public personal criticism, or failure of the teacher to keep his word or live up to a promise. He is quick to recognize injustice practiced by students against a teacher as well. In a senior class, students were asked to write anonymously on the theme "An Injustice I Experienced." One boy wrote: "The greatest injustice I experienced was the way the boys treat Mr. R. in the gym." A senior girl, who chose to identify herself despite the offer of anonymity, charged a teacher with a grave injustice for advising girls that they would be much prettier if they would "take the make-up off" their faces.

The adolescent is beset by many if not all of the problems of the adult. In addition, he is subjected to explosive forces from within and to relentless pressure from without—peers, home, school, and society. We have discussed the former briefly. We now turn to an examination of cultural forces as they impinge on the high-school student.

THE ADOLESCENT SOCIETY

Typically, adolescents develop a society of their own, probably as a protective device against the failure of the older generation, both at home and in school, to appreciate their special problems. "In order to strengthen his ego and to give himself self-confidence, he allies himself with a group of his peers."[10] Excessive telephoning, that bane of the life of every adolescent's parents and siblings, lies in the instinct of self-preservation. A need for identification with the strong and the successful may be the reason for the hero-worship which is a part of adolescence in all countries and in all cultures. The same needs explain the adolescent drive for identification with a friend, for association in clubs, for distinctive dress, speech, manners, and mores.

Adolescence is the time of close and warm friendships, deep as they never will be again. Adolescents have an enormous need for one another because they need security and support in order to make the crucial adjustments necessary for life.

In a comparative study of ten Midwestern high schools, Coleman asked, "What does it take to get into the leading crowd in these schools?" He found that though the elite often consisted of college-bound boys and girls, "It takes athletic prowess, know-

[10] Gerald H. J. Pearson, *Adolescence and the Conflict of Generations* (New York: Norton, 1958), pp. 41, 72, and 86.

ing how to dance, owning a car or having a good reputation or liking to go to parties, and it often takes not being a prude (for girls) or a sissy (for boys). Good grades are mentioned, but not very often, not as often as any of these items."[11]

The author of this study suggests that:

> If there were systematically organized games, tournaments, and meets in all activities ranging from mathematics and English through home economics and industrial arts to basketball and football, and if promotional skills were used, the resulting public interest and student interest in these activities would undoubtedly increase sharply.[12]

The point is made that this approach might give the needed impetus to adolescent acceptance of academic achievement as worthy of recognition and acclaim. Many educators feel, however, that this type of motivation is less effective than that resulting from self-propelled intrinsic interest.

Moreover, there is no reason to suppose that it takes the same kind of qualifications to get into the "leading crowd" in *all* high schools. While the high-school adolescent develops his own subculture, this climate may vary considerably from one part of the country to another, from rural area to suburb to city and from one part of the city to another. For example, the special schools studied by Conant in *Slums and Suburbs*[13] (Bronx High School of Science; Central High School, Philadelphia; Evanston Township High School, Illinois; Great Neck High School, New York; Newton High School, Mass.; and Scarsdale High School, New York; as well as the Bronxville High School, New York; Horace Mann School, New York; New Trier Township High School, Illinois; and the University of Chicago High School) undoubtedly have a student climate in which the criteria of acceptance and recognition are far different from those which prevail in the typical middle-class Midwestern schools studied

[11] James S. Coleman, "Style and Substance in American High Schools," in *The American Secondary School* (New York: College Entrance Examination Board, 1959), pp. 12–13. This study, sponsored by the Cooperative Research Program of the Department of Health, Education and Welfare, and published by the Department in 1961 under the title *Social Climates in High School* concludes: "Adolescents today are cut off, probably more than ever before from adult society" and ". . . . adolescents are not looking to the adult community for their social rewards, but to each other."
[12] *Social Climates*, p. 74.
[13] (New York: McGraw-Hill, 1961), p. 116.

by Coleman. In Conant's schools, the "leading crowds" stand out because they rank high academically.

Unfortunately, a student body of high academic caliber may be driven to react with apathy or even with disdain against a school program that fails to challenge its talents, awaken its potential, or promote its interests. The type of extra-class activities in which students engage and the type of student they attract may throw some light on this problem.[14]

It is common to find that high-school students who score in the upper half of the distribution make little progress after the tenth grade on tests of understanding and ability to apply concepts and principles. Their scores level off to a plateau. Interviews with samples of these students indicate that they turn increasingly to the extracurricular activities because these have proved more stimulating and meaningful to them than their courses in the eleventh and twelfth grades.

Additional illumination of the adolescent world is found in fiction. Intimate glimpses into the way the teenager sees the world, the problems he faces, and the life he leads can often best be found in imaginative literature. Among outstanding works in this category there are the following:

The Catcher in the Rye by Jerome David Salinger; *David Copperfield* and *Great Expectations* by Charles Dickens; *Prairie Town Boy* by Carl Sandburg; *The Diary of a Young Girl* by Anne Frank; *Seventeen* by Booth Tarkington; *A Tree Grows in Brooklyn* by Betty Smith; *Cress Delahanty* by Jessamyn West; *The Member of the Wedding* and *The Heart is a Lonely Hunter* by Carson McCullers; *The Challenger* by Frank Waldman; *The Dark Adventure* by Howard Pease; *City Boy* by Herman Wouk; *The White Circle* by John Bell Clayton; *The Grass Harp* and *Other Voices, Other Rooms* by Truman Capote; *Death of the Heart* by Elizabeth Bowen; *The Sky is Red* by Berto Giuseppe; *Devil in the Flesh* by Raymond Radiquet; *A Prospect of the Sea* by Dylan Thomas; *The Red Carnation* by Elio Vittorini; *Seventeenth Summer* by Maureen Daly; *Tea and Sympathy* by Robert Anderson; *Compulsion* by Meyer Levin; *My Mother* and *The Counterfeiters* by André Gide; *I'm A Fool* by Sherwood Anderson; *Paul's Case* by Willa Cather; *A Portrait of the Artist as a*

---

[14] Ralph W. Tyler, "New Criteria for New Curriculum Content and Method" in *The High School in a New Era*, Francis S. Chase and Harold A. Anderson (eds.) (U. of Chicago Press, 1958), p. 172.

Young Man by James Joyce; *Father and Son* by James T. Farrell; *The Way of All Flesh* by Samuel Butler; *Fathers and Sons* by Ivan Turgenev; *Look Homeward Angel* by Thomas Wolfe; *Sons and Lovers* by D. H. Lawrence; *Young Man With A Horn* by Dorothy Baker; *The Adventures of Augie March* by Saul Bellow; and *End as a Man* by Calder Willingham.

We have already alluded to the pattern of the club or association of adolescents as a protective device. Less tangible but nonetheless real is the language, dress, dancing, dating customs, food, fads and other mores of this age group, which are constantly changing but which are sufficiently standardized in any group to unite its members and to separate them from the out-group of adults or other adolescents. Although parents, teachers, social workers, and others who work with teenagers and enjoy their company often delight in these oddities of speech, dress, and manner, no other than an actual member of the group can participate in or understand these activities. Emerson sums it up when he says: "Do not think that youth has no force because he cannot speak to you and me. Hark! in the next room his voice is sufficiently clear and emphatic—to his contemporaries."

Influence of the Home

For a child, there is no adequate substitute for a happy home. A boy came home from school and reported to his father, "My teacher doesn't like me." To which the father replied, "What do you care? I like you." A home where the parents are happy with each other and with the children affords a girl or boy the best opportunity for adjustment to life's problems. Conversely, where there is friction between the parents, the children are bound to suffer. Divorced, unhappy, overworked, physically or mentally ill parents pose an additional burden to boys or girls trying to find themselves during adolescence. Here a teacher may indeed stand *in loco parentis*—to listen to the child's problems, to give a word of advice, encouragement, or consolation.

The home may offer security to each child, or it may permit sibling rivalry or favoritism to do serious injury to one or more of the children. Parents are often insensitive to the damage they do by favoring a bright or a handicapped child, or a "baby." Here, again, the school can help by giving each girl or boy a feeling of belonging, of being wanted and appreciated for what he or she is and can do.

Consider the obstacles the adolescent must overcome. He is dependent on his elders for support; he has been taught obedience as a legal and moral precept; and he is becoming an adult and seeking selfhood. His parents and teachers make the rules for his behavior, for the use of his time, for the selection of his clothing, for the choice of his playmates, for decisions about his vocation, for his leisure-time activities, about the place where he is to live, and for the religious, political, and economic views he is to accept.

Sometimes, of course, the reverse is true. Often the adolescent makes the decisions for the family, or at least the family inconveniences itself to accommodate the adolescent, but such a reversal can lead to undesirable consequences for parents and adolescents. More frequently, however, it is the parent who sets restraints and restrictions and the adolescent often revolts, insisting on the freedom to become sufficiently independent so that he can grow into maturity.

The concept of the conflict of generations is a familiar one in psychiatry.[15] This conflict is present in some degree at all ages and in all societies. Occasionally it is pronounced, as it was in the rivalry between Oliver Wendell Holmes senior and junior. In other instances it is latent. Adolescents in our culture encounter the conflict because for the most part, we postpone the privileges and responsibilities of adulthood long last puberty.

A sixteen-year-old high-school girl writes:

> We learn not to be prejudiced, that everyone is equal no matter what their race or religion is. I am not prejudiced but what can we do about parents who are?
>
> It is not so much my mother as my father. If he so much as sees me talking to a boy that is not of my religion he gets very mad. I try to talk to him but he does not understand. He says boys of different religions will not have respect for me, which I find from experience is not true. One time I was going out with a boy that was not of my religion. My father caught us and actually had a fist fight out in the street with the boy. He even gets mad when my girl friends are not of my religion.

---

[15] For discussion of the thesis that the conflict of the adult male with the adolescent boy is rooted in homosexuality, see Friedenberg, pp. 175.

The only thing I can do is not go out with any boys of another religion. It gets a bit confusing at times when you are taught in school not to be prejudiced and at home there is nothing really you can do about it.

During a lesson on human relations one native-born tenth-grade girl reported that she was unhappy because her parents (Greek immigrants) would not let her be friends with "American" girls. She was advised by a member of the class to invite one very nice "American" girl to her home so that her parents could see they were mistaken.

Many parents require their children to take after-school instruction in music, dancing, Hebrew, Greek, religion, and so on. One boy traveled a total of three hours daily to a night school to study Italian because it was not taught in the day school he attended. Middle-class parents in suburban high-school districts often subject their children to pressure to attain school grades that will insure admission to prestige colleges. The first conclusion listed by Conant in summarizing the results of his study of schools is: "The main problem in wealthy suburban schools is to guide the parent whose college ambitions outrun his child's abilities toward a realistic picture of the kind of college his child is suited for."[16]

Often parents prevent their children from becoming weaned psychologically in order to protect them. This overprotection extended into adolescence may result in permanent dependence. The child may never become a man or woman, a husband or wife. If maturity is to be attained, the battle between the generations must result in a victory for the younger. Wisdom demands that the adolescent be given every opportunity to learn from his mistakes. Parents, of course, must be ready to help when they are needed, but restraint, forbearance, sympathy, patience, and understanding will give the child an opportunity for self-esteem, help him to make the necessary transitions and to become a mature and independent adult. The result will be not less but greater love between the generations.

The adolescent wants to be independent, but he finds himself dependent. Parents either can help develop or can inhibit his capacity for making independent judgments. This capacity

---

[16] Conant, *Slums and Suburbs,* p. 144.

may be planted in early childhood and can flower in adolescence and bear fruit if it is allowed to develop and gain
strength.[17] But it is in this very area of making basic decisions—
involving the choice of a vocation, a mate, a college, friends—
that the conflict between the high-school student and his parents is most pronounced.

Making wise judgments about problems requires a high
degree of maturity. Perhaps there is no greater challenge to the
home and the school than guiding and fostering the development of mature judgment in the young. In the home it can be
started very early by permitting—indeed, requiring—the child to
make simple choices on his level. As he gains in confidence and
competence, the range and complexity of his decisions may be
increased. The parent must restrain himself so that he does not
intervene, especially in adolescence, when such intervention results in a maximum of friction.

Influence of the School

High-school youngsters often find their lives rigidly regu-
lated in and out of school. Some activities are required while
others are prohibited, and their decisions are overruled repeatedly. They may be subject to ridicule, severe punishment, or
harsh criticism. Their dignity and self-respect is not enhanced by
being required to ask the teacher's permission to leave the room
or having to carry a large wooden "pass" to and from the lava-
tory. These and other rules—silence in the study hall, detention
for lateness to class, appearance before a student court for such
infractions as failing to pick up a paper that someone else had
thrown down in the lunch room, and so on—are often imposed
without more than token approval by the student council. The
writers recall an incident in which a high-school boy was reported to the dean for walking on the wrong side of a pole in the
basement during change of classes. The guilty student had just
returned to school to complete his education after four years in
the service during which he had spent nineteen months in a pris-
oner of war camp.

---

[17] See Morris Gall, *Judicial Decision and Practical Judgment* (New York: King's
Crown Press, 1946), for a discussion of aspects of judgment and what may be
done to develop competence in this area.

Unfortunately, this is not an isolated case. Some secondary-school teachers seem to believe that adolescents are evil beings from whom the devil must be exorcised, and that they are the unhappy but chosen instrument of redemption! Yet many times praise is the most useful thing a teacher can give a high-school student. One principal found a simple formula in redirecting delinquents: "They must be praised, praised, praised." Another advised his faculty to give tests from time to time on which most of the youngsters scored 100 percent. "Appreciate every good piece of work," he urged. "Praise it, post it, have it read aloud, tell other classes, teachers, and the principal about it." One teacher entered only the spelling grades of those children who had scored 90 or 100 percent. Another wrote the names of honor-roll students on the board. One teacher made sure to compliment every child he knew who made the honor roll.

Of course, teachers must be careful not to substitute praise for standards of excellence. Children, especially bright children, will be the first to resent this. But no boy or girl can be expected to do his best if adults are emphasizing errors instead of being warmly appreciative of achievement.

The adolescent is worthy of respect. He deserves the same courtesies that mature, democratically oriented adults accord each other. The adolescent is consolidating a *new* self—a new bodily self and a new social self. He is finding him*self*, a task often painful, generally protracted, and always difficult.

Remmers and Radler asked 2,500 teenagers, "What is the most important thing that young people should get out of high school?" and received the following answers: vocational skill, 14 percent; skill in basic subjects like English or math, 14 percent; sense of discipline and responsibility, 33 percent; knowledge about our society, 3 percent; knowing how to get along with other people, 36 percent.[18] The item placed first by the largest number of adolescents would be placed last by many of their teachers.

Our culture tends more and more to prolong childhood and to lengthen the period of dependence. In this country the school as an institution plays a greater role in the life of the individual than it does in any other country. Every child must

[18] Remmers and Radler, p. 256.

adjust to classmates and teachers in six years of elementary school and six years of secondary school. A potentially traumatic transition occurs as each new school is entered. New people, new procedures, new requirements, new standards, and a new environment must be met and assimilated.

The school is a place of authority. Its rules—often irrational from the student's viewpoint—must be obeyed. Its standards must be met. These are enforced by the social sanctions and by the moral and sometimes physical suasion of parents.

Competition between students complicates school life. In our culture it is all-important to compete and to excel. Some youngsters are preparing for the competitive economic-social world in which they will soon be on their own. Those who are college-bound must vie with each other for grades that will insure college entrance. Examinations are highly competitive, with all the tensions this implies.

The school itself is a community, with all the interpersonal tensions a community generates. Indeed, since attendance is involuntary and the regulations imposed are sometimes severe, it may assume to some degree the character of a prison. At best, it is not unlike a small town.

In an average town of one thousand there are likely to be several criminals. Similarly a high school with this number of highly emotional and volatile human beings will not be entirely free from crime. Hence those who work with our adolescents should not be surprised to find boys and girls who steal, forge, cheat, engage in vandalism, and otherwise break the law. For the most part, it is the rare adolescent who is beyond redemption, and the work of teachers, administrators, guidance personnel, psychologists, and psychiatrists must be directed at prevention and at redirection. If we can lead a student to see himself as a respectable and respected citizen, he may respond accordingly.

The adolescent is expected to learn increasingly complicated skills at the same time that he is trying to deal with his own internal conflict. It is all important, therefore, that teachers attempt to develop a relaxed classroom atmosphere in which each child has a sense of belonging, a sense of pride, and a feeling of pleasurable achievement. In this type of classroom the best will be brought out of each boy and girl, and the dividends to the teacher will be priceless.

Influence of Our Culture

Adults often fail to realize that adolescents inhabit a turbulent world. Lacking the perspective that comes with years, they tend to exaggerate every slur, every criticism, every failure. The imminence of war, violence, unemployment, home disturbances, injustice, pressure of school, of work, of relations with peers—all these and more constantly confront them. Furthermore conflicts in values within our culture are disturbing factors in the development of the adolescent personality. Our ideal of freedom guarantees to each boy and girl the right to choose his mate, his religion, his politics, his vocation, his residence, his friends—in short, his way of life. But the growing child soon discovers contradictions in the culture. He may disagree with one or even both of his parents, with friends, or with teachers on matters of politics, economics, religion, social practices, and personal goals. The security of a stable, monolithic culture is not available to him. Instead, he is tossed in a sea of disquieting uncertainty, and it is not surprising that he may become rebellious, subdued, neurotic, aggressive, repressed, or otherwise unstable.

In other respects, too, the world outside of school exerts influence on the development of the teen-ager. He becomes increasingly aware that the expanding horizons of science, international rivalries, national and local political conflicts, labor-management relations, and racial and religious differences and prejudices are important to him. These aspects of our world are brought insistently to his attention by our highly developed mass media—the movies and television programs he sees, the records and radio programs he listens to, the magazines and newspapers he reads.

Ours is a world of movement. The population of California, for example, is growing at the rate of 1,500 per day, partially as a result of interstate migration. About 12 million Americans move from one state to another every year. Never before have teen-agers seen so much of the world through one or another of the many other agencies of travel—a school supervised trip, a summer camp, scouting experience, a family vacation trip, a student exchange opportunity, a summer work program, and so on. Familiarity with other people and places has tremendous potential in developing an understanding, a tolerance, and a competence which can overcome the limitations of provincialism.

DELINQUENCY

If teenagers were organized, their first objective might well be an attack on the label "delinquent." In proportion to the population, the percentage of teenage offenders is relatively small, and in comparison with other times and other places, the American teenager is a model of propriety. In fact, in the face of the many tensions—natural and imposed—from which teen-agers suffer, it is a tribute to their self-discipline that their in-fractions are so few.

Nonetheless, delinquency is a problem because damage is done to innocent people and because a young offender is lost to himself and to society if he does not follow a constructive path. Delinquency occurs in the city and in rural areas, among rich and poor, native- and foreign-born, girls and boys, the rigidly disciplined and the unrestrained.

Obviously, the reasons for delinquency are not easily dis-covered.[19] While there are no absolute indicators of potential de-linquency, the teacher should be alert to any sign of disturb-ance. Truancy is one such sign. An abrupt change in the quality of a student's work is another. Unusual behavior may be a third. Others may be a decline in health or change in peer group ad-herence. In delinquency, the adage, "an ounce of prevention is worth a pound of cure," is particularly true.

As we have suggested, the teacher is often confronted with problems that arise in the home or that derive from conflicts in our social structure. This is both a challenge and an opportu-nity. Since learning proceeds, if at all, under severe handicaps when children are disturbed, the high-school teacher's first task is often one of therapy. He must establish an atmosphere of calm. He must give each child a sense of security, of belonging, of being accepted and wanted. Those who come to school with whole personalities no less than those who need more than their share of sympathy and attention reflect the forces of home and society that have been at play during their young lives. Unfortu-nately, the school can do little to redirect either. But it can and must do a superhuman task in helping each child find himself and realize his potential. That the task is easier with some than

[19] See Gertrude Samuels, "Why the 'Assassins' Can't Be 'Punks,' " *New York Times Magazine*, August 16, 1959, and "World Wide Story—Juvenile Delin-quency," *New York Times Magazine*, February 14, 1960.

with others is but a reflection of the many forces for good and ill at play on each child in a society which is itself torn by incessant pressures and conflict.

THE ADOLESCENT IN OTHER CULTURES

Throughout most of the world today, higher education is still the privilege of the few. In the older countries of Europe and Latin America, education is traditionally a privilege of aristocracy,[20] and despite attempts by legislation to extend opportunities to gifted children in all ranks, secondary education and colleges are reserved to the upper class. The better positions in science, the arts, the professions, industry, and politics are reserved to these children, while children of the masses begin their working lives early in their teens or before. The traditional Hebrew "Bar Mitzvah" ceremony in which the boy is vested with the status and the responsibilities of manhood on his thirteenth birthday is symbolic of the practices of other countries.

A second group of countries in which education into and beyond the teens is reserved for the few are the new Communist "empires" of Russia and China. The traditional Russian and Chinese education was reserved for the few of the privileged classes. The rationale is different today, but the result is the same. In these countries, each attempting to lift itself into the rank of a first-rate industrial power, the luxury of extended education for all is too expensive. Membership in the Communist Party is now the path to preferment. Early manifestation of talent, especially in science and technology, may lead to a higher education, but in general the adolescent is expected to assume the burden of work as soon as he is able.

In those countries which have recently won independence in Asia, Africa, the Middle East, and elsewhere, the problem is not unlike that of the Soviets: to raise the standard of living by rapid industrialization. The demands of their economies dictate that an investment in continued education through and beyond adolescence for more than a very small percentage is at present prohibitive.

[20] In Mexico, for example, architecture is a profession reserved for the aristocracy. In her biography *Orozco,* Alma Reed describes his feeling of relief when he lost a hand in an accident in the chemistry laboratory and felt free to leave architecture and pursue his chosen work of fresco painting.

Despite these problems, however, a high-school explosion, similar to that experienced during the past half-century in the United States, may be on the way throughout the world. The *New York Times,* reporting a recent UNESCO study states:

> Although the total number of children in high schools now represent only 2.6 percent (71,000,000) of the world's estimated total population, the study forecasts an "explosion" of the enrollment in the near future. For example: the percentage of young people aged 15 to 19 enrolled in secondary schools in the United States has risen in recent years from 50 to 73 percent; in Ceylon from 11 to 42 percent; in the Netherlands from 35 to 87 percent; in France from 13 to 42 percent; in Chile from 12 to 27 percent; in Australia from 25 to 65 percent; and in Morocco from 1.5 to 5.3 percent.[21]

FOR DELIBERATION and DISCUSSION

1. "The American adolescent has more in common with adolescents in other communities and indeed in other parts of the world than he has with the adults in his own family." Comment and explain.
2. The program of academic studies in our schools tends to become increasingly rigorous and demanding as students pass through adolescence. Is this consonant with what we know of the physical, mental, and emotional development of teenage girls and boys? What revision, if any, in current school practice seems indicated?
3. In what respects are the problems of teenage boys similar to those of teenage girls? How do they differ? What are the relative advantages and disadvantages of co-education at the high-school level?
4. Is a permissive classroom atmosphere conducive to the best education of the adolescent? Why?
5. What factors in the growth and development of adolescents suggest reasons for their preference for extracurricular activities instead of traditional classroom activities at the high-school level?
6. "Adolescents in our culture are subjected to undue regimentation and restraint." Is this an unfair or inaccurate statement? Explain.
7. Read and report on two or more of the novels mentioned on pages 36–37 (or two other works of literature depicting problems of adolescents).
8. From what we know about the development of high-school students, it would seem that they would have a greater interest in

[21] *New York Times,* May 6, 1962, Sec. 4, p. 5. Report on the *World Survey of Education* (New York: UNESCO, 1962), III.

sex than in almost any other subject. Does sex education have the place it should in the high-school curriculum?

9. Which seems to play the most crucial role in the development of the adolescent: self, family, school, peers, society, other? Explain.

10. What seem to be the common elements of adolescence? What are the variables? What implications does this have for the high-school curriculum?

FOR ADDITIONAL READING

BLOS, PETER. *On Adolescence: A Psychoanalytic Interpretation.* New York: Free Press, 1962. Detailed account of the phases of adolescence. Copius citations of "cases." The usefulness of this volume depends on the psychoanalytic background of the reader.

BRAYTON, MARGARET. "The Problems, Worries, Fears, and Anxieties of Physically Handicapped Junior and Senior High School Adolescents." *Bulletin* (National Association of Secondary School Principals), 46, No. 271 (1962): 268–269.

COLEMAN, JAMES S., JONASSOHN, KURT, and JOHNSTONE, JOHN W. D. *Social Climates in High Schools.* Washington, D.C.: United States Department of Health, Education, and Welfare, 1961. The principal author studied ten Northern Illinois high schools. Questionnaire and interview techniques were used to disclose statistically the differences between adolescent and adult values. (The report in its entirety, called *The Adolescent Society,* was published by the Free Press in 1961.)

CONANT, JAMES B. *Slums and Suburbs.* New York: McGraw-Hill, 1961 This second report on the American high school is as much a book on sociology as on education. It takes a realistic view of the problems of the high school. Seventeen concluding recommendations.

"Disaffected Children and Youth," *Educational Leadership* (Journal of the Association for Supervision and Curriculum Development, NEA), 20, No. 5 (February, 1963). Devoted to the problem of the "dropout" who remains in school.

FRIEDENBERG, EDGAR Z. *Vanishing Adolescent.* New York: Beacon, 1962. An original and provocative study based on psychoanalytic concepts. Well-written. Scholarly. Draws many of its illustrations from literature.

HAVIGHURST, ROBERT J. *Developmental Tasks and Education.* New York: Longmans, Green, 1948. An original work on the concepts of interrelationship of psychological and social factors in the growth of the individual.

HAVIGHURST, ROBERT J., *et al. Growing Up in River City.* New York: Wiley, 1962. A team from the University of Chicago, working with the Community Youth Development Commission made a ten-year study (1951–1960) of public-school children during their adolescent years (11–20) in a mid-western city of 45,000 to throw light on the question "Under what conditions do boys and girls grow into competent young adults and under what conditions do they become incompetent young adults? Makes recommendations for adapting programs in school and society to meet the needs of youth.

HECHINGER, GRACE and HECHINGER, FRED M. *Teen-Age Tyranny*. New York: Morrow, 1963. Argues that adult society is fostering teenage tyranny by catering to the immature.

KELLEY, EARL C. *In Defense of Youth*. Englewood Cliffs: Prentice-Hall, 1962. Describes programs in student government. Suggests appraising curriculum on basis of youth's needs and interests.

KRAVACEUS, WILLIAM C. *Juvenile Delinquency*. Washington, D.C.: Department of Classroom Teachers, American Education Research Association, NEA, 1958. A booklet including bibliography outlining research on juvenile delinquency. Gives a checklist for appraising teacher competencies in working with potential delinquents.

LICHTER, SOLOMON O., RAPIER, ELSIE B., SIEBERT, FRANCES M., and SLANSKY, MORRIS A. *Drop-Outs, The: A Treatment Study of Intellectually Capable Students Who Drop Out of High School*. New York: Free Press, 1962. Reports a three-year study in depth of one hundred and five Chicago adolescents of at least average mental ability who were referred to the Scholarship and Guidance Association (counseling agency) on the verge of dropping out of high school. Contains a guide for teachers and bibliography. New view of the emotional problem of children who do not complete high school.

NEUMEYER, MARTIN H. *Juvenile Delinquency in Modern Society*. 3rd ed.; Princeton: Van Nostrand, 1961. A thorough discussion of the subject based on the latest research. Considers extent of the problem, causes, control, and treatment. The author subscribes to no special "school" in either cause or treatment.

PEARSON, GERALD H. J. *Adolescence and the Conflict of Generations*. New York: Norton, 1958. An introduction to the contributions of psychoanalysis in the understanding of adolescence.

REMMERS, H. H. and RADLER, D. H. *American Teenager*. Indianapolis: Bobbs-Merrill, 1957. A study of the thoughts and mores of the high-school boy and girl based on a sampling of 2,500 students among grades nine through twelve, urban and rural.

RIESSMAN, FRANK. *The Culturally Deprived Child*. New York: Harper, 1962. A sympathetic but not sentimental analysis of the problems and possibilities of education for the underprivileged. Strongly recommends that the positive aspects of the culture of the disadvantaged be recognized in educational practice. Contains more than a score of practical suggestions for working with the deprived child.

3 Dynamics of the Curriculum

THE IMPORTANCE OF THE CURRICULUM

One of the basic differences between the high school and the elementary school, at least in the United States, is that the high school programs students individually rather than *en bloc*. Through the elementary school, and even the junior high school, the basic program is designed to be, as far as possible, the same for all children.[1] Some schools, of course, do accelerate the abler pupils or, more commonly, provide enrichment for them through additional experiences. The program of the senior high school, however, is based on the premise that all students have widely differing abilities, interests, and goals, and that different patterns of experience and different courses of study are necessary. Experiences which are desirable for all youth and those which are suitable only for those with similar aptitudes, interests, and goals must be included in the curriculum. In large school systems it may be necessary to decide whether it is possible or desirable to meet all of the different needs adequately in the same secondary school.

The curriculum of the high school in practice, if not always

---

[1] As in other respects, the junior high school occupies an intermediate position. There are wide curricular variations from class to class within each grade but, in general, each student in a class follows the same program. The tendency, however, is in the direction of flexibility and individuality of programs approximating the high-school pattern. The junior high school is discussed on pages 59–61.

in theory, must be built around all the experiences of school life. Major and minor courses, extracurricular and cocurricular activities, the homeroom experience, the cafeteria, study halls, assembly programs, informal social contacts, and the amount and kind of homework all constitute the functioning curriculum of the high school. All of these are directed to provide each student with experiences that will best equip him for life. If the curriculum is successful, at graduation the students are ready for college, for suitable employment, or for whatever further educational opportunities the community offers. They are prepared for lives of maximum usefulness and satisfaction in the homes, the communities, and society.

It is usual for the high school to divide its curriculum into two sections—a required "core" of subjects, including English, social studies, mathematics and science, which are assumed to provide knowledge and skill needed by all youth; and a group of electives designed to prepare selected students for further formal education, for employment, or for homemaking. For many years curricula were based on completely false assumptions that there was a great similarity in abilities of high-school students, but today courses of study, required and elective, are adapted to the widely varying abilities of students.

THE BASIC DETERMINANTS OF THE CURRICULUM

In America the high-school curriculum is considered far too important to be left solely to educators. Newspaper editorials, magazine articles, and radio and television commentators direct a constant stream of criticism at the secondary schools and offer a wide variety of suggestions for its improvement. The sales of the *Conant Report* and of such books as those of Keats, Rickover, and Woodring witness the degree of public concern. Such interest is entirely proper in view of the American tradition of local control of the schools.

Courses of study and curricula are, in fact, a composite of the work of legislatures, boards of education, school administrators, teachers, students, and interested civic, religious and fraternal groups. Each group attempts to use its influence and authority to insure a school program most compatible with its own interests, which are conceived as being synonymous with public interest.

The Values of Society

Obviously, the basic determinant of curriculum is the American system of values. Since not all Americans always agree on these values, there have been, are, and will be differences of opinion about what should be included or omitted, but generally, our fundamental concepts of nationalism, civic virtue, and economic organization appear in courses of study. In varying degrees, English courses stress communication as a social process or as a means for self-realization. The literature to be studied by students as a group reflects the values of mid-century America. Since this is a scientific age, stress is given to science. The rapid development of technology and the demands of the cold war require emphasis on theoretical rather than applied science. In an age enriched by greater leisure, high schools have larger bands and more athletic teams (though many teachers and principals may be less than enthusiastic about these developments). In our practical industrial society, vocational education is emphasized. The degree and kind of foreign languages taught reflect in part the social aspirations of the community, as well as the needs of international relations. Some critics of our schools object to the dominant position of middle-class values and virtues in our schools, but these values are the values dominant in our culture.[2]

The Force of Tradition

American educators frequently discuss dynamic change and progressive adjustment, but the nature of the school makes it a highly traditional social institution. It is easy for us to think of the French *lycée* or English public school as examples of how traditionalized secondary education can become, but few of us realize that the American high school, too, is subject to conservative pressures. If an American in his forties or fifties thinks about his own high-school experiences, he will realize how many of today's educational patterns were established in his youth. The number and general pattern of required courses, the daily schedule, the homeroom, report cards, examinations, assemblies, study halls, and the plan of administration and of extracurricu-

[2] See *Balance in the Curriculum* (Washington, D.C.: 1961), Association for Supervision and Curriculum Development, for a detailed discussion of the questions raised in this section.

lar life have changed only in degree and detail. Students themselves are eager to follow traditions. Even in new high schools it is remarkable to see how readily student life is organized in the familiar American matrix. Teachers, too, generally are a conservative force. They often cling to older procedures and older textbooks to an extent that disturbs and frustrates forward-looking supervisors. The latter, of course, include their share of traditionalists who dampen the ardor of classroom teachers. Parents, too, are likely to be fairly complacent about the outcomes of their own education, and frequently urge the school to reproduce for their children a carbon copy of their own educational experiences.

The Interests and Needs of Youth

Fortunately or unfortunately, in a free society youth is relatively articulate about its own interests. If education is too traditional or if it is permeated with the values of only a segment of adult society, teachers may be confronted by a degree of resistance to the educational process that will seriously interfere with its effectiveness. Parental complaints, high dropout rates, truancy, and perhaps even delinquency may be the storm signals of an outmoded and inadequate curriculum. Since educators are properly concerned with the most effective motivations for pupils, and since we are learning more and more about how to measure the effectiveness of our procedures, the schools must try to discover the needs and interests of youth if we are to get students more interested and more involved.

Students, like adults, vary enormously in their ability to discern distant and ultimate goals, and the curriculum designer is always faced with conflict between the student's ultimate and immediate interests and needs. As the character of the high-school population changes, the differing needs of a broader range of student abilities and interests properly and inevitably will be reflected in broader and more varied courses of study.

Of course, traditionalists who consider the high school as an institution with fixed standards will regard this as a watering down of the curriculum. It is often difficult for the resident of the brick (if not ivory) tower to understand the full significance of the now trite maxim that, in learning one must start where the learner is. On the other hand, some who have lived by that maxim have abused it, interpreting "start" as "stay." More important, we know precious little today about *where* the pupil is when he starts secondary school and *what* his needs are. Yet one is the indispensable guidepost of the curriculum-maker and the other is, in its fullest sense, what the curriculum is about. The imperative need for research in these two areas is obvious.

Competence and Preparation of Teachers

Basically, the meaning and effectiveness of the curriculum depends on the skills and competencies of our teachers. For example, though there is good reason to require wide and extensive instruction in Russian and oriental languages in our schools the actual number of classes will depend on the number of available and accredited teachers who are competent in these areas. Of course, despite the necessity for competency, changes in society may result in alternatives in these requirements. For example, after World War I, hundreds of German teachers found themselves teaching English or civics. The great shortage of mathematics and science teachers and the emphasis on these subjects may necessitate the in-service retraining of some teachers.

Newer procedures—core programs, the use of visual aids, unit and committee procedures, team teaching, and educational TV—and the introduction of new subjects or experimental practices in the high school always depend on whether the staff members are able and willing to undertake innovations. Thus, advanced placement classes, or special areas, such as journalism, dramatics, radio and television, modern geometry, physical chemistry, and any of the less common foreign languages, can be introduced only if there are competent teachers who are at least willing and preferably anxious to make the attempt. Similarly, experiments or innovations in method can be introduced only if the staff is ready and eager to participate.

New Insights

Inevitably, in a society committed to the scientific method, education will grow and change with research and the emergence of new insights. As scholarship develops, subject matter will change. The most obvious recent changes are those which have taken place in science courses, and all indications are that the process of change there is just beginning. Mathematics, long one of the most static subjects, is now receiving attention in curriculum revision. Language instruction has felt the impact of new techniques; the use of multiple tape recorders in language laboratories is a vivid illustration of how method can influence subject matter. The extension of foreign language instruction to the elementary schools, if it comes about, will have enormous effect on teaching in the secondary schools. New ideas about psychology will undoubtedly continue to change our concepts of method. Studies of the effects of our traditional courses in history and government on civic behavior ultimately may cause much greater emphasis on the participation by students in civic enterprises in both the school and the community. Increased knowledge in such areas as mental health and the social sciences, and more accurate diagnoses of the occupational needs of our society all will affect our courses of study. These changes inevitably will conflict with tradition.

Outside Pressures

In a country where schools are subject to local administration and control and where the people are deeply committed to democratic government, the weight of pressure groups will continue to be felt by the schools, just as they are by other agencies. Indeed, the absence or diminution of such pressures usually is indicative of indifference to education rather than to faith in the wisdom of educators. Patriotic groups may want more narrative history of the nation's early beginnings and more local history extolling the virtues of the ancestors of the oldest residents. Business and labor groups may agree that more economics should be taught, but disagree about the point of view. Other groups will want stress on conservation. National groups may want particular languages taught. Religious groups may want released time for religious instruction and may insist on a veto involving literature or science that they feel conflicts with the tenets of their faith. Groups interested in foreign policy and international affairs will demand more emphasis on international understanding.

Since an increasing proportion of students plans to attend college, colleges exert more influence on the high-school course of study. In the late 1930's the famous Eight Year Study seemed to prove rather forcefully that the specifics of the high school curriculum seemed to have little or no effect on the success of students in college.[3] For two decades after, the colleges seemed to be less interested in what students had studied than in their potential ability and the level of their achievement. But there are some indications that the situation is changing. Certainly, as students compete more intensely for places in prestige colleges, the ideas of those institutions about which high-school courses are most desirable will have a great influence on the curriculum.

Available Facilities

Finally, the physical plant of the school—buildings, grounds, and equipment—has important effects on the courses of study. Where schools are equipped with shops there naturally will be greater effort to program students for courses that utilize this equipment. Swimming cannot be taught if swimming pools are not provided. The presence or absence of gymnasiums and of athletic fields naturally affects the nature of the health-education program. The inventory of textbooks has an obvious effect on what is taught. The nature of the classrooms and the amount and kind of visual aids and laboratory equipment affect not only the kinds of courses taught, but their nature and quality. The adequacy of a school's library has important consequences for the curriculum. The extent and variety of the physical facilities that a normal community can afford is greatly affected by the size of the student population, and usually the curriculum will be restricted in a very small high school.

THE CONTENT OF THE CURRICULUM

The Traditional Academic Curriculum

The traditional academic curriculum is based on the European system of secondary education, though the American form is very different from the original. Traditionally, in Europe the secondary school's main curriculum ingredient is the study of Latin and Greek. This basic plan has been largely abandoned in the United States, even in the most traditional private schools.

[3] Wilfred M. Aiken, *The Story of the Eight Year Study* (New York: Harper, 1942).

Usually four years of Latin is the maximum requirement, and Greek has been replaced by a modern language. In many high schools, even Latin has yielded to one of the modern languages. In fact, recently there has been concern because so many students take only two years of a foreign language.

The format of the American high-school program was rather definitely established when the Carnegie Foundation, in 1906, defined a unit as a course of five periods a week throughout an academic year.[4] College admission was determined by the completion of a given number of such units. This convenient administrative practice firmly established a requirement of sixteen units for graduation and the five-period-a-week course in our schools. The pattern of an academic course in a four-year high school became four years of English, three to seven years of foreign languages, ancient and modern, with the remaining units to be selected from science, mathematics, and history (which later came to be called the social studies).

In science the first offerings usually included botany, zoology, physiology, physics, and chemistry. Later the natural sciences were consolidated into general science and biology. Mathematics began with algebra and proceeded through plane geometry and more algebra to solid geometry and trigonometry. At the turn of the century the usual social studies offerings included geography, political economy, American history, English history, and ancient history. Modern European history and economics appeared in the first decades of the twentieth century, and varying types of fusion courses developed. This traditional course was usually enriched by electives or minors in art and music or, as became popular at the turn of the century, by courses in manual training. Physical education was usually a required part of the program.

While the Carnegie units no longer are the established requirements for graduation, many schools maintain the traditional elements of the curriculum they prescribed.

Developments in the Twentieth Century

The twentieth century has been a period of tremendous expansion of secondary education in America, and the second-

---

[4] Ellsworth Tompkins and Walter H. Golemitz, *The Carnegie Unit: Its Origins, Status, and Trends* (Washington, D.C.: United States Office of Education, 1954), Bulletin No. 7.

ary school is now regarded as a necessary educational experience for all American youth. The expansion of the secondary school to serve the great majority of youth made it a useful instrument for adaptation to the social, industrial and commercial changes taking place in America. The traditional academic curriculum is still widespread in our schools, but many courses of study necessary to meet the needs of the greatly increased number of students have been introduced.

Commercial Courses.   Commercial courses were among the first of the new vocational courses designed for the secondary schools. Courses in typing, stenography, and bookkeeping rapidly established a place for themselves. The success that the graduates of these courses achieved in gaining employment ensured the popularity of this curriculum. Standard sequences of these courses were quickly set up so that commercial diplomas could be awarded.

Technical and Vocational Courses.   A similar growth took place in other vocational and technical courses. While separate technical and vocational high schools were organized only in the larger cities, courses in industrial, vocational, and technical subjects were widely established. The passage of the Smith-Hughes Act in 1917 gave great impetus to this development. The Smith-Hughes Act (supplemented and extended by the George-Barden Act of 1946) resulted in a vastly expanded program of vocational education at the secondary level by providing federal aid for instruction in agriculture, home economics, trades and industry, and the distributive occupations (retailing), as well as teacher education in these fields. Communities were able to receive federal funds as soon as they inaugurated programs meeting the requirements of this law. Industry and labor unions were eager to help the development of sound technical and vocational courses and to help design these programs.

One misconception that arose early, and has remained to vex educators, is the notion that vocational education is the unfailing answer for all students who are not interested in or capable of succeeding in academic courses. Students with low IQ's are often as little interested in and as relatively incapable of reasonable success in vocational courses as they are in academic studies. Obviously it is poor policy to spend the extra funds needed for vocational education for students whose sole qualification is their inability to adjust to the traditional academic program. This concept has also resulted in an image of the vocational schools as second-class schools.

Work-Study Plans.   Another promising innovation of the twentieth century has been the attempt to design school programs that combine work in school with on-the-job experience in industry or business. There have been a variety of successful patterns. One plan provides one job for two students, who alternate a period in school with a period of full-time employment. More commonly the school day is abbreviated so that the student can have a part-time job in industry. The student is under some school supervision and receives school credit for the job. Obviously these programs require cooperation between school and industry, and support and assistance from labor organizations.

General Courses.   As the high school was made available to almost all adolescents, it became obvious that there were many students who apparently were not interested in, or able to succeed in academic, commercial or vocational programs. Sometimes their feelings were passive, but sometimes they became hostile. Other patterns of education were needed to meet their interests and abilities. In most large schools this alteration took the form of a "general" course, which often was a watered-down version of the traditional programs.

Students who were unsuccessful in other courses were permitted to enroll in the easier versions, where languages usually were not required and where science and mathematics were made easier and more "practical." In general courses English and social studies courses were modified, and special courses in business practice, crafts, and industrial arts were provided. Electives that would appeal to these students were offered. (These appealing, easy courses sometimes are elected by students capable of the more academic work.) In many instances, of course, these general courses have not succeeded in eliciting interest and maximum effort from some students.

It may be that some of our current programs are still too restricted to the classroom and the textbook. Many students may need broader and more elastic programs than we have yet developed—programs that may mean more involvement with the adult world in the home, in industry, and in government.

The Specialized High School.   As these varied curricula developed, larger cities began to establish specialized high schools, following a pattern that had been established in European secondary education. Many of the larger cities established not only academic, commercial, and vocational high schools, but also separate high schools for particular vocational activities. These schools have been criticized on the basis that they tend to become too socially homogeneous, and that grouping students from one social class and generally of the same ability level is not democratic. Another criticism is that, specialized as they may be, they often tend to become neighborhood schools, selected by students for their proximity rather than their special interest in the industry. There is some question as to whether a sufficient proportion of the graduates of these schools work in the particular industry to justify their courses of study.

Another type of specialized high school, designed for the abler students, has been established in several American cities, including Boston, Philadelphia, Cincinnati, and New York. These high schools are organized to meet the needs of abler students with particular interests in science, music, and art. There is no doubt that these specialized high schools have been successful, but some feel that concentrating gifted students in separate high schools has a perceptibly adverse effect on the tone of the neighborhood high schools.

THE JUNIOR HIGH SCHOOL

One of the most outstanding organizational changes in secondary education has been the change from the four-year high school either to a six-year "junior-senior" high school or to separate three-year junior and senior high schools. The term junior high school is believed to have been used first in Columbus, Ohio, when the Indianola Junior High School opened there in 1910. This type of organization did not attain prominence until after World War I. The movement gained momentum in the second decade of the century, until by 1963 more than twice as many students were attending six-year or three-year schools as were attending the traditional four-year high school.[5]

[5] *Public Secondary Schools: Statistics of Education in the United States 1958–59 Series* (Washington, D.C.: United States Office of Education, Government Printing Office, 1961), pp. 8–9.

Since there are now over 5,000 junior high schools in the United States, it is well to consider the needs this institution is designed to serve. These include: a recognition of the special problems of early adolescence, speeding of college-entrance preparation, experimentation in education, coping with the dropout problem, flexibility in school building programs, bridging the gap between elementary school and high school, and dissatisfaction with the traditional high school.[6]

The junior high school was conceived as a transitional school where young adolescents could get a broader and better designed program than in the upper two years of the traditional elementary school. Also, the adoption of the 3–3 system (grades 7–8–9 and grades 10–11–12) proved a useful device when high-school buildings became too old and too crowded. Junior-high-school personnel usually are freer and more eager to adopt curriculum changes, since they are convinced that a separate school can design better programs to meet the special needs and interests of the younger adolescent. At one time, the junior high school was considered to be a terminal school for many students who would complete their education on reaching sixteen, but as the percentage of students remaining in school increases, this function has less importance.

The Effect of the Junior High

The junior high school has had several operational and philosophic effects on the curriculum: (1) There has been general acceptance of the idea that the program of the ninth year should have a large degree of uniformity, whether the student is enrolled in a junior or senior high school. Marked specialization in course of study should not take place until the tenth year. (2) Junior high schools have been far more ready than senior high schools to adopt core or unified studies programs,

[6] V. T. Thayer, *The Role of the School in American Society* (New York: Dodd, Mead, 1960), refers to five aspects of early adolescence which the flexible program in the junior high school was to meet: (1) rapid changes in interests and aptitudes, (2) budding social interests, (3) intellectual interests centering on concrete rather than abstract, (4) individual differences in interests and life goals becoming prominent, and (5) concern with the immediate environment. See also "How the Junior High School Came To Be" in *Educational Leadership*, 18, No. 3 (December, 1960). For an expression of junior-high-school vitality, see *Educational Leadership*, Journal of the ASCD, 18, No. 3 (Dec. 1960), on the theme, "Junior High School: Issues and Prospects."

perhaps because this pattern is closer to the traditional self-contained classroom of the elementary school. (3) The wide diversity in student ability, maturity, and interests has tended to stimulate the use of ability grouping in the junior high school.

The junior high school can be conceived as a step from the self-sufficient classroom of the elementary school to the more traditional subject-matter approach of the senior high school. At best, the junior high school is a school especially designed for the young adolescent where he is neither the ranking senior of an elementary school, nor the callow freshman in a senior high school. He is not inappropriately referred to as a "tweenager"—between elementary and secondary school, between the immature child and the mature adult. The junior high school provides a variety of curricular and extracurricular experiences that will identify and develop his abilities at his own level.

THE JUNIOR COLLEGE

At about the same time the junior high school emerged as a popular pattern of educational organization, the junior college was conceived as a means for extending the education of students who could not (or felt no need to) complete a full four-year collegiate program. William R. Harper, first president of the University of Chicago, championed the junior college as a means by which students could begin their professional education at an earlier age. Advocates of the junior college hoped that it might become an established and integral part of the public school system. They envisaged a 6/3/3/2 organization that would add a thirteenth and fourteenth year to public education.[7] Recent demands for increased facilities for higher education have led to a renewed emphasis on the junior college.

In 1962, there were 677 junior colleges with a total enrollment of over one million students. At the present rate of increase the number of junior colleges may reach 1,500 by 1970, with a total student enrollment of close to four million. And, in the light of pressures in secondary and post-secondary education, these figures may prove conservative. The population explosion, unemployment of youth, the need for greater educational preparation in the attainment of vocational goals, the

[7] Ellwood P. Cubberley, *Public Education in the United States* (New York: Houghton Mifflin, 1934), p. 557.

increase in relative and absolute numbers attending high school and applying for college, the insufficient facilities of the colleges to absorb the applicants in the first two years, the prohibitive cost of attending college as a boarding student, the uncertainty of many high-school graduates about vocational goals, and the inability of many to undertake rigorous college-level work have combined to promote the growth of the community junior college.

Junior colleges provide occupational training for those who wish two years of post-high-school education on a terminal basis. For those seeking a four-year college education, it provides the first two years on an experimental basis, supplying the four-year college with a quota of upper-classmen who have demonstrated the capacity and the motivation for college work. For example, Atlantic University in Florida now offers only upper-class and graduate study because the students are drawn from junior colleges. Others may adopt this pattern.

The Community Junior College

The community junior college[8] stands ready to take any and all high school graduates, regardless of their academic achievement, and provide them with further education on condition that they give evidence of profiting from additional schooling. Nor is the condition difficult of fulfillment, for the community junior college is committed to adjusting its curriculum to the needs and interests of all who apply. The principles underlying the community junior college are enumerated by Thornton as follows:

> To make higher education available to qualified students of all ages, all social classes, all varieties of ability; to develop a sufficient variety of curriculums to meet the educational needs, at this level, of the community and of the individual students; to provide counseling and guidance services to help students choose appropriately from the available offerings; to devote concerted attention to effective teaching; and then to require the highest standards of achievement of its students.[9]

[8] The "community" junior college refers to the college established and financed by a local community, often with state support, to serve the post-secondary-school needs of the community. The term "junior college" is the all-inclusive term subsuming both the community junior colleges and the colleges established under private, religious, state or other auspices.

[9] James W. Thornton, Jr. *The Community Junior College* (New York: Wiley, 1960), p. 44. Reprinted by permission.

The policy of admitting all who would come means that the community junior college must offer a college preparatory program geared to those of the nearby colleges and universities, as well as an occupational program based on the economic characteristics of the community. Another curricular area must be designed for those whose interest is neither college preparatory nor vocational preparation but general or cultural education.

This wide span of curriculum acts as a bar to pretensions for degree granting, and indicates an urgent need for expert guidance facilities. The community junior college, even more than the high school, is beset by student demands for aid in planning a program of studies appropriate to their capacities, interests, and objectives. In many cases guidance at this level means helping students understand their capacities and find their interests and objectives.

RECENT TRENDS IN CURRICULUM

Despite changes in organization, the basic patterns of curriculum of the secondary school have changed relatively little during the twentieth century. Major and minor subjects, homerooms, assemblies, and extracurricular activities are almost identical with those of the high school of the turn of the century. Despite tracking, audio-visual aids, improved teaching materials, better laboratories and libraries, the subject-specialist teacher is still the norm. Compared with the major reconstruction of elementary-school practice, patterned on the child-centered school of Dewey and Kilpatrick, the secondary school of today is a generation or more behind the times. Yet there is reason to believe that it will not be long before the curriculum of the high school will be radically reconstructed. Directions of change are discernable.

Unified Studies

The trend toward unified studies, such as humanities, core, block-time, common learnings, is particularly strong in the junior high school, though many senior high schools are experimenting with this curricular innovation. Two or more subject areas (generally English and social studies) are taught by the same teacher to a class that is together for two periods or more each day. An analysis of the rationale for this development and a discussion of its implementation will be found in Chapter 15.

At this point we merely note this as a major curricular innovation in the secondary-school program.

Provision for the Individual

A society committed to education for each individual to the extent that he is able and willing to learn must of necessity develop suitable programs for the gifted, the talented, the slow, the mentally retarded, the physically handicapped, and the emotionally disturbed. Each of these special areas will find its representatives in every comprehensive high school. Hence the school of today, unlike its predecessor of a quarter-century ago, is developing special programs to meet the needs of these and other groups.

Advanced Standing

A massive attack on the problems of the gifted high-school boy or girl (2 or 3 percent of the total high-school population) and of the talented (15 percent) is yielding new insights, new techniques, and gratifying results.

One approach to meeting the special needs of the gifted and talented is *enrichment;* another is *acceleration.* The latter is represented by the advanced standing program sponsored by the College Entrance Examination Board, and is participated in by a growing number of secondary schools and colleges. Under the impact of this and similar programs it will not be long before the traditional eight-year, high school—college sequence is shortened to seven or even six years for large numbers of gifted and talented students.

This trend will help in part to obviate the tendency of postponing the completion of professional education to the late twenties, while the average age for marriage is lowered. It will also have the effect of measurably increasing the holding power of schools and colleges for those best able to profit from academic and professional education. Finally, it will necessitate a revision of traditional curricular patterns and methods of teaching, studying, testing, and grading.

College Entrance Pressure

In the forseeable future (1975) the number of qualified college applicants probably will exceed the number of places in accredited colleges. The mounting pressure on high-school students to achieve excellent academic records is being felt down into the junior and sophomore years and will probably affect students and teachers down into the junior high school. Whether this is a salutary development or whether, as many believe, it is detrimental to the best interests of the coming generation, there is no doubt that pressure on students from their school administrators and teachers, from their parents, from the community, and from the competitive situation will become greater during the next decade or two.

Modification of Compulsory Education Laws

An interesting development is the relaxing of compulsory education laws. Recently there has emerged a recognition of the evils of requiring attendance of students who are not profiting from high school, who are actually developing anti-social habits, and who may be making high school a nightmare for earnest, conscientious teachers and fellow students. Such adolescent girls and boys command a disproportionate amount of the time and energy of the professional staff. They do no one, including themselves, any good in school.

Attendance laws are being modified both *de facto* and *de jure* to permit separation of this small number before the age of compulsory attendance is reached. Sometimes these students are removed to special institutions, sometimes to the custody of parents, children's bureaus, employers, or detention homes.

Neither laws insisting that these students remain in school, nor the relaxing of the laws are the answers to the problem of the "problem" students. Instead they are interim measures. The school may—indeed must—properly undertake the education of the deviate, but it cannot fairly be required to educate those who make education for the rest well-nigh impossible.

Juvenile Delinquency

This factor is closely associated with but not identical with the problem discussed in the previous section. The juvenile delinquent may be amenable to education in school while participating in organized law breaking outside school. He is not necessarily emotionally disturbed in the narrow sense of the term. He is a member of organized crime of the adolescent or post-adolescent variety.

With the extension of compulsory school attendance into

the late teens and with the emergence of the secondary school as the school of all youth, the school has become a major social agency for combating juvenile delinquency. Attendance teachers, counselors, psychological personnel, special teachers, administrators, coaches, and other members of the secondary-school staff are combining to develop a program of prevention, substitution, sublimation, and correction in meeting the problems posed by anti-social teenage group activities.

Integrating School and Community

The combined efforts of school and community in solving the problem of juvenile delinquency is just one phase of a union which is certain to have increasing influence in the education of secondary-school students. The community is becoming an integral part of the school, and vice versa. Members of the community who are specialists in their fields are being invited increasingly to share their information and skill with students. Talks, demonstrations, informal meetings, illustrated lectures, debates, and panel discussions by local attorneys, physicians, and other professional, business, and community specialists are a strong influence on the education of children in their community schools. Teachers are taking groups of children into the community to view and examine the art, religion, economic life, and cultural activities which constitute the life of their community. The high-school student is being encouraged to participate in the politics, business or agricultural life, social and cultural activities of the community as part of his school work.

Increasingly, then, the school and the outside community are merging into a union of organized experiences designed to further the education of the student. These are some of the trends that may be projected for the next decade or two in the changing curriculum of the American secondary school.

FOR DELIBERATION and DISCUSSION

1. "The Conant Report turned back the clock so far as curricular change in the high school is concerned." Discuss this remark, giving evidence for your position.
2. "Curriculum-making is not the business of the layman." To what extent are laymen involved in curriculum-making? To what extent should they be involved? Why?

3. Should high-school students participate in curriculum-making? At what stage? What are the implications of involving students in curriculum-making?

4. To what extent is the high-school curriculum influenced by (a) tradition, (b) teachers' competencies and interests, (c) concept of the worth of specific subject matter (see Herbert Spencer's *What Knowledge is of Most Worth* for an expression of this philosophy)? To what extent do you think each of these should influence the high school curriculum?

5. State and explain your opinions of the relative advantages of various types of school organization (6–6, 6–3–3, 6–2–4, 8–4, or others) in secondary education.

6. Advanced placement, combined with the junior college, may result in telescoping fourteen years of education into twelve for the talented youth of the next generation. Is this a desirable trend? Why?

7. In what respects is the curriculum of the junior high school similar to that of the high school? Of the elementary school? Has it followed the better or the less desirable aspects of each? Explain in detail.

8. Distinguish between "curriculum" and "course of study." What is the relationship, if any, between them? Which is the broader term? Explain.

9. Bestor says: "The idea that there can be a 'curriculum expert' is as absurd as the idea that there can be an expert on the meaning of life." (*Educational Wastelands,* p. 40) Do you agree? Explain.

FOR ADDITIONAL READING

AIKEN, WILFORD M. *The Story of the Eight Year Study.* New York: Harper, 1942. Vol. I. The first of a five-volume study of the attempt to practice "progressive education" in thirty selected secondary schools throughout the country and its results. Evidence supports the premise that students were better educated than those in the traditional high school during the same period (1933–1941). The other volumes of the study are: Vol. II, *Exploring the Curriculum;* Vol. III, *Appraising and Recording Student Progress;* Vol. IV, *Did They Succeed in College?;* Vol. V, *Thirty Schools Tell Their Story.*

ALCORN, MARVIN D. (ed.). *Issues in Curriculum Development.* Yonkers: World Book, 1959. All aspects of curriculum considered by leading contemporary American educators.

AMERICAN ASSOCIATION OF SCHOOL ADMINISTRATORS, COUNCIL OF CHIEF STATE SCHOOL OFFICERS, AND NATIONAL ASSOCIATION OF SECONDARY SCHOOL PRINCIPALS. *Testing, Testing, Testing.* Washington, D.C.: The Association, 1962. Raises serious questions about the validity of standardized tests and about the warrant for time, money, and effort spent by school districts in selecting and administering them and in attempting to use their results.

Balance in the Curriculum. Washington, D.C.: Association for Supervision and Curriculum Development, 1961. In eight chapters the subject is examined on the basis of content, method, organization, and so on. The last chapter analyzes the roles of all individuals and groups in curriculum-making. (See also the 1951 Yearbook of the ASCD, *Action for Curriculum Development,* and the 1957 Yearbook, *Research for Curriculum Development.*)

CONANT, JAMES BRYANT. *The American High School Today: A First Report to Interested Citizens.* New York: McGraw-Hill, 1959. Based on a survey of over one hundred comprehensive high schools in twenty-six states. Makes recommendations. Known as *The Conant Report.*

Education in the Junior High School Years. Princeton: Educational Testing Service, 1960. Contains fourteen recommendations for the junior high school.

Evaluative Criteria. Washington, D.C.: National Study of Secondary School Evaluation, 1960. Consists of a manual followed by detailed criteria for evaluation of a high school including philosophy and objectives, school and community, program of studies (by subjects), student activity program, and so on. This volume is used as the basis of high-school evaluation by regional accrediting associations.

FRAZIER, ALEXANDER (ed.). *New Insights and the Curriculum.* Washington, D.C.: Association for Supervision and Curriculum Development, 1963. Two chapters on each of the following: potentiality, knowledge, self-management, relationships, across cultures, citizenship, creativity. Many ideas and insights on the practice of educational thinking and research.

GLEAZER, EDMUND J., JR. *The Junior College Directory of the American Association of Junior Colleges.* (Published annually at 1777 Massachusetts Ave., N.W., Washington, D.C.) Contains addresses, names, and information about all junior colleges in the United States. Includes other data in the area of the community junior college. Also by the Association the *Junior College Journal* published monthly from September to May inclusive.

GREER, E. S. and HARBGER, RICHARD M. *What High School Pupils Study: A National Survey of the Scholastic Performances of Various Abilities.* Washington, D.C.: United States Department of Health, Education, and Welfare, 1962. A statistical study pointing the way to improvement in program planning in the high school.

"The Junior High School Idea in Theory and Practice,"

Bulletin (National Association of Secondary School Principals), 46, No. 276 (October, 1962). A selection of articles summarizing the goals, achievements, and problems of the junior high school.

SMITH, B. OTHANEL, STANLEY, WILLIAM O., and SHORES, J. HARLAN. *Fundamentals of Curriculum Development*. rev. ed.; New York: World, 1957. The best available theoretical discussion of curriculum. The issues in curriculum construction and development are examined with keen insight.

STRATEMEYER, FLORENCE, *et al. Developing a Curriculum for Modern Living*. New York: Bureau of Publications, Teachers College, Columbia U., 1957. A large work containing many suggestions. The authors state their position frankly, ". . . that the needs and purposes of learners must be central in designing a curriculum. . . ."

THORNTON, JAMES W., JR. *The Community Junior College*. New York: Wiley, 1960. An informed, judicious discussion of every aspect of the institution: its background, organization, curriculum, and prospects.

VENABLE, TOM C. *Patterns in Secondary School Curriculum*. New York: Harper, 1958. A concise treatment of the traditional high-school curriculum. Brief separate chapters on each high-school subject. Good bibliographies.

What The High Schools Ought to Teach. Report of a Special Committee Prepared for the American Youth Council, and published by the American Council on Education, Washington, D.C.: 1940. A provocative report containing a brief historical account, keen analysis, and recommendations still very much worth considering.

WOODRING, PAUL. *A Fourth of the Nation*. New York: McGraw-Hill, 1957. A consultant for the Fund for the Advancement of Education attempts to resolve recent conflicts in education. (See also his *Let's Talk Sense About Our Schools*, 1953.)

4 The Secondary-School Teacher

RECRUITMENT

Traditionally, secondary-school teachers in the United States have been recruited from three major sources: (1) the education departments of liberal arts colleges; (2) the secondary-education departments of teachers colleges; and (3) the elementary-school faculty. The first was a major source until the 1920's, when teachers colleges began converting to degree-granting institutions. In the 1940's and early 1950's, as the need for secondary teachers increased rapidly, teachers colleges expanded their offerings to help meet the rapidly expanding demand. The third source, the ranks of the elementary profession, has furnished a relatively small percentage of secondary-school teachers, and it is likely to recede in importance as the need for elementary teachers continues to grow, as the single salary schedule becomes universal, and as specialized training of each division makes retraining more complicated.

Economically and socially, the secondary-school teacher traditionally has come from the middle and lower-middle class. The security factor, the teacher's social status, and (in times of depression and economic stress) the relatively high income have made teaching on the secondary level attractive to these groups. Children of immigrants, working men, small business men, and professionals have gravitated to the teaching profession. Of course, this does not deny the idealism which has at-

70

tracted young people from all socio-economic groups to answer the "call" to teach.

Through the 1930's, graduation from a liberal arts college was sufficient in most states to qualify one for a secondary-teaching certificate in the area of the graduate's major work. During the past quarter-century, however, state departments of education have adopted certification requirements of courses in professional education. These vary from state to state, but generally they demand a strong major in the subject to be taught, plus a number of courses in education, including student teaching.

A reorientation of recruitment and training began after World War II. The first impetus to change was the tremendous increase in secondary-school enrollment, with a corresponding increase in the need for qualified secondary-school teachers. The second was the cold war and the challenge of Russian education which sparked an American rededication to excellence and turned the emphasis in secondary-teacher certification to specialization and heavy subject-matter concentration. Finally, a relatively long period of economic prosperity and inflation reduced the status of the teacher in the socio-economic scale, making recruitment to teaching more difficult. These factors have had the overall effect of making the staffing of secondary schools with well-qualified teachers a difficult national problem.

Experimental Programs

Recognizing that the staffing of our schools with qualified teachers, particularly at the secondary level, is a national necessity, the Fund for the Advancement of Education has supported new techniques in recruitment, training, staffing, and teaching.[1]

[1] The Ford Foundation *Annual Report* for 1962 lists the following grantees with national programs to strengthen preparation of teachers for elementary and secondary schools. The grants vary from $100,000 to $2,000,000: Brown University, Central Michigan University, University of Chicago, Claremont College, Cornell University, Converse College, Duke University, George Peabody College, Goucher College, Harvard University, University of Hawaii, Johns Hopkins University, University of Kansas City, Kansas State University, Miami University (Ohio), Michigan State University, Middlebury College, New York University, Northwestern University, University of Notre Dame, Oberlin College, University of Pittsburgh, San Diego State College, U.C.L.A., Stanford University, Temple University, Wayne State University (Michigan), Webster College, University of Wisconsin, Yale University. The Ford Foundation has also made a grant of $5,000,000 for teacher-education internship programs to the Oregon System of Higher Education, administered through the Oregon State Department of Education, beginning in 1963.

Other organizations also have made grants to colleges and school districts for experimental programs designed to meet the needs in secondary education. The premises on which these grants are made include the following factors:

1. There is a vast reservoir of potential for secondary-school teaching personnel which needs to be tapped. This includes graduates of liberal arts colleges in the following groups: homemakers, business men and women, people engaged in other occupations or professions, retired civil service personnel, and recent college graduates with liberal arts degrees but no course work in education.
2. There are many practices on the job performed by trained professional teachers which can be done equally well by semi-skilled, less thoroughly prepared, people.
3. Technology is making available resources which can be used in education to alleviate the need for the present small teacher-pupil ratio.
4. The traditional pattern of classroom instruction and organization needs re-examination.

Sex and Age Factors

Historically, secondary-school teaching in the United States has been a man's profession, just as the elementary school was and continues to be staffed primarily by women. The more extensive period of training required of high-school teachers limited the number of women entrants, since teaching was for many a temporary commitment terminated by marriage, and since some state and school district policies until the first quarter of the twentieth century prohibited employment of married women as teachers.

With the revision of these policies, women entered the secondary school as teachers in increasing numbers. During World War I a sharp rise in the percentage of women secondary-school teachers was necessitated by the shortage of men. In the postwar period, rising costs and economic opportunities worked against attracting men to the profession. The trend was reversed in the 1930's, however, when the depression again made teaching economically and socially attractive to men.

The traditional domination of the secondary schools by men served to limit the opportunities of women to attain supervisory and administrative positions. While this tradition still prevails to some extent, it is passing rapidly. Today approximately 47 percent of the nation's high-school teachers are women, and a smaller but significant percentage occupy positions of leadership—principals, chairmen, curriculum directors, and so on.[2] Women have dispelled the belief that they are not the equal of men in the discharge of supervisory and administrative responsibilities.

Opening the profession of secondary education to women on an equal basis has resulted in a number of obvious advantages. The source for recruitment is appreciably enlarged. Gifted secondary-school teachers, who might otherwise be lost to the profession, are being recruited. This also increases the potential for leadership. Secondary-school staffs display a healthy representation of men and women, married and single, inexperienced and experienced.

Age has also operated as a restricting factor because of law and prejudice. Many states have established a maximum age for entrance into the profession and a compulsory retirement age. Realistically, age should be secondary to competence. The assumed superiority of the older, experienced teacher does not always hold true. Many young teachers attain a high degree of mastery during their first few years on the job, and some old teachers decline in competence and actually are superannuated before the age of compulsory retirement. School administrators need discretion in hiring, assigning, and retiring personnel. The test of age is realistic only insofar as it yields a varied staff of well-qualified individual teachers working at maximum potential. Obviously, every consideration should be given to a man or woman who has devoted twenty years to successful teaching in a secondary school, but who seems to be declining in competence while only middle-aged.

The welfare of the students demands that teachers be reasonably secure, since they are expected to devote their lives to a profession with demands which by far exceed its economic return. The staffing of our secondary schools with well-qualified personnel requires that the factor of age, like that of sex, be con-

---

[2] "There are 857,353 elementary-school teachers, comprising 125,477 men and 731,876 women; and 551,609 secondary-school teachers comprising 285,632 men and 265,979 women." NEA *Research Bulletin*, 39, No. 1 (Feb. 1961): 28.

sidered only in maintaining a balanced faculty, not in preju-
dicing the hiring of otherwise competent individuals.[3]

A Continuing Problem

Student enrollment in the public schools annually increases
by 1 million, necessitating some 35,000 new teachers. In addition, to relieve overcrowding and part-time instruction, some
30,000 new teachers are needed. Some 25,000 more need to be
added to replace those not properly prepared, and finally, 25,000
more are necessary to provide special instruction not now being
given. Add to this replacements for the 125,000 who leave the
profession annually (the attrition rate is about 8 percent and
there were 1,409,000 public-school teachers in 1961), and we
have the basis of the NEA-estimated demand for 240,000 new
teachers annually.

Less than half of this number entered teaching in 1962.
Moreover, the situation actually became worse in mathematics,
foreign languages, English, physical education, library service,
music, business education, and industrial arts, as well as in the
general staffing of the elementary school. Emergency certification and lowered requirements actually hurt recruitment by
discouraging able people from entering the profession. As we
are confronted by the need for some 2 million new teachers in
the next decade, the magnitude of the problem becomes obvious. And if we consider the consequences of a decline in the
quality of teaching personnel, the importance of finding new
sources of well-qualified teachers becomes equally obvious.

The solution most often suggested is raising salaries. That
this will have a powerful effect in recruitment of well-qualified
candidates cannot be denied, but other avenues need to be explored. We need accurate information, for example, about the
people coming into the profession from sources other than recent college graduates. Future Teachers of America clubs in colleges and secondary schools should be encouraged. Above all,
the public image of the teacher needs to be modified. Books like
A Teacher Is A Person, by Charles H. Wilson, can do tremendous good in this direction. The attitude of current teachers in
representing the profession to the young must somehow be al-

---

[3] "The average age of public-school teachers is about 41 years, of superintendents, about 52 years. The average age of beginning teachers is about 24 years."
Ibid.

tered in the direction of a positive presentation. An increase of freedom, self-respect, and general morale of the staff will bring this about. Research is needed to tell us which groups influence young people in occupational choices.

We also need more scholarships to enable young people to pursue college work leading to teaching. Raising the standards—intelligence, academic achievement, commitment to the profession—is another means of reducing the shortage of qualified people. Something like Gresham's law seems to be in operation, so that an increase in the number of incompetents actually has the effect of driving the more able and desirable applicants away from the profession.

PREPARATION AND CERTIFICATION

The preparation of the secondary-school teacher has always been a function of the liberal arts college, and more recently it has been assumed by the teachers college. Almost all of the more than 500,000 secondary-school teachers hold college degrees, and state certification requirements now uniformly require a degree from a four-year college as a minimum for certification.[4]

College preparation of the secondary-school teacher falls into three categories: liberal studies, specialization in a major field, and professional education. Many liberal arts colleges have education departments in which the prospective teacher may pursue a program leading to certification; others do not. Graduates from the latter who wish to enter teaching must pursue a sequence of courses in professional teacher education at a college or university other than their own after graduation.

Generally, fifteen to thirty semester hours in professional courses are required for certification as a teacher of a secondary-school subject. These may include one or more courses in each of the following areas: philosophy or history of education, adolescent psychology, methods of teaching, survey or principles of secondary education, curriculum, guidance, and student teaching. (Table 6, from Armstrong and Stinnett, lists the required hours in professional education for each state.)

Fifteen to thirty-six semester hours of college work in the subject which the student is preparing to teach comprise a major for certification. Generally this is broken down into more

[4] See T. M. Stinnett, "A Vast Overhaul of Teacher Certification," in *Saturday Review*, March 17, 1962.

specific requirements. For example, a student hoping to be certified as a teacher of English may need thirty-six semester hours of English—six in composition, six in speech, six in American literature, with the balance in world literature, English literature, Shakespeare, mass media, and the like. Other majors have similar specific requirements.

Thus the combined requirements of professional education and specialization leave about half the four-year college course for electives in liberal education. This is a recognition of the fact that a secondary-school teacher needs a broad liberal education if he is to be effective in working with adolescents. All disciplines are interrelated. For example, all secondary-school teachers are English teachers, for they must be concerned with the reading, writing, speaking, and listening competencies of their students. Similarly, while contemporary world affairs are taught in the social-studies class, they enter into the work of all subjects, so that a teacher of science or of modern languages who attempts to exclude world affairs or who lacks a background in social sciences will be inadequate in teaching his own subject.

TABLE 6

Specific Minimum Requirements for High-School Certificates Based on Degrees[5]

State	Degree or College Years of Preparation Required	General Education Required, Semester Hours	Professional Education Required, Semester Hours	Directed Teaching Required, Semester Hours (Included in Column 4)
Alabama	B	36	24	3
Alaska	B	—	18	C
Arizona	5	—	18	6
Arkansas	B	48	18	5
California	5	40	22	6
Colorado	B	AC	AC	AC
Connecticut	B	45	18	6
Delaware	B	60*	18	6
District	5	30	18	6
Florida	B	45	20	6
Georgia	B	40	18	6
Hawaii	B	100	18	AC
Idaho	B	—	20	6

[5] W. E. Armstrong and T. M. Stinnett, *A Manual on Certification Requirements for School Personnel in the United States* (Washington, D.C.: NEA, 1961), p. 28.

TABLE 6 (continued)

State	Degree or College Years of Preparation Required	General Education Required, Semester Hours	Professional Education Required, Semester Hours	Directed Teaching Required, Semester Hours (Included in Column 4)
Illinois	B	104	16	5
Indiana	B	30	18	5
Iowa	B	40	20	5
Kansas	B	50	20	5
Kentucky	B	45	17	8
Louisiana	B	46	18	4
Maine	B	39–48	12	0
Maryland	B	—	18	6
Massachusetts	B	—	12	2
Michigan	B	—	20	5
Minnesota	B	—	18	4
Mississippi	B	48	18	6
Missouri	B	25	20	5
Montana	B	—	16	AC
Nebraska	B	—	18	3
Nevada	B	—	18	4
New Hampshire	B	—	21	6
New Jersey	B	—	21	6
New Mexico	B	48	18	6
New York	5	60	18	6
North Carolina	B	—	18	3
North Dakota	B	—	16	3
Ohio	B	100	17	6
Oklahoma	B	50	21	6
Oregon	B	—	24	6
Pennsylvania	B	60	18	6
Puerto Rico	B	—	29	5
Rhode Island	B	—	18	6
South Carolina	B	45	18	6
South Dakota	B	—	30	5
Tennessee	B	40	24	4
Texas	B	45	24	6
Utah	B	48	22	8
Vermont	B	—	18	6
Virginia	B	—	15	4–6
Washington	5	AC	AC	AC
West Virginia	B	—	20	5
Wisconsin	B	—	18	5
Wyoming	B	40	20	C

LEGEND:—means not reported; AC means approved course; 5 means bachelor's degree and 30 semester hours of appropriate postbaccalaureate preparation, not necessarily completion of master's degree; B means completion of the bachelor's degree of specified preparation; C means completion of a course in the field.
*Professional requirements listed are the basic requirements for degree or lowest regular certificates. Some variation from the professional requirements as stated in this table may be found in the requirements for specific certificates listed for the respective states in Chapter 11.

There is, in fact, a current of opinion, bolstered by experimental evidence, among many secondary-school teachers that the teaching of two or more subjects by one teacher, provided that teacher has a good liberal education, is more effective than the teaching of these subjects separately.[6]

State Education Departments and Certification

The state education department promulgates certification requirements and issues teaching certificates for the state. Thus there are fifty sets of requirements for certification in each secondary-school subject. To minimize the chaos, some state education departments have entered into reciprocity arrangements for accepting each other's teaching certificates.[7] Even so the requirements vary so widely that it is possible to get a certificate to teach English, for example, in one state with less than half the college credits in English required in another. The same disparity is apparent in requirements both for general liberal education and for professional education.

Since the state education department is concerned with the maintenance of standards in the certification of teachers, it must work closely with colleges and with school superintendents to bring teacher education in line with the best professional thought and practice, and it must set realistic standards that will make possible the staffing of the schools. Occasionally pressure from boards of education which cannot attract qualified personnel has resulted in the state departments issuing emergency certificates which disregard minimum standards. However, the general requirement that the hiring official attest that he cannot find a qualified teacher for the vacancy before the state education department will issue the emergency certificate makes it unlikely that he or his board will bypass a better-qualified candidate in favor of a less-qualified one.

In its work with liberal arts colleges and teachers colleges, the state education department, like the regional accrediting

[6] Margaret Willis, *The Guinea Pigs After Twenty Years: A Follow-up Study of the Class of 1938 of the University School at the Ohio State University* (Columbus: Ohio U. Press, 1962).

[7] Eighteen states report in 1962 being members of reciprocity compacts. The Eleven State Reciprocity Compact includes the six New England States and New York, New Jersey, Delaware, Maryland, and Pennsylvania. The Central States Conference includes Illinois, Iowa, Kansas, Missouri, Nebraska, South Dakota, and Wisconsin.

associations, exercises some authority in the maintenance of professional standards, in curricula, and in the general pattern of higher education which is reflected in the preparation of personnel for the profession.[8] Presumably the state education department helps the colleges under its general surveillance in developing programs designed for the preparation of well qualified teachers. By granting or withholding approval of college programs for teacher certification, it can exercise influence on the formulation of programs and on general policy in teacher preparation.

PROFESSIONAL ASSOCIATIONS AND TEACHING STANDARDS

The National Commission on Teacher Education and Professional Standards was established in 1946 by the NEA for the express purpose of developing national standards of professional teacher education and certification. The Commission holds national and regional meetings, issues reports, sponsors research, and publishes a yearbook and numerous pamphlets, brochures, and releases designed to raise standards in teacher education and influence state education departments to adopt uniform regulations for teacher certification. Its influence has grown over the years. Hundreds of state and local TEPS bodies have been organized to cooperate with the National Commission in raising standards of "recruitment, selection, preparation, certification, and advancement" of teachers. It has attracted leaders in the profession, especially from the teachers colleges which are in agreement about the importance of the problem and the general direction in which the solution should be sought.

A powerful influence on standards in teacher education is exercised by the National Council for Accreditation of Teacher Education (NCATE). This autonomous body was organized in 1954 on a broad base of representation from five agencies— The American Association of Colleges for Teacher Education, Council of Chief State School Officers, The National Association of State Directors of Teacher Education and Certification, The

---

[8] There are six regional accrediting associations in the United States. They are the Middle States Association, the Northwest, Western, North Central, Southern, and New England. For details on membership and function see J. B. Edmonson, *The Administration of the Modern Secondary School* (New York: Macmillan, 1957), pp. 463–465.

National Commission of Teacher Education and Professional Standards, and the National School Boards Association. Thus NCATE represents teachers colleges (AACTE), teachers (TEPS), state bodies, and the public. Accreditation by NCATE is prized by teacher-education institutions.

The American Association of School Administrators and subject-centered organizations, such as the National Council of Teachers of English, have also tackled the problems of establishing suitable standards for certification on a national level. Indirectly, the American Federation of Teachers works toward raising standards and establishing greater uniformity by pressing for higher salary schedules and other benefits designed to make teaching a more attractive profession.

SALARY SCHEDULES AND IN-SERVICE EDUCATION

Salary schedules for teachers are constructed not only with a view to attracting superior teachers but with three additional objectives in mind: (1) the retention of teachers through regular annual salary increments; (2) a differential for advanced professional education; and (3) a differential for supervisory and administrative personnel.

In some school districts the teacher's annual increment is not automatic but is based on continued professional preparation after appointment. Sometimes the retention of the certificate during the early years of teaching is contingent on the completion of a certain number of college credits. The certificate when first issued may be described as "temporary," "probationary," "provisional," or "limited." After a period of time or after the teacher has met additional requirements, the certificate may become standard or permanent. In some communities only courses taken in accredited colleges (sometimes only on the graduate level) are acceptable. Elsewhere courses given by teachers or supervisors under the auspices of the school system (in-service courses) are accepted. These are generally workshop type courses, and often are established as a result of teacher demands.

There is a specific salary differential in most school systems based on the completion of a master's degree or of thirty credits beyond the baccalaureate, and another differential for an additional thirty credits. Some school systems include salary differentials for fifteen credits beyond the bachelor's and/or the master's level. Many school systems recognize the doctorate with still another salary differential. If a teacher is preparing for a certificate in supervision, guidance, or administration, he may be required to take special courses to qualify for added remuneration. This may be one justification for a salary differential, but it is generally based on the rationale that the position entails greater responsibility.

A few school districts have established the category of "master teacher" and have granted additional salary on this basis. The question of merit pay is mentioned here since salary schedules are under discussion, but this topic is treated more fully in a later section in this chapter.

In *The Education of American Teachers* Conant makes a number of recommendations for improvement in teacher education. He proposes that the onus and responsibility for teacher preparation be placed on the college and university, that practice-teaching be enlarged and structured to become the major phase of teacher preparation, that piecemeal, part-time course work leading to graduate degrees be discontinued, that newly appointed teachers receive special consideration and assistance during a four-year probationary period, and that a valid teaching certificate issued by any state be accepted on a recriprocal basis by all states.

CONTROL OF ENTRY INTO TEACHING

Some educators argue that education can never be a profession until teachers control entry.[9] A comparison with the medical profession is made, where the American Medical Association, through its state affiliates, establishes high standards for entry into the profession and enforces rigid adherence to them. Thus the number of licensed physicians remains low enough to ensure a large amount of economic independence to the elect while the professional competence of each practitioner is reasonably uniform and uniformly high. Equally uniform and high standards of competence are enforced by the profession itself in the various specialist categories. Teachers, on the other hand, argues Lieberman, are in the unenviable position of having

[9] Myron Lieberman, *Education As A Profession* (Englewood Cliffs: Prentice-Hall, 1956).

membership in the profession determined by a wide variety of
sources—legislatures, boards of education, colleges and universities, state education departments—whose members often are
laymen and whose interests often foster a resort to expediency in
certification, with the result that the number of incompetents
and unqualified who are granted entry depresses both the status
of the profession and the economic independence of its members. This undesirable situation may well discourage qualified
people from entering teaching and further downgrades the profession.

There is no denying the validity of this argument. Whether
the solution lies in militant teacher organization or in increased
awareness and appropriate action by existing bodies, such as the
NEA and its affiliate, the National Commission on Teacher Education and Professional Standards, or in some other approach,
such as action by the United States Office of Education or by the
Congress, the fact remains that until standards of entry into the
teaching profession are made fairly uniform and high, the body
of competent teachers will continue to be corrupted both in
status and in income by the omnipresence of the unqualified
but certified members.[10]

THE PAID INTERNSHIP AND
SECONDARY TEACHER EDUCATION

A very promising approach to the problem of recruitment
of qualified teachers from new sources is being made throughout the country by cooperative arrangements between colleges
and public-school systems. The paid internship is the main feature of these programs. The other and even more significant
feature is that students in many of these programs simultaneously take professional education courses and have laboratory
experiences with pupils. These experiences precede the internship.

In the intern program itself, the trainee is supervised and
oriented by experienced teachers and supervisors in the participating school and by members of the college department of
education. Some internship programs are for one year; others

---

[10] Some school districts rely on the National Teacher Examination administered
throughout the country each February by the Educational Testing Service
of Princeton, New Jersey, as a partial criterion for the selection of teachers.

for as long as two years.[11] Some lead to the bachelor's degree and others to the master's degree. The internship stipends vary widely; some offer about $1,000, others as much as $4,000 for the year. In some of the programs special personnel called "intern consultants" are given total assignments to supervise the work of the intern teachers.[12] When we recognize how little help is actually provided for the beginning teacher by the average school system, this new program is a significant step toward progressive professional training. The stipend paid the intern, often coupled with partial tuition scholarship or loan, makes it possible for men and women who could not otherwise afford to continue their education to complete work for their teaching credentials.[13]

Teachers who have been trained under an internship program and cooperating personnel in the public schools who have participated are impressed with the results of giving the beginning teacher responsibility from the start. With careful screening of candidates where the practitioner also assumes responsibility for selection, it has been found that permitting a beginner to assume actual teaching duties is a very effective method of developing confidence and competence in a trainee.[14]

In this system of teacher education, the college assumes the traditional role for formal course work in the program, and teachers and administrators in the school system are afforded a far more active part in teacher preparation. They help prepare and are consulted frequently about the college curriculum. They take and give lectures, colloquiums, seminars, and courses at the college level, and provide a diversified field experience for the interns. Thus intimate professional cooperation between college and field personnel helps give direction and depth to internships while upgrading participating personnel in the schools. Although other short-term or even long-term experimental projects have been undertaken with the combined resources of the school and the college, the value of these is in-

[11] See *Strengths of the S.T.E.P. Program* (College of Education, Michigan State University), for a description of a highly successful internship program.
[12] *Ibid.*
[13] "The Teaching Internship Program," a report of November, 1961, United States Office of Education, provides a summary of intern programs in operation in the United States.
[14] *Strengths of the S.T.E.P. Program.*

creased when school and college find their staffs working together directly in establishing and directing internships. The intimate working relationship between the school district and the
college is a direct by-product of the internship plan of teacher
education. It may be expected to be extended in the years ahead.

THE MORALE OF THE SECONDARY-SCHOOL TEACHER

Administration

Probably the most important factor in the establishment
and maintenance of high morale among secondary-school teachers is the school administration. It is impossible to have a good
school without a good principal. As administrative head of the
school, the principal is expected to provide educational leadership within the framework of established policy. He is the chief
public-relations officer of the school, and he must establish those
relationships among the faculty and between students and faculty that will make possible the most effective implementation
of the school's program.

Since high staff morale results in the release of the creative
energies of teachers, it is probably the first goal toward which
the administration should work. This objective is attained by
instituting democratic practices and a democratic atmosphere in
school relationships. This means respect for the individual
teacher, equal treatment of faculty members, an opportunity for
all to participate in the formulation of school policy, and the
right to criticize without fear of recrimination. When morale is
high there will be a minimum of criticism and a maximum of
constructive suggestion.

In one school the principal is a friend to whom teachers
may come with professional and even personal problems. He is
not afraid to call them by their first names. He seeks advice from
his assistants and from his staff members, and generally acts on
it. Faculty meetings are run in a businesslike manner but are
concerned with problems the staff considers important, and an
atmosphere of give-and-take prevails in lively discussions. Criticism is given privately and orally to his teachers in a spirit of
help and encouragement.

In some schools the principal has a few favorites who are
rewarded with preferred assignments, rarely speaks to teachers

except to criticize their work, governs the school by edict and expects every order to be carried out without question, holds faculty meetings only to tell his staff what they are to do, interrupts lessons, send notes to teachers for real or fancied infractions, and generally runs his school on the principle of fear. Obviously the morale of the staff in such schools will be low.

Teachers' morale can be seriously affected by the degree and kind of support they receive from their principal in controversial situations. Working day-to-day with some two hundred adolescents is like sitting on a powder keg, at best. When a student complains to the principal of a real or fancied injustice, what position will the principal take? Will he ask the teacher to change a grade or to administer a re-examination? Will he transfer the complaining student to another room? Will he give tacit approval to the student? Or will he support the teacher in the face of all but uncontrovertible evidence?

The most difficult challenge occurs when some educational or personal act of the teacher becomes a public issue. The teacher recommends a book by an author who is thought by some self-appointed censor in the community to be a socialist or communist sympathizer, too liberal, too conservative, and so on. Unless the principal and the school authorities support teachers in such public controversies, the staff cannot be expected to have feelings of security.

Recognition

Each of us needs recognition and approval. A good administrator knows how effective a few words of praise or a laudatory letter or memorandum is in building the morale of a teacher. Many school systems publish newsletters in which original and creative teacher practices are reported, along with other professional activities of staff members. Here teachers receive recognition for special work.

Many administrators encourage their teachers to work for higher degrees, to publish books or articles, to apply for scholarships, teacher exchanges, and fellowships, to take sabbaticals for travel or study, to join and become active in professional associations, and to achieve recognition and upgrading in other ways. A liberal policy of permitting teachers to attend conventions and defraying part or all of the expenses is effective in raising morale. Often merely appointing a teacher to membership in a faculty committee can do much for his morale. Within a school or school system recognition can be accorded in many other ways. Assignment to teach a special (honors) class or a new course or to act as a part-time guidance aide or program advisor—all are morale builders.

Merit Pay.   Some systems give special recognition to outstanding teachers in the form of merit rating. Such rating officially designates a small percentage of teachers in the system as outstanding and entitled to additional compensation on this basis. While it is generally recognized in the profession that certain teachers are masters worthy of such recognition, no objective system of selecting such teachers has yet been developed. As a result, merit rating has had a negative effect on morale, has been abandoned in many places, and is losing rather than gaining ground. A recent NEA *Research Bulletin* states:

> The basic reason for giving up plans of merit pay appeared to be that *no satisfactory plan had been developed for selecting the superior teachers.* The corollary, stated with equal frequency, was that *the plans had created dissension.* Words such as *ill will, friction, resentment, misunderstanding,* and *suspicion* were used in reporting the negative reactions of the staffs.[15]

Opportunity for Experimentation.   The opportunity to do original work, to experiment, to revise the curriculum, or in other ways to be responsible for introducing creative innovations may serve as a morale builder for a group of teachers. Experimenting with new material and new techniques makes teaching an adventure and gives the teacher a feeling of being a real professional.

Regular meetings of teachers involved in experimental work or a teachers' committee devoted to a common problem is itself a morale-builder. If, in addition, the group is really free to implement its decisions, the effect on morale is electric.

Salaries

A teacher's income is a vital factor in his morale. Until teachers' salaries are high enough to make it unnecessary for them to take on additional jobs, all other efforts to improve morale may fail. It is too much to expect anyone, even a dedicated

[15] NEA, *Research Bulletin,* 39, Number 2 (May 1961): 62.

professional, to give his all when he feels the community is exploiting him under existing economic conditions, especially if the average business and professional man in the community is earning substantially more than he is.

Teaching, Clerical, Supervisory Duties.   Only those who have been classroom teachers can know the tensions and pressures attendant on teaching and counseling six or more groups each day, preparing lessons, keeping records, supervising the study hall, and sponsoring a cocurricular activity. Teachers reach the weekend or holiday much in the condition of a crew that has just finished a race—exhausted and in need of recuperation. There must be a realistic appraisal of the extent of teacher responsibility if teacher morale is to be high.

Facilities.   School facilities available to the teacher may constitute an important morale factor. In crowded, double-session secondary schools, office space, classrooms, study halls, and counseling rooms are at a premium. The teachers' lounge in overcrowded schools may be too small to accommodate faculty needs. In contrast, especially those in newer buildings, in other schools there are adequate offices arranged in departmental areas, a fine library, laboratories, adequate classrooms, extra student and teacher work space, good gymnasiums, swimming pools, soundproof music rooms and practice booths, language laboratories, an auditorium, service offices, and perhaps a little theater. Good facilities can help attract and hold well-qualified teachers.

Academic Freedom.   The question of controversy is related to the broader question of freedom of teachers outside school. Are teachers free to attend any or no church, to belong to any political or economic party, society or organization not committed to the overthrow of our government by force? Are they free to speak their minds out of school as citizens of the community or to advocate unpopular causes?

Teacher Organizations

The American Federation of Teachers, affiliated with the A.F.L.-C.I.O., has a membership of approximately 80,000 teachers in several hundred locals throughout the United States. It is committed to the principle of collective bargaining and is reluctant to sanction strikes except in extreme circumstances. Its history of more than forty years shows a slow but steady gain in membership and in acceptance by the profession as a means for the attainment of adequate salaries, working conditions, and status.

The National Education Association (NEA) and its affiliates, the largest professional organization in the country, with a membership of about 800,000, opposes labor patterns and practices as unprofessional and ill-designed for the profession of education. Instead, the NEA advocates an upgrading of the profession through improved teaching, more perceptive evaluation procedures involving teachers, better supervision and administration, more adequate school supplies and facilities, and a better program of school-community relations. The NEA and its affiliates maintain active lobbies and sponsor conferences and educational workshops, publications, and excellent professional research pointed toward the improvement of educational practice and the consequent advancement of teachers. In 1962 the NEA at its national convention approved the use of sanctions, a policy of disapproving a school district for employment of its members where conditions are deemed poor, where administrative officials are highly dictatorial and autocratic, or where elements of the community control the board of education in a manner which prevents effective teaching. The extent to which teachers join together in professional organizations to improve themselves, their standards, teaching conditions, and economic status has a positive influence on morale.

The Status of Teaching.   Teacher organizations work toward the upgrading of teaching as a profession. When teachers are impotent to influence salaries, working conditions, and professional rights of members, they are at the mercy of society. In some cases, society will employ those whom it can get for the lowest salary, who will work under adverse conditions, and who will remain silent in the face of repression. NEA takes the position that the public will recognize quality, competence, and professionalism, and will treat teachers as professionals to the degree that they earn this treatment by their performance. The American Federation of Teachers holds the view that teachers will be treated as professionals when they are strong enough to enforce their demands for higher salaries, excellent working conditions, and professional treatment and status.

NEA believes that real professionalism is being retarded by the labor approach of the AFT, and that as long as teachers adopt the tactics of force, they will be met by counter force and postpone the day when teaching will everywhere be recognized and treated as an honored profession. The secondary-school teacher must decide whether to join either, both, or neither of these organizations. At this point we merely note that both groups are concerned with improvement in the status of the teacher and that this constitutes an important morale factor in teaching.

Opportunities for Advancement

Many teachers will seek some form of advancement within the profession. Some will seek supervisory or administrative positions. Others will endeavor to become guidance counselors, team leaders, remedial reading specialists, curriculum consultants, audio-visual specialists, or research workers. Whatever the direction of advancement, it is important that the avenues be kept open and that reasonable opportunities be available to teachers for the attainment of normal objectives.

The profession is seriously remiss, however, in permitting skilled classroom teachers to seek advancement only for higher salaries and more desirable working conditions. Admittedly, some teachers are better suited for administration, guidance, and other functions, but this should be the only grounds for the change. When higher salaries are paid for a position, the position carrying the higher salary is considered more important and may attract those best suited to perform superior service in the classroom.

An analogous situation exists in our colleges and universities, where teachers accept administrative positions as advancement opportunities. The results are the same, as John A. Hannah points out:

> All universities suffer a constant attrition that might be slowed down or stopped altogether. I refer to the common practice of making academic administrators of good teachers and research workers. For reasons of convenience or expediency, we take them out of their fields of professional competence, and as a consequence, most of them are lost to the world of scholarship forever.[16]

---

[16] John A. Hannah, *Economic Problems Facing Michigan State University and Other State Universities in the Next Decade* (Address to the Fifth Annual Meeting of the Advisory Committee for Economical and Statistical Studies of Science and Technology, National Science Foundation, April 4, 1963).

Secondary-school teaching as a profession faces problems of recruitment, preparation, morale, and organization. These have been discussed in some detail in this chapter. They are problems to which teachers, leaders in education at all levels, as well as local school administrators will need to give careful and continuing attention. They are questions which the beginning teacher faces as he seeks the fulfillment of his various potentials in the profession of education.

FOR DELIBERATION and DISCUSSION

1. Proposals are sometimes advanced to pay higher salaries when there is a scarcity of teachers, as in women's physical education, mathematics, or physics. What is your position with respect to this proposal?
2. If you were empowered to determine certification requirements for the certificate for which you are preparing, what changes would you make? Why?
3. Examine Professor Lieberman's arguments for control over entry into teaching. Are they sound? Explain.
4. Internship programs have encountered some opposition from educators in traditional teacher-preparation programs. What are the issues.
5. Teacher-education departments and schools have often met opposition from liberal arts departments and colleges. What are the issues?
6. List the morale factors discussed in this chapter in descending order of importance. Explain your arrangement.
7. What, if any, is the relationship of morale and effectiveness in teaching? Is the correlation between the two greater, the same or less in education than in industry? Explain.
8. Teachers' salary schedules generally call for a long period (sometimes as high as twenty years or more) before the attainment of maximum. Is this justifiable? Compare with other occupations.
9. What are the advantages and disadvantages of basing teachers' salary schedules on a ratio principle?
10. What rationale is there for basing teachers' salary schedules on graduate work beyond certification requirements? Can you defend a better principle of salary differentials?

FOR ADDITIONAL READING

ARMSTRONG, W. EARL and STINNET, T. M. *A Manual on Certification Requirements*. 1961 ed.; Washington, D.C.: National Commission on Teacher Education and Professional Standards (TEPS) of the NEA, 1962. Published biennially. Contains latest information on certification requirements for teachers, supervisors, administrators, and special school service personnel arranged by states. Also a summary of certification practices and trends.

CHANDLER, B. J. *Education and the Teacher.* New York: Dodd-Mead, 1961. Considers the importance of teaching, preparing for teaching, the work of the teacher, and the profession of teaching.

CHARLES, DON C. "Stereotypes of the Teacher in American Literature," *Educational* Forum, XIV (March, 1950): 299–304. Examines the works of representative American writers from the Puritan period to the twentieth century.

CONANT, JAMES B. *The Education of American Teachers.* New York: McGraw-Hill, 1963. Reports results of a two-year study. Makes recommendations involving selection, preparation, certification, and in-service education of elementary- and secondary-school teachers.

Decade of Experiment. New York: Fund for the Advancement of Education, 1951–1961. A description of the various educational experiments that the Fund supported and a discussion of the reasoning behind the commitments made by the Fund.

ELSBREE, WILLARD S., *et al., Principles of Staff Personnel Administration.* New York: Bureau of Publications, Teachers College, Columbia U., 1959. Analyzes problems of teacher preparation and certification, personnel policies of school districts, legal aspects of teaching, teacher organization, and so on.

FAUNCE, ROLAND C. and CLUTE, MORREL J. *Teaching and Learning in the Junior High School.* San Francisco: Wadsworth, 1961. A comprehensive analysis of the junior high school from a "child centered" point of view. Chapters on learning process, student activities, and guidance. Annotated bibliographies with each chapter.

FIELDS, RALPH R. *The Community College Movement.* New York: McGraw-Hill, 1962. Traces the historical development of the junior college. Presents depth studies of four "outstanding" colleges—Long Beach (Calif.), Tyler (Texas), Orange County (N.Y.), and Bridgeport (Conn.). Discusses problems resulting from the admission of a broad range of students and the types of vocational programs offered.

HODENFIELD, G. K. and STINNETT, T. M. *The Education of Teachers.* Englewood Cliffs: Prentice-Hall, 1961. A report of three TEPS conferences, 1958, 1959, and 1960. Reports progress in healing the schism between the liberal arts faculties and the schools of education.

Journal of Teacher Education, (National Commission on Teacher Education and Professional Standards (TEPS) of the

NEA). Published quarterly. Reports opinion and research in matter related to teacher education and the improvement of teaching.

KERSHAW, JOSEPH A. and MCKEAN, RONALD N. *Teacher Shortages and Salary Schedules.* New York: McGraw-Hill, 1962. Presents the case against the single salary schedule.

KOERNER, JAMES D. (ed.). *The Case for Basic Education.* Boston: Little, Brown, 1959. A collection of essays by laymen and college professors of content "disciplines" ("citizenship," English composition, philosophy, speech, and so on) explaining what the high school ought to be doing and berating the high school for its concern with "life adjustment."

The Miseducation of American Teachers. Boston: Houghton Mifflin, 1963. Develops the "findings and prejudices" that education as a discipline is inferior to liberal studies; that the "educationists" have a vested interest in the *status quo* and therefore oppose reform; that the education faculty is of "inferior intellectual quality"; and that teaching tends to attract students of inferior academic ability.

LIEBERMAN, MYRON. *Education As A Profession.* Englewood Cliffs: Prentice-Hall, 1956. A provocative discussion. The author has keen analysis, forceful style, and original approach.

The Future of Public Education. Chicago: U. of Chicago Press, 1960. The author presses his demand for teacher organization, control over entry into teaching, limiting of lay participation, federal control, and similar "unorthodox" views.

LINDSEY, MARGARET (ed.). *New Horizons for the Teaching Profession.* Washington, D.C.: NEA, 1961. A new look at teacher preparation from the traditionalist point of view. Emphasis on scholarship.

MEDSKER, LELAND L. *The Junior College: Progress and Prospect.* New York: McGraw-Hill, 1960. One of a series of studies on "The Diversification of American Higher Education" sponsored by the Carnegie Corporation. Reports the objectives, programs, students and services of two-year colleges in fifteen selected states.

PARKER, FRANKLIN. "Fifty Years of the Junior High School; Preface to a Bibliography of 131 Doctoral Dissertations," *Bulletin,* National Association of Secondary School Principals, 46, No. 271 (February 1962): 435–445. Includes the bibliography listing 131 studies giving author, title of study, university, and date of award of degree.

RADCLIFFE, SHIRLEY. *Teacher Education Fifth-Year Programs: A Selected Bibliography.* Washington, D.C.: United States Department of Health, Education, and Welfare, 1959. Annotated bibliography of 154 books and articles.

Recommendations: Composite Report of Findings. (Golden Anniversary White House Conference on Children and Youth March 27–April 2, 1960.) Washington, D.C.: United States Government Printing Office, 1960. Reports and describes one hundred and twenty-five resolutions pertaining to education adopted by one or more of the eighteen forums composed of 7,600 delegates representing grass roots education and religious groups, professional and voluntary organizations, and scientific and scholarly societies. An excellent sounding board for public opinion re-education, employment, health, social welfare, law enforcement, etc.

SMITH, ELMER R. (ed.). *Teacher Education, A Reappraisal.* (Report of a conference sponsored by the Fund for the Advancement of Education). New York: Harper and Row, 1963. Educators associated with the Fund pool their experience in answering basic questions about teacher education, and sharply criticize current practices.

STABLER, ERNEST (ed.). *The Education of the Secondary School Teacher.* Middletown: Wesleyan U. Press, 1962. Essays on the history of education, comparative education, philosophy of education, educational psychology, and the preparation of secondary-school teachers of English, history, foreign languages, science and mathematics.

STILES, LINDLEY J., BARR, A. S., DOUGLASS, HARL R., and MILLS, HUBERT H. *Teacher Education in the United States.* New York: Ronald, 1960. Discusses the current status of teacher education, the structure of teacher preparation institutions, undergraduate and graduate studies of prospective teachers, in-service education, and other related problems.

Teacher Supply and Demand in Public Schools, 1961. Washington, D.C.: Research Division, NEA, 1961. Statistical report and interpretation of factors and trends involved in supply and demand of teachers in all states on all levels and in all subjects.

WHITELAW, JOHN B. *Teaching As A Career.* Washington, D.C.: United States Office of Education, 1959, Pamphlet No. 122. Presents the advantages of teaching the prospects open to career teachers.

WILSON, CHARLES H. *A Teacher Is A Person.* New York: Holt, 1956. A warm, witty book by the Superintendent of Schools of Grosse Pointe, Michigan. Autobiographical. Makes no apology for the profession but leaves the reader with the feeling that education is a worthy calling and a potentially satisfying one.

5 Special Aspects of the Secondary-School Program

The Meaning of Extra-Class Activities

The traditional high-school program consists of major and minor subjects which a student is required to take and pass in order to earn a diploma. A number of electives are also offered to give each student an opportunity to enrich his formal school program in accordance with his interests and talents. This program is supplemented in every high school by a less formal series of experiences ranging from the required home room and assembly to a host of voluntary activities—clubs, squads, teams, and other school associations—to which the terms *extra-class,* *cocurricular,* or *extracurricular* may be interchangeably applied.

When we examine the subject offerings, required and elective, of any large high school, it is obvious that the "regular" curriculum shades imperceptibly into the cocurricular program. In English, for example, there may be special classes not only in dramatics and journalism but in one or more of the following: creative writing, radio and TV workshop, library science, debating and public speaking, Shakespeare, poetry, literary criticism, and playwriting. The social-studies programs of the school may include, beyond the traditional geography, world history, economics, and American history, such offerings as problems in American democracy, psychology, introduction to college social science, contemporary world history, the Western Hemisphere, communism, United Nations, and parliamentary procedure.

In the science department a student may find electives including advanced biology, chemistry, physics or earth science, botany, zoology, organic chemistry, elementary nuclear physics, meteorology, independent supervised experimentation, science fiction, geology, and archaeology. The latter may be given as a combined offering of the science and social-studies department as may a course in the interrelationship of science and politics, or a course in the history of science.

The mathematics department may offer, in addition to the traditional high-school algebra, geometry and trigonometry, courses in number theory, analytics, introduction to calculus, mathematics of finance, calculating machines, mathematical literature, and mathematics research. In the language departments students may find electives in linguistics, literature, speaking, writing, translating, international relations, and the United Nations.

Space does not permit a description or even an enumeration of the variety of course offerings in vocational schools. It should be noted, however, that many if not most of these courses have elements of initiative and creativity similar to the academic cocurricular programs.

In the academic high school the minor subjects—music, art, health education—have offerings that are indistinguishable from the extra-class activities. Band, orchestra, chorus, painting, sculpture, and the various courses in the industrial-arts department may be "regular" curricular offerings in one school and "extracurricular" offerings in another. In many schools membership on a team which engages in interscholastic competition may be accepted for credit in place of class attendance in physical or health education.

Among major subjects, core (generally English and social studies) most closely resembles the extra-class program in its philosophy and procedures. In any modern high school the curricular and cocurricular activities merge so that the entire school program is integrated and designed to give each student maximum opportunity to develop all his capacities.

As we have noted, many high schools have work-study programs which combine the theoretical instruction of the classroom with practical experience in a related job, and school credit is allowed for satisfactory performance on the job. Pupils are supervised by teachers specializing in work-study education, and they are paid prevailing wages. Thus there is no absolute dividing line between the formal curriculum and the extra-class program.

Extracurricular experiences, coupled with the formal program can be developed into worthwhile out-of-school activities, even during the high-school years. For example, the first two years of the regular English curriculum may lead a gifted student with the proper predisposition to elect journalism or dramatics in his junior or senior year. This student may then join the staff of the school newspaper or participate in the work of the dramatics club. This experience in the informal extracurricular activity might lead to a professional opportunity with the local newspaper or with a local theatre group.

Similarly, the social studies program can take a student with talent from the regular history class to the elective "problems in American democracy." The student may attain an office on the Student Council, write a contest essay on American government, or begin to participate in the work of a local political organization in the community.

A similar line of development from the formal class program to the informal extra-class activity may be traced in each of the major and minor subjects. The mathematics club or team, the science project entered in the Westinghouse competition, the foreign language "pen pal" program, the school orchestra, the student art work and industrial art creations that adorn the school, the intramural and interscholastic athletics program— all indicate the interrelationship between the "regular" curriculum and the extracurricular program of the school.

Of course, not every activity, nor even a majority of the co-curricular activities, is expected to have vocational outlets. As we shall see, the rationale for the extra-class program is much more extensive than the merely vocational. The adolescent is learning simultaneously not only from the formal school program and from the informal extra-class activities in which he participates, but perhaps even more from the less formal out-of-school experiences to which he is subject a majority of the hours of the day. The school often exercises a high degree of control over these out-of-school influences through homework assignments, directed reading, listening, and viewing, and the cultivation of tastes and interests which carry over into the home and community.

Scope of the Extra-Class Curriculum

A closer look at the extra-class program of the modern high school reveals an almost endless variety of activities in which the youngsters are engaged. Each extra-class activity must have a faculty sponsor. These activities are limited only by the time, inclination, and talent of the faculty. School teams provide an outlet for the interests and aptitudes of many students and an opportunity for interscholastic competition which may have great educational worth. Students compete for places on the school team. The team develops skill in practice under expert guidance. Basketball, football, baseball, tennis, track, swimming, and other athletic contests bring out large cheering sections with organized cheerleading and all the excitement attending victory, or the disappointment attending defeat. The team has a manager, assistants, business director, and so on.

Often students are organized into a service squad. A lunchroom, study-hall, or school-patrol squad helps keep order and sees that school rules are obeyed. A traffic squad in the school will perform a similar service. An audio-visual squad can ensure a high-quality school audio-visual program. Squads to assist in school programming, stagecraft, makeup, printing, and record keeping also exist.

Individual students serve as teacher aides in a variety of ways. The most common is the teacher's "secretary," who helps take attendance, keeps records, writes notes, and runs errands. Others assist in the various school offices doing chores at the direction of the principal's secretary, department chairman, guidance counselor, school nurse, or dietician. Student aides operate mimeograph machines, repair equipment, act as library assistants, prepare laboratory materials, care for supplies, and help direct visitors to appropriate parts of the building.

In more than 5,000 secondary schools the National Education Association sponsors chapters of The Future Teachers of

America with a total membership of close to 200,000 students. Members work in elementary schools under teacher direction gaining information about requirements, opportunities, and problems in teaching. Through discussions, lectures, tours, and films they discover their own interests, capacities, or disabilities. Meanwhile this phase of the school's extra-class program offers many students an excellent opportunity for service and guidance.

Student government has many ramifications in addition to the activating of large numbers of students in important cocurricular activities. During the elections of student council officers, the student body may be organized into political parties, with activities ranging from the choice of candidates and the campaign posters and slogans to the rallies and the election assembly, with its speeches and excitement. Often there are regular ballotings, victory speeches, inductions into office, and inaugural speeches.

The student council holds regular meetings, follows prepared agenda, adopts resolutions and reports to the student body in assemblies. It may exercise some authority over expenditure of student council funds, school activities, and regulations pertaining to student dress and conduct. There may be a student court holding sessions regularly to try offenders, make findings, and assess penalties. Interscholastic discussion groups and summer-camp programs have brought student government officers from different schools together.

Another important aspect of the extra-class program is the school assembly, which in many schools is organized to give students a major opportunity for useful experience. Students may plan and carry out an entire assembly program organized around a school event—for example, a forthcoming varsity show—or around the work of a department or club. The assembly is one of many school-wide activities that activate large numbers of students.

Student organizations also may sponsor school dances and socials. Here the students begin to practice the social amenities essential to their development in our culture. Clubs, trips, and school outings are also calculated to develop these social competencies.

School-wide dramatic undertakings, concerts, and operettas are among the most educative enterprises in which high schools engage. Often there are trial runs in school assemblies prior to the official weekend performances before parents and the community. The sale of tickets, printing programs, preparing stage scenery and sets, making costumes, actors' makeup, lighting, sound-effects, and many other by-products, such as writeups in school and community newspapers, make these enterprises invaluable sources of worthwhile experiences for high-school girls and boys.

Other extra-class activities that may involve large numbers of students include charity drives, the "adoption" of a foreign school, "pen pals," or an extended trip in the senior year.

Obviously, an extensive series of activities consuming the time and energy of administration, staff, and students requires justification, and we turn, therefore, to a discussion of the rationale for this program.

The Rationale for Extra-Class Activities

The high-school student has reached the point in his education at which he is able to initiate and to accomplish a program with a worthwhile goal. In addition, he is reaching for freedom from adult domination. Finally, he is approaching adulthood, with its demands of increasing responsibility. Psychologically he is ready for the opportunities and experiences provided by extra-class activities. In these activities student initiative, ingenuity, and responsibility are released. Faculty supervision is provided to give assistance and direction where necessary. The cocurricular program provides the opportunity for the adolescent to try his wings in an atmosphere like that of the adult world. These activities, often sponsored by the student council, are extremely important in the total educational program. In the school spirit engendered, in the social learnings promoted, and in the energy, enthusiasm, and altruism generated, these activities constitute a significant part of the education of adolescents.

It is the justifiable contention of some that the extra-class program is potentially more important in the total education of the high-school student than is the traditional class program. It is impossible to overestimate the importance of the extra-class activities in the total program of the high school. In fact, to the extent that the classroom fails to provide opportunities for self-direction, initiative, and individuality it loses the interest of talented students, who then turn to the extra-class activities as a place to find release for their talents in initiating and executing projects in a relatively free atmosphere.[1] Many talented high-school students who find no challenge either in the curricular offerings or in the extracurricular activities drop out of school. Lawrence G. Derthick, former United States Commissioner of Education, points out that

> The need for professional and technical personnel in our society will increase by almost 40 percent by 1965 . . . Yet 40 percent of our young people are still selling their future short by dropping out of high school before graduation. And each year an estimated two hundred thousand of the most talented of our young people fail, for a variety of reasons, to carry their education beyond the high school.[2]

The need for recognition is strong in the adolescent as, indeed, it is in all ages. The extra-class program with its officers, awards, displays, its appeal to originality and initiative, and its endless variety often helps fill this need for the individual child.

Another of the adolescent's needs which the extracurricular program is admirably designed to fulfill is the requirement for independence. The student joins a group of his own choosing, uniting with other students of similar interests. This, rather than age or proficiency in a "subject," is the basis for the association. There is no formal "course of study." The agenda is determined democratically by the members. There are no recitations, no tests, no grades. The faculty is there as a "sponsor" or "advisor" not as a "teacher" in the traditional sense. Often the students will choose an activity because the sponsor is known to be sympathetic toward girls and boys. The sponsor provides advice when it is sought, helps secure a place for meeting, obtains needed materials, and satisfies the adminis-

---

[1] "It is common to find that high-school students who score in the upper half of the distribution make little progress after the tenth grade on tests of understanding and ability to apply concepts and principles. Their scores level off to a plateau. Interviews with samples of these students indicate that they turn increasingly to the extra-curricular activities because they have proved more stimulating and meaningful to them than their courses in the eleventh and twelfth grades." Robert S. Gilchrist, "Innovations in the High School Curriculum," in *The High School In A New Era*, Francis S. Chase and Harold H. Anderson (Chicago: U. of Chicago Press, 1958), p. 172.

[2] *Ibid.*, p. 38.

trative requirement for appropriate supervision. The freedom may extend also to the time and place of meeting, sometimes including weekend and holiday get-togethers in the homes of members or of the sponsor.

Another adolescent need that can be met by the extra-class program is the social need. Unlike the formal class atmosphere, where students rarely get to know each other well, the informal extra-class atmosphere brings together students of similar interests more intimately. Moreover, a warm relationship more readily develops between the students and the faculty sponsor. Clubs that have a religious purpose—Newman Club, Bible Club, Hillel Club—serve the social function in another way.

The extra-class program is generally better able than the regular curriculum to provide for individual differences. Particularly in the smaller high school, the number of curricular offerings may be quite limited, while the extracurricular program can be very diverse. When a student selects an activity, his interest probably is strong enough to overcome limitations—mental, physical, or emotional—that operate against his maximum development in an assigned curriculum. This is not to say that students should be permitted to select only those courses in which they are interested, but rather that the more flexible and informal extra-class program offers opportunities for each child which the formal curriculum sometimes fails to give. In fact, it is the recognition of this limitation in meeting individual needs that has caused and is causing the traditional curriculum to develop a flexibility resembling the extra-class program.

Along with the satisfaction of the social needs of the adolescent, the extra-class program serves to meet his recreational and leisure needs. Originally these were the prime objectives of the extra-class activities; hence, the term is traditionally associated with athletics, games, and sports. In fact, even where the extracurricular program is curtailed these activities are the last to be disbanded.[3] Undoubtedly there are factors other than the need to meet the recreational needs of adolescents involved. The athletic program is well entrenched, is often self-supporting, has come to be recognized as providing a necessary supplementary income to the health education staff, is virtually demanded by

[3] Rosalind Zapf, *Democratic Processes in the Secondary Classroom* (Englewood Cliffs: Prentice-Hall, 1959).

the community, and provides a tremendous outlet for adolescent energies.

The vocational function of the extra-class program must also be considered. A student who acts as a teacher's secretary, operates the school switchboard, acts as a library aide, assists with laboratory equipment, or tutors a backward class may be well on his way to a career in the adult world. In the many extra-class activities of the school his classmates, too, may be attaining vocational experience at an age when they are ready to benefit most and under conditions where trial and error will be least costly.

Finally, association with peers in these voluntary group activities is often the best education for democratic living. Qualities of leadership emerge and are developed. No less important are the qualities of followership—adherence to law, critical attitude toward policy and toward the method of its implementation, cooperation in a common cause, respect for the rights and personalities of others.

Why does every high school have a program of extracurricular activities? Why do administration and staff exert effort to have as many students as possible participate in one or more extra-class activities? Why do many schools require a minimum of such participation as a prerequisite for a diploma? The answer to all of these is that the extra-class program is the means by which a full and well-rounded education is made available to all students.

THE HOME ROOM

Definition

Typically each high-school student is assigned to a home room where he meets with the home-room teacher and with a group of his classmates each day at a regular time and place. During the time spent together—which may be from ten minutes or less to a half-hour or more—school administrative functions, such as taking attendance, distribution and collection of report cards, reading of notices, election of school officers, and other school activities are discharged.

There is disagreement among educators about the place of the home room in the total high-school program. Some schools are organized without home rooms. A few minutes of classroom time are set aside each day for announcements to be made over the public-address system and for the collection of attendance records which are processed by clerks. In other schools home rooms meet for ten minutes or so each day with longer meetings when necessary. Obviously, if the home room is nothing but a record-keeping device, this function can be performed better in other ways with less strain and less time wasted.

The discussion here will describe those schools in which the home room is recognized as having important guidance functions and contributing significantly to the emotional, social, intellectual, and moral development of the student.

The key to understanding the importance of the practice is the word *home*. The home-room teacher really stands *in loco parentis* for his students. The home room is their haven, their home in the school. To it they come each day for attendance, reports, study, guidance, programming, notices, student activities, and many other intimate activities of school life. The home room is the liaison between each student's home and the school. The student's attendance, report cards, and notices of school community activities are communicated to the parents via the home room.

The home room also functions as liaison between the student and the rest of the school. The home-room teacher may intercede to help one of his students out of difficulty with a teacher or administrator. He enters current data, including grades, on each of his student's permanent records and brings items of importance in the life of the school to the attention of his students.

Ideally the home room should have a guidance-oriented teacher, a small, compatible student group, an attractive room in which to meet, and a large amount of time (perhaps half an hour) together each day. The group should remain together with the same teacher during the three or four years the students are in the high school. Under these conditions, the home room may be one of the most productive aspects of the school curriculum.

Management of the Home Room

It is essential that proper discipline be established in the home room. Too often it is a noisy, even rowdy, place where students and teacher wait nervously for the bell to ring. With proper discipline, the teacher can establish a real study situation and use the time for remedial work, tutoring, or study help. Here the teacher's function is one of assisting students informally and of organizing the room into a cooperative academic home.

The mechanical requirements of the home room may be delegated to students as learning activities. Thus one student may be responsible for keeping attendance records, another for preparing absentee post cards, another for reading school notices, and one or two others for maintaining a bulletin board. One student may collect dues and another be responsible for special drives such as Red Cross or Christmas Fund. Each home room as a class will elect a representative to the school council and its own class officers. It may wish to prepare an assembly program, have a party, adopt an overseas orphan, write a class letter to the press, or petition the principal for permission to go on a trip.

With competent teacher leadership a home room, particularly if it stays together for three or four years, may develop an *esprit* and achieve an educational benefit. Students can learn democratic procedures, self-discipline, and mutual respect in the home room. The home room will be a friendly but businesslike place, where students will not only feel at home but may learn as they do in a regular classroom.

Guidance in the Home Room

The home-room teacher is in a unique position to provide guidance. He meets his students in an informal atmosphere each day for three or four years. He is responsible for entering all data —academic grades, test results, citizenship, family information, IQ, attendance, and awards—on the permanent record cards. He issues report cards, helps prepare each student's program, and literally shepherds the flock to graduation. This day-to-day contact with its responsibility and opportunity is a natural setting for guidance.

The home-room teacher is the initial agent in preparing each child's program for the next semester or school year. A sensitive performance of this task requires a knowledge of all school offerings and requirements, information pertaining to college and professional requirements, the abilities, aptitudes, interests, and competencies of each child, and sympathetic insight into the most effective combination of each child's talents with the objective possibilities of the curriculum and of future potentialities and opportunities. The teacher will need to know the vocational situation in the community and elsewhere; he will need to confer with parents, guidance counselor, administrators, and other teachers. Above all he will need to have a fine understanding of each child, and he will need to enjoy the confidence of each child. Given the will, the intellect, and the energy to do all this, the home-room teacher will be able to perform an invaluable service.

The home-room teacher may also guide the social development and the emotional stability and growth of his charges. He will be consulted about dress, dating, and the more intimate details of boy-girl conduct. He will be challenged by day-dreaming, taciturn, sullen, boisterous, aggressive, shy, recalcitrant, morose, timid, overweight, handicapped, unhappy, and anxious adolescents. The more he knows about adolescents, about psychology, and about this girl or that boy, the more he will be able to help them. When the challenge is too great, expert psychological or psychiatric help will need to be summoned, and not the least of the home-room teacher's competencies will be the ability to recognize this need, the knowledge of where to go for help, and the courage to get the help at once.

Organized and Informal Home-Room Programs

When the home-room period is limited to ten or fifteen minutes, no organized program can be developed, since the minutiae of attendance, notices, and collections will occupy a large part of the time. When the home-room schedule calls for daily meetings of half an hour or more, however, the school philosophy obviously regards the home-room period as a time for creative learning. This may be achieved through a planned program of formal class "lessons" or through an informal, but carefully planned, approach.

In some schools the home-room teacher is expected to prepare and teach lessons like a teacher of a subject class. The lessons may be a series on human relations, school regulations and requirements, curricular and extracurricular offerings, or community affairs. The theme for one series might be vocational, for another colleges, for a third study habits, and for a fourth the world we live in. Other themes could be family relations, personal problems, health, or personal economics.

In contrast with the formal unifying theme developed through regular lessons, some schools program a long home-room period so that the teacher may use the time for a less structured approach to the problems of the adolescents in his room. Some of the problems clarified in this type of program are study habits and progress, relations with one another and with teachers, students' mental outlook and physical well-being, their social and emotional adjustments, and their overall success in meeting the problems of growing up in their environment.

In some schools each student, at least in the ninth year, and sometimes in the tenth and beyond, is scheduled for a block of time with one teacher for English and social studies. This teacher is often designated as the home-room teacher and guidance counselor of the group. It is of the utmost importance that the teacher be a well-adjusted and dedicated person skilled in working with adolescent girls and boys. Of course, every high-school teacher should possess these attributes, but when a student is with one teacher for a block of time and when the same person is his home-room teacher and his guidance counselor, it is obvious how much good (or bad) the teacher can do for each of his students. The reason for this type of programming is that teacher and student can get to know each other in a way that is not possible when the student has several teachers each day and sees his guidance counselor for fifteen minutes a semester.

The home room, then, can be used effectively as a place where students are truly at home, where important learning goes hand in hand with necessary school mechanics, where real guidance takes place, and where some of the fondest memories of the high-school years are made.

GUIDANCE AND COUNSELING

Aspects of Guidance

In the sense that every teacher is a guide and counselor, everything he does in relation to each of his students may truly come under the head of guidance and counseling. Thus to say that the classroom teacher's function is guidance is to describe the relationship correctly when the term *guidance* is understood in its widest meaning.

Generally, however, the term *guidance* is meant to describe a situation in which a student comes to a teacher or advisor with a problem or with a question seeking help from an older, more experienced person. The student may be seeking an answer to a question of fact, such as "Do I need to take a language in order to get an academic diploma from Southside High School?" or "How does one go about getting a reference from the school for a position?" Again, the student may be seeking advice on a matter of judgment. He may ask "Is it a good idea to try to graduate from high school in three and a half years?" or "Is Spanish a more useful language than French?" He may present a problem, such as "Should I concentrate on my studies and try to get a college scholarship or should I take a part-time job and save up for my college education?"

Each of these is an example of a formal "Guidance" situation, in which a student seeks help from a teacher. The questions asked by high-school students generally will fall into a number of distinct categories: academic competence, curriculum, and college entrance; vocational aptitude, preparation, availability, and choice; personal and social problems; and psychological concerns.

Guidance in the Classroom

Since the person who comes in closest contact with each student for the longest period of school time is the classroom teacher, it is logical to expect that the student will consult him first about his problems. This is especially true if the classroom teacher is also the home-room teacher. And if the home room stays together semester after semester, it may be expected that the home-room teachers will be the first resort of the student in quest of counseling.

When a group is scheduled for a block of time with one teacher, as in core or common-learning classes, it is inevitable that this teacher also will be consulted by students more often than the teachers wtih whom they spend only half as much time. In some schools the core teacher is also the home-room teacher. In some he is actually designated as the students' guidance counselor or advisor. Thus, in every instance the classroom teacher tends to be the key person in guidance, insofar as his students are concerned. He is the heart of the school's guidance function, and the classroom is the place where the most effective guidance takes place.

Guidance, like all learning, proceeds best in an informal situation. Guidance effected by precept and by example is especially effective in matters of personal conduct (which may help explain and even justify the concern the community shows in the personal life of the teacher). Students will be guided—particularly when they admire and like a teacher—by his speech, dress, manners and mannerisms, associations, and general deportment and preferences. These intangibles constitute a constant and very important aspect of guidance.

The widespread use of the anecdotal record by classroom teachers and the introduction of the new open-end report card in the high schools indicate a recognition of the guidance function of the classroom teacher. Similarly, the development of self-evaluating devices and techniques by core and other teachers recognizes the guidance function of the classroom teacher as an essential phase of his responsibilities.

These guidance features make the classroom teacher a mediator between the student and the rest of the school, his parents, and his out-of-school environment. So far as the rest of the school is concerned, there are the student's relations with classmates, with other teachers, with specialized guidance personnel, and with the administration. A sensitive, devoted teacher will get to know all he can about each of his students and help them adjust to the demands of each of the other forces listed above. He will intervene when he is consulted or when he senses the need. He can reduce tensions, provide information, or use his influence to secure the maximum in healthy adjustment for each student whenever the need or the opportunity offers. For example, if a student suddenly begins to slump in a subject, is rated unsatisfactory by one of his teachers in citizenship, or is the subject of an adverse comment by a teacher at lunch, a friendly teacher may be able to avoid serious consequences by judicious intervention in the form of guidance. This does not imply condoning misconduct. On the contrary, it may mean helping an offender to recognize the error of his ways and to avoid a recurrence.

The Guidance Specialist

Today, most high schools have guidance specialists as regular staff members. Many secondary schools are attempting to increase the number and quality of guidance personnel until there is one full-time guidance counselor for every 250 pupils. If the objective is to remove guidance from the classroom, it is contrary to sound educational practice. If, on the other hand, it means that each high school should have specialists on the staff who are expert in handling adolescent problems of curriculum, college entrance, testing, vocational matters, personal and social problems, and psychological and psychiatric problems, this type of expertness is highly desirable. It must be recognized, however, that to be an effective counselor of adolescents one must be close to them, and the person removed entirely from the classroom is likely to be at some disadvantage in this respect.

Unfortunately, most high schools find it expedient to designate certain members of their staff as guidance specialists. Sometimes these are part-time teachers and part-time guidance persons. They may have small offices where they interview each of some five hundred or more students for ten or fifteen minutes once a semester. This kind of "guidance" is generally ineffective.

Originally the guidance teacher was a "grade advisor," who counseled a large group of students about their academic programs. His secondary function was vocational counseling, which was intimately related to the former, since the course or subjects chosen by a student often determined or was determined by his vocational direction. During the past quarter-century many states have established certification requirements for guidance specialists. Certified counselors are now required to have competence in vocational counseling, group and individual testing, the interview, and in the use and interpretation of personal data sheets, sociometric devices, scattergrams, role-playing, and similar counseling aids.

Increasingly guidance specialists also are moving into the areas of psychological training, social work, and clinical experience. This development is due in part to the increased responsibility undertaken by the American high school for meeting all the adolescent's needs. It has become highly desirable—indeed necessary—for a counselor to be skilled in recognizing the existence of social or emotional disturbance and the more serious mental disorders. He must be able to make proper and prompt referral to the school or clinical psychologist or psychiatrist. Referral to the proper school or community agency or the proper recommendation to classroom teacher, parent, or community resource is a major function of the guidance specialist. Another is to help arrange for changes in the child's school environment —for example, a change in course of study, placement in a special class or group, or physical rehabilitation. He also may interpret results of objective tests and explain the reason for the reassignment of the student to a special class or group. A kind, sympathetic counselor can be of great psychological assistance merely by listening as a youngster unburdens himself. An occasional question may lead the student to see his problem in a new light.

A guidance specialist who is skilled in the various functions of his position can be invaluable in helping the student make adjustments to his educational, social, and emotional environment. To the extent that the counselor is successful, he serves the best interests of the child, his teachers, his home, and his community.

An Integrated High-School Guidance Program

Every staff member—the principal, the specialists in curriculum and teaching, and guidance personnel of all types—is involved in implementing the school guidance program. The administration's responsibility is to provide both the personnel and the conditions for an appropriate program of guidance. The home-room and classroom teacher, as we have seen, are the heart of the guidance program. A guidance-conscious faculty, supported by the administration, informed by reading, course work, conferences, and experimentation, and supplemented by a competent staff of specialists can be instrumental in the total effectiveness of the school program. Specialists, including counselors, social workers, psychologists and psychiatrists, in sufficient numbers complete the picture of a potentially effective program of guidance.

A competent guidance director, with the support of the school administration and with tact and wisdom in enlisting the support of the teaching staff, can organize a school program of instruction, testing, counseling and referral by which each child's academic, social, and emotional needs and problems can be attacked and in most cases resolved.

TRACKING

Origin and Development

The European school provides a common education during the first few years, after which those students with wealth or talent are transferred to a middle school, *lycée,* or *gymnasium.* In these schools, students are separated into groups, and each of these groups proceeds on a separate "track," the first reaching a terminus at about age twelve, the second at about age eighteen. There may be an additional separation at about fifteen, when one group is transferred to a technical school which terminates at age twenty, while the second proceeds in a different "track" leading to the university and the professions.

The American system of the nineteenth and early twentieth century was often called the "stepladder" system, in which each child proceeded along the same ladder as far as he could go—elementary, junior high school, senior high school, college and university. Most pupils dropped out after graduation from elementary school, if not before. After World War I, however, as an increasing percentage of children went on to junior and senior high school, the wide range of capacities and purposes of the student body forced a differentiation in the curriculum which resulted in an American form of tracking.

The earliest elements of tracking took the form of homogeneous grouping and was adopted on all levels. Using the IQ as a basis, the children in the third grade, for example, were assigned to separate classes—slow, average and above-average—and the curriculum was adapted to the needs of each. If a child remained in the above-average group through elementary school, he would probably be placed in an accelerated group in the junior high school and go on to an academic senior high school. If he was in a slow group in elementary school, his formal schooling would be likely to terminate at graduation, though he might go on to a vocational school or to a general course in junior and senior high school. The middle group might go either way, depending on the motivation of family and child.

Types of Tracking in the High School

The type of high school a student attends may itself constitute a track. In urban areas there are vocational, commercial, specialized, academic, and technical, as well as comprehensive high schools. For example, a student attending a vocational high school has a limited chance of going on to college. In the comprehensive high school the same result is achieved through a variety of *courses of study,* each of which is, in effect, a track. The academic course is reserved for those of high IQ and reading ability who intend to go to college. The commercial course, generally for girls, leads to a position in a business office after graduation. The industrial-arts course may lead to a trade, and the general course for the less gifted leads to a position as an unskilled worker.

In general, the high-school curriculum consists of both common learnings (general education) and electives. The former, including English, social studies, basic mathematics and science, health education, and orientation in art and music, are required of all students. The latter, including modern and classical languages, advanced mathematics and science, industrial arts and homemaking, business education and other areas of specialization, such as agriculture and vocational education, differentiate students into the college-bound, office-bound, and so on.

An extension of the idea of tracking is the segregation of students in the common-learnings subjects into homogeneous groupings. For example, if a high school has 240 students taking tenth-year English, they may have eight classes which include one or two "honors" classes, two or three "special" classes (retarded, slow, or reluctant learners), and three or four "regular" classes. This too is a form of tracking, for the "honors" classes are college-bound, while for the "slow" the high school will be terminal. The basis for the segregation is generally IQ, reading level, previous achievement in the subject and, sometimes, intensity of purpose.

Advantages of Tracking

As the high school becomes a school for all American youth it will have to differentiate its program to meet the diverse needs and talents of its students. When all high-school students were college-bound, the academic college-preparatory course was the only one the high school needed to offer. But since at least half of all high-school students are not college-bound today, the school must offer different programs for those preparing for industry, business, agriculture, homemaking, and other general objectives.

Homogeneous grouping developed as a practical approach to the problem of educating children of vastly different abilities. Teachers soon discovered that the traditional curriculum in history, for example, was too difficult for the increasing percentage of youngsters who were severely retarded in reading. To "water down" the curriculum would be unfair to the bright, college-bound youngster. To insist on the maintenance of high standards for all would lead to frustration and perhaps even to truancy and delinquency for the retarded. The solution of homogeneous grouping was adopted to make it possible to place each student in a group with comparable ability.

Since the high school is organized on a departmental basis, with each student taking four or more subjects in separate classes, it is theoretically possible for a student to be in a "talented" group in science, an "average" group in social studies, and a "slow" group in English. When a flexible program is maintained, so that a student may move from one type of group to another on the basis of effort, motivation, and improvement in reading, the charge that some children are being labeled as permanently retarded is unwarranted. In a well-administered school no stigma is ever attached to a student because he is in the slow group, for it is recognized that each person has worth and that the school's philosophy is to place each student where he can get the most from his education and give his best to society in return.

Arguments Against Tracking

Serious objections have been raised against homogeneous grouping, particularly in the general education phase of the curriculum. The argument is succinctly stated in *The High School We Need:*

> In the high-school program, the general education phase of an individual's schedule should be in classes that are heterogeneously grouped. A priority purpose of general education is to develop qualities that will make the student a good citizen. One aspect of this process is getting to know what the various segments of the population are like, and developing skill in working with people who are different from one's self. The student needs to have this portion of his time in heterogeneously grouped classes so that he will develop the ability to work with many types of people; skill in communications; means of effective leadership; and an understanding of the purposes, points of view, and values held by others.[4]

Proponents of homogeneous grouping argue that the need to learn to associate with all types in a democracy is met in the physical education, art, and music classes, in the lunch room, assembly, home room, study hall, library, and in cocurricular activities.

Many of the arguments for and against homogeneous grouping discussed above are answered by the introduction of new teaching techniques and, in fact, by a new philosophy for the general education phase of the high-school program to which the term "core" or "common learnings" is applied. Undoubtedly there is a warrant for continued ability grouping in the high school, but experimental practices with new methods and new curricular materials may set desirable limits to the tendencies toward rigid tracking and universal homogeneous grouping.

PROVIDING FOR INDIVIDUAL DIFFERENCES

Identification of the Talented

Approximately 20 percent of all high-school students are academically talented—that is, they have IQ's of 120 or more and can excel in the academic college-preparatory program. Many of these students have social, artistic, or athletic talents as well. Some excel in one area but not in others but generally

---

[4] Kimball Wiles and Franklin Patterson, *The High School We Need,* A Report from the ASCD Commission on the Education of Adolescents (Washington, D.C.: Association for Supervision and Curriculum Development 1959), p. 14.

talent in one field goes along with talent in others. Some 2 to 3 percent of high-school students are not only bright or talented but possess rare endowments of intellectual or other potential which classifies them as "gifted." It might appear that these youngsters would be easily identified in any high school, but unfortunately this is not true. Often failure to identify them causes them to be placed in unchallenging learning situations where they lose interest, do mediocre work, or drop out of school. It is estimated that "about half of our most able youth do not now go to college."[5]

Every effort must be made to identify the talented and the gifted and to challenge them to the point where they achieve to capacity. Methods of identification are being developed and refined. Standardized tests of special abilities and talents are available as supplements to intelligence tests. Anecdotal reports, observation by teachers, conference with parents, school grades, and extra-school activities all yield clues to identification.

> All able youth will not be the same. There are many kinds of abilities. . . . In our identification, we must consider the background to which the individual has been subjected, the way in which he is superior to others . . . the depth and nature of his interests, his energy level, the strength and persistence of his motivation and the kind of chap he really is.[6]

The Mentally Retarded

The mentally retarded are those whose IQ is about 75 or below. Students with IQ's from 75 to 50 are regarded as *educable*. Below an IQ of 50 they are said to be *trainable*. It is the task of the high school to provide the instruction and environment which will make it possible for these students to adjust to the demands of society and to achieve some vocational competence and satisfaction.

A great deal of research and experimentation and considerable financial assistance has been devoted to the problems of the mentally retarded. Classifying children as "mentally retarded" is difficult because of the variety of types of retardation. There

---

[5] John M. Stalnaker, "Methods of Identification—The Complexity of the Problem," *The Identification and Education of the Academically Talented Student in the American Secondary School* (Washington, D.C.: NEA), p. 18.
[6] *Ibid.*, p. 26.

are those who suffer from inherited or congenital deficiencies, and those who are retarded as a result of illness or injury. Others have had limited opportunity, either social or educational, and these might achieve normally if given a chance. There are still others who are so emotionally disturbed that they have been unable to learn or to acquire the necessary basic educational tools. Whatever the cause of retardation, every high school must provide for those youngsters who are so retarded that they cannot profit from the ordinary instruction or high-school curriculum.

"Slow Learners"

Every high school also enrolls a large number of boys and girls who are three or more years below the reading grade of their class. Such children are classified as "slow" or "reluctant" learners and are placed in separate classes under the same principles of homogeneous grouping applied to the talented. Teachers adept at working with this type of child and in giving remedial diagnosis and instruction in reading, arithmetic, and other subjects are or should be assigned to these groups. The IQ of these students may range upwards from about 75 or 80. Their interest level may be adolescent but their reading and comprehension level may be retarded several years. In some high schools the percentage of such youngsters may be fifty or more; in others, it may be very small. In any event, special provision must be made for them in their own interest, in the interest of the more able in the school, and in the interest of society. Some of these students can be upgraded by skillful remedial instruction; all can be helped to acquire the maximum education possible for them.

The Emotionally Disturbed

Every high school has some students who are categorized as emotionally disturbed, on the basis of their anti-social and often unpredictable behavior. These students are a constant problem for teacher and administrator. They break school rules, refuse to obey teachers, upset classroom procedure, and not infrequently attack other students or teachers or engage in vandalism. Causes for this behavior may be traced most frequently to unfavorable home environment. Other causes may include physical disabilities, adolescent tensions, membership in unde-sirable groups, school conditions, and occasionally mental re-tardation.

The high school's weapons for attacking the problem of the emotionally disturbed include available psychiatric and psycho-logical help, a skillfully administered testing program, a sym-pathetic guidance program, specially trained teachers, and the enlistment of community agencies—police, social workers, recre-ational programs, financial assistance—to relieve some of the difficulties. In some instances, it may be necessary to place a dis-turbed child in a special school.

An administration and faculty that is able and willing to undertake the education and rehabilitation of the emotionally disturbed can save society and the student from serious future problems. In fact, some of these students may become strong positive forces once their energies are redirected into construc-tive channels. It is, however, easier to discuss these problems ob-jectively than to try to solve them while attempting to carry on the normal routine of class and school activities.

The Physically Handicapped Student

Most high schools make provisions for the education of chil-dren who are physically handicapped. Wherever possible these children should be required to do the work of the normal child with a minimum of dispensation. Of course, the homebound, the cardiac, the blind, and others with severe handicaps may need special instruction. Generally the health education de-partment is actively involved in the program for such students. The object in every case is to provide opportunities for rehabili-tation, and at the same time to make it possible for each child to develop his capacities and to secure the best high-school edu-cation of which he is capable.

Special Education

The term "exceptional" is applied to the mentally retarded, emotionally disturbed, and/or physically handicapped as well as to the gifted. The preparation of teachers for any of these cate-gories of students is called *special education*. The problem of educating the exceptional child is part of the general problem of individualizing instruction. The goal is clear—to help each child realize his potential as an individual and as a citizen. We have made huge strides in this direction, but we still have much to learn about the exceptional child and how the school can best foster his development. Teachers preparing to specialize in any of these areas may look forward to participation in programs of dynamic change in the decades ahead.

FOR DELIBERATION and DISCUSSION

1. In interviewing how much weight should a principal attach to a teacher's potential for directing extra-class activities? Explain.
2. Should teachers be required to sponsor extracurricular activities as a part of their jobs? Should this be regarded as a professional task to be performed without compensation?
3. In most states there are special requirements for certification to teach either the mentally retarded or the emotionally disturbed. Few require special certification for teaching the talented or gifted. Should a special certificate for teaching the gifted be required? Why? What preparation should be required of such teachers?
4. The extracurricular program of the high school cuts across grade lines. What are the implications of this for curriculum?
5. What are the arguments for and against homogeneous grouping in the high school? How may the disadvantage be minimized?
6. Since the classroom teacher has the advantage of daily contact with each student, what justification is there for special guidance personnel?

FOR ADDITIONAL READING

ARBUCKLE, DUGALD S. *Guidance and Counseling in the Classroom.* Boston: Allyn and Bacon, 1957. An introduction to counseling containing a section on "Teachers as Guidance Workers."

CHASE, FRANCIS S. and ANDERSON, HAROLD S. (eds.). *The High School in a New Era.* Chicago: U. of Chicago Press, 1958. Leading American educators discuss aspects of the high-school program, including guidance, homogeneous grouping, and so on.

DOUGLASS, HARL R. (ed.). *Education for Life Adjustment.* New York: Ronald, 1950. Twenty-one articles by various specialists organized by subjects and specialities around the concept of life adjustment.

FEATHERSTONE, WILLIAM R. *A Functional Curriculum for Youth.* New York: American Book, 1950. A dynamic approach to curriculum derived from a consistent philosophy of education. Emphasis on student needs.

GORDON, IRA J. *The Teacher As A Guidance Worker.* New York:

Harper, 1956. Abounds in information and concepts useful to the classroom teacher in his capacity as guidance worker.

"Guidance Practices in the Secondary School," *Bulletin*, National Association of Secondary School Principals, No. 277 (November, 1962).

JOHNSTON, EDGAR and FAUNCE, RONALD. *Student Activities in the Secondary Schools.* New York: Ronald, 1952. Detailed discussion of many phases of extra-class activities. Concrete illustrations presented throughout.

MCKOWN, HARRY C. *Extra-Curricular Activities.* 3rd ed.; New York: Macmillan, 1952. A comprehensive discussion of the subject. Includes consideration of secret societies, manners, commencement, and many other activities.

WILES, KIMBALL and PATTERSON, FRANKLIN. *The High School We Need.* Washington, D.C.: Association for Supervision and Curriculum Development, 1959. A forthright statement of beliefs about virtually every aspect of high-school education by twenty-five specialists in secondary education.

PART II: THE SECONDARY-SCHOOL PROGRAM

6 Teaching and Methodology

Reaching the Student

All high-school teachers today face the major problem of establishing a solid relationship with all the students in the class. Unless the students are with us, we have a situation in which curriculum material is imposed on students who have little or no interest in it, and who therefore exert no effort to relate to it, and who waste their time and talent. It is important, therefore, to understand the student, to know as much about him as possible, to seek to involve him in the work of the school and to work at this task sensitively and unremittingly as a key in curriculum building.

The professional term *motivation* is too often narrowly construed to mean that it is enough to suggest to a group of students some reason—usually the teacher's—for studying, and they will learn. A more substantial approach to motivation recognizes two factors. The motivation which is internal or intrinsic —that is, the student's own motivation—is the one that will carry him through difficulties in making advances in learning. Furthermore, the motivation which is most comprehensive is likely to have the most worth in the learning process. Thus, if a student himself finds the value in formal schooling, each task or subject will acquire interest for him. If the desire to learn French is the student's, the need to "motivate" a lesson on irregular verbs is minimized. How this extensive motivation is achieved is, of course, a field of inquiry which needs to be fully explored. Known sources of motivation include the home, friends, some accidental experience, and the school itself.

Good teaching is achieved by the teacher who has a genuine interest in the student—his background, capabilities, ambitions, and potential interests. A truly sympathetic teacher will have little difficulty motivating the students, for he will accommodate his teaching to the student. If he is to achieve this level of good teaching, however, the teacher must have some freedom in curriculum planning. Subjects designed for the select student of the early twentieth century are not suitable for the average high-school student of the 1960's or 1970's. The material tailored for the average high-school student is far removed from the potential of the non-verbal student and too elementary for the prowess of the gifted. Thus, the sensitive, creative secondary-school teacher will have an openminded concept of curriculum and develop it as each individual, group, and situation demands.

Love of Learning and of the Subject

In a well-motivated classroom situation, with rapport between teacher and students, there is a good possibility that a major objective of all secondary-school teaching—the love of learning and of the subject being taught—will be achieved. This is especially true when the teacher has a high degree of competence in the subject and radiates a love for it because his feeling is communicated to students. Many high-school teachers attribute their choice of vocation to an inspiring teacher of the subject in their own high-school days.

It is important as well for teachers to communicate a love for learning beyond the confines of their own subject. The well-educated teacher, who is at home in disciplines other than his own, will convey this general love of learning to students if there is a spirit of understanding and mutual respect in the relationship.

Fundamental Tools: Reading, Writing, Speaking

The statement "every high school teacher is an English teacher" should be taken seriously. Students' reading, writing, speaking, listening, note-taking, and other aspects of the traditional English curriculum should be of concern to every teacher. The teacher of health education must insist on the highest possible standards of written and oral English in his classroom, and the teacher of English must be concerned with the health habits of his students. The work of the school is a co-operative venture, and it will succeed best as each teacher accepts students' progress in the basic tools of reading, speaking, and writing as one of the goals of his own subject.

Thinking and Inquiry

The old idea that certain subjects—Latin and mathematics, for example—are uniquely designed for developing thought processes has yielded to our realization that all subjects, including the arts and vocational subjects, embody unlimited potential for teaching students to think. Increasingly today the good teacher helps develop the creative potential of his students. In every subject, activities involving imagination, intuition, planning, research, investigation, reasoning, and criticism must be utilized. The older method of guiding students through the steps of an experiment to its inevitable conclusion is giving way to discovery, the process in which students pose their own problems and find solutions by applying one or more of the processes of thinking and inquiry—inductive or deductive reasoning, comparison, classification, analysis, and creativity.

Aesthetic Appreciation

Here, again, no subject has a monopoly. The teacher of English, social studies, science, or mathematics knows the aesthetic appeal of his subject. He helps develop this appreciation in his students just as does the teacher of art or music, if he himself is sensitive to and works consciously toward this objective.

Intellectual Interests and Pursuits

In every subject there is an intellectual content which may be said to have its own *raison d'être*. To stimulate and develop the intellectual capacity of each student so that he is provided with continuing interests is one of the tasks of the high school. The awakening of intellectual curiosity in as many as possible of the 50 percent who do not go on to college is to help them lead richer lives and thereby to enrich our entire culture. The teacher must accept this responsibility as he does the task of developing intellectual potential of the college-bound.

Moral Values

Finally, all teachers face the task of developing students of strong moral character. Through precept, practice, and analysis, attitudes of integrity, self-respect, respect and appreciation for individuals and groups, adherence and loyalty to democratic practices, cooperation, sympathy and other character traits the high-school teacher will contribute to the moral development of his students.

Working With Slow Learners[1]

One of the growing problems of modern secondary education is provision for the slow learner. Some educators merely reject the slow learners as a poor educational risk. Yet, if we accept the democratic ideal that each individual is precious and deserves the optimum development of his potential, we must find ways to educate these students.

To the teacher who is faced with the daily problem of meeting slow learners, the problem is an acute one. It is essential that the teacher of the slow learner develop perspective in meeting the problems that arise daily in the classroom. This section is designed to identify these problems, analyze them, and acquaint the teacher with the more enlightened approaches to their solution.

A teacher who understands the mental and emotional makeup of the slow learner is in a better position to channel the energies of these pupils along constructive and creative lines. In fact, the establishment of good rapport is a basic aspect of a teacher's work with slow learners. The following analysis may help give the teacher insight into the behavior characteristics and emotional drives of the slow learner.

In general, the most striking differences between the normal and the slow learner are found in the higher mental processes. Slow students

have difficulty making and understanding abstractions.

---

[1] The section on working with slow learners is adapted from *Teacher's Manual* for *Going Places With Mathematics,* 2nd ed., pp. 1–9 by M. Peters. © 1956, 1962, by Prentice-Hall, Inc., Englewood Cliffs, N.J. By permission of the publisher.

are very weak in forming associations between words and ideas.

are weak in seeing relationships and in making generalizations.

have limited imagination.

have inadequate memories.

have difficulty following a logical argument.

have a short attention span.

The plight of the slow student is worsened by these facts:

The social stigma of poor school performance over a long period of time has a corrosive influence.

Because of poor school achievement, the educational goals of the slow are either blurred or non-existent.

The disapproval of teachers and parents has a demoralizing effect.

Children of low socio-economic background may be culturally deprived and may be influenced by group values which tend to derogate education.

Thus it is not surprising that some slow pupils rebel against school work and that this rebellion sometimes takes the form of overt manifestations of anti-social behavior. More often it is an inward reaction, resulting in an outward mechanical conformity characterized by listlessness, indifference, and an attitude of hopelessness. The teacher of the slow must counteract these tendencies toward maladjustment and must provide an emotional climate conducive to learning.

The teacher should not start the semester with the attitude that working with slow pupils is an unpleasant, unwanted assignment: this feeling is quickly sensed by the students. Slow learners can provide the teacher with many satisfactions in his work. No group is more appreciative of kindness, consideration, and understanding. Teachers who have had successful experiences with slow learners often ask for slow-learner classes rather than average or bright classes.

Secondary-school teachers have been working with special classes of slow learners for more than a generation, and during this time a number of procedures have been established. Reading material, especially textbooks, must be geared to the reading level of the students. A number of texts have been and are being prepared for this level, but there is still a dearth of suitable material for the slow learner. It is better to give a slow class a book, such as *Boy Meets Girl,* of proper interest and reading level, though it is only remotely connected with the course of study, than to attempt to give these students a difficult textbook beyond their comprehension. Of course, the ideal is an appropriate text of low reading-grade and high-interest level.

No child should be placed only in slow classes. He may be in a slow group in social studies, an average group in mathematics, and possibly a bright group in some other subject, but he should be in one or more average groups during the day. It is equally important to permit some fluidity in grouping, so that at the end of each semester, as a result of tests and teacher recommendation, some students will move from retarded to normal or the other way.

No student should be placed in a slow group as a punishment, nor should a stigma be attached to membership in such a group. Occasionally a bright but emotionally disturbed pupil is placed in a slow group. Nothing could have less educational merit. Not only does this tend to aggravate his emotional difficulty, but his conduct often deteriorates and he disrupts the work of the slow but otherwise diligent students. Parental pressure should not be permitted to influence the school's decision. If a pupil is really slow, it is better to let him work with a group whose abilities are like his own and where a competent, sympathetic teacher will make his schooling a source of pleasure and possible growth for him.

THE EDUCATION OF THE GIFTED
AND THE TALENTED

A deep concern about the education of the talented high-school student is not new; the studies of Lewis M. Terman go back more than three decades. But the American high school during the second quarter of this century was so preoccupied with the retarded that the gifted and talented were neglected. During this time the number of college courses in education of the retarded was ten times that of courses in education of the gifted. The same ratio obtained in professional literature and in the amount of money spent on the special education of each of these groups. In 1951, Paul Witty wrote of the gifted high-school student: "He is frequently permitted to drift along aimlessly for four years denied the stimulation and the guidance which could enable him to make the most of his gifts."[2]

The conference on the academically talented high-school student, held in Washington under the auspices of the NEA in 1958, sounded a keynote marking the revival of interest on a high professional level and with broad and sustained attack on all aspects of the problem. The conference was attended by more than a hundred leaders in education of the talented in all fields. It resulted in the publication of an excellent booklet which has been followed by special statements relating to each high-school subject.[3]

Identification

No two children have the same kind or the same degree of talent in one or all high-school subjects. Selecting talented students as a result of an arbitrary rating on a group IQ test is much too crude a procedure, for it will rule out some who should be included and include others who do not belong. The individual IQ test generally is a more refined instrument. This, coupled with the judgment of teachers based on cumulative records and performance, should come closer to giving a valid basis for identification. A high degree of academic competence should be complemented by creativity, originality, and imaginativeness. No one should be permanently classified as gifted or average, nor should work with the vast middle group fail to utilize those materials and procedures which prove effective with the gifted.

It also may be advisable to draw a distinction between the 2 or 3 percent who are gifted and the 15 or 20 percent who are talented. The latter will probably be sufficiently challenged if they are placed in a homogeneous group and taught by a talented and devoted teacher. Their program should be based on their needs and interests, and it should be sufficiently varied, extensive, and intensive to require each student to apply himself fully in accordance with his ability.

[2] Paul Witty, *The Gifted Child* (Boston: Heath, 1951), p. 240.
[3] *The Identification and Education of the Academically Talented Student in the American Secondary School* (Washington D.C.: NEA, 1958), and various reports of the NEA "Project on the Academically Talented."

As for the much smaller number of truly gifted, it may be that they can find a congenial and challenging program in the special area in which their gifts lie. The school is bound, under penalty of allowing human resources to remain undeveloped or to be destroyed, to re-examine its program for the gifted continuously.

A few principles stated by Woolcock[4] are sufficiently clear and important to be restated here: (1) The gifted and talented should be identified as early as possible, in the first years in school. (2) They should be taught by superior teachers. (3) Small classes are essential. (4) Acceleration and enrichment are both advisable, but the former is virtually indispensable (at least two years should be gained by the talented during the first twelve years in school). (5) As far as possible, motivation should be inner directed, not imposed. (6) Leadership should be an explicit goal. (7) Intense competition fostered by examinations and grades should be avoided. (8) A vertical guidance program, in which a counselor stays with a child throughout his schooling, is advisable. (This is one area in which better integration between the work of elementary, junior, and senior high school is needed.) (9) Every effort should be made to foster creativity and originality. Opportunities for self-direction will foster the development of the latent talents of the gifted.

While these principles apply equally to all subjects and indeed to all students—ordinary as well as gifted—it is clear that their implementation for those with special talents will go far toward improving the work of the secondary school.

Enrichment

We have already discussed homogeneous grouping, the device most frequently employed to bring together in separate classes children with special talents. For any such class, however, the term "homogeneous" may be a tragic misrepresentation, for a group of thirty boys and girls in an English or mathematics "honor class" may include the extremes of one or more with slightly above average talent (or even below average but with high motivation), and the boy or girl whose talent borders on genius. So-called homogeneous grouping can never replace the

[4] Cyril W. Woolcock, *New Directions in the Education of the Gifted* (Morristown: Silver Burdett, 1961).

challenge to the teacher for recognizing individual differences and adjusting the curriculum to accommodate them.

Too often the enriched class is taught by a teacher who is not qualified to work with talented youngsters. It is a mistake to suppose that a talented class is easier to teach than an average or retarded group. Each demands special training and skills. Unqualified teachers of the talented generally assign more of the same—*more* reading, *more* homework, *more* oral reports, with little imagination—and no real challenge to the treasures committed to them.

"The teacher of the academically talented should have in exceptional degree some of the qualifications expected of all teachers: a good mind, broad intellectual curiosity, creativeness, energy, experience, enthusiasm, emotional balance, personality and a deep interest in students."[5] Such a teacher will provide for individual difference through enrichment in a flexible curriculum designed to challenge each student to the highest degree. In studying a piece of imaginative literature, the slow student may be expected to achieve a minimum of understanding and appreciation, the average student a deeper insight and more complicated responses, the talented a mature perspective and the stimulation to make original responses to the author's message, and the gifted an inspiration to proceed as far as his endowments permit.

There is a growing body of material devoted to meeting the challenge of the gifted high-school student. Competent teachers are using creative study guides to reach each child on his own level of ability. Colleges and universities are beginning to offer courses in educating the gifted. A report entitled "The Gifted Student in the New York City Schools"[6] contains a section on "effective instructional procedures." The Bureau of Secondary

---

[5] John M. Stalnaker, pp. 95, 121, and 130. The report stated, for example, that "Teachers working with the academically talented in social studies should have a scholarly knowledge of their subject or area, be liberally educated, have a deep understanding of the nature of learning and of the learning process, a belief in and an understanding of the needs of academically talented students, and a keen desire to teach such students; they should also have grappled with the philosophical problems of the meaning and purpose of education and have a knowledge of the history of American education." p. 121.

[6] *The Gifted Student in the New York City Schools:* A Memorandum and Bibliography (New York: Bureau of Curriculum Research, New York City Public Schools, 1959).

Curriculum Development of the New York State Education Department issues a list of "Fiction for High School Students of Superior Ability" and another entitled "More Books for High School Students of Superior Ability" listing poetry, plays, Shakespeare, essays, biography, history, travel, and miscellaneous. The National Council of Teachers of English sponsors much curriculum material suitable for the gifted especially its *Books for You.* The National Council for the Social Studies issues considerable curriculum material including its *World History Book List for High Schools.* The NEA is a major source of curriculum material much of which is useful in working with the talented or gifted high-school student.

Acceleration

We have been considering enrichment as one approach to the education of the talented. We turn now to another concept which is gaining wide acceptance as a partial solution to the challenge presented by youth of superior ability—*acceleration.*

A recent study indicates that 76.1 percent of all school districts in the nation make some special provisions for the gifted in senior high schools, including one or more of the following: enrichment, separate classes, acceleration.[7] Many junior high schools are organized so that the upper third or quarter can complete the seventh, eighth, and ninth grades in two years by pursuing an accelerated curriculum in special classes. For many years high schools have permitted students to accelerate by carrying a heavier course load and attending summer school.

Another growing trend is that of attendance of talented high-school students at special summer programs conducted by colleges. Selected students are attending special seminars on Saturdays and even after school. Many of these, too, are held at colleges. This integration of high school and college for the benefit of the gifted has great promise. A few curriculum experiments in high school are designed specifically to permit each child to proceed at his own pace and to complete the high-school course in as little as two and a half years. This movement is bound to grow, for it is soundly grounded in an educational philosophy that will break the deadening traditional lock-step.

[7] NEA *Research Bulletin,* 38, No. 2 (May 1960): 47–48.

Another form of integration between the high school and college is the Advanced Placement Program of the College Entrance Examination Board. The Board conducts examinations in centers throughout the country during the spring. In 1960, over ten thousand candidates, including some of the most gifted high-school juniors and seniors, took examinations for college credit (advanced placement) in American history, biology, chemistry, English, European history, French, German, Latin, mathematics, physics, and Spanish. Over 350 colleges throughout the country accepted one or more of these candidates for advanced placement by previous agreement with the College Entrance Examination Board.

Nevertheless, though there has been a vast expenditure of research funds, special training for teachers, and special classes for the mentally retarded, no such concerted effort has been made to meet the needs of the gifted. Lyle Spencer, President of Science Research Associates, explains:

> Most citizens stand ready at any time to help a handicapped person—particularly if that person is a child. . . . But the obverse of this attitude—that academically superior school children *also* need special school help—is a thought that requires a complete change of mental set to gain acceptance. . . . An added problem to surmount is that superior teaching of superior students also requires superior teachers and somewhat increased school budgets.[8]

Not only do the gifted have the normal problems of growing up—the need for sympathy, understanding, encouragement, the need to feel they belong—but they frequently have additional problems. These may include a discrepancy between their intellectual and their physical or emotional development, rejection or ridicule by their peers and even by adults who feel challenged or threatened by their gifts, parental pressure, and expectation of adult behavior because of their advanced intellectual development.

An all-out attack on the problems of the gifted high-school student is gaining momentum. In addition to the practices already described, the following are being attempted in various schools: (1) one teacher assigned the task of coordinating the

[8] *Identification and Education of the Talented*, pp. 41–42.

entire high-school program for the talented; (2) an attempt to have gifted students assigned as assistants to teachers in their free time so that the teacher in turn may give part of this time to special tutoring of the gifted student assistant; (3) a regular honor roll published after each marking period, with various rewards by administration, teachers, and parents; (4) special attempts to encourage independent study and research by the talented; (5) regular exhibits of the work of the gifted; (6) awards, scholarships, citations, and other types of recognition; (7) experimentation especially for helping the talented; (8) the home, community agencies, and colleges with special programs for these students; (9) using the school homeroom and guidance program as an adjunct for upgrading the gifted.

We will not have solved the problem until the gifts of each child are identified as early as possible and developed to their limit by expert teaching.

SUPPLEMENTING THE SCHOOL PROGRAM

Homework

The limited time and the restricted space available to a teacher and class in any subject can be appreciably extended by a well-planned supplementary program. The most common and time-honored device for achieving this is homework. Most schools consider it not only appropriate but essential that a high-school student spend approximately the same amount of time outside of school as he does in school on each of his major subjects. Homework assignments can include reading the textbook; answering specific written questions; reading supplementary texts, novels, essays, plays, and so on; library research; preparing for special examinations and contests; radio, television, and theater programs; visits to museums and historic buildings and sites; writing letters; interviewing or consulting specialists; and special individual or group projects.

If these assignments are carefully and specifically made, properly motivated, thoroughly checked, and adequately recognized, they may well be as effective as class work. Not all of the above need be unsupervised homework. The textbook lesson may occasionally be completed in class under the watchful eye of the teacher, thus constituting a supervised study lesson. From time to time the written homework of the student should be carefully inspected and guidance for improvement offered. An occasional visit of class and teacher to the school library with the objective of teaching one or more techniques—use of card catalog, use of vertical file, comparison of textbooks, contents of reference books, location of fiction, biography and non-fiction —will be carried over to more effective individual use of libraries. Each of the other suggested supplements to the formal work of the class occasionally may be carried out under teacher supervision.

Testing and Evaluation

Any program of evaluation must be related directly to the educational objectives of the school. If we examine the general aims of a school program or of a specific subject, we will see the difficulties inherent in attempting to determine whether and to what extent these aims have been achieved. For example, in social studies, how do we get a quantitative evaluation of "appreciation for our democratic heritage" or "appreciation of the cultural heritage of the ages, of different peoples and civilizations" or of the other basic general aims of social-studies teaching?

The traditional means of evaluation are written examinations designed to test as thoroughly as possible the quantity and quality of the mastery attained by the student in the subject. While written examinations cannot test many of the intangibles, it is a mistake to assume that such examinations, properly constructed, are entirely inadequate in this respect. Too, with the rapid expansion of national examinations—Merit Scholarship, Scholastic Aptitude, College Entrance Examination Board —as well as standardized achievement tests, such as the Iowa Examinations and statewide examinations, it is possible to get some idea of the success of a school program at least in meeting the standards set by the respective examinations.[9]

There are, of course, other means of evaluation, though none is as "objective" as those described above. If a school has consistently large numbers of scholarships won by its students, if its students are successful in interscholastic competition, in

[9] See the critical report *Testing, Testing, Testing* (Washington, D.C.: National Association of Secondary School Principals, The American Association of School Administrators, and The Council of Chief State School Officers, 1962).

debate, journalism, essay writing, and so on, it is reasonable to attribute this, at least in part, to the quality of the program. If students read, write, and study on their own, if their use of the library is increased, if they prepare their work willingly, volunteer for special assignments, seem to take keen interest and pride in their work, and give every indication of desirable growth, these results may be taken as an indication of the success of the school program.

Tangible evidence of a good program includes written homework, essays, bulletin boards, class log, notebooks, related art projects, and the like. Supervisors, alert to what is going on, will regard these tangible results as significant evidence of the work of a teacher and class. Parents, too, will be able to distinguish the interest and effort generated in one class from the routine motions of another.

Finally, children's self-evaluation should play a major role in judging their progress. High-school boys and girls can be taught to develop standards against which to measure their own work and the class program. The following self-evaluation checklist is one sample of the type of questionnaire a social-studies teacher may find valuable.

Student Self-Evaluation Checklist in Current Events

Do I: *Yes   No*

1. Prepare current events assignments with the same care and effort I use on other assignments?
2. Read carefully the main news stories in my school current events periodicals each week?
3. Study the news shorts to see what big stories are in the making?
4. Listen to at least one radio or TV news program every day?
5. Read at least one news magazine each week?
6. Read a daily newspaper regularly for news?
7. Read the important news stories on the front page of my newspaper and follow those I consider significant to their conclusion in the back pages?
8. Follow significant news stories as they develop?
9. Think about the meaning of a news story and relate it to what I already know?

10. Study news headlines and subheads to get an idea of what a story is about before reading it?
11. Study news pictures, graphs, and maps for the information they contain?
12. Read editorial columns and study cartoons to get the "political slant" of papers?
13. Keep alert to editorializing in news columns and through news selection and use of pictures?
14. Consider news sources in terms of reliability?
15. Consider all the information I have obtained on important problems and then arrive at my own tentative solutions?
16. Relate the news to my study of history, science, and other subjects?
17. Sometimes write to my representatives in Washington and the state capital stating my views on current problems?
18. Attend lectures or discussion groups on current affairs held in my community?
19. Keep myself informed on important community events and problems?
20. Participate actively in helping solve current problems in my community?

When students participate, at least to some extent, in developing their curriculum and when they are taught to evaluate their achievement in each aspect of their work, they will be more sensitive to the extent of their progress and attainment. As a result, students will have a more realistic approach to the problems presented and greater pride in the progress made, no matter how far short of perfection it may fall.

FOR DELIBERATION and DISCUSSION

1. The text describes seven basic goals of high-school teaching. Give specific illustrations to show how each of these goals may be attained through the subject you teach or are preparing to teach.
2. What special qualifications should a teacher possess for working with retarded students? With talented or gifted youngsters? What are the advantages or disadvantages of teaching each group? Assess your own qualifications and attitudes in this respect.
3. What objection, if any, is there to placing a student in a "slow track" or any other track in all subjects in a secondary school?

Heterogeneous grouping in academic subjects? How can the apparent contradiction be resolved?

4. Some teachers say, "I teach English"; others "I teach boys and girls"; and still others say, "I teach boys and girls English." What are the implications of each statement?

5. Self-direction (inquiry, independent study, and self-evaluation) are becoming increasingly important in the secondary-school program. What are the implications for the teacher?

FOR ADDITIONAL READING

Bulletin, National Association of Secondary School Principals, 47, No. 281 (March 1963) is devoted to the theme "Student Differences and Secondary School Offerings," and contains a number of articles describing programs for the gifted and a number describing programs for the retarded.

BRUNER, JEROME S. *The Process of Education.* Cambridge: Harvard U. Press, 1961. One of the most challenging books in education in the twentieth century. A magna carta for investigation of the learning process and for bringing method and content in line with findings.

CLARK, HAROLD F. *Cost and Quality of Public Education.* Syracuse: Syracuse U. Press, 1963. This pamphlet in the Syracuse series "The Economics and Politics of Public Education" summarizes many recent studies. Lucid and keenly critical.

CONANT, JAMES B. (ed.). *The Identification and Education of the Academically Talented Student in the American Secondary School,* Washington, D.C.: NEA, 1958. Some two hundred leaders discuss the identification and education (curriculum) of academically talented high school students. The NEA Project in the Academically Talented Student also has published bulletins in the following: Mathematics, Social Studies, Science, English, Modern Foreign Languages, Music, Art, Guidance, Business and Economic Education, Research and Administration.

DEHAAN, R. F. and HAVIGHURST, R. J. *Educating Gifted Children.* Chicago: U. of Chicago Press, 1961. Up-to-date evaluation.

EVERETT, SAMUEL (ed.). *Programs for the Gifted: A Case Book In Secondary Education.* New York: Harper, 1961. This fifteenth yearbook of the John Dewey Society contains contributions by some dozen distinguished educators including William H. Kilpatrick, Goodwin Watson, Paul Witty, *et al.* Describes programs for the gifted in selected high schools throughout the country.

GARDNER, JOHN W. *Excellence: Can We Be Equal and Excellent Too?* New York: Harper, 1961. A discourse on problems associated with recognition and reward for a variety of talents in contemporary America and elsewhere. Spells out an affirmative answer to the question in the title.

Labels and Fingerprints. Washington, D.C.: NEA, 1961. A brief statement on individualizing instruction by five affiliates of the NEA including the NASSP.

LARSON, KNUTE and KARPAS, MELVIN R. *Effective Secondary School Discipline.* Englewood Cliffs: Prentice-Hall, 1963. Comprehensive treatment of discipline in Rhode Island's Cranston High School East—both critical and practical.

MAGER, ROBERT F. *Preparing Objectives for Programmed Instruction.* San Francisco: Fearon, 1962. Instructs the reader, step-by-step, in stating objectives for teaching any content in such a way that the objective cannot be misunderstood. An original contribution to the improvement of instruction in all subjects.

OJEMANN, RALPH H. *Personality Adjustment of Individual Children.* rev. ed.; Washington, D.C.: NEA, 1962. Helpful suggestions to teachers in coping with personality problems of students.

PASCHAL, ELIZABETH. *Encouraging the Excellent: Special Programs for Gifted and Talented Students.* New York: Fund for the Advancement of Education, 1960. An extremely lucid statement describing a number of Fund-sponsored programs for the gifted.

TROW, WILLIAM CLARK. *The Learning Process.* rev. ed.; Washington, D.C.: NEA, 1963. One of the "What Research Says to the Teacher" series. Guideposts in a relatively uncharted area.

WOOLCOCK, CYRIL W. *The Hunter College High School Program for Gifted Students.* New York: Vantage Press, 1962. A description of the program and philosophy of a well-established high school for gifted girls by its principal.

_____. *New Approaches to the Education of the Gifted.* Morristown: Silver Burdett, 1961. Based on the latest research, this book clarifies the problems and possibilities of curricular reform.

7 Social Studies

THE SOCIAL-STUDIES CURRICULUM

Objectives of the Social Studies

In addition to the general aims of education described in Chapter 4, the social-studies teacher recognizes special objectives to be attained in his subject. While these are stated somewhat differently each time a conference report, syllabus, curriculum bulletin or textbook is issued, the aims of social-studies teaching may be summarized as follows:

Appreciation of our Democratic Heritage.   This patriotism goal is basic to all social-studies teaching. Appreciation includes understanding, and that implies critical analysis, so that a realization that our history is not without its shameful pages is not only compatible with appreciation of our democratic heritage, but essential to it.

Appreciation of the Cultural Heritage of the Ages, of Different Peoples and Civilizations.   Since our culture is a product and extension of the world's, especially the Western world's, culture, an understanding of world civilization is important to an appreciation of our own institutions.

Competence in Social Practice.   Beginning with the family, the peer group, the class, and the school, and widening to include the rights and duties of citizenship of the worker and con-

sumer of the member of a local, state, national, and world community each student should know his rights and responsibilities
and discharge them effectively.

Social Skills and Attitudes.   Skill in democratic processes, patience in seeking solutions, cooperation, tolerance of other
points of view, ability to suspend judgment, commitment to orderly processes of change, and readiness to seek justice are skills
and attitudes which the social-studies program attempts to develop.

Competence and Confidence in Handling Social Material.
The ability to get along with people of varying backgrounds
and to resolve social conflicts presupposes the development of
skill in reading and interpreting newspapers, magazines and
books; in understanding political, social, and economic movements; in interpreting data, charts, maps, graphs, symbols, and
propaganda; in having a well-developed sense of chronological
and geographical relationships; in understanding the vocabulary of the social sciences; and in comprehending relationships
among social movements.

Curriculum Reform

Revision of the curriculum to bring social-studies teaching
in line with research developments and current trends is long
overdue. Other disciplines—mathematics, science, and languages—have made huge strides in this direction during the past
few years. In fact, the National Science Foundation has only
recently elevated the social sciences to the level of the other sciences in its program.

What discernable directions will these curricular changes
take? Several emphases may be anticipated on the basis of current trends. American history, and perhaps all history as such
probably will be de-emphasized, while such studies as world
geography, sociology, psychology, and anthropology will find a
larger place in the curriculum. Correlation of studies both
within the area itself and in combination with other subjects—
English, the arts, modern languages and so on—will be developed far beyond the present limited scope of core programs.
Closer integration between the social-studies programs of elementary, junior high, senior high, junior college, senior col-

lege, and graduate school will be another target of curriculum reform.[1]

METHODS IN SOCIAL STUDIES

Planning the Social-Studies Lesson

The basic pattern of high-school organization continues to be the standard 45–50 minute period with the teacher meeting a class of approximately thirty-five students five times a week. The lesson appropriate to this schedule will be discussed here. Other curricular arrangements will be treated briefly in this chapter and more thoroughly elsewhere.

The elements of the traditional lesson are aim, motivation, pivotal questions, brief review, medial summary, final summary, application, evaluation, and assignment. These are the basic elements of the developmental lesson. The major points in the lesson are listed or outlined on the chalkboard as the lesson proceeds, with the class taking notes.

A typical lesson of this kind might be taught from the following lesson plan:

AIM (Students') *To see how the Civil War started.*

TEACHER'S AIM   To help students learn to identify with all Americans; to develop understanding for other points of view; to stimulate reflective thinking about why men fight; to teach the events, personalities, and motives surrounding the outbreak of the "War Between the States."

MOTIVATION   What similarity do you see between the situation in the U.S. in 1861 and the world situation in the 1960's? ("House divided" "Cold war.")

REVIEW   Prior to 1861, what bloodshed had occurred between

[1] See Richard E. Gross, "Emerging Horizons for Social Studies" in *Social Education*, XXIV, No. 1 (January 1960): 21–24; Richard E. Gross and Jack Allen, "Upside Down But Not Backwards," *The Social Studies*, XLIX, No. 5 (October 1958): 180–183; John H. Haefner, "Proposals for a Social Studies Curriculum," *Social Education*, XXIV, No. 5 (May 1960): 200–204; and Stanley P. Wronski, "A Proposed Breakthrough for the Social Studies," *Social Education*, XXIII, No. 5, 215–218; *The Social Studies and the Social Sciences* sponsored by The American Council of Learned Societies and the National Council for the Social Studies. (New York: Harcourt, Brace, 1962); Committee of the National Council for the Social Studies, "The Role of the Social Studies," *Social Education*, Vol. XXVI, No. 6, (October 1962): 315–318, 327.

the pro-slavery and anti-slavery forces? How do you account for the success of the new Republican Party in the election of 1860? Since the Republican platform did not advocate the abolition of slavery, why did the election of Lincoln result in the secession of South Carolina and other southern states?

DEVELOPMENT (pivotal questions)   Did all the slavery states secede? Which did? Which did not? Why? Why did the new government of the South call itself the Confederate States of America? What provisions in its constitution differed radically from those of the United States Constitution? What does this tell us about the causes of the secession? Read Lincoln's First Inaugural Address (previously assigned). Would this statement encourage or discourage secession?

MEDIAL SUMMARY   Was the outbreak of the war inevitable? Why? Why not?

FURTHER DEVELOPMENT   Could the Confederacy permit Fort Sumter to remain in the hands of the Union? Explain. Could the Union permit it to fall to the Confederacy? Explain. What similar situations do we have in the world today? (Germany, Laos, Cuba, others.)

FINAL SUMMARY   What factors were driving the country to war? What factors were at work for peace? Why did the former prevail?

EVALUATION   Basing your comments on the lesson just studied, give your reaction in a written statement of not more than 250 words to a recent cartoon showing a poor Southern white farmer saying "This country hasn't had a good president since Jefferson Davis."

ASSIGNMENT   To study the conduct of the Civil War—economic, military, political, social.

It will be obvious that a complete treatment of the questions in the lesson just described could hardly be achieved in one 45–50 minute period. Nor could the lesson assigned for next time be completed in one period. The fact is that any attempt to teach *all* of American history (or world history or any other of the social studies) in one year must prove unrealistic. The teacher will be forced to select and give emphasis to specific points. He must employ his philosophy of teaching social stud-

ies as the basis for such selection and emphasis. The treatment
of the material in the above lesson indicates a concern with
thought questions and a lesser interest in facts. Often, much material may be presented graphically in outline form as the lesson
evolves to help the students see relationships.

Among the key areas in which social-studies teaching, especially history, seeks to develop mastery are the following:
causal relationships, vocabulary of social concepts, chronological
relationships, biographical understandings and a knowledge of
basic facts.

The Social Studies Unit

A functional approach to the teaching of social studies is
the organization of a semester or a year's work into a few large
units. For example, a year survey course in world history might
be built around the following units: prehistoric man (optional),
ancient times, the medieval world, the Renaissance and the Reformation, nationalism, the Industrial Revolution, the French
Revolution, democracy, imperialism, world wars and dictator-
ship, the modern world.

In a one-year course approximately one unit per month
can be studied. Often a teacher will find it helpful to give the
students concrete guidance as the unit is developed. A work
sheet, such as the one on "The Pioneer in America" will help
give direction to students in their readings and research and will
help them evaluate their work.

Work Sheet on *The Pioneer in America*

A. Three motives that caused the American pioneer to settle
the frontier were   1. _____
2. _____   3. _____
B. A place is said to be frontier territory if its population is less
than _____
C. Five difficulties encountered by the American pioneer were
1. _____   2. _____
3. _____   4. _____
5. _____
D. Three characteristics of the pioneer are   1. _____
2. _____   3. _____

E. The influence of the American West (frontier) has been reflected in our way of life. It has moulded our national

Item	Illustrations
character	
art	
music	
literature	
movies	
TV and radio	
other factors	

F. In learning about the pioneer in America I have already seen
or done the following: (lessons studied, books read, places
visited, movies seen, lectures attended, etc.) _____

_____

_____

G. In addition I would like to do the following: (choose at least
one) prepare a project, read a book, write a report, visit a
museum, study a special topic, other activity (specify). _____

_____

H. Suggested reading list on the Pioneer in America

Author	Title of Book
Aldrich	*A Lantern in Her Hand; Song of Years*
Binns	*The Land is Bright*
Cather	*My Antonia; Oh Pioneers; Death Comes for the Archbishop*
Clark	*The Oxbow Incident*
Davis	*No Other White Men*
Fast	*The Last Frontier*
Garland	*A Son of the Middle Border*
Grey	*The Last of the Plainsmen*
Guthrie	*The Way West; The Big Sky; Mountain Medicine*
Hough	*North of '36; The Covered Wagon*
LaFarge	*Laughing Boy*
Parkman	*The Oregon Trail*
Pease	*The Long Wharf*
Richter	*The Light in the Forest; The Trees*
Roberts	*The Great Meadow*
Rolvaag	*Giants in the Earth*
Schaefer	*Shane*
Taylor	*The Travels of Jaimie McPheeters*
Wister	*The Virginian*

It is advisable to prepare a guide for students whenever the assignment or class undertakings are lengthy or complicated. This is especially true when a unit of work is in progress. The guide should be duplicated and given to each student at the beginning of the unit, and a detailed discussion of the unit conducted at the outset so that each student understands the work, is suitably motivated, and finds a challenge sufficiently difficult to require his best efforts and yet possible of accomplishment. The following study guide was used in a three-week unit in American history with a group of slow eighth graders.

STUDY GUIDE

Silver for General Washington: A Story of Valley Forge

by Enid LaMonte Meadowcroft

Scholastic Book Publications

You will be reading this fascinating story about Americans during the War for Independence (Revolutionary War) in your social studies work. As you read this story and work out the answers to the following questions you will learn much about our history that is not included in your textbook. Write the answers in your notebook *and* be prepared to discuss your findings orally in class.

Assignment for the Entire Class

1. Read the book. Write the story in your own words (no more than 300 words); or write the events of one chapter in your own words (no more than 100 words). This is a composition that should be written in your best English.

2. Who is the hero (main character of the book)? Do you like him (or her)? Why? Name *3* other fictitious people in the book Tell why you like or dislike each of the 3.

3. Name 3 real people from American History who appear in the book. What do we learn about each of them? (Check with textbooks or other fact books to find out which are historical characters).

4. Did all Americans help Washington and his men? What do we call those who did? Those who did not?

5. Name 3 difficulties Washington had to overcome. How did he overcome them? What help did he get from different people?

6. What facts about American History do we learn from this

book? Compare this story with your textbook story of Valley Forge.

7. On a map show the places mentioned in the book—Valley Forge, Philadelphia, etc. (To be done in class.)
8. Make a list of 10–25 new words you learned from this book. Use each in a sentence and tell what each means.
9. Read Uncle Benjamin's remark on page 186. What does it mean? Do you agree? Why?

Additional Assignments (Do as many of these as you can.)

10. Compare the British forces with Washington's as to numbers, equipment, supplies, leadership, morale. What military facts does this story bring out?
11. Various dialects are spoken in the book—southern, soldiers (Seth), Hessian. Select one passage and translate it into correct modern English.
12. Draw 3 more illustrations for the text. Make a jacket (cover) drawing in color.
13. Did doctors know as much in 1778 as they do today? Prove it from the story.
14. Describe the means of transportation and communication in Revolutionary days.
15. Select a scene from the story and write a short play about it.
16. From this book we learn much about the way people lived —homes, customs, etc. in Revolutionary times. Give examples from the book of customs of the time which we no longer find.

Volunteer Activities (To be selected by individuals in the class and approved by the teacher.)

17. Choose *one* of the following topics and tell what you learned about it from reading this book: furniture of the Revolutionary Period, clothing, food.
18. Prepare to sing in class (words and music) 3 songs sung in the story.
19. What does the author tell us about climate, weather, animals, etc.?
20. People made their own food, clothing, tools, etc. Give 2 examples of home arts and explain how each was done.

Types of Social-Studies Lessons

In addition to the developmental lesson, social studies teachers use a variety of approaches to vary the pace and to adjust the method to the demands of the content. These include supervised study, socialized recitation, audio-visual aids, group activities, student panel discussions, debate, dramatization, drill, review, current events, newspapers, book report, and radio and television.

A few words about each of these may help the social-studies teacher see his work in perspective. The supervised study lesson can best be understood if we imagine the teacher sitting next to the student as he does his homework. In the study hall the teacher may work with individual students on school subject lessons. In the classroom the teacher may assign a lesson to be finished while he watches the students at work, observes their study habits, and helps them improve their methods of study. Teachers can learn much about the way students work at their subjects by this technique. They can make useful suggestions to students about reading, analyzing questions, note-taking, seeking information, writing answers, and taking written examinations.

The socialized recitation is a variation of the developmental approach. Here the teacher encourages free discussion among the students without requiring that the ball be thrown back to him each time. Success in this method requires that students' skill be developed gradually, so that an orderly discussion may be conducted without constant or obvious teacher domination. A further extension of this procedure is the student discussion panel. Good results are often achieved by asking one or more students to prepare to "teach" the class, that is, to lead the discussion. High-school students enjoy this and often show amazing aptitude in conducting an orderly and fruitful developmental lesson. Of course, the teacher should be available for help and should be ready to interrupt when necessary.

Improvement in Method

Although methods cannot readily be divorced from content, they are treated separately here for emphasis. In the near future, today's concern with individualized instruction will result in more seminar (small group) work, more tutoring, and more independent study, especially for the gifted. Schedules will be made sufficiently flexible to permit a variety of class size and in time periods for class meetings. For example, in addition to small seminar groups there will be lecture groups of a hundred or more students. In addition to the 45–50 minute class meeting, there will be large blocks of time scheduled for correlated studies, experimentation, independent and supervised study, visits, and so on. School architecture is being accommodated now to the new methods of providing social-studies laboratories, audiovisual rooms, seminar rooms, and lecture halls.[2]

Innovations in social-studies methods will affect the whole school environment. Social-studies teachers will be trained differently, and thus should approach their work with greater enthusiasm. Students will work cooperatively with teachers on long-term projects, participate in the solution of social problems, read widely, write creatively, and experience a sense of meaning and reality about social studies. Of course, some of these new elements exist today, but the future may be expected to offer all of our students and teachers what relatively few are fortunate enough to experience at present.

Since the social studies stand midway between the humanities and the sciences, they may act as a link for unifying knowledge for approaching learning. The fragmentation that has gone on may be responsible in part for our difficulties. It will be through a unified approach cemented in the area of social studies that some degree of unity may be restored.

Some social-studies teachers have modified the traditional developmental approach by group (committee) work, panel discussion lessons, debates, dramatization, and similar methods generally associated with unified studies (core) teaching. These will be discussed in detail in Chapter 8, since they are perhaps more applicable in an English–social studies setting and are more effective when a block of time longer than the single period is available.

SPECIAL PROBLEMS IN TEACHING SOCIAL STUDIES

Teaching Current Affairs and Controversial Issues

Current affairs and controversial issues are treated together here because so much of the current social scene—elections, foreign affairs, economic theory, labor management, federal aid, and so on—is controversial. Of course, almost any period or aspect of history may be controversial.

[2] *High Schools 1962* (New York: Educational Facilities Laboratories, 1961).

The social-studies teacher must be ready to guide discussion of controversial questions in his classroom. The discussion should be based on as complete information as the students are able to obtain. It should be conducted in an orderly fashion, with each side having as much opportunity as possible to present its position. No *ad hominem,* derogatory remarks should be tolerated. If asked to state his position, the teacher should offer to do so at the end of the discussion. No student should be penalized by the teacher in any way for holding an unpopular view on a controversial issue.

Teaching current affairs has always been a difficult problem for the social-studies teacher. Probably the most effective approach to it is the functional one of discussing any controversial topic when it arises naturally in connection with another topic under discussion. For example, in a lesson on the Spanish-American War, it would be natural to direct the discussion to Cuba today. In a lesson on ancient Egypt, the subject of Nasser and the Arab world would naturally arise.

Of course, though these natural sequences cover some current issues, they leave others untouched, and the teacher must seek an approach in which all current topics of importance are studied. Many teachers set aside one day a week for this purpose, using a daily newspaper or a special newspaper issued for school use as a text.[3] Some teachers prepare their own weekly current-events material.

Metropolitan newspapers with large circulations have special programs for building circulation in schools and colleges. They offer attractive rates, bonus items, and aids of various kinds, including speakers, to help build effective current events programs. "How to Teach Current Events," a thirty-two-page booklet published by The American Education Publications, offers helpful suggestions. The "How To" series of the National Council for the Social Studies includes a useful pamphlet on "How to Teach Current Events," and another on "How to Handle Controversial Issues."

[3] Scholastic Magazines (33 West 42nd Street, New York 36) issues *Junior Scholastic* (grades 6–8), *World Week* (grades 8–10), and *Senior Scholastic* (grades 10–12). Civic Education Service (1733 K Street, N.W., Washington 6, D.C.) issues *American Observer* (grades 10–12), *Weekly News Review* (grades 9–11), Junior Review (grades 7–9), and *Civic Leader* (for teachers). American Education Publications (Columbus 16, Ohio) issues *Our Times* (grades 11–12), *Every Week* (grades 9–10), and *Current Events* (grades 6–8).

Teaching Social-Studies Skills

One of the aims listed at the beginning of this chapter is "competence and confidence in handling social material." Throughout the six-year secondary program in social studies, it should be a conscious purpose of instruction to build mastery in each of the following skills: reading and understanding newspapers, magazines, and books in the social studies, including familiarity with sources and with elementary research; having a sound grasp of chronological relationships; having clear ideas of places and of space relationships; identifying with the stream of American and world history; understanding current events and having a continuing interest in them; having clear concepts of common terms in social studies; having insight into and competence in problems of human relations; having an understanding of and a commitment to democratic processes; and having a knowledge of basic facts of man's past.

These and other social skills are taught by giving each child an opportunity to develop under guidance. Time-lines, map work, group activities, reading, writing, speaking and listening, problems of graduated difficulty, sympathetic correction and suggestion, constant evaluation—these are the activities and procedures for the teacher and class in building competence in social skills. Diagnostic tests can help. A sympathetic teacher is important. Some students will need the special help of a guidance counselor, reading specialist, or psychologist. In the end, the competent teacher who presents each child with problems difficult enough to challenge him but not so difficult that they discourage him and who guides the individual's progress firmly yet sympathetically is the gift that each child deserves.

A resource which has come into its own during the past decade and which has vast implications for social-studies teaching is the paperback book. Originally, this medium offered few useful titles, but today there are thousands of suitable titles at prices which virtually every high-school student can afford. The teacher has but to scan the publication lists of Pocket Books, Bantam Books, Dell Books, and The New American Library to find essays, novels, histories, biographies, plays, poems, and anthologies appropriate to whatever the class may be studying. *Paperbacks in the Schools* (Bantam, 1963) is a useful source for teachers.

TEACHER PREPARATION

The social-studies teacher of the future will be prepared in a teacher education program very different from that of today. His general education will be strong both in the sciences and in the humanities because his teaching will need to extend beyond the confines of social studies. Within the social studies he will have a broad grasp of anthropology, sociology, geography, economics, and political science, areas which some of his predecessors neglected in favor of history. He will be recruited on the basis of his personality and potential success as an artist-teacher rather than on the attainment of certain college grades. He will be trained as an apprentice to a master teacher observing creative work with students in a democratic, permissive atmosphere free from the rigidity, fear, empty formalism, "recitation" and "testing and grading" which dominates so much of the work with secondary-school students today.

The teacher of the future will be encouraged to try new methods, to visit other teachers in his own and other fields, to continue his studies, and to report original work in professional literature. He will be on his way to the status of "master" after travel, study, and teaching abroad, gaining a fellowship or using a sabbatical leave to develop professionally, participating in the work of the National Council for the Social Studies and other professional bodies.

The social-studies teacher must: (1) maintain a wide acquaintance with developments in all areas of human culture, including the humanities and the sciences; (2) keep abreast of contemporary affairs; (3) maintain contact with scholarly developments in the various social sciences; and finally, (4) know and practice the latest and best in professional methodology. No one who aspires to excellence in all these can ever be content with his achievement. The only realistic approach is to do one's best, to strive for improvement and to accept realistic goals, however short they may be of perfection.

FOR DELIBERATION and DISCUSSION

1. Make a critical comparison of the aims of social studies given in this text with those described in a book on the teaching of social studies.

2. What techniques and procedures may be used in social studies to individualize instruction? What type of organization—self-contained classroom, core, team, other—is best suited for these techniques and procedures? Explain.
3. How can the social-studies teacher determine whether and to what extent he has succeeded in attaining his objectives? Construct an evaluative instrument (test) to measure the degree of attainment of a social-studies objective with one class in one semester.
4. How does the teaching of controversial issues present a special problem to the social-studies teacher? What opportunities does it offer?
5. Should current events be taught separately or should they be taught only in context—that is, as they arise in connection with other content being taught?

FOR ADDITIONAL READING

COMMITTEE ON TEACHING OF THE AMERICAN HISTORICAL ASSOCIATION. *Preparation of Secondary-School History Teachers.* Washington, D.C.: The Association, 1963. A summary of the thinking of college professors of history.

FRASER, DOROTHY MCCLURE and WEST, EDITH. *Social Studies in the Secondary Schools.* New York: Ronald, 1961. Comprehensive treatment of high-school social-studies teaching.
Handbook for Social Studies Teaching. rev. ed.; New York: The Association of Teachers of Social Studies in the City of New York, 1963. A thoroughly practical book. Over 200 pages of suggestions useful to the social-studies teacher.

HIGH, JAMES. *Teaching Secondary School Social Studies.* New York: Wiley, 1962. A good modern treatment of major aspects of secondary-school social-studies teaching, including method, content, and materials. Annotated bibliographies at end of chapters and other source items.

HUNT, ERLING M., et al. *High School Social Studies Perspectives.* Boston: Houghton Mifflin, 1962. Chapters by scholars on each of the following: Changing perspectives in the Social Studies; Anthropology, Sociology and Social Psychology; Economics; Geography; Political Science; United States History; Western Civilization; Africa South of the Sahara; East Asia; Latin America; The Middle East; India and Pakistan; The U.S.S.R. Each chapter is a careful statement of the potentials for high-school teaching and each includes a valuable annotated bibliography.

HUNT, MAURICE P. and METCALF, LAWRENCE E. *Teaching High School Social Studies.* New York: Harper, 1956. An original approach to problems in the teaching of high-school social studies.

JOHNSON, EARL S. *Theory and Practice of the Social Studies*. New York: Macmillan, 1956. A thoughtful rather difficult book that will repay careful study.

KENWORTHY, LEONARD S. *Guide to Social Studies Teaching in Secondary Schools*. Belmont: Wadsworth, 1962. A successful "attempt to relate theories about social studies teaching to specific classroom situations." Highly recommended for social-studies teachers because of simplicity and wealth of material.

MCLENDON, JOHNATHAN C. *Teaching the Social Studies*. Washington, D.C.: NEA, 1960. An excellent summary; one of the NEA pamphlet series "What Research Says to Teachers."

PATTERSON, FRANKLIN. *High Schools for a Free Society: Education for Citizenship in American Secondary Schools*. Glencoe: Free Press, 1960. A study, conducted under Ford Foundation grants, of policies, practices, and possibilities in citizenship education in the American high school.

PRESTON, RALPH C., SCHNEYDER, J. WESLEY, and THYNG, FRANK J. *Guiding the Social Studies Reading of High School Students*. Washington, D.C.: National Council for the Social Studies, 1963. Contains many useful suggestions about reading, an ever-present problem.

SHEPARD, DAVID L. *Effective Reading in the Social Studies: A Handbook for Secondary Teachers*. Evanston: Row, Peterson, 1960. Chapters on each of eleven basic skills in the social studies including the ability to read for a purpose, skill in using parts of a book, the ability to recognize propaganda, and so on. Each chapter includes transcript of an actual lesson to illustrate the special skill under discussion.

Social Education. Published monthly October through May by the National Council for the Social Studies. Reports experimentation, research, books, speeches, and so on in social studies, K–12.

Social Studies and the Social Sciences, The. New York: American Council of Learned Societies and National Council for the Social Studies, Harcourt, Brace and World, 1962. Chapters by scholars in each of the social sciences—history, geography, political science, economics, cultural anthropology, psychology, and two area studies—Asia and Russia including Eastern Europe. A concluding chapter discusses "Revising the Social Studies." The emphasis throughout is on the secondary social-studies curriculum.

SUTTLES, P. H. and HARTLEY, W. H. *Educator's Guide to Free Social Studies Materials*. 2nd ed.; Randolph: Educators Progressive Service, 1962. Lists 1,913 free items: films, filmstrips, slides, tapes, scripts, transcriptions, pamphlets, magazines, maps, and books.

TYLER, FRED T., COOK, WALTER W., GOODLAD, JOHN I., and SCHOOLING, HERBERT W., *et al. Individualizing Instruction.* Chicago: National Society for the Study of Education, U. of Chicago Press, 1962, Part I. Section III contains four chapters under the general heading "Current School Practices for Individualizing Instruction: Values and Limitations."

8 English

The teaching of English is a major part of the program in all American high schools. Each student is generally required to take and pass at least three years of English as a requisite for a diploma from a four-year high school. Since this constitutes from one-fourth to one-fifth of the major work of his high-school program, it is reasonable to expect that the work in English will be appropriately challenging and rewarding, that the objectives of the program will be comprehensive and realistic, and that the outcomes will be worthy of the time and energy expended by students and teachers. In this section, an attempt will be made to describe briefly the problems and procedures relating to the English program in the high school. The approach focuses on those practices and trends which seem to embody greatest promise for the attainment of desirable goals.

Reading—Spelling—Vocabulary—Sources

Of the four major areas of concern to the English teacher—reading, writing, speaking, and listening—the first is perhaps the most basic to our culture. Much of what we do in our vocational life as well as in our leisure time involves reading. The student who comes to the ninth grade is presumed to have attained a degree of speed and comprehension in reading material of certain difficulty and complexity. Ideally, he is also favorably disposed to reading and is actively interested in seeking both enlightenment and entertainment from printed material. Often, however, the student has failed to reach the degree of reading skill and maturity of his age and grade. In many schools he is then classified (if as much as two years below grade on standardized tests) as a retarded or reluctant reader and assigned to a special class for remedial work. Others are well in advance of their grade in speed and comprehension and in the type of material they can absorb. For these gifted and talented, special work is also indicated.

Children of normal intelligence, with no physical impediment to their vision and no emotional block, will learn to read and will grow in competence regardless of whether the earliest method used with them is the phonic, the recognition of words and phrases, or a combination of these. Given effective teachers, encouragement at home, and a variety of reading material of the proper level of difficulty and interest, they will make strides commensurate with their normal growth and with the time spent in reading. The function of the high-school teacher insofar as these students is concerned is to extend their range of reading interests, to deepen their comprehension and to open to them the pleasures of good reading—in short, to make habitual readers of them.

Fortunately, the teacher has several useful allies in the pursuit of this objective. Excellent texts (anthologies and single works) newspapers and magazines, the world of paperbacks, libraries (including the classroom library and the student's home library), guides to reading, such as the pamphlet *Books For You* issued by the National Council of Teachers of English, book clubs (such as those sponsored by Scholastic Publications), and special magazines published for school use, help the classroom teacher in building reading competence in his students.

Closely allied to progress and prowess in reading is competence in spelling and vocabulary. The former is treated here rather than in the section on composition (written English) because of the close relationship between ability in reading and spelling. We rarely hear words spelled. We spell them as we see them in our reading. Hence extensive and intensive reading is very important in the development of good spelling. The spelling list should be an individual item which each student makes for himself derived from his reading and based on his needs— that is, the words he needs to know and is not sure of.

The need for an individual list is equally, if not more true for vocabulary. No one but the student himself knows which words he knows, which he meets in his reading and listening, and which he wants to add and can add to his vocabulary. The teacher can and should show each student how to find new words, how to look them up, how to study them, and how to use them.[1] The teacher can devise tests to evaluate progress, but only the student can build his own vocabulary. The traditional standardized grade lists for spelling and vocabulary can serve as a guide to teacher and student, but the individual lists developed by each student for his own needs are best. Vocabulary development, too, should be a natural, not an artificial process. The student should learn the meaning of new words *when he needs them* in reading and writing.

Literature and Literary Forms

From the simple sentences and rhymes of children's literature to the profound subtleties of style, symbolism, and allegory, the English teacher can awaken the student to the wonders of literature. How best to do this is the challenge of method. Arguing that "any subject can be taught to any child in some honest form," Bruner states, "If it is granted, for example, that it is desirable to give children an awareness of the meaning of human tragedy and a sense of compassion for it, is it not possible at the earliest appropriate age to teach the literature of tragedy in a manner that illuminates but does not threaten?"[2] The same, of course, may be said of comedy, history, melodrama, farce, satire, and fantasy.

With each class a work of literature should be studied in appropriate depth. For example, *The Adventures of Huckleberry Finn* can be studied in the junior high school for the story, and in an advanced class in the senior high school for its deeper human connotations. In any group, no matter how much homogeneity is sought, there are variations in the intellectual and emotional maturity which students bring to the study that help determine what each can reap from it. It may as well be said here

---

[1] Many teachers have found that the paperback by Wilfred Funk and Norman Lewis, *30 Days to a More Powerful Vocabulary* (New York: Washington Square Press), is an effective aid to teaching vocabulary.

[2] Jerome S. Bruner, *The Process of Education* (Cambridge: Harvard U. Press, 1961), pp. 52–53.

as later that English is one of the humanities (arts) and that teaching is an art; and therefore that teaching English requires great insight into both content and method. The experienced teacher is often the most humble, for never is the same work taught twice the same even to similar groups that follow one another immediately.

In the literature program great works of English, American and foreign language (both ancient and modern) writing are introduced, and every literary form—essay, novel, poetry, drama, non-fiction, and declamation—is studied. Obviously the task of selection and balance is difficult. It is further complicated by the wide range of competence of the student body. Hence both the selection of works and their presentation present a constant challenge which the experienced teacher meets by adapting both content and method to his students.

Composition and Creative Writing

Frantic and even phrenetic denunciation of our schools' failure to teach writing are symptoms of a number of unhealthy situations. The business community is indeed short of competent writers when neither the boss nor his secretary can compose a satisfactory letter. Yet the task of the school is extremely complicated and its achievements not inconsiderable.[3]

As with literature, the English teacher's role in composition is to introduce the student to its various forms—the letter, essay, short story, poem, play, and so on. But whereas the goal in literature is understanding and appreciation, in composition it is creativity. This function has both a formal and a substantial aspect—that is, the writer must have something to say (substance) and must say it correctly (form).

The school teaches communication best by having students write. Continual opportunity for encouragement of inclination for writing by all students is the best practice for building competence in writing. Conant recommends that high-school English teachers teach no more than one hundred students so that they can correct written compositions with care. Of course, there is some doubt that meticulous correction of composition errors accomplishes its purpose. The chief job in writing is to learn

---

[3] See Norman Cousins, "Why Johnny Can't Write," *Saturday Review,* June 15, 1963.

how to explore a subject, to find what there is to be said about it. Until the student learns to say something interesting and of value, there is little point in picking away at mechanical and grammatical "errors."

Often a heavily blue-penciled paper will serve to inhibit rather than to encourage improvement in writing. This is not to say students' errors need no correcting nor that teachers' time so spent is wasted, but much research is still needed to find the most effective procedures for improving composition.

Students who like to write and who write well should be encouraged, of course. Most high schools have a special journalism class, and some have special classes in creative writing, radio and television script writing, and so on, for the talented and gifted. Creative teachers are alert to detect talent in substance—originality, humor, insight, plot, forcefulness, vocabulary, choice of subject—regardless of the degree of competence the student may or may not have attained in the formal aspects of writing. A student anxious to improve can learn punctuation and conventional grammar more readily than he can develop originality.

Language structure (grammar) can be learned either "by ear" or by analysis. We learn to speak by listening and imitation. If we hear good speech, we are most likely to speak well. And if we read good literary style—Churchill, for example, in the twentieth century or the great English novelists in the nineteenth—we will have good models. We will probably write well without knowing anything about the formal aspects of language structure. Many teachers today feel that grammar, spelling, punctuation, and word study are best taught in context, not as separate items.

Imitation also can be raised to the level of understanding by analysis. Hence the English program in the high school calls for some formal work. This may consist of exercises, for example, in the use of "who" and "whom," "its" and "it's," "their," "there," and "they're," with a minimum of explanation. In one school, at the beginning of the year, the teacher and the class examined the table of contents of their text and decided which chapters would best serve the needs of the majority of the class. Any student who wished to complete a chapter not included in the class curriculum would receive individual instruction in that chapter. Thus, formal grammar was approached in a less formal and more palatable fashion.

Speech and Communication—Dramatics

Speech is a matter of imitation, and the English teacher must be a worthy model. Students also should listen to a Laurence Olivier and a Helen Hayes, and must regard their speech as a worthy model and seek to emulate it. Hence a climate of acceptance and admiration needs to be built.

It is regrettable that some youngsters are graduated from high school without the ability to express themselves before a group. The English teacher, as well as teachers of other subjects, should make every effort to encourage each girl and boy to speak easily and freely before the class. The opportunity to address larger groups, such as the school assembly should also be offered. In most areas the days of debating teams are no longer, but individual and group reports to the class, assembly announcements, speeches and declamations, oratorical contests, radio forums, panel discussions, simulated United Nations meetings and, most of all, class and school dramatics involve large numbers of our youth and give them an opportunity to develop poise and skill in addressing their fellows on subjects of common interest and concern.

Listening and Observing—Notetaking

Communication in the spoken word may be as effective in conveying information, arousing emotion, stimulating the imagination, giving pleasure, and providing relaxation as that of the printed page. We often hear people say "I'm eye-minded, not ear-minded; I can understand what I read much better than what I hear." An important objective of the English language-arts program is to build competence in listening and—in the case of cinema, drama and television—of combining this with skill in observing.

Research studies reveal that listening is a factor in scholastic achievement, that poor listeners can be helped to improve their skills, that listening is subtly modified by attitudes toward the speaker, the situation and the audience, that mass listening is modified by the social nature of the situation (the same listener responds variously to the same speech in different audience contexts), that poor listening with or without hearing impairment retards normal language development, and that listening is so important in business and industry that many large enterprises have offered to their employees (at all levels) training courses in listen-ing.[4]

While reading skills have been sought and taught for ages, an interest in listening skills has only recently been developed. Yet we know that children can and should be taught how to listen and what to listen for. An excellent device is to require the class to listen to an assembly program, student council election speeches, a radio program, or a record, and to have each student reconstruct what he heard in content, manner of delivery, and fine points of communication. Repeated experience in listening to lectures by the teacher, a guest, or a radio commentator, and practice in notetaking to reconstruct the main points of the argument will help develop this skill. The teacher should demonstrate the technique of capturing the structure of a speech in a skillfully written outline. Fine points of delivery—pause, emphasis, voice modulation, gesture, facial expression—should be noted.

Since the theater, the lecture hall, the classroom, the movies, television, and forums combine the spoken word with the dramatic act, students should be taught to analyze such aspects of performance as facial and bodily expression, control of voice, subtleties of language, along with the content of oral expression. The development of skill in listening and in appreciation of the spoken word can yield great dividends in satisfaction to the conscientious and competent English teacher. Recent emphasis on linguistics—the study of nuances of language—indicate a recognition of the importance of the factors mentioned above in the development of good oral and written English.

The Mass Media[5]

Much of our discussion of reading and listening involved the mass media as sources of material for building competence in the English language arts and for evaluating the success of

---

[4] National Council of Teachers of English, *The English Language Arts in the Secondary School* (New York: Copyright © 1956 Appleton-Century-Crofts, Inc., prepared by the Commission on the English Curriculum, The Council), pp. 253–254.

[5] National Society for the Study of Education, *Mass Media and Education*, (Chicago: U. of Chicago Press, 1954), Part II.

the program. These media include books, newspapers, magazines, radio, television, moving pictures, and audio records. Technology is constantly improving each of these media. Newspapers are now available on microfilm, television is in color, records are stereophonic and on tape, and movies are becoming more realistic visually.

The English teacher needs familiarity with what is available and what is happening in the mass media. He must be selective in what he will use to assist him in teaching. His objective is quite clear: he must acquaint his students with the products of these media, awaken their interest in seeking information, inspiration and pleasure from them, and above all, raise their level of appreciation, so that each student will distinguish between the artistic and the tawdry and develop a commitment to the former. The mere statement of the goal is sufficient to indicate how much is yet to be accomplished in this area. Higher and higher levels of excellence will always be in sight, and as public taste improves, the challenge to better performance is increased.

Criticism

The art of literary criticism can and should be taught to high-school students. They should be taught and required to report more than merely story content, especially in their independent or supplementary reading. Matters of style, construction, consistency, suspense, emotional power, and originality should be discussed with as much insight as possible. Often it is feasible to have students research the original reviews by critics. For example, if the class is studying *The Grapes of Wrath, Arrowsmith,* or *Gone With the Wind,* students can compare their reviews with those of professional critics. In this way the elements of literary criticism are taught, and its quality is steadily improved.

One of the authors once distributed to a senior class an annotated reading list on which *Laughing Boy* was described by the phrase "life on an Indian reservation." A boy of average ability read the book and correctly commented that a more appropriate description would be "a great love story." This is genuine literary criticism in its humble beginnings.

Related Studies—Translation, Social Studies, Other Humanities

To be effective, the teaching of English requires familiarity with and sympathy for other disciplines. The reason is twofold. Language is used for communication, but usually the subject matter of the communicative vehicle is derived from or related to some other area. For example, good literature may be associated with such areas as history (*Henry V*); psychology (*The Red Badge of Courage; Catcher in the Rye*); sociology (*The Scarlet Letter*); human relations (almost any good piece of literature); science (*Microbe Hunters*); art (*The Moon and Sixpence*); law (*The Nature of the Judicial Process*); education (*Democracy and Education*), and so on. Whether it be diary, short story, letters, drama, poetry, the novel, or scenario material, the subject matter of literature, after analysis, involves one of the many areas of human thought and study. Hence the English teacher who is at home in other disciplines is best able to teach the masterpieces of English and at the same time to stimulate and inspire his students to explore and create ideas of greater variety with deeper insight. In the social studies and the humanities—philosophy, language and literature—the well-rounded, alert English teacher will find endless sources from which he can motivate and inspire his students.

A fertile but neglected field for teaching is found in translation. English and foreign-language teachers create translation projects by which the quality of understanding, skill, and appreciation in the native as well as the foreign language is improved under challenging and enjoyable conditions. Colleagues in other departments should be encouraged to support these efforts. For example, social-studies teachers could alert their students to quality composition in their disciplines by occasional reading and comment on the works of Gibbon, Macaulay, O. W. Holmes, Jr., Churchill, Becker, Commager, and other writers of distinguished prose. In the section on core teaching we treat the idea of unified study of literature in greater detail.

AIMS AND EVALUATION

Generally a discussion of the teaching of a subject starts with aims and ends with evaluation. Since the two are so closely related—we evaluate in order to see how well our objectives have been attained—they are treated together here.

In his discussion, Hook quotes a United States Bureau of

Education report listing the following general aims of education: health, command of fundamental processes, worthy use of leisure, and ethical character. The English teacher shares the obligation of helping to realize these common aims with his colleagues in other departments. Hook indicates further that studies of the special aims of the English language arts program in the high school have resulted in the listing of some 1,581 special aims. He goes on to say, "To attain two thousand aims is impossible; to attain one large and worthy aim is not only possible but desirable. The aim of improvement of communication is both large and worthy."[6]

The traditional mode of evaluation may be ill-suited to determine the extent of achievement of such objectives as healthy personality, worthy home membership, ethical character, or improvement of communication. Objective tests are generally designed to test command of fundamental processes and even those —for example, effective presentation of a theme, orally or in writing—are not easily tested by the traditional methods. Still we must know how well we are succeeding. Hence written and oral examinations—class, schoolwide, city and statewide, college entrance, scholarship and the like—must be supplemented by whatever techniques we can develop.

Student self-evaluation, discussion with parents, employers, and college officers, follow-up of achievements of graduates, examination of cumulative records, comparison of the work of present seniors with that of seniors a generation ago, as well as comparison with standardized national norms, will all help to tell us what we are accomplishing and what more needs to be done. As a group, teachers of English need no apology for the quality of their achievements in the light of the tremendous task confronting them. The quality of the national product in the creative arts is high because generations of students have been subjected to creative experiences in high school.

SPECIAL METHODS IN TEACHING ENGLISH

Unit and Lesson Planning

The syllabus, curriculum bulletin, or course of study is a guide for the classroom teacher in planning the year's work.

[6] J. N. Hook, *The Teaching of High School English* (New York: Ronald, 1959), pp. 27–34.

Ideally, the teacher should have participated in its formulation or at least he must be thoroughly familiar with and sympathetic to its philosophy and content. Taking the syllabus and his class and putting them together without doing violence to either is the main objective of the teacher in planning his work. Most English teachers have found that they can best accomplish this assignment by planning a number of inclusive units. The number will vary, but if an average unit runs about three weeks it should be possible to teach some eight to ten units in a year.

Today, instruction by the teacher is supported by a great variety of teaching aids. To the textbook—which is often beautifully printed and illustrated with end-of-chapter questions and teaching materials—and the chalkboard, have been added films, filmstrips, television, tape recordings, printed or mimeographed study guides, programmed material, and teaching machines (see Chapter 17). The English teacher should have reasonable familiarity with what is available, how it may help fill a need in his work, and the technique of using the device or material.

The Library and Classroom Library in the English Program

The library is an important adjunct of the English department, for it provides students and teachers with facilities for reference, research, reading, and study. The librarian should be a consultant for book purchases, reading lists, classification of materials, and display of student work and language arts materials. The librarian should assist individuals, small groups, and classes in developing technical skill in finding and using library facilities.

The modern library is a pleasant, attractive place with plenty of room and easily accessible materials. Liberal lending policies, ample pamphlet and paperback material, a vertical file, magazines and newspapers, record and tape collections, and other modern aids distinguish it from the library of past generations. Some modern high-school libraries provide carrels where students may spend part of the school day in independent study and research.

In his classroom, the progressive English teacher maintains a miniature of the school library. It should contain basic reference works, one or more copies of a variety of suitable textbooks, volumes from his own home library, and a large number of paperbacks, and magazines appropriate for the age and reading level of his students. A class librarian in each class may supervise the arrangement of the books and the borrowing procedures.

A resourceful teacher can prevail readily on parents, friends, and students to contribute to the classroom library. These materials can circulate among the students in connection with units of work or for their leisure reading and enjoyment. If one of the keys to improvement in reading is more and more reading, the teacher who inspires his students to read widely, regardless of the "subject" he is teaching is making a major contribution to the reading growth of his students.

PREPARATION OF THE ENGLISH TEACHER

In discussing the attributes of a good English teacher, J. N. Hook lists the following seven *academic* qualifications and eight *professional* qualifications of the capable English teacher:

Academic Qualifications
1. To read well both silently and aloud.
2. To speak and write clearly and agreeably.
3. To be widely read.
4. To have a knowledge of literary history.
5. To know how to show the present social implications of literary selections.
6. To have some idea of the relationship between English and other areas of learning.
7. To be more than dimly aware of the existence of movies, stage plays, newspapers, and radio and television programs.

Professional Qualifications
1. Ability in planning a course of study in English.
2. Skill in providing for individual differences.
3. Competency in improving students' reading.
4. Competence in arousing interest in literature and appreciation of it.
5. Skill in improving students' oral and written English.
6. Ability to teach satisfactorily listening habits.
7. Skill in guiding cocurricular activities.
8. Ability to lead classes through semester after semester filled with stimulating, broadening, and pleasant hours.[7]

---

[7] Based on Hook—*The Teaching of High School English*, Second Edition, pp. 20–23, Copyright © 1959. The Ronald Press Company. See also John S. Lewis and Jean C. Sisk, *Teaching English: 7–12* (New York: American Book, 1963), pp. 20–25, for an excellent discussion of this area.

If these requirements seem impossible of attainment, it should be understood that the beginning teacher in English, as in any other subject, has a background of study and experience which needs to be forged and molded in the classroom. Here he will learn where his background needs reinforcement, what adolescent boys and girls are really like, and what methods and materials are applicable to his particular situation. He will be well-advised to take courses to supplement his background, to continue to read widely, to welcome opportunities to teach a variety of courses in his own and other departments, to visit the classrooms of master teachers, to accept student teachers from nearby universities, to participate in curriculum projects, to experiment constantly with new approaches and new content in teaching, and to sponsor at least one cocurricular activity.

Teaching activities should be supplemented by professional undertakings, such as giving a course or occasional lecture in-service or at an institution of higher learning, affiliating with professional bodies, or participating in the work of a local, state or national committee.[8] Other recommended activities are: conducting a joint controlled research project or an individual action research project and reporting the results of findings in professional journals; writing for publication, and participating professionally or commercially in any of the arts comprising the English program. As the teacher attains status in the profession, his self-esteem and prestige will tend to increase his effectiveness in the classroom and in the school.

THE ENGLISH DEPARTMENT

The English department exerts a major influence in the life of the school because generally it has a relatively large enrollment and because (1) the language arts are basic to all subjects, (2) the English department traditionally has a high status, and (3) the extra-class services of the language-arts department are of tremendous importance in the life of the school.

This latter item deserves brief amplification. The mere enumeration of extra-class activities sponsored by the English

[8] National Education Association (1201 Sixteenth St., N.W., Washington 6, D.C.) and National Council of Teachers of English (508 South Sixth Street, Champaign, Ill.) are the two professional bodies to which the beginning teacher of English would most likely wish to belong.

faculty is impressive—periodicals, yearbook, dramatics, assemblies, handbooks, book fairs, sales of paperbacks, and book auctions, and so on. Any of these may involve large numbers of students who will be gaining specialized vocational experience and competence by virtue of participation under expert guidance. Thus the influence of the English program extends far beyond the formal classroom instruction. In fact, the activities enumerated above often exert significant influence in the informal education of adult members of students' families and other adults in the community. This is as it should be, for a good school English program should raise the level of appreciation and performance in the language arts throughout the community.

FOR DELIBERATION and DISCUSSION

1. Make a lesson plan for a topic you will have an opportunity to teach. Use the plan in student teaching or in your regular classroom. Evaluate the results.
2. Prepare ten thought questions for use in a specific unit in English. Why do you consider these thought questions? How do they differ from fact questions?
3. How may the English teacher serve as a resource person for other subjects, for the home, and for the community in attaining one or more of the objectives of the language arts program?
4. Since the English curriculum is so diverse, what is the best preparation one may get for teaching English in the secondary school?
5. How are curriculum and method in English responding to the major changes in our way of life?

FOR ADDITIONAL READING

AUSTIN, MARY C. *The Torch Lighters: Tomorrow's Teachers of Reading.* Cambridge: Harvard U. Press, 1962. Contains recommendations for teacher preparation with special reference to the teaching of reading.

COMMISSION ON THE CURRICULUM OF THE NATIONAL COUNCIL OF TEACHERS OF ENGLISH. *A Check List for Evaluating the English Program in the Junior and Senior High School.* Champaign: National Council of Teachers of English, 1962. Reprinted from the *English Journal,* April, 1962. A guide to evaluating procedures in planning the English curriculum, teaching conditions, literature, reading, writing, language, speaking and listening, nature of classroom instruction, and evaluation.

Educational Leadership, Journal of the Association for Supervision and Curriculum Development, 19, No. 5 (February, 1962). Contains half dozen articles of importance to high-school English teachers.

FAY, LEO C. *Reading in the High School.* Washington, D.C.: NEA, 1956. Pamphlet summarizing research on reading problems in high-school subjects.

High Points (in the Work of the High Schools of New York City). Published each month of the school year. Board of Education, 110 Livingston Street, Brooklyn, N.Y. A high calibre periodical reporting criticism, action research, and books in the field of secondary education.

JENNISON, PETER. *Freedom to Read.* New York: New York Public Affairs Committee, Inc., 1963, Pamphlet No. 344. Summarizes controversy over the freedom to read. Names the prosecutors and defenders of this freedom and analyzes the implications of the controversy.

Paperbound Books in Print. New York: R. R. Bowker Co. Issued quarterly. Paperbacks in all fields indexed by subject, author, title. Gives publisher and cost of each volume. List of publishers and addresses included.

Reading in High School and College. Chicago: National Society for the Study of Education. Research and recommendations for classroom practices in reading development.

SAUER, EDWIN H. *English in the Secondary School.* New York: Holt, Rinehart, and Winston, 1961. A readable book on method. Part I is devoted to "grammar"; Part II to "literature"; concludes with a "Selected Reading List for High School English Classes."

SHANE, HAROLD and MULVY, JUNE GRANT. *Improving Language Arts Instruction Through Research.* Washington, D.C.: Association for Supervision and Curriculum Development, 1963. Reports in ten categories the findings resulting from examination of reports of over 1600 research studies compiled 1955–1962 in reading, handwriting, creative writing, spelling, language usage, children's literature, listening, mass media, foreign languages, and oral English. Discusses the findings of 844 studies and lists appropriate items alphabetically at the end of each chapter.

Standards for School Library Programs. Chicago: American Association of School Libraries, 1960. A major work involving cooperation of many interested professional associations. Part I—"The School Library as an Educational Force"; Part II—"Planning and Implementing School Library Programs"; Part III—"Resources for Teaching and Learning." An invaluable study containing data and suggestions that offer something to every school library.

STRANG, RUTH, MCCULLOUGH, CONSTANCE, and TRAXLER, ARTHUR. *Problems in the Improvement of Reading.* 1955. Authorities attack a major problem in the high school with light instead of heat.

The English Journal. Published monthly September through May by the National Council of Teachers of English, 508 S. Sixth St., Champaign, Ill. Articles, book reviews and reports of interest to high-school teachers of English.

The English Language Arts in the Secondary School. Champaign: National Council of Teachers of English, 1956. An authoritative treatment of the entire field.

WOOLF, JEANNE A. and WOOLF, MAURICE D. *Remedial Reading.* New York: McGraw-Hill, 1957. Suggested practices for working with retarded high-school readers.

9 Science

THE SCIENCE CURRICULUM

Basic alterations in the entire structure of the science curriculum, as well as in each area of science teaching are in progress. Science teaching in the elementary school is developing, and it will be possible to undertake more advanced work in the junior and senior high school. Thus, it will be necessary to provide continuity and integration in the science program of the twelve or fourteen years of public education so that elementary concepts, experiments, techniques, and facts learned in the first six years will not be repeated in the second six.

The science curriculum in any school or school district should be developed in and for the school by its science teachers in cooperation with other interested and qualified persons, including supervisors, administrators, parents, students, resource persons, state and national authorities, college specialists, and curriculum consultants. It should be the result of planned, protracted study, and it should be introduced experimentally, evaluated carefully, and revised constantly.

The curriculum is a blueprint for action, but it can never replace the actual learning experiences of children; hence the teacher-artist should be free to modify the curriculum in practice. The prescribed curriculum should be only a guide, never a straitjacket, for the living curriculum.

Among the factors that need to be considered in making a high-school science curriculum are the following:

Objectives of the science program.

Students' backgrounds, interests, and goals.

Community, state, and national needs.

Interrelationship of science and other areas (notably social studies).[1]

Provision for individual differences.

Special provision for the gifted.

Special provision for the retarded.

Integration of grades K through 12 or 14.

Provision for student activities (laboratory, self-directed, experimental, creative).

Utilization of community resources.

Functional orientation.

College and vocational provision.

Utilization of professional resources (books, pamphlets, audiovisual aid, commercial products, and so on).

Concern with basic learnings (concepts, scientific method, thought processes, hypotheses); recognition of ethical moral issues in science; practical aspects—taking into consideration limitations of time, materials, teacher competence and other aspects of the curriculum.

Unity of the sciences (and indeed of all knowledge); illustrations of specific items (lessons, units, sources of materials and sources of reference).

Relationship to extra-class activities.

In discussing the senior high-school science program, the recent booklet of the National Science Teachers Association points out that

The majority of students should take a balanced program of physical and biological science courses as part of their high-school curriculum.

The notion of teaching completely different sets of ideas to different groups of students is unrealistic.

---

[1] "Science and social studies must merge at some points in the curriculum. This view is expressed by those who see the widest ramifications of science—the scientists." Paul DeH. Hurd, "Critical Issues in the Teaching of Secondary School Science," *California Journal of Secondary Education*, 33 (March, 1958): 135; see also Morris Gall, "Science Paperbacks in Social Studies," *Social Education*, 24, No. 8 (December 1960): 369–371.

> Students often face problems and wrestle with them more successfully in the laboratory than in the classroom.
>
> High school science laboratory learning needs great improvement.
>
> The task of translation of strong but general guidelines into a science education program is not one primarily for professional scientists and technologists.
>
> Too little is known about the readiness of students for different concepts.[2]

The second of the above points refers to the watered-down courses in science offered to slow learners in the high school. "General biology," "applied chemistry," and "special physical science" are names often used for those science courses so elementary that they have little in common with traditional high-school science. These courses are often decried, but experience has shown that the slow or retarded student is unable to master difficult high-school courses in biology, chemistry, physics, or earth science. Hence courses have been developed for the retarded with special reference to their level of comprehension, interest, and ability. This is not to say that science is completely beyond the ken of these students. In fact, resourceful teachers are able to motivate them to a high level of interest and to improvement in comprehension commensurate with their talents. Since the characteristics of the slow learner generally include reading retardation, short attention span, difficulty with abstract thinking and resistance to the intellectual approach, these factors need to be taken into account in planning a science curriculum for these students.

At the other extreme, the challenge is no less striking. The great potential for future scientists and science teachers is to be found among our gifted students, particularly those whose talents lie in scientific thought and action. The special abilities of this group include a high degree of competence in abstract thinking, the ability to think in mathematical terms, a talent for formulating hypotheses, a curiosity about biological or phys-

---

[2] *Planning for Excellence in High School Science* (Washington, D.C.: National Science Teachers Association, 1961), pp. 41–49 (excerpted). On the general question of readiness and learning, see Jerome S. Bruner, *The Process of Education* (Cambridge: Harvard U. Press, 1961).

ical phenomena, reasoning (both inductive and deductive) ability, strong power of observation, a predisposition to investigate and experiment, and the courage of one's convictions. The school must identify these youth as early as possible, preferably in the first few grades of the elementary school, and provide them with instruction which will challenge their abilities. This will require special instruction and specially trained teachers.

The high-school science curriculum can make provision for the gifted and talented in a number of ways. Special classes for the gifted, small in size and taught by talented teachers, are scheduled in high schools. In some schools these classes are scheduled so that lecture, discussion, and laboratory work may go on uninterruptedly for half a day, three days a week. These students can be permitted to work on projects of their own choosing under faculty guidance and encouraged to do a great deal of independent study.

Some of the best science teaching and learning goes on in the science laboratories and offices, where student's work as assistants to teachers during unassigned periods. Here they learn to handle equipment, talk with professionals, become familiar with periodical literature, and in general absorb a feeling for scientific thinking and research.

Another avenue for developing the talents of the scientifically gifted boy or girl is the extra-class activity program—the science club, rocket club, scholarship club (in which Westinghouse or Merit candidates may be coached), science fair, or assembly program.

Recently a number of acceleration procedures have been introduced to supplement these enrichment practices. Chief among these is the advanced placement program of the College Entrance Examination Board. The gifted are programmed in special classes, and the four-year science curriculum is completed in three. The fourth year may include a college-level course in beginning astronomy, zoology, geology, physical chemistry, or advanced physics. In some places, high-school students pursue such work on college campuses after school, on Saturday, or during the summer. These arrangements need to be carefully organized so that the student will find a challenge in the advanced course, and yet not find it so far removed from his background that the work results in failure and disillusionment.

SPECIAL METHODS AND MATERIALS IN SCIENCE

Special teaching methods in the science classroom include lecture, demonstration, developmental problem-solving project or research, supervised study, committee or group investigation, laboratory or field trip, and case study.

The problem-solving method is possible in science when materials are available for immediate experimentation to test the validity of one or more hypotheses advanced to resolve a stated problem. The case-study method enables students to review both the history and the scientific thinking and investigation involved in the solution of a specific scientific problem.

In science even more than in other areas, the use of concrete supplementary aids in teaching is essential. These may include the chalkboard, charts, maps, posters, films, filmstrips, slides, microprojector, magnifiers, tools, models, and mock-ups.

A well-equipped science laboratory requires items too numerous to list here.[3] The teacher should be familiar with standard items, with sources of materials, with the relative merits of competing items, with sources of free materials, and with new materials as they become available.

The school library should have a science section with encyclopedias, reference books, periodicals, books on science hobbies, the history of science, and science fiction. Suggestions for locally available material, science book clubs, science fairs and so on, should also be made available in the library.

PLANNING FOR TEACHING

The Unit

In the teaching of science as in other subjects it has been found that the psychological advantage of relating various activities to one large topic makes for a functional approach, sustained interest, better comprehension, and better retention. Thus a course in eighth- or ninth-year general science may be organized around the following units: Health and the Human Body, the Earth and the Universe, Obtaining and Improving

---

[3] See Nathan S. Washton, *Science Teaching in the Secondary Schools* (New York: Harper, 1961) for checklists of equipment and supplies in biology, pp. 155–59; in physical science, pp. 177–81, and suggestions for "improvising for lack of equipment" in the biological and physical sciences.

our Food Supply, Natural Resources, Matter and Energy, The Atomic World, Transportation and Communication.

If possible, the teacher should find or prepare a resource unit on the topic before working out the teaching unit. The resource unit should be as comprehensive as possible, and should include many aims and objectives, lesson topics, materials and resources, supplementary aids, teaching methods, suggestions for evaluation and application, and other matters relating to content and method in teaching the unit. From the resource unit the teacher can select a number of lesson topics, prepare the motivational approach to the unit and to each lesson, make assignments, and determine leading questions, activities for the class, devices for reaching the individual, culminating activities, evaluation, and application. This plan should guide teacher and class throughout the unit and be flexible enough to permit modification and variation as the work unfolds. It is often advisable to enlist the aid of the class in making the plan or at least to apprise the class of the plan at the outset of the unit.

EVALUATION

The effectiveness of the high-school science program is a matter of deep concern to teachers and students and to local, national, and international groups. How can the program be evaluated? There is both a formal and an informal approach. The former is the competitive examination—class, school, city, state, or national; the latter is an *ex post facto* procedure based on questionnaire, observation, and performance.

Obviously, evaluation must be directly related to the stated objectives. It makes no sense to begin with certain goals and then to test for others. Since both objectives and the quality of a program change, evaluation must be a continuous process. It is fair to ask how well students in a given high school do on examinations in science courses, on school, local or state examinations, in winning science scholarships, in gaining admission to college and succeeding there (especially in science work), and in going on to advanced work and to careers in science. Informally, it is important to discover changes in attitudes toward science, scientific thinking, interest in and knowledge about current developments in science, initiative, and independence in scientific activity—reading, research, and experimentation. These can be discerned to some extent through questionnaires, observation and recording by teachers, administrators, and parents, consultation with guidance personnel, and follow-up studies.

THE SCIENCE TEACHER

A good science teacher needs to be a scientist, a social scientist, and a humanist, as well as a psychologist and an educator. Obviously, this is more than we can require, yet the education of the science teacher should include liberal amounts of these components if he is to be well-equipped for his role in the modern secondary school.

As a result of the advent of the atomic-space age and the dramatic success of Russia in equalling, and in some respects surpassing, the achievements of American scientists, our science teachers carry a heavy burden of responsibility for the survival of the free world. To help discharge this responsibility, the science teacher needs to be well-educated, a specialist in one area of science, competent in others, and conversant with the most modern methods and materials in teaching. He must also have the cultural background and the social awareness to appreciate the place of science in the total complex of civilization. Only then can his teaching lay the groundwork for a new generation of scientists and of science-educated laymen who will be equal to any challenge.

High-school science teaching includes at least four areas: earth science (including geography, geology, meteorology, astronomy and oceanography), biology, chemistry, and physics. Since it is virtually impossible for the teacher to specialize in all of these, it is expected that he will concentrate in one or two and have some background in the others. Because of the interdependence of science and mathematics, the science teacher should also have a good background in the latter.

In discussing the preparation of the science teacher a recent statement suggests the following requirements:

1. A good command of subject matter.
2. Contact with the history and philosophy of science.
3. A liberal education.
4. Keeping abreast of the happenings and discoveries in science.
5. Skills and techniques in the teaching process.
6. Knowledge of psychology and the learning process.

7. Contact with education in action and the results of educational research.[4]

The same pamphlet suggests that the science teacher's familiarity with developments in science

> can be accomplished through membership in scientific societies, visitation to research and field activities, enrollment in college or graduate level courses in advanced science, systematic study of books and journals, attendance at conferences, development of hobbies, and even through on-the-job research.

and that keeping abreast of educational developments

> . . . can be effected by encouraging the teacher to become actively affiliated with professional organizations, attend conferences, read extensively in science education, and enroll in in-service training courses and summer institutes.[5]

Excellence in Science Teaching

A comprehensive statement of "characteristics of an effective science teacher" is contained in *Planning for Excellence in High School Science*. It is quoted here as a checklist for the beginning teacher by which he can evaluate his work from time to time.

The Effective Science Teacher

Provides students with opportunities to identify and solve problems related to science learning (as contrasted to merely telling students how scientific information is acquired).

Provides his students some experience with the unverified and hypothetical (as contrasted with only the relatively certain).

Gives his students opportunities to select and construct equipment, to develop experimental procedures, and to design (as distinguished from the "laboratory manual" method).

Devotes proper attention to limitations of measurement and observation and, hence, to the tentativeness of conclusions (as distinguished from presumed finalities).

Provides students opportunities in developing generalizations for themselves (as contrasted with handing them out or dictating them).

Emphasizes the development of generalizations (as distinguished from the mere memorization of discrete facts).

---

[4] *Planning for Excellence in High School Science,* pp. 62–64.
[5] *Ibid.,* pp. 63–64.

Helps students develop true understanding of generalizations by broad and numerous applications and illustrations (as contrasted to contentment with verbal facility).

Permits and encourages students seriously to explore questions of interest to them whether or not these questions are directly related to the logic of the course (as contrasted with confining everyone to the same learning sequence).

Is selective and creative in the learning experiences he employs in the light of the maturity and intellectual ability of his students (as distinguished from a formal or routine following of a text or course of study).

Insists on standards of performance at least slightly above those which evidence indicates his students are capable of (as contrasted with aiming his instruction at the average student).

Transfers the responsibility for the learning process from teacher to student by training the student in the process and mechanics of self-initiated learning (as contrasted to continually leading the student by the hand).

Makes evident to his students his conviction that science, generally and in particular, is a matter of supreme importance and satisfaction to him (as distinguished from the appearance of being noncommittal or dutiful).

Consciously provides guidance for his students, helping them to identify and meet their own learning goals and their own occupational goals (as distinguished from merely helping them learn science and leaving guidance functions up to counseling specialists or to the students).[6]

Professional Growth

A number of professional affiliates should be familiar to the science teacher. These include the National Science Teachers Association (a division of the NEA), American Association for the Advancement of Science, National Association of Biology Teachers, National Science Foundation, and American Educational Research Association. A number of specialized journals, such as *Science Education,* published at the University of Tampa and *The Bulletin of the Atomic Scientists* are devoted to the social implications of science. *The Journal of Chemical Education* reports developments in its own field and others. Each of these publications reports scholarships, fellowships, grants, research,

[6] *Ibid.,* pp. 59–62.

literature, summer and all-year institutes and other opportunities that may be of interest to the science teacher. Taking and
giving courses, conducting experiments in science and/or science
teaching, sponsoring student activities, attending lectures, serving on school committees, maintaining active membership in
professional bodies, contributing occasionally to a learned journal, reading one or more journals regularly, attending conventions, and acting as a public-relations representative for the profession are among the many avenues for professional growth.
Professional growth is based on excellence in teaching, and excellence in teaching is dependent on continued professional
growth.

FOR DELIBERATION and DISCUSSION

1. Is there a body of science content to which *every* high-school
   student should be exposed? What does it include? Why?
2. What qualities are characteristic of the scientist? Which of these
   (and to what extent) are inherent? Which (and to what extent)
   are acquired or developed? What techniques or clues are there
   for the early identification of talent or giftedness in science?
3. Read Schwab's essay on "The Teaching of Science as Enquiry."
   How does the method he describes differ from the one by which
   you were educated? What problems would its implementation
   present in the high school?
4. How can the science teacher help boys and girls think clearly
   about current world problems? Is this part of his responsibility,
   or is it exclusively the province of other departments in the
   school?

FOR ADDITIONAL READING

BARNARD, J. DARRELL. *Teaching High School Science.* Washington,
    D.C.: NEA, 1956. A summary of research findings. Very use-
    ful for the beginning teacher.
    Planning for Excellence in High School Science. Washing-
    ton, D.C.: National Science Teachers Association, 1961. A
    report resulting from a conference of fifty specialists in edu-
    cation, science, and science education. Sponsored by the Na-
    tional Science Foundation.
SCHWAB, JOSEPH J. *The Teaching of Science as Enquiry.* (The Ing-
    lis Lecture.) Cambridge: Harvard U. Press, 1962. An in-
    formed appeal for revolutionizing the teaching of high-
    school science. Textbooks and teaching methods would be

open-minded, emphasizing "fluid enquiry" and teaching the
student how to learn by himself.

"Science in the School," *Educational Leadership,* 19, No. 4
(January, 1962). Contains articles on methods and materials
in science education.

The Two Cultures and the Scientific Revolution. New York:
Cambridge, 1959. Pleads for a reunion of science and the humanities.

WASHTON, NATHAN S. *Science Teaching in the Secondary Schools.* New
York: Harper, 1961. A practical guide for high-school science
teachers. Contains much useful information directly applicable to the work of the classroom teacher.

10 Mathematics

HISTORICAL CONSIDERATIONS

Mathematics, the oldest of the sciences, dates back to ancient times both as a field of speculative study and as a practical resource. It had great influence on the life of ancient China, Egypt, Babylonia, and Greece. In the medieval university, arithmetic and geometry formed, together with music and astronomy, the higher studies (quadrivium) of the curriculum. The American academy of the eighteenth century gave mathematics a place of importance as a practical study. The secondary school of the nineteenth and early twentieth centuries made algebra and geometry compulsory, justifying their inclusion on the grounds of "mental discipline," since they had long since ceased to serve a functional role in the lives of most students. Until quite recently, elementary and intermediate algebra and Euclidean plane geometry were taught to all college-bound high-school students. Although electives in trigonometry, solid geometry, and advanced algebra were offered in academic courses, they were taken by relatively few students.

Unfortunately, the fundamental principles of these studies were rarely understood by teachers, and almost never grasped by the students. Hence mathematics at the high-school level, until very recently, was the deadest of subjects, a stumbling block to many students and a drudgery to most. In 1954, MacLane described high-school mathematics in *The Bulletin* of the National Association of Secondary School Principals as follows:

My subject is vacuous; the highly modern development of mathematics has had no impact on the content or on the presentation of secondary-school mathematics. Algebra and geometry, as covered in schools, consist exclusively of ideas already well known two hundred years ago—many of them two thousand years ago—The pupils can conclude only that there is no such thing as a new mathematical idea.[1]

MacLane could not have foreseen that within a decade the subject would be in the vanguard of academic progress. So thoroughly are the teaching and learning of mathematics being revolutionized that the curriculum of a half-century ago is no longer recognizable—and the change is only beginning.

Our schools have always placed proficiency in arithmetic on a par with that in reading and writing. Mathematics has played a key role in science, technology, industry, business, and agriculture. Its study has been associated with habits of effective thinking, intellectual independence, aesthetic appreciation, and creative expression. Yet we allowed these objectives and opportunities to become stagnant until the challenges of the modern world startled us out of our complacency.

In 1956 a careful study reported:

Over the years there have been repeated recommendations for changes, but by and large the offerings at the secondary level have remained static. . . .

The substance of these recommendations has varied in detail, but there have been three persistent themes: First, take the traditional subjects of algebra, geometry, and trigonometry out of their watertight compartments and unify the mathematically important topics into one naturally related development; second, bring such subjects as analytic geometry, statistics and the calculus into the secondary school curriculum; and third, set up a double-track program—applied mathematics for the student not headed for college, and a two-to-four year integrated sequence for the college-bound student.

. . . By and large, most students who stick with mathematics throughout the four years of high school follow the same ruts their grandfathers followed before them. The high school curriculum today shows few, if any, signs of the important develop-

[1] *The Bulletin*, 38 (May, 1954): 66–70.

ments that have taken place in mathematical science since the seventeenth century.[2]

While this statement is still true for many of our high schools, developments of the last half-dozen years have been moving our high-school curriculum in new directions. Since no more than passing reference is made to mathematics in the elementary school, it should be noted that the curriculum there, too, is in process of basic revision and that the quality of work completed by secondary-school students is directly related to their experiences with mathematics during the elementary-school years.

THE REVOLUTION IN MATHEMATICS TEACHING

In a stimulating paper, Robert B. Davis identifies seven conditions to which the changes in mathematics teaching may be ascribed: The growing importance of technology, the rapid rate at which new mathematics is being discovered, the ever-lengthening number of years involved in completing one's education, the unfortunate degree of illegitimate specialization (that is, the teacher who becomes a "specialist" in Algebra 1), neglect stemming from ignorance, a confusion of democracy with egalitarian anti-intellectualism, and the sociological fact that a good mathematician who is also a good man can find more remunerative work in a more congenial atmosphere than he can in teaching.[3]

We can assess only the causes of the revolution. Its course, since we are in its midst, can be discerned dimly, if at all. As for the outcome, we can know only that the revolution in method, content, and preparation of teachers in secondary-school mathematics will go on, perhaps with increased tempo, for many years and that its full impact will not be felt until the generation now entering elementary school is middle-aged. The new methods of teaching will open vistas of comprehension and creation to the young which were closed to their elders. The possibilities of the new mathematics will begin to be realized only when those educated by the new methods become teachers.

---

[2] *Problems in Mathematical Education* (Princeton: Educational Testing Service, 1956), pp. 21–22.
[3] Robert B. Davis "The Mathematics Revolution: Causes and Directions" in *Frontiers of Secondary Education III*, Paul M. Halverson (ed.) (Syracuse: Syracuse U. Press, 1958), pp. 52–63.

It is a mistake to suppose that the revolution in mathematics dates from and owes its beginning to Sputnik. Late in 1954, the Carnegie Corporation asked the Educational Testing Service to investigate the kinds of research activities that would lead to a better mathematics curriculum in the elementary and secondary schools. The resulting report briefly described the work of the University of Illinois Committee on Secondary School Mathematics, the School and College Study of Admission with Advanced Standing, the establishment of a Commission on Mathematics by the College Entrance Examination Board, the Science Teaching Improvement Program of the American Association for the Advancement of Science, and the work of the Curriculum Committee of the National Council of Teachers of Mathematics. The report's twenty-page bibliography lists 250 studies, indicating ferment in mathematics education in the early fifties.[4]

The National Science Foundation (NSF), established by Congress in 1950, makes grants for basic research and provides scholarships for teachers, students, and advanced scholars, establishes institutes for group study for teachers, supports projects designed to produce up-to-date course content materials, and maintains a National Register of Scientific and Technical Personnel. NSF also supports the work of the School Mathematics Study Group (SMSG), instituted at Yale University during the summer of 1958, in which a group of forty top-level research mathematicians and secondary-school teachers prepared experimental material for grades seven through twelve. Subsequent conferences and work sessions of the SMSG have been conducted every summer since 1958. The curriculum materials developed at these conferences are being tried experimentally by thousands of teachers throughout the country.

The National Defense Education Act of 1958 provides funds for the purchase of equipment for aid in teaching science, mathematics, and foreign languages, and provides assistance to states for supervision in these areas. Under the stimulus of this act many states have undertaken programs designed to improve and upgrade the instruction of science and mathematics on all school levels.

The Secondary School Curriculum Committee of the National Council of Teachers of Mathematics issued its compre-

[4] *Problems in Mathematical Education.*

hensive report on the secondary mathematics curriculum in 1959.[5] The report addresses itself to key questions in mathematics education and discusses objectives, content, and implementation in detail.

These are but a few of the organizations and groups that have been studying mathematics education at the high-school level. With so much activity in progress, it is to be expected that rapid change will occur and that divergences and conflicts will develop. Such indeed is the case, as we shall see in the next section.

THE CURRICULUM

The University of Illinois Committee on School Mathematics

Since 1952 a group of university professors, psychologists, and secondary-school teachers have been developing a curriculum so radical in its nature that it bears little resemblance to what was standard for centuries. Max Beberman, the leader of this movement, describes the new curriculum which is being tested by trained teachers in high schools throughout the country.

Our program begins by leading the student to an awareness of the distinction between things and their names—in particular, of the distinction between numbers and numerals, and of the need when writing about numerals (or other expressions) to have names for them. . . . Finally, he studies Euclidean plane geometry from an informal point of view. . . .

The second year deals, first, with the notion of ordered pair and a study of the solution sets of equations and inequations in two variables. . . . Recursive definitions and proof by mathematical induction are treated at length, and illustrated by the use of notation and the theory of arithmetic progressions.

Our third year begins with a study of exponents. . . . Finally, the student considers polynomial fractions and studies such aspects of the theory of equations as the factor theorem, synthetic division and curve tracing.

[5] *The Secondary Mathematics Curriculum.* Report of the Secondary-School Curriculum Committee of the National Council of Teachers of Mathematics (NCTM). Reprinted from the *Mathematics Teacher,* (May, 1959): 389–417. The NCTM, founded in 1920, is the mathematics affiliate of the NEA. The Mathematical Association of America, with headquarters at University of Buffalo, is a national organization of persons interested in mathematics on the college level.

> The fourth year contains a treatment of the circular functions based on a winding function. . . . The remainder of the course is devoted to a study of plane geometry and solid geometry by analytic methods.[6]

Even this brief description indicates how far a functional course in mathematics departs from the traditional approach. The course being developed by the Illinois group is under continual revision. Other experimental groups, notably that of the School Mathematics Study Group, are developing programs of their own which depart in varying degrees from the traditional secondary-school curriculum. In this sense the report of the Secondary-School Curriculum Committee of the NCTM is disappointing. Its recommendation is for the college-preparatory course:

> Ninth grade, algebra; Tenth grade, geometry (plane with some solid); Eleventh grade, algebra, trigonometry; Twelfth grade, any two of the following semester courses: Probability and statistics; analytic geometry; mathematical analysis based on a study of functions (algebraic, trigonometric, exponential, and logarithmic). (Some schools might find desirable a strong course in analytic geometry and calculus as preparation for Advanced Placement examinations.)

Essentially these follow the traditional secondary-school curriculum. This may be no more than a recognition of the fact that few teachers of high-school mathematics are prepared to depart radically from the content or method in use for generations. Naturally, unless curriculum revision and in-service training proceed in the direction of our best practice known, no progress toward a better program in secondary-school mathematics can be anticipated.

Other Experimental Programs

The School Mathematics Study Group (SMSG) has been preparing units for use with the academically talented in grades seven through twelve. Textbooks based on the findings of teachers using these units probably will replace those now in use and ultimately will have the effect of curriculum revision, with new

---

[6] Max Beberman, *An Emerging Program of Secondary School Mathematics.* (Cambridge: Harvard U. Press, 1958), pp. 39–43.

topics, such as deductive reasoning, measurement, and probability and statistics gaining in importance and others being sloughed off.

The Commission on Mathematics of the College Entrance Examination Board has brought together distinguished mathematicians and gifted secondary-school teachers in an effort to upgrade secondary-school mathematics teaching (especially for the talented) and to integrate it with college mathematics. Their tentative findings seem to imply the following recommendations summarized by an observer:

> (1) Where possible, modernize. (2) Where obsolete, discard. (3) Emphasize fundamental concepts and unifying ideas. (4) Stop the present overemphasis on drill and computation. (5) Combine solid geometry, plane geometry, and analytic geometry into a single one-year course. (6) Introduce a course in statistics in the twelfth grade. (7) Require more mathematics for admission to college. (8) Keep the door open for further experimentation.[7]

The College Entrance Examination Board also conducts the "Advanced Placement Program" designed for talented college-bound high-school students. In this program the student completes the four-year high-school mathematics sequence in three years and takes the college freshman course in calculus in his senior year. While this does not constitute basic curriculum revision, it has been found that the introduction of a course in calculus has a salutary effect on the entire mathematics program of the school.

General Mathematics

Long before a basic revision of the mathematics curriculum began, the problems raised by the growing number and percentage of slow and retarded high-school students forced minor curriculum revisions in order to provide for the needs of this group. A ninth-grade course called "General Mathematics" for non-college bound youth was well-established in the secondary-school curriculum by the middle of the twentieth century. However, there was no agreement about what this course should be. One position maintained that every high-school student should be exposed to the elements of algebra and geome-

---

[7] Davis, p. 57.

try, and a simplified course of this nature was designed. It was felt that without an understanding of elementary terminology, concepts, and processes in algebra and geometry, a student would lack one of the essential components of a general education. Another view conceded the wisdom of including these elements in general education, but took the position that a large number of students entering our high schools were deficient in simple arithmetic, and that it was therefore impossible, to expect them to master algebra and geometry.

Perhaps here, too, a realistic approach which disregards subject names as well as student labels will make possible the development of course material appropriate for the slow learner in high school. Our culture demands that every citizen have competence in making monetary computations, understanding time and space relationships, reading simple graphs and charts, making and reporting accurate measurements, and solving simple mathematical problems.[8] Whether the term "arithmetic," "algebra," or "geometry" is applied is less important than that the material presented be within the grasp and interest of the boys and girls.

Mathematics in the High-School Program

Each school must adjust its program to the ability, needs, and interests of its own students. Good guidance demands that students able to do advanced work in mathematics be directed to college-oriented classes, just as it does that the slow learner be spared the humiliation and frustration of attempting such work.

In most high schools, general mathematics is required through the ninth year, but not beyond, for graduation. Some colleges will admit students who have had only elementary algebra, though most require the completion of a high-school course in plane geometry, and the prestige colleges generally require three, four, or five years of high-school mathematics. In his first report, Conant decried the failure of many high schools to provide an impetus to elect this program. His recommendation of one year of general mathematics for the non-college-bound called for a course with elements of algebra and of geometry, rather than the usual remedial arithmetic.

[8] See M. Peters, *Going Places With Mathematics* (Englewood Cliffs: Prentice-Hall, 1962), for a practical course in ninth-year general mathematics.

The sciences, industrial arts, and commercial and vocational studies depend heavily on competence in mathematics. Nevertheless, attempts to unite science with mathematics—for example, in core programs—have not been successful, since it is impossible to prepare curriculum units which will provide for the sequential teaching of each of these subjects.

Ability grouping is widely practiced in high-school mathematics classes, particularly in the larger schools. An accelerated group may be studying a combination of elementary and intermediate algebra while an average group moves more slowly, a general math class touches the subject lightly, and a retarded group studies remedial arithmetic. In the smaller school the problem sometimes is met by grouping the talented and gifted in one mathematics class regardless of grade. The same result is achieved internally in many schools by the extra-class activity called the "math club" or "math team."

As in other subjects, the use of outside resources—college professors, representatives of industry, authors, visits to places of interest, such as a computer laboratory, appropriate audio-visual materials, and supplementary reading—can enrich the study of mathematics. In this connection there is a growing body of low-cost paperback books of high caliber which illuminate almost every phase of mathematics—its history, biography of great mathematicians, and current developments.

THE STUDENT AND THE LEARNING PROCESS

More than a generation has elapsed since Piaget investigated "judgment and reasoning in the child," but we still know very little about the learning process, particularly as it relates to mathematics. "Teaching mathematics to most children is akin to teaching speech to children who are deaf. Their daily life does not provide readiness, and the entire task devolves upon us."[9]

The University of Illinois group is concerned at least as much with the learner as it is with the material it wants him to learn. Beberman is constantly preoccupied with "maintaining interest in mathematics," and he asserts that sensible problems and opportunities to invent solutions are the two key aspects in

[9] Davis, p. 56.

this connection. It is exciting to hear a mathematician speaking to mathematicians say,

> The child's world is, of course, different from the adult's. It is rich in fantasy and not at all bounded by the exigencies of making a living and providing for old-age security. A child delights in the what-would-happen-if type of question, and, if he can give consistent answers to such questions, he regards this work as being eminently practical.[10]

One of the most fruitful attacks in problems posed by the learning process is reported by Bruner, who summarizes the work of a ten-day meeting of scientists, scholars, and educators in 1959.[11] In less than a hundred pages the author discusses the importance of structure, readiness, intuition, and motives in the learning process. The concern for the learner while based on a kind of non-invidious opportunism is consonant with the highest ethic of democracy.

Children can grasp fundamental principles of mathematics —for example, set theory—in the lower grades, and it is preferable to present concepts and strategies in the form of intuitive geometry at the outset rather than to confront the student with a set of axioms and theorems.

> Much more attention needs to be given to the development of students who have a good intuitive feel for geometry, students who are skillful in discovering proofs, not just in checking the validity of or remembering proofs with which they have been presented.[12]

If Bruner's categorical statement that scientific and mathematical aptitudes can be discovered earlier than other intellectual talents is true, we have a mandate to identify the talented *and* to use all we know about the learning process in developing their talents and for continuous experimentation and teaching to improve the process of education. The pendulum has been swinging in the direction of heavy commitment to education of the gifted. Our curriculum studies, the Advanced Placement Program, a host of scholarship programs, independent study, special college-campus courses for talented high-school students,

---

[10] Beberman, p. 37.
[11] *The Process of Education.*
[12] *Ibid.,* p. 78.

conferences on the gifted and special projects, yearbooks, and reports indicate a deep interest on the part of the profession for meeting its responsibility to the talented and gifted high-school girl and boy.

The report of the 1958 conference on the academically talented recommended that ninth-grade algebra be moved down to grade eight, and that the conventional four-year program of algebra, plane geometry, intermediate algebra, solid geometry, and trigonometry be compressed into three so that the talented, in the twelfth year, might study probability, statistical inference, set theory, and polynomial calculus.[13]

The ferment in mathematics education is an inevitable reaction to the long standing static nature of the mathematics curriculum. In the words of Justice Holmes "To rest upon a formula is a slumber which prolonged means death."

THE MATHEMATICS TEACHER

The increased high-school enrollment, coupled with the national need for trained personnel in science and mathematics, has resulted in a steadily mounting demand for teachers in these areas. At the same time, attractive offers in engineering, government service, business, and industry have tended to siphon off qualified personnel from education. The result has been a severe shortage of competent mathematics teachers. This has resulted in curtailment of the high-school program, particularly in the junior and senior years, in the junior college, and even in the four-year colleges. The high schools have had to resort to the employment of teachers under emergency certificates and the assignment of teachers holding certificates in other subjects to the mathematics programs. This practice may be disastrous, since a teacher poorly prepared in content and method and lacking interest in or enthusiasm for the subject is not likely to be effective with students. When one considers the preparation required, teaching conditions, and the opportunities available in other fields, it is small wonder that the demand for qualified mathematics teachers in our high schools has for many years far exceeded the supply.

---

[13] *The Identification and Education of the Academically Talented Student in the American Secondary School*, p. 78.

Preparation for Teaching High-School Mathematics

The following recommendations, embodied in the official report of the National Council of Teachers of Mathematics, have been adopted in substance by many states:

> In view of curriculum demands, teachers of mathematics in grades seven through twelve will need to have competence in (1) analysis —trigonometry, plane and solid analytic geometry, and calculus; (2) foundations of mathematics—theory of sets, mathematical or symbolic logic, postulational systems, real and complex number systems; (3) algebra—matrices and determinants, theory of numbers, theory of equations, and structure of algebra; (4) geometry —Euclidean and non-Euclidean, metric and projective, synthetic and analytic; (5) statistics probability and statistical inference; (6) applications—mechanics, theory of games, linear programming, and operational research. . . .
>
> These programs in mathematics should be supplemented by a basic program in education and psychology. As a minimum, a teacher should have completed successfully eighteen semester hours, including student teaching in mathematics, in such courses as: a methods course in the teaching of mathematics; psychology of learning (with particular reference to adolescents); psychology of adjustment (mental hygiene); and tests and measurements. This total program of specialization should be based on a strong program of general education.[14]

The problem of staffing our secondary schools with mathematics teachers of this level of preparation is complicated and requires: (1) the establishment of high-level teacher preparation programs in our colleges; (2) identifying, attracting, and retaining qualified potential teachers in large numbers into these programs; (3) upgrading the profession through better working conditions, status, and salary to make the job sufficiently attractive to competent teachers; and (4) development of in-service programs designed to bring existing teachers up to the levels of the newer requirements.

A number of fruitful attacks on the problem of bringing quality teachers into the profession have been underway. The Ford Foundation programs have been attracting people with mathematics majors and liberal arts degrees into fifth-year training programs in colleges throughout the country. Many

---

[14] *The Secondary Mathematics Curriculum*, pp. 414–15.

of these men and women have been out of college for ten years or more, but want to teach. They find it possible to bridge the gap through one of these programs, which offer opportunities involving "earn while you learn" features. Many schools are offering married women an opportunity for part-time service so that their talents may be utilized even though their home responsibilities preclude full-time assignments.

In the long run, the supply of qualified teachers will depend on the in-service situations. An attractive professional status will have the dual effect of halting the exodus from the profession and bringing in a sufficient number of qualified people.

In-Service Conditions and Opportunities

On the negative side we find teachers suffering from low morale due to a real or fancied grievance based on one of the following: overwork, underpay, improper utilization of talent, or lack of status. That there may be some truth in each of these charges is apparent when we realize that the teacher carries a load of five classes and other assignments daily, is expected to teach large classes, sometimes including several retarded groups, receives an average salary of $5,516, and spends an inordinate amount of time keeping records, making reports, policing study halls, collecting money, and attending faculty meetings.

The picture, while still not so bright as it might be, has been changing for the better. The revitalizing of the curriculum, involving many teachers in work with mathematicians and college professors on revision and in experimental teaching practices, has played an important part. These curricular revisions have set in motion a vast program of in-service courses, seminars, workshops, institutes, and conferences financed by foundations and by local, state and federal agencies. The more able teachers have found their talents recruited for curriculum revision committees, writing textbooks, workbooks and programmed material, giving in-service courses and lectures, teaching on television, serving as team leaders in the newer team-teaching situations, acting as consultants, teaching some classes in college, preparing testing materials, serving on evaluating and other professional committees, and assisting on various research projects. In short, the opportunities available to many able mathematics teachers are making their work at least as challenging and rewarding as it would be in government, industry, or self-employment.

The average teacher in service has benefitted from many of these activities. Scholarship opportunities for attending courses, seminars, and conferences have been made available. The beginning teacher may be assigned to a team where he can benefit from working closely with more experienced teachers. Non-professional teacher-aides may be assigned to do the time-consuming non-professional chores connected with teaching. The more ambitious may aspire to advanced degrees, and in time to positions of leadership in curriculum, instruction, or administration.

An interesting experiment in upgrading mathematics teaching is under way in central New York State, where the Sloan Foundation is financing an operation called the Syracuse Plan. Participating teachers work at their usual jobs half-time, study at a nearby university half-time, and continue to receive their full salaries. Having the time and energy for advanced study without loss of pay is, for most teachers, the nearest thing to heaven on earth. If some plan can be worked out to give every teacher of every subject an opportunity for this kind of in-service development, the level of the profession and the quality of education will be vastly improved everywhere.

FOR DELIBERATION and DISCUSSION

1. Why should a high-school mathematics teacher be well grounded in the elementary-school instructional program in mathematics?
2. College professors of mathematics, science, and other content areas have cooperated with high-school teachers in efforts to modernize high-school curricula in their respective disciplines. What effects may this be expected to have on the work of the modern high school?
3. Why is the quotation from Beberman (p. 192) significant? How would this point of view influence content and method?
4. Why is the National Council of Teachers of Mathematics less inclined than the various college study groups to make major revisions in the curriculum?
5. What hurdles must a mathematics teacher overcome in order to teach successfully the new secondary curriculum?

FOR ADDITIONAL READING

BEBERMAN, MAX. *An Emerging Program of Secondary School Mathematics.* (The Inglis Lecture) 1958. Cambridge: Harvard U. Press. A description of the radical revision of the secondary curriculum in mathematics developed by the Illinois Committee on School Mathematics. Emphasizes the place of "precision of language" and "discovery" in the learning process.

BUTLER, CHARLES F. and WREN, F. LYNWOOD. *The Teaching of Secondary Mathematics.* New York: McGraw-Hill, 1960. A comprehensive, conservative statement of all phases of mathematics, grades seven through fourteen. Part I emphasizes professional matters. Part II concentrates on content.

DYER, HENRY S., KALIN, ROBERT, and LORD, FREDERIC M. *Problems in Mathematical Education.* Princeton: Educational Testing Service, 1956. A booklet which includes a bibliography of 258 studies reviewing the work in mathematics education. Makes recommendations.

FEHR, HOWARD F. *Teaching High School Mathematics.* Washington, D.C.: NEA, 1955. Summary of research in content, method, and special problems in teaching high-school mathematics.

"Mathematics in the School," *Educational Leadership,* 19, No. 6 (March, 1962). Contains articles on curriculum and instruction in mathematics.

Secondary School Curriculum, The. Report of the Secondary School Curriculum Committee of the National Council of Teachers of Mathematics, *Mathematics Teacher* (May, 1959): 389–417. A careful statement including orientation, content, and implementation of the curriculum. Represents the thinking of in-service teachers and administrators in secondary-school mathematics.

11 Foreign Languages

THE CHALLENGE OF
FOREIGN LANGUAGE INSTRUCTION

The world is a family and it behooves all of its members to learn to communicate with one another. Yet fewer than 50 percent of our high schools offer any foreign-language instruction at all, and only one in four high-school students in the entire country studies any foreign language. Although over 500 million people in the world speak Chinese, 150 million Hindi-Urdu, and 150 million Russian, only a few thousand high-school students study the latter language, and a few hundred the former. Equally meager is our preparation to communicate with the 100 million speaking Japanese, the 70 million speaking Indonesian, and the 65 million speaking Portuguese (Brazilian).

Even the record for those modern languages which have been taught in our schools traditionally—French, Spanish, German, Italian, Greek, Hebrew, and Polish—is not particularly satisfying. In 1929, the Coleman Report stated that most students who studied a modern foreign language in high school did so for only two years. The profession accepted this as the standard and geared instruction to reading, grammar, and translation.

During World War I, German was eliminated from the curriculum of many schools as a "patriotic" gesture. In Germany, on the other hand, the study of English and French increased sharply during the war. During the 1930's the attitude that our country was self-sufficient and had no need for foreigners prevailed to the detriment of foreign-language programs in our schools. Prior to World War II there was virtually no foreign-language instruction in the elementary school and very little in the junior high school. What little there was rarely attempted to develop competence in oral communication. Furthermore, social pressures discouraged millions of immigrants from any attempt to perpetuate their language among their children. As a result, America found itself in the 1940's and 1950's a nation of foreign-language illiterates.

In contrast, Germany and Japan and later Soviet Russia, as well as other countries in Europe and elsewhere, were far better prepared to meet the needs of communicating with and understanding other peoples in their language. Conservative estimates indicate that 10 million Russians can speak basic English. (Some place the figure at many times that.) Yet until recently we numbered our Russian-speaking population in only the thousands. The tradition in the European secondary school, is to teach at least two foreign languages throughout the course to every student. Those majoring in humanities will take at least six foreign languages and develop competence in listening and speaking as well as in reading and writing these. The degree of competence developed is often high enough to approximate native speech.

In the past Europeans have perhaps had greater need to be polyglot than we have. However, in today's world the situation demands that we give high priority to language instruction. The stories told in *The Ugly American* point up the stark fact that in many uncommitted countries around the world we may lose the battle for men's minds because we are far less competent than are the Soviets in the use of a basic tool—language. Aside from the advantage the Communists have over us for practicing deception through skilled use of Pakistani, Malay, Urdu-Hindi, and other languages in which they far excel us, there is the obvious fact that people will be more amenable to friendship with those who speak their language well than with those who do not.

The need during World War II for engaging in propaganda, reading enemy material, questioning prisoners, engaging in sabotage, and espionage, effectively infiltrating enemy lines and practicing other war strategy forced our armed services to develop a crash program for teaching Japanese, German, Russian, Chinese, and other languages. The ASTP (Army Specialized Training Program) or Army Method impelled the Modern Language Association to re-examine the objectives and methods of language instruction in our schools.

In 1952 the United States Commissioner of Education, Dr. Earl J. McGrath, strongly advocated that language instruction emphasize competence in speaking and asserted that there were ". . . cogent psychological, social, pedagogical, and national reasons for intensifying and increasing the scope of language instruction in the American school system."[1] The Commissioner's recommendations included an examination of the place of foreign-language study in the elementary school; revision of the language curriculum in teacher education institutions; combining language study with broader programs of international understanding; modernizing instruction, with emphasis on the spoken language; convening a representative body of language teachers along with representatives of other disciplines (history, sociology, anthropology, education, psychology) as well as administrative and guidance specialists to re-examine the entire language curriculum and seek means for extending language instruction into the lower grades. Many of these suggestions were implemented as a result of the Modern Language Association's Foreign-Language Program financed by a $250,000 five-year (1953–1958) grant by the Rockefeller Foundation. Sputnik gave added impetus to the program, and probably played a major role in the passing of the National Defense Education Act (1958), which has provisions for the support of foreign-language programs.

The NDEA, extended in 1961 for three more years, includes two sections relating to language programs. Title III appropriates $70 million for assistance to states in strengthening science, mathematics and, through the equipment of language laboratories, modern foreign-language instruction. Title VI authorizes the United States Commissioner of Education to administer four interrelated programs: (1) the establishment of area centers to expand and improve instruction in neglected modern foreign languages; (2) to provide fellowships for graduate students of these languages; (3) to conduct research on meth-

[1] Earl J. McGrath, "Language Study and World Affairs," *The Modern Language Journal*, XXXVI, No. 5 (May, 1952): 207.

ods of teaching and to develop teaching materials; and (4) to establish foreign-language institutes for advanced training in new methods and materials for elementary and secondary-school teachers of modern foreign languages.

Modern foreign languages judged critical and necessary include Arabic, Chinese, Hindi-Urdu, Portuguese (Brazilian), Russian, and Spanish (Latin American). The Latin American Studies Program, inaugurated in 1961, coordinates and intensifies federal aid to instruction in Latin American languages and related studies. Under Part B of Title VI, language institutes have been conducted for public- and private-school teachers of Spanish, French, German, Russian, Italian, Hebrew, Chinese, and Japanese.[2]

FOREIGN LANGUAGE CURRICULUM AND INSTRUCTION

Opportunities for Students

It is not enough for language teachers to be convinced of the need for Americans to have competence in foreign languages. School administrators, guidance counselors, and students also must be convinced. The serious difficulties which still impede the progress in this area include restricted offerings or even no offering at all, poor counseling, lack of administrative support, short duration of study or failure of continuity in offering, poorly prepared teachers, and faulty objectives, materials, and methods.[3]

For students foreign-language study offers social, cultural, aesthetic, intellectual, vocational, academic, and humanistic advantages. The social aim is to increase status among peers and opportunity for social contacts. The cultural advantages are increased familiarity with the history, customs, and civilization of another people and increased pleasure in foreign travel. Aesthetically the students experience the pleasures of entering more intimately into the creative life—art, music, literature, and so on—of another people. Studying linguistics, translation, compo-

[2] See *The Language Development Program: Title VI National Defense Education Act* (Washington, D.C.: United States Department of Health, Education, and Welfare, Office of Education, 1962).

[3] Adapted from Kenneth Mildenberger, "The National Picture of Modern Foreign Languages in the High School," (Washington, D.C.: United States Department of Health, Education, and Welfare), *Bulletin,* 1958, No. 16, pp. 48–49.

sition, criticism, philology and other aspects of advanced language study provides them with an intellectual challenge.

The advantage most frequently mentioned is the vocational or practical, which includes opportunities in teaching, research, as a travel agent or guide, or as an interpreter or translator, and government service. There are vocational possibilities also in business, industry, journalism, science, and engineering. The technical assistance and Point IV programs of the federal government, as well as the Peace Corps and Alliance for Progress, demand specialists in many fields, but foreign-language skills are essential.

Many colleges require three years of a foreign language for admission. A major in English, business, or public administration may require competence in a foreign language. Advanced study on the doctoral level, scientific research, and other specialized studies require a foreign language. Finally, from the humanistic point of view, foreign-language study is perhaps the most broadening of pursuits.

The School Program

The school should start language instruction as early as possible, give each child adequate opportunity to progress in a language, identify talent, and provide a continuous and excellent instructional program. The following is a comprehensive summary of the responsibilities of the local school system:

1. Providing a sequential, continuous program through the high school years.
2. Articulating the junior- and senior-high-school programs with each other and with the work of the elementary school and of the college.
3. Counseling students in the light of the increased need and opportunity for persons with language competency.
4. Encouraging students of foreign backgrounds to study their mother tongue in school.
5. Surveying and utilizing community resources in languages.
6. Making the most effective use possible of superior teachers— through closed-circuit television, teacher aides, or other means.
7. Giving material encouragement for teachers' professional activities and foreign travel.

8. Arranging for interschool visits and teacher exchanges.
9. Providing language laboratory facilities.
10. Maintaining a language library, including foreign publications and tape recordings, either for the classroom or as part of the school library.
11. Keeping courses of study and instructional materials in accord with objectives.
12. Setting policies for interdepartmental planning and co-operation.
13. Initiating experimental programs and demonstrations of new teaching techniques.
14. Allowing flexible schedules for advanced classes and the special language needs of gifted students.
15. Recognizing outstanding achievement in foreign language with awards comparable to honors in athletics, science, journalism, and other fields.[4]

A typical modern curriculum bulletin in secondary foreign languages was issued by the Connecticut State Department of Education in 1960.[5] It is a good example of the way one state is attempting to implement the above recommendations. The bulletin states:

"An ideal program would consist of six years of language instruction begun in the seventh grade and continued through the senior year of high school . . . Students showing interest and aptitude should be encouraged to begin a second foreign language in grade 9."[6]

Four plans for grades 7–12 are suggested: six full years; five years over a six-year period (that is, two or three periods a week during grades 7 and 8); four years over a six-year period (that is, two or three periods a week in grades 7, 8, 11 and 12); and four full continuous years beginning in grade nine. Thus each plan includes language instruction through grade 12, and, except for the last, instruction starts in grade 7 and continues for six years. Articulation with college is facilitated. "It is one of the utmost

[4] Marjorie C. Johnston and John R. Ludington, "Post Conference Reflections," Modern Foreign Language in the High School, (Washington, D.C.: United States Office of Education, 1958), pp. 160–161.
[5] Foreign Languages Grades 7–12 (Hartford: Connecticut Board of Education, 1960), Curriculum Bulletin Series.
[6] Ibid., p. 7.

importance that schools provide instruction in advanced classes
even if the enrollment is small."[7]

Under the heading of "first principles," the bulletin makes
the following observations:

> Language is first of all something you say. All languages were
> spoken long before they were written, and some have never been
> written down.
>
> . . . No matter how complicated the sound system and the
> syntax of a language may seem to an outsider, every five-year-old
> speaker of that language knows them thoroughly. . . .
>
> A period of ear and tongue training *without the aid of sym-
> bols for the eye* is the essential foundation for effective language
> learning. . . . From the start, the learner should hear only authen-
> tic speech, speak only what has been heard, read only what has
> been spoken, write only what has been read, analyze only what
> has been heard, spoken, read, written, and learned. . . .
>
> Books should be out of reach for a part of the time in *every*
> class and for *most* of the time in most classes.[8]

The curriculum outline discusses skills, structure, content,
and class program for each of six "levels," corresponding to six
years of instruction in the modern foreign language. On the first
level the suggested time allocation for the four skills is hearing,
40 percent; speaking, 30 percent; reading, 20 percent; writing, 10 percent. On the second level: hearing, 30 percent; speaking, 20 percent; reading, 40 percent; writing, 10 percent. On
the third and fourth levels: hearing, 20 percent; speaking,
20 percent; reading, 40 percent; writing, 20 percent. On the fifth
and sixth levels, "Literary, artistic, and politico-economic developments are discussed entirely in the foreign language."[9]

The bulletin includes a seventeen-page outline devoted to
Latin which, after many years of decline, has been experiencing
a revival. The discussion includes pronunciation, morphology,
syntax, vocabulary, derivatives, and reading. The latter begins
with simple sentences and stories in the first year and goes on to
Caesar (still preferred, though some choose Nepos) in the second; Cicero (or Ovid) in the third, and Virgil in the fourth. Advanced standing groups are advised by The Advanced Placement Program to include a substantial amount of prose at a

[7] *Ibid.*, p. 9.
[8] *Ibid.*, p. 10.
[9] *Ibid.*, pp. 12–20.

level of difficulty comparable to that of the philosophical works of Cicero, the writings of Livy and Tacitus, a Latin comedy, and a substantial amount of poetry of Horace and Catullus.

Problems of Instruction

Too many of the language programs in our high schools are still limited to the languages of western Europe and need to be expanded to include the living languages of the Near East, India, China, Japan, Central Africa, and Indonesia. In many of our smaller high schools, no foreign language is offered at all. In many schools a fourth year or even the third year is not offered. Often a language is taught by a teacher who speaks it poorly or who is out of touch with modern methods and materials. Counseling fails to inform students of what is available to them or to enroll girls and boys with special aptitudes in the program. Finally, a language begun in elementary school may not be continued through failure to provide a coordinated program, or articulation in the language program between elementary, junior high school, and senior high school may be inadequate. These problems are being overcome, however, through the combined efforts of the profession itself, the colleges, government, foundations, and public interest.

RECENT ADVANCES

As in other subject areas, a recognition of the potential of the gifted and talented high-school student has spurred the development of special programs. Early identification, language study in the lower grades of the elementary school, and continuance through grade twelve, small classes that cut across grade lines, independent study both in the laboratory and in the library, and opportunities to hear and speak the language through foreign films are enriching school programs. Foreign travel and contact with resident foreigners, enrollment in special college courses, and encouragement to use the language in correspondence, creative writing, and other available occasions are extending the depth of language skill and competence of the talented. Better training of teachers, experimentation and research, imagination and daring, experience and exchange of information will combine in the years ahead to raise the level of our national effort and accomplishment in foreign-language instruction.

Not only the talented but all students in a foreign-language

class can benefit immeasurably from the many out-of-school opportunities available. Among these are travel, listening to foreign-language broadcasts, including short wave broadcasts from
the foreign country and direct contact between "ham" radio op-
erators, foreign films, theaters for foreign audiences, church services, choral groups, folk festivals, foreign-language story hours in
the public library, foreign restaurants, visits to foreign embas-
sies, phonograph records, and tape recordings. Student clubs
may undertake such projects as performing a foreign play or op-
era, writing and producing an original play, or organizing a
trip. Foreign newspapers, magazines, and books can easily be secured. Correspondence with pen pals in a foreign language and
exchange of records and tapes, stamps, maps, photographs, sports
and travel items, or whatever the students may be interested in
will promote realistic use of the foreign language.

There are many opportunities for correlating foreign language work with other subject areas. Social-studies classes study
the history and culture of all peoples and learn words and expressions from the language of the people being studied. Modern European history can be studied in a core curriculum combining history, language, music, art, and literature. "As a matter of fact, in many ways the foreign-language teacher is a social-
studies teacher who has specialized in the language, culture,
and civilization of a particular country."[10] There are unlimited
possibilities for combining foreign-language work with music,
art, science, physical education, history, geography, and other
subjects.

There is evidence of an increased concern about proficiency
in foreign language. Webster College in St. Louis, in a course designed for prospective teachers of Foreign Language in the Elementary Schools (FLES), provides tables in the dining room
where only a foreign language may be spoken and a special section of the dormitory is assigned to foreign-language students.
Following their junior year eighty Indiana high-school students
went to France, Mexico, or Germany during the summer of 1962
as outstanding foreign-language students under a grant from The
Carnegie Corporation to Indiana University. Films and records
made in native villages in India are being used as the basis of be-

---

[10] James P. Soffietti, "The Exploratory Study of a Foreign Language and Culture," The Modern Language Journal, XLII, No. 1: 3–7.

ginning courses in Hindi-Urdu under the auspices of the University of California. The material, linking social anthropology with linguistics, has enabled students to move on to the second year of the curriculum after twelve weeks of intensive summer study.

These innovations, coupled with improved textbooks, independent study arrangements, programmed material, better teachers, awakened public interest, and the proper use of the language laboratory, are revolutionizing the study and teaching of modern foreign languages throughout America.

The Foreign Language Laboratory

The foreign language laboratory, more than any other one thing, is responsible for upgrading the teaching of the language skills of listening comprehension and of oral communication. The rapid improvement of technical facilities in the 1940's and 1950's, coupled with the financial support of the National Defense Education Act, has resulted in the installation of language laboratories in many of our high schools.

Typically a teacher's console is connected with individual student booths so that the teacher can communicate with any one student, or with several, or with the entire class as he chooses. Students listen through earphones to records or tapes prepared by native speakers. These may be played over and over again. Often they consist of material programmed so that the student is required to respond to a question and hears the correct answer immediately thereafter. Students may record their own voices and play them back while the teacher listens and comments.

A realistic appraisal of the strengths and limitations of the modern-language laboratory is given in a United States Office of Education report:

> The following are things the language laboratory facilities can do: 1. Provide for active simultaneous participation of all students in a class in listening and listening-speaking practice in or out of class. 2. Provide a variety of authentic native voices as consistent and untiring models for student practice. 3. Provide for individual differences through guided practice in individualized group, small group, or individual study situations with facilities for student self-instruction and self-evaluation at his own learning rate.

4. Free the teacher from the tedious task of presenting repetitive drill material, thus allowing him to perform a dual role simultaneously. 5. Afford the teacher an opportunity and convenient facilities for evaluating and correcting the performance of individual students without interrupting the work of others. 6. Provide intimate contact with the language, equal learning conditions for all students, and facilities for simultaneous grouping of different activities through the use of headphones. 7. Provide a reassuring sense of privacy, reduce distractions, and encourage concentration through the use of headphones and partitions. 8. Provide facilities for group testing of the listening and speaking skills. 9. Provide for special coordination of audio and visual materials in sequential learning series or in isolated presentations. 10. Provide aid to some teachers, who for various reasons do not have adequate control of the spoken language, in improving their own audio-lingual proficiency. . . .

The language laboratory makes its greatest contribution as an integral part of a program in which audio-lingual instruction forms the basis for the progressive and continuous development of all the language skills. The language laboratory is at its weakest (1) when used as an adjunct to a traditional grammar-translation type of program, (2) when it is expected to fulfill requirements other than its basic function of helping develop and maintain the listening and speaking skills, (3) when used only for enrichment or peripheral activities, (4) when it is expected to perform the miracle of teaching the listening and speaking skills alone without the coordination and integration of classroom activities and materials, (5) when the teacher is expected to prepare all the recorded practice materials, (6) when it is used to further unsound pedagogical practices, and (7) when it allows the machine to interfere with the teacher-student rapport. But, chiefly, it is at its weakest without the humanizing influence of the teacher over the machine. . . . Superior teaching is still an art which gains much of its strength through intuitive and empirical procedures.[11,12]

[11] Joseph C. Hutchinson, *The Language Laboratory, Modern Foreign Languages in High School* (Washington, D.C.: United States Government Printing Office, 1961), pp. 8–10.

[12] For additional discussion of the role of the language laboratory see Patricia O'Connor, *Modern Foreign Languages in High School: Pre-reading Instruction,* Bulletin 1960, No. 9, U.S. Office of Education "The Classroom Teacher and the Machine: A Division of Labor" pp. 5–7. Also, *Foreign Language Laboratories in Schools and Colleges,* by Marjorie C. Johnston and Catherine C. Seerely, Bulletin 1959, No. 3, U.S. Office of Education, "Purposes of Language Laboratory" pp. 13–17.

PREPARATION OF FOREIGN LANGUAGE TEACHERS

The discussion of methods and materials in foreign-language instruction has emphasized the importance of the teacher. Without superior personnel, no program can attain its full potential. In a statement entitled "Qualifications for High School Teachers of Modern Foreign Languages," prepared under the auspices of the Modern Language Association of America and endorsed by the leading professional associations, specific criteria for a teacher of modern foreign languages are described under the headings: Aural Understanding, Speaking, Reading, Writing, Language Analysis, Culture, Professional Preparation. Under each heading there are descriptions of three levels of preparation labeled "minimal," "good," and "superior." For example, under Aural Understanding, we have:

Minimal: The ability to get the sense of what an educated native says when he is enunciating carefully and speaking simply on a general subject. *Good:* The ability to understand conversation at average tempo, lectures, and news broadcasts. *Superior:* The ability to follow closely and with ease all types of standard speech, such as rapid or group conversation, plays, and movies.[13]

The level of competence described as "good" or "minimal" under each heading is approved only as long as there is a shortage of qualified personnel. But since a minimum often tends to become the standard, only the superior qualifications will be cited here.

Speaking: The ability to approximate native speech in vocabulary, intonation, and pronunciation (for example, the ability to exchange ideas and to be at ease in social situations).

Reading: The ability to read, almost as easily as in English, material of considerable difficulty, such as essays and literary criticism.

Writing: The ability to write on a variety of subjects with idiomatic naturalness, ease of expression, and some feeling for the style of language.

Language Analysis: Ability to apply knowledge of descriptive, comparative and historical linguistics to the language-teaching situations.

Culture: An enlightened understanding of the foreign people

---

[13] *Modern Foreign Language in the High School,* pp. 163–166.

and their culture, achieved through personal contact, preferably by travel and residence abroad, through study of systematic descriptions of the foreign culture, and through study of literature and the arts.

Professional Preparation: The personal qualities which make an effective teacher; a well-balanced education, including a knowledge of our own American culture, and appropriate training in professional education, psychology and secondary-school methods, including a mastery of recognized teaching methods, and the ability to experiment with and evaluate new methods and techniques.[14]

Nothing short of a national effort along many fronts will achieve the level of language instruction described above. It will be necessary to identify talent quite early, motivate young people to prepare for language teaching, raise the status of the profession, extend scholarship aid, improve the program of teacher preparation in colleges and universities, expand and upgrade the in-service program, and enlist the active support of guidance and administrative personnel.

The goal is clear. Every child who has the talent and inclination should be given an opportunity to study at least one foreign language for an extended period of time in order to attain mastery in understanding, speaking, reading, and writing the language, as well as a familiarity with the culture and history of the foreign people. Every major language of the globe should be studied by a representative segment of the American school population.

Many wheels are now in motion to make this goal a reality. Federal, state, and foundation funds are supporting college programs—research, institutes, area studies, development of curricula and materials—foreign travel, scholarships, in-service courses, purchase of equipment and other spurs to the upgrading of language study and teaching. The modern-language teacher of the future probably will have spent a year or more in the foreign country or countries of his specialization. The vast increase in the number of Americans who will be studying and attaining mastery in foreign languages will stimulate foreign travel, student and teacher exchange, establishment of foreign-culture centers, increasing interest in foreign books and maga-

[14] *Ibid.*

zines, records, films, theater, the dance, and other cultural media of international understanding. It is to be hoped that a familiarity with the history and culture of a foreign people through the medium of its language will encourage amicable relations and foster attitudes of appreciation and amity. In any event, we must face the need for building this resource in our own culture. The schools are our only hope for success in this venture. Given an understanding and acceptance of the responsibility and the necessary public and financial support, the goals will be achieved. The high school is the necessary fulcrum of the total program. Its teachers will therefore need to perceive the problem clearly, accept the responsibility unequivocally, and extend the necessary effort toward its attainment.

FOR DELIBERATION and DISCUSSION

1. What effect may the introduction of foreign-language study in the elementary school be expected to have on the secondary-school language program?
2. Comment on the statement that ". . . the foreign-language teacher is a social-studies teacher who has specialized in the language, culture, and civilization of a particular country."
3. Speaking of our national effort in foreign-language competence, the text says: "The high school is the necessary fulcrum of the total program." Do you agree? Explain.
4. Since it is impossible for any school or even school district to teach all the foreign languages we need, what procedures can be followed to meet the national needs?
5. The shrinking globe will force us to adapt to the need for learning foreign languages. Do you agree with this statement? Explain.

FOR ADDITIONAL READING

ALDEN, DOUGLAS W. (ed.). *Materials List for Use by Teachers of Modern Foreign Languages.* New York: Modern Language Association, 1960. A basic document of annotated books, periodicals, audio-visual materials and so on, by grades for French, German, Russian, Italian, and Spanish.
HUTCHINSON, JOSEPH C. *Modern Foreign Languages in High School: The Language Laboratory,* Bulletin, No. 23, Washington, D.C.: United States Office of Education, 1961. A brief comprehensive report on rationale, equipment and operation of language laboratories. Includes glossary of laboratory terms in English and foreign languages and list of references.
JOHNSTON, MARJORIE C. (ed.). *Modern Foreign Languages in the High School.* Bulletin, No. 16. Washington, D.C.: United States

Office of Education, 1958. Report of a conference called by United States Commissioner of Education in 1957. Surveys the situation and reports recommendations.

JOHNSTON, MARJORIE C., REMER, ILO, and SIEVERS, FRANK L. *Modern Foreign Languages: A Counselor's Guide.* Bulletin, No. 20, Washington, D.C.: United States Office of Education, 1960. An excellent report on guidance aspects of school language programs. Gives foreign-language entrance and degree (B.A.) requirements for all colleges. Appendices include statistics of languages of the world and bibliography.

Modern Techniques in Teaching Foreign Languages. Annual Bulletin No. 19, New York: Educational Film Library Association, 1959. Contains thirty recent articles and reports on language laboratories and other audio-visual techniques. Includes bibliography and references.

WALSH, DONALD D. "A Dozen Do's and Don'ts for Planning and Operating a Language Lab." *Bulletin,* National Association of Secondary School Principals, 46, No. 272 (March, 1962): 120–122.

12 Art

ART IN THE HIGH-SCHOOL CURRICULUM

Objectives of the Art Program

The goals of the high-school art program have two aspects: (1) what art education does for the individual girl or boy, and (2) what the individual can or should do with his art education. From the first point of view the art program can promote mental hygiene, personality adjustment and growth, and personal integration; it may release the creative potential of the student, cultivate aesthetic appreciation, and lead to achievement and satisfaction. These varied emphases are, in a sense, part of the same general objective—the development of an integrated personality.

In art education the girl or boy, particularly the adolescent, should be allowed to work creatively to express what he sees, thinks, and feels. The product is uniquely his, always good, there to be examined, explained, approved, and admired. No two works are ever alike. Each is a challenge for other and perhaps better work. The process builds competence and self-confidence, encourages aesthetic appreciation, cultivates a sympathy for the struggle and achievement of the artist, results in identification with other creative artists, and inevitably helps build a healthy personality.

Other goals of the high-school art program are based on what the individual does with art. Here again a number of specifics may be distinguished. Art is an end in itself, a means of communication, a field of knowledge, a medium for self-expression, for the development of good taste, and for the reorganization of the environment. Art education promotes the development of the mind through sharpening the power of observation and providing challenges for problem-solving and critical thinking. The art program seeks to discover talent, to present vocational opportunities, and to develop interests and competencies for the worthy use of leisure time.

Watch a girl or boy at work on a problem in art. The extent of concentration and absorption of all his faculties marks the effect clearly as one that develops critical thinking, planning, experimenting, creating and evaluating. This is not to say that the visual arts call for little discipline. The preparation and use of materials and of the instruments of visual presentation require understanding and experience. This, too, is a lesson the student learns in art—that achievement is 90 percent perspiration and 10 percent inspiration.

Given a high standard of living such as ours and a truly effective art program in the schools, in a matter of years we could elevate public taste, produce creative artists, and develop a consciousness and predisposition to excellence in the general public so that life for all our people would be immeasurably enriched. These are the ultimate objectives of art education in the schools.

Art Offerings in the High School

Many schools still offer art as a required minor course for all freshmen. At best, this general art course gives the student an opportunity to work in several media, to get a "smattering" of information about art history and appreciation, and to discover talent which may be developed by further study. At worst, the designation of art as a minor subject tends to stigmatize it. Art has a further disadvantage because usually it is an elective and often is not credited toward college.

Guidance personnel in the high school rarely promote the fine arts program. The counselor may be unfamiliar with the fine arts offerings or even unsympathetic to the program. Thus, Ziegfeld urges that "the art teacher should be actively engaged in the counseling process," and that "persons outside the art field who are involved in counseling artistically talented students should be thoroughly familiar with the art program and with talented students."[1]

The elective art program in the American high school is so varied that it defies description. The specialized courses offered in any one school depend chiefly on the interests and competencies of the staff. Often the basic tenth-year electives include theory of line, color, composition, form and perspective, experimentation with various media and materials, and art history and appreciation. In the eleventh and twelfth years electives in drawing, painting, sculpture, and crafts (applied art) may be available. Students draw in crayon, charcoal, and pencil; do etching; paint in oil, water colors and pastel; sculpt in clay, wire, stone, wood, and metal; work with tile, leather, paper, plaster, and straw; and engage in such applied arts as ceramics, pottery, lettering, silk screen, collage, block printing, posters, illustration, colored ink, air brush, and lithograph. Other elective specialties may include textile design, decorating, furniture, and architecture. The elective art program is generally supplemented with a variety of enriching experiences. Visits to museums, field trips, artistic masterpieces, contact with artists through attendance at art shows, extensive reading, independent study and special programming of double period "studio" sessions all enhance the effectiveness of art instruction. Some teachers invite students to their own studios and permit the students to work on some project—for example, preliminary carving in sculpture work. The student who completes a three-year elective sequence in art has taken strides toward the development of a well-integrated personality and has developed a knowledge of art history, an appreciation and taste for art, competence in self-expression, and a disposition to create. Indeed, some will mature as creative artists.

Correlation of the Arts

The visual arts are akin to the other arts—music, literature, and so on—in their potential for attaining the educational objectives previously described. The art teacher must be at home in

---

[1] Edwin Ziegfeld (ed.), *Art for the Academically Talented Student in the Secondary School* (Washington, D.C.: NEA and National Art Education Association, 1961).

the other arts and be able to correlate them. For example, a good motion picture or play will give the art teacher an opportunity to discuss theme, development, form, representation, and other aspects of creative expression. Each will enhance the capacity of the student to solve problems and to express himself more effectively in the medium in which he is working.

A play, poem, piece of music, trip to the country, or movie —any aesthetic or novel experience—may provide the impetus for creation. The good art program fosters a correlation with the other arts. The art teacher who is well-read, widely traveled, a lover of music and the other arts, and adept at correlating them in his work is the most effective. While it is perhaps too much to expect a student to pursue advanced work in more than one field of art in the curriculum, the student who majors in the visual arts should be encouraged to read good literature, attend theater, dance, and the cinema, and listen with understanding to good music. Correlation among the arts will be discussed further in connection with the extra-class program.

Correlation with Other Subjects

While correlation with other arts must, in general, depend on supplementary or peripheral opportunities, there is constant opportunity for teachers of major subjects (particularly English and social studies, but also science, modern languages, and mathematics) to correlate with art. Most people who view the secondary-school curriculum objectively are in agreement that it is too academic. "Our education," says Munro, "has been on the whole too exclusively verbal, intellectual and practical. For an adequately balanced, diversified program in general education it needs more emphasis on the aesthetic and creative side."[2]

In the elementary school it is quite common for drawing, painting, sculpture, and other art work to be related directly to the work in English, social studies, or other subjects. Children's drawing or painting will often be inspired by a story in English class, an event in history, or a phenomenon in science. On the

[2] Thomas Munro, "The Interrelation of the Arts in Secondary Education," in *The Creative Arts in American Education* (Cambridge: Harvard U. Press, 1960), p. 5.

secondary level, the great value of correlated learning is often lost by the departmentalization of instruction. Teachers in one department either do not know what their colleagues are doing or feel insecure about crossing subject boundaries. The result is isolation instead of correlation. There are, fortunately, many exceptions. Teachers of English, social studies, and the other major subjects occasionally encourage and even require students to illustrate, make models and replicas, perform, and otherwise correlate their academic work with aesthetic representation. It should be noted also that there may be and often is a strong emotional appeal in literature, history, science, foreign-languages, and mathematics.

Art in the Extra-Class Program

It is in the extracurricular and cocurricular aspects of high-school work that correlation is most fully realized. For example, an operetta, variety show, Christmas, or Easter program involves selection or writing of a script, casting of characters, and direction of performance by the English and speech departments. The design and execution of costumes, scenery, furniture, and makeup are provided by the fine and industrial arts departments; orchestra, chorus, soloists and compositions by music; printing of programs and tickets, advertising, selling, decoration of hall, ushering, and so on, by business, health, or other departments. The art club, school museum, election of student officers, and various fund drives call for extracurricular art efforts which correlate with other aspects of the school program. These functional activities are self-motivating and often inspire creative effort of a high order. Creative art work is encouraged in many schools by contests culminating in exhibits and awards. Outstanding works often are included in shows where amateurs are invited to exhibit.

In almost every high school, opportunities for extracurricular art work are provided by school publications (newspapers, literary magazines, yearbooks), which rely on art majors for their illustrations and art work. Brochures, programs, announcements and other school releases also provide opportunities for the student artist. Display cases, poster contests, and similar activities are a challenge to student enterprise and ingenuity.

The Industrial Arts Program

The industrial arts occupy a position intermediate between the fine arts and vocational subjects. There is no definite dividing line, but usually the applied or industrial arts are taught in a department separate from that of the fine arts, though occasionally the two departments are united. The industrial arts may include homemaking (cooking, sewing, home management) for girls, and shop (mechanical drawing, wood, metal, glass, foundry) for boys. At the extreme such subjects as automechanics, electrical, home repairs, carpentry and so on may also be included in the industrial-arts department. (See Chapter 16.) The small classes, double periods, studio setting, activity orientation and individualized program of instruction in industrial arts offer unlimited possibilities for promoting the educational growth of the student.

THE ART TEACHER

Preparation and Certification

Usually the art teacher is educated as an artist and as an art teacher. Schools such as the Rhode Island School of Design, Parsons School of Design, Pennsylvania Academy of Art, and Yale School of Fine Arts prepare sculptors, painters, designers, engineers, architects, and art teachers. Each art teacher is qualified in performance as well as in teaching. To a lesser degree the same is true of art teachers prepared at schools like Teachers College Columbia University, Brooklyn College, Kutztown (Pa.) State Teachers College, Ohio State University, Florida State University, Michigan State University, and the University of Texas. Neither the English teacher, the social-studies teacher, nor the science teacher is expected to be as proficient in creative performance as is the art teacher.

In the classroom this requirement has both a positive and a negative effect. To the extent that the art teacher is able to demonstrate excellence in his own artistic area so that he gains the confidence and admiration of students, colleagues, and the public, he is in a better position to influence his students and to achieve the objectives of the art-education program. However, preoccupation with creative work and the tendency to assume that "art is caught, not taught" sometimes results in the teacher's failure to realize the potential of a good art-education program.

The difference between the artist and the art teacher is not inherent in the teacher's preparation, for many an artist with no preparation for teaching has shown a strong bent and often great skill in directing and fostering learning, while many trained art teachers have neglected teaching in favor of performing. Nonetheless, in recent years the certification of art teachers has followed the pattern set by other high-school subjects, so that in most states today the requirements for a certificate to teach high-school art include a college degree with a major in painting, sculpture, architecture, or applied art, and courses in the history or philosophy of education, psychology of adolescence, methods of teaching art, and ten or more weeks of supervised student teaching in a secondary school.

Placement and Advancement

There has been and is likely to continue to be a shortage of qualified art teachers for our schools at all levels. This is the result of several factors: (1) a shortage of college art programs designed to meet increasingly rigid certification requirements; (2) the rapid increase in the size of the secondary-school population; (3) a growing recognition by the public and by school authorities of the importance of art education in the total education of boys and girls; and (4) the tendency for art teachers to leave the teaching profession for more lucrative or more congenial opportunities in commercial art, self-employment, design, engineering, and other fields. Thus the certified or certifiable teacher of art will have little difficulty securing employment in a junior or senior high school or, if he has taken courses in child development and in elementary-school teaching methods (and has had some student teaching in the elementary level), as a special teacher in the elementary school.

The elementary-school specialist is not assigned to a class but works with a number of teachers and classes in giving demonstration lessons, selecting materials, organizing and motivating projects, developing curricula, evaluating children's work, and strengthening the art program of one or more classes and/or schools. The art teacher in the secondary school is a classroom teacher who probably meets a home room, teaches a number of classes (often different aspects of art and different types of students), gives tests, enters grades, proctors school examinations, patrols halls, polices the lunch room or study hall—in short, assumes the same obligations in the school as do his colleagues in other departments. The good teacher is willing to accept these assignments because the program gives him an opportunity to work with adolescents in what is to him the most inspiring field of all—art education.

In the small school system the classroom teacher may in time aspire to the position of coordinator or department head. Often this means a small increase in salary, reduction of the teaching load, and an addition of supervisory and administrative responsibility. In the larger school system the department head may have a sufficiently large responsibility to be a non-teaching professional whose work entails leadership in curriculum and instruction. The very large school system is likely to have a director (or even an assistant director) of art education. Of course, the classroom teacher of art is not prevented from seeking an administrative position as principal, assistant superintendent or superintndent, and many art teachers throughout the country have found their professional bent to be in this direction.

Status and Working Conditions

The art teacher's status is an anomaly. Often he is looked on as the embodiment of special native talent enhanced by uncommon training and experience—a maverick, a radical or at least a non-conformist. Or he may be looked on as a teacher of a minor (dispensable) subject which is included in the curriculum as a concession to the public conscience, but which should not be elected by the more able students lest it interfere with their academic careers. There is also the notion that the art teacher, more than his colleagues, would find employment practicing his art if he really had talent. Of course, the individual teacher, in his manner and attitude, will establish his own status among his colleagues. If he has self-esteem based on substantial achievement in his work, he will receive the recognition he deserves.

In most schools the secondary-school art teacher wll teach five classes each day, have a home room, and supervise a lunch room or study hall. His starting salary wll be similar to that of teachers in other departments. There will be yearly increments, tenure after three years of satisfactory service, pension, sick leave, vacations, sabbatical leaves, advancement, and other professional opportunities similar to those in other subject areas. The art teacher, again like his colleagues, will often seek after-school, weekend and/or summer employment, either as a supplement to his income or as an outlet for his energy and talent. If he is fortunate, he will be able to engage in creative work in art.

Other art teachers teach in private schools, in public summer schools, at camps or in their own studios. Many paint homes, finish basements, frame pictures, or do other work (lettering, card designs, sign painting, and so on). However, a background in art often leads to opportunities for work as museum curators, advertising illustrators, interior decorators, designers, creators of fashions, art buyers or dealers, architect or engineer. In short, the vista of the trained art teacher opens on many opportunities outside the immediate field of teaching for creative use of leisure time or exciting and remunerative avocations.

Opportunities and Responsibilities

Art as a subject area offers unlimited opportunities for influencing adolescents. In art classes the teachers and students work in an atmosphere of relative freedom, personal intimacy, and potentially high creativity. Almost every child has natural curiosity, an eagerness to explore and experiment, and a high degree of imaginativeness and creative potential. The sensitive art teacher is in a unique position to encourage originality, freedom of expression, and creativity. Operating on the assumption that he is helper, not censor, he will accept the student, appreciate his product, and encourage his efforts. He will broaden his student's horizons by exposing him to excellence in artistic achievements through books, displays, demonstrations, trips, films, and visits to studios and museums. By encouraging the student, he fosters creativity and aids immeasurably in building self-esteem and adjustment. By permitting the student to express his emotions and to explore his own interests, he promotes integration and mental health.

The art teacher may make healthy in-roads into a dark area that touches the adolescent most profoundly. Munro has this to say about art and sex:

> It is also obvious that one of the main distinctive characteristics of adolescence is the development of sexuality. . . . Adolescent sex interests, both masculine and feminine can be expressed in almost any art. Teen-age students are especially attracted—and perhaps disturbed, if their home environment has been puritanical—by art which suggests erotic images and impulses. . . . Art of this sort is, of course, mostly avoided in schools. Instead, the secondary school student is given a rather tame and pallid diet of respectable, often tedious, classics and studio exercises devoid of any erotic suggestiveness such as painting still lifes or abstract designs. . . . There is no level in our educational process on which the content of formal education diverges as widely from the normal interests of students as it does on the secondary level. . . . The result of ignoring sex in high school art is not only to lose a potential source of interest in art studies, but to lose the recognized values of great art in refining and harmonizing the sexual impulses and attitudes. . . . The school evades the delicate responsibility of guiding adolescents through these difficult situations.[3]

It is not implied that art is the only subject suited to help the adolescent gain understanding about problems of sex. The suggestion is that art education offers an excellent opportunity for giving students some help in this area and that the opportunity is often unnecessarily lost in current practice.

Finally, the art teacher opens direct channels to vocational opportunity for his students through building special competencies, developing marketable skills, informing students of needs in the world of commerce and industry (perhaps placing them in direct contact with vocational opportunities), and counseling further study in the community college, college, or university.

As a Colleague

The art teacher is a resource person to his colleagues in a variety of situations. Generally he sets the pace in style of dress, particularly if he specializes in commercial illustrating, window dressing, fashion design, or related areas. He will be consulted in the art education of his colleagues and of their children. His ad-

[3] Munro, pp. 26–29.

vice also will be sought in art purchases and home decorating. He may be commissioned by a colleague to do a portrait, paint a scene, sculpt a statue, bas-relief or lamp base, or do a work in ceramics or other craft in which he may be considered expert. Should he be known to have a collection of paintings he may be asked to exhibit or to have a showing. Such questions as what art galleries to visit, art shows to see, art books and magazines to purchase and art works in which to invest are among those his colleagues will feel free to ask. Much as a spiritual adviser is at the call of his congregation, so the art teacher is the guide of the staff in matters pertaining to the arts.

As a Faculty Member

Related to the above but in a somewhat different category are the duties of the art teacher as a faculty member. He is expected to sponsor extra-class activities (such as the art club), act as art adviser to one of the school publications, help decorate the school—library, lounges, offices, and corridors—and plan museum trips and visits. When the school program is well-integrated he may work closely with teachers of music, literature, history, or other subjects on common projects. He may be curator of a small school art museum, a member of the principal's council on school purchases, or chairman of a faculty committee in an area of his special competence. In short, the art teacher's special talents will find outlet in and be utilized through many aspects of creative work in the school.

In the Community

Particularly in a small community (under 25,000) the high-school art teacher may be an important public figure. He will be called on to judge art contests, to serve on the board of amateur or even professional art groups, to help found a community museum and contribute to it, to display his work in exhibits or in a one-man show, to serve as art consultant to the town or city government, and to teach adult classes either at the high school or privately.

The high-school art teacher is clearly an important factor in the education of students, colleagues, and community. His responsibilities as well as his opportunities for making a significant contribution in the lives of many people—encouraging creativity, building competence, upgrading taste and appreciation, and fostering the development of wholesome personality—are therefore incalculable.

FOR DELIBERATION and DISCUSSION

1. What conflict arises in programming a high-school student who is talented both academically and in art? How can this conflict be resolved?
2. Give reasons, pro and con, for uniting the fine arts and the industrial arts in one department. What is your own position? Why?
3. Comment on the quotation from Munro (p. 222). To what extent is this challenge being met in high-school practice? What more might be done?
4. "The art teacher in the United States works under a severe handicap because our culture gives a low priority to art." Comment on this statement, showing if possible, the rationale for the opposite point of view.
5. To what extent is the caliber of a high-school art program influenced by conditions in the school? In the community? What can a teacher do to overcome obstacles and strengthen the program?

FOR ADDITIONAL READING

BROUDY, HARRY S. "Aesthetic Education in a Technological Society." Ithaca: Cornell U. School of Education, 1962. (Lecture delivered on May 17, 1962.) Philosophical consideration of art in our culture.

CONANT, HOWARD and RANDALL, ARNE. *Art in Education*. Peoria: Charles A. Bennett, 1959. A factual discussion for the prospective art teacher. Includes teacher preparation, curriculum, agencies for exceptional children and similar data.
Educational Leadership. Published monthly October through May by Association for Supervision and Curriculum Development. Each issue concentrates on a theme—for example, Vol. 19, No. 7 (April, 1962) focuses on "Arts in the School."

JEFFERSON, BLANCHE. *Teaching Art to Children: The Values of Creative Expression*. Boston: Allyn and Bacon, 1959. Excellent for theory and practice in art, continual emphasis on freedom and creativity. 120 illustrations of children's work.

NATIONAL ASSOCIATION OF SECONDARY SCHOOL PRINCIPALS. *The Arts in the Comprehensive Secondary School*. Washington, D.C.: The Association, 1962. Reprinted from *The Bulletin* (September 1962) of the Association. A succinct statement of goals and their implementation in secondary-school practice.

ZIEGFELD, EDWIN (ed.). *Art for the Academically Talented Student in the Secondary School.* Washington, D.C.: NEA and National Art Education Association, 1961. (Part of the NEA projects on the Academically Talented Student.) Part I discusses the high-school program in general. Part II describes programs for the gifted in Houston (Texas), Pittsburgh (Pa.), and Hillsdale (N.J.).

13 Music

MUSIC IN THE HIGH-SCHOOL CURRICULUM

Music, another of the so-called minor subjects, can have major importance in the lives of many students. Among values of the music program are the aesthetic satisfaction of listening, learning, doing, and creating; the social contact in orchestra, band, and chorus; the personal satisfaction of accomplishment; the opportunity to serve the school and to gain recognition. As each student is exposed to a variety of musical opportunities, he discovers his potential for enjoyment, for talent, and possibly for a vocation.

Typically the high-school curriculum includes one year of music required for all and a series of electives. The general course may meet only one or two periods a week, though the more favorable practice is to meet four, or preferably five, times a week for one semester rather than two periods a week for a year. This gives the subject the same status as other courses and gives teacher and students an opportunity to get to know each other and to pursue an organized program. This program may include listening to music, playing, singing, individual and group work, projects, and any other undertakings that teacher and class find appropriate and interesting.

Usually the electives in vocal music concentrate on boys' and girls' glee clubs, mixed chorus, choir, solo work, vocal ensembles, and voice classes. The electives in instrumental music usually include instruction in specific instruments and playing in chamber groups, band, small ensembles and orchestra. In large schools it is possible and advisable to have a beginning and an advanced group in both band and orchestra. Additional electives may be offered in music theory, composition, appreciation, history, conducting, or any other areas for which the staff has special competence or for which there is a demand.

In addition to the advantages enumerated above, the high-school music program is important as a force for stabilizing and harmonizing the personality of the adolescent.[1] A varied music program is also a means of reaching the handicapped student and helping him make the most of his abilities. Music affords each student the opportunity to be integrated in the work of the group and to have his contribution accepted and valued, regardless of how meager it may be. The appreciation of his efforts fosters self-confidence, mental and emotional well-being, and improved performance.

MUSIC FOR GIFTED CHILDREN

While it is not too late to start special music programs in the secondary school, it is fortunate that many forces—elementary and junior high schools, music foundations, and mass media—are at work to promote early discovery and development of musical talent. The music teacher has a responsibility for identifying special talents in his pupils. An examination of each student's record, conferences with other teachers, with administrative and guidance personnel, with the student and with his parents, and finally administering a good music-aptitude test, such as the Drake Test of Musical Talent, should disclose information that will help the teacher discover musical talent in his students. Then it is the responsibility of the teacher to inform the student and his parents of the facts and to see that the student gets every opportunity to develop his potential. The piano and violin require years of application before a fair degree of technical skill can be achieved. In some elementary and junior high schools and in private homes young children are receiving instruction and encouragement which brings them to the high school in an advanced state of musicianship. Summer schools, camps, clinics, and private studios are all working toward extending and expanding music education for all, but especially

[1] See Paul R. Farnsworth, "The Present Status of Music Therapy," *The Social Psychology of Music* (New York: Dryden, 1958), pp. 258–259.

for those children whose talents show great promise. Increasingly, summer schools are cooperating with colleges to develop programs for musically talented high school girls and boys. The gains not only in musical attainment but in social and emotional growth are incalculable.

CLASSROOM INSTRUCTION

Music instruction may be enriched by a variety of supplementary materials and procedures. It is impossible to do more than mention a number of these in this discussion. The audio-visual facilities of the school, the instructional program in other subjects, the cultural life of the community, and mass media may all be used effectively to supplement and support the high-school music class. Student scrapbooks, charts, and bulletin boards; magazines, such as *Metronome,* and books; special aids, such as music maps, the Magne Music Board, flash cards, and charts of keyboard or music terms; listening rooms with a library, phonographs, and tapes; educational radio, closed-circuit television, films, and filmstrips; display cases, posters, and overhead opaque projectors are some of the materials and devices available to the classroom music teacher to vary and enrich instruction.

Correlation

There are virtually unlimited opportunities for correlating instruction in music with other curriculum areas. For example, since musical composition is a function of the culture in which the composer lives, a definite relationship between social studies and music can be demonstrated. The biography of a composer or performer, fictionalized or factual, can give a picture of the age and place in which he lived. Music may be used to illustrate an event or period—for example, the *1812 Overture* by Tchaikowsky.

Social studies and humanities today include units called intellectual history, in which there is a study of the great writers, artists, scientists, musicians and other contributors to cultural life. The social studies and music classes can cooperate closely and effective correlation may be worked out by reading, listening to and studying music, and by writing, composing, and dramatizing.

English classes will find common ground with music in reading, listening, creative writing, dramatization, and aesthetic criticism. Foreign-language classes are uniquely related to music, since many of our great composers and performing artists are of foreign origin. In fact, correlating the work of foreign-language classes with music is virtually a necessity. The affinity of music and mathematics is a relationship well known at least since the time of J. S. Bach.

The effectiveness of each of the arts—the visual, industrial, theatre, literature, and dance—is enhanced by correlation with the others. Sculpture and painting of musicians, musical instruments and musical subjects, music drama and dance, musical accompaniment to films and program music, are all examples of correlating music with the other arts.

The music teacher is interested in awakening music appreciation in his students, fostering their growth, and realizing the emotional potential of his subject. Proficiency in technical aspects is the least of his concerns. Hence his approach is informal, and he should come to his class with no rigidly preconceived idea of what the students must absolutely accomplish during that period in listening and appreciation.

THE EXTRACURRICULAR PROGRAM

In music, more than in any other high-school subject, the class program and the extra-class program are united. While some schools still have music clubs which meet after school on a voluntary basis, most music activities meet as regular classes. After-school rehearsals and performances are, therefore, extensions of class work. Thus, while the work of other subjects is confined to the classroom or to homework, the music class continues to function as a group in after-school activities. There is great value in this situation. The adolescent is part of a social group in orchestra, band, or chorus. Much of the work of the special music class culminates in performances. The marching band at the Saturday football game, the jazz band at the Friday evening "stag and hag," the symphony and chorus at the annual concert, the vocal and instrumental groups on the local radio, the student operetta in the school auditorium before a capacity audience of parents and friends, the orchestra's performance in the assembly, and the semi-professional youth orchestra are all part of the regular high-school music program. These public performances are applauded by age-mates, parents, teachers, and community.

THE MUSIC TEACHER

The high-school music teacher is required to meet the same standards of academic and professional preparation as his colleagues in other departments. Because of the degree of musical expertness required, however, his preparation tends to be more rigorous. In addition to a broad liberal education and professional courses, the music teacher is required to demonstrate proficiency in sight reading, piano playing, score reading and conducting, music theory, vocal and choral techniques, and a basic knowledge of orchestral and band instruments and instrumentation. He is also expected to specialize in either vocal or instrumental music. The former requires extensive knowledge and competence in selection and training of voices, reading of vocal scores, training and conducting chorus, choir, and vocal ensemble, knowledge of the history and literature of choral works, and considerable competence in vocal performance. The teacher who specializes in instrumental music is required to be sufficiently competent on most instruments to teach beginners, to have the ability to organize band and orchestra, to read scores, to conduct, and to transpose. A knowledge of the history of orchestral music, familiarity with the literature, including current and contemporary developments, and competence on the piano and on one or more standard instruments are among the requirements for certification in music.[2]

The high caliber and sound preparation of high-school music teachers during the past quarter-century has elevated music education to its proper place as an integral part of the high-school curriculum. Educators have come to recognize the great values inherent in music education and have begun to expect expert preparation of music teachers.

Responsibilities of the Music Teacher

The effective music teacher, as we have seen, must have a sound cultural background in all liberal studies if he is to be effective as a teacher of his own subject. His contribution will

[2] For a more detailed discussion see William R. Sur and Charles F. Shuller, *Music Education for Teen-Agers* (New York: Harper, 1959), pp. 265–284.

be measured by many criteria—his concern with the welfare of the individual student, his willingness to give of himself, his skill and competence in working with colleagues and administrators, his participation in professional activities, his contact with professional musicians and music activities, and finally his contribution to the advancement of music in his own community.

These activities should not be looked on as additional burdens. While they represent an expenditure of time and energy, they are a source of gratification to the true professional teacher of music. Membership in the Music Educators National Conference (MENC), the Department of Music of the NEA, attendance at conferences, and occasional participation in panels, research projects, and reports are duties which each owes the profession. Within the school, helping a student teacher, serving on school committees, sponsoring extra-class activities, and working with problem students are sources of personal and professional growth. Of course, each teacher's opportunities will depend on the school and community in which he finds himself. In very small schools a music teacher may be the only special teacher on the staff. In a large system he may be only one of a hierarchy of music specialists headed by a city director with several assistants. The former may be hard pressed to rescue from oblivion a musically gifted child and to give each of his students some experience with the possibilities of music for recreation and enjoyment. The latter may find ample opportunity for introducing an elective course into the curriculum, for working with gifted underprivileged children, or for organizing a school or community project. The teacher's own concept of his function in the total scheme of education will open possibilities for service and for achievement.

A feature story by Beatrice Z. Heddericg in the February 10, 1962 issue of *Mark* magazine (Southern New England) opens as follows:

> Walk into Stamford High School any Tuesday evening from about 7:15 on! Don't bother to ask how to get to the small auditorium where the Youth Orchestra is rehearsing. Just listen a moment! You'll hear the unmistakable rhythm of Mozart, the sweeping, soaring strains of Wagner or the intricate counterpoint of a Handel fugue, and your ear will lead you directly to the Schubert Club Youth Orchestra.

Through the high-school music program, school and community are united in common undertakings for the welfare of both students and adults. Thus, the high-school music teacher is in a key position to make an impact on the life of the community.

ADMINISTRATION OF THE MUSIC PROGRAM

In a small school district which employs only one music teacher, responsibility for teaching and administration of the music program will be combined. In larger systems the administrative function is more divorced from teaching. Even in the largest system with a director of music and one or more assistant directors, the classroom teacher will have administrative functions. He will, of course, be responsible for the details of classroom management, seating pupils, collecting information, administering aptitude and achievement tests, keeping records, distributing and collecting books, materials, and instruments, and allocating resources. The music teacher often is consulted by the school administration in determining curricular offerings, scheduling classes, processing student applicants for advanced courses, and allocating space.

Another function of the music teacher is the care and repair of musical instruments and materials. Public performances involving admission charges raise the problem of management of finances. The teacher whose effort makes possible a successful fund-raising concert has a right to an accurate accounting of income and expenditure entailed by the affair. If he is equally skillful in human relations, the music teacher should be able to get a substantial share of the income from such performances allocated for the purchase or repair of musical instruments and equipment, and the establishment of music scholarships or other benefits related to music education.

The music teacher should be prepared to make suggestions to the school administration for budgetary provisions, including audio-visual equipment, instruments, books and magazines, teaching aids, attendance at professional meetings, and repair and replacement of equipment.

Finally, the teacher may be consulted in questions involving school architecture. These will arise when modernization of an old building is in prospect, when a wing or other addition to an existing structure is being contemplated, or when a new building is being planned. Proper placement of music rooms, size, shape, acoustics, equipment, practice and listening rooms, teacher's office, storage rooms, library, proximity to auditorium, and similar factors are of great importance in the effective conduct of a music program.

The alert music teacher will be devoted to his students, to mastery of his subject, and to the world of art and of ideas in all times and places. Yet the everyday needs of working with colleagues and administrators, the importance of contact with the community, and demands of administrative know-how will not be lost on him. For the success of his work with students will depend in no small measure on an awareness and competence in these other aspects of his work. No high school can afford to be without a substantial music program. The good high schools seek competent professional music personnel and actively support their efforts to develop a superior music program.

FOR DELIBERATION and DISCUSSION

1. "There are virtually unlimited opportunities for correlating instruction in music with other curricular areas." Support this statement with appropriate specific illustrations.
2. Describe the music education of the average high-school student. Evaluate this program and make appropriate recommendations.
3. A dynamic secondary-school music program has many points of contact with the community. Illustrate.
4. A deep love of music may constitute a liability as well as an asset in teaching music in a secondary school. To what extent may this be true?
5. What part may each of the following play in the school music program: the library, audio-visual equipment, budgetary considerations?

FOR ADDITIONAL READING

FARNSWORTH, PAUL R. *The Social Psychology of Music.* New York: Dryden, 1958. A scholarly, readable book on topics that bridge music and psychology including language aspects of music, the nature (and the measures) of musical taste, the nature (and the measurements) of musical abilities, application of music to therapy and industry.

HENRY, NELSON B. (ed.). *Basic Concepts in Music Education,* Chicago: U. of Chicago Press, 1958, Part I. Fifty-seventh Yearbook of the National Society for the Study of Education. A series of papers by authorities. A comprehensive survey of music education, its foundations, and its practice in school curriculum and instruction.

Journal of Research in Music Education, VIII, No. 1 (Spring 1959). Published semi-annually by The Music Education National Conference, this issue is devoted to "Music Education Materials: A Selected Bibliography."

MURSELL, JAMES L. *Music and the Classroom Teacher.* New York: Silver Burdett, 1951. An elementary survey by a nationally recognized authority.

SUR, WILLIAM R. and SHULLER, CHARLES F. *Music Education for Teenagers.* New York: Harper, 1958. Includes a sixty-page appendix of instructional materials and sources. A comprehensive treatment of all phases of music in the junior and senior high school. Chapters on the music teacher, school music and community, administration, audio and visual.

14 Health and Physical Education

THE HIGH-SCHOOL PROGRAM

Objectives

The general aims of high-school health and physical education are similar to, if not identical with, those of other subjects— that is, promoting the growth and development of the individual in harmony with the ideals and practices of American democratic society. A Cincinnati curriculum bulletin makes the observation that "the word *health,* itself, implies an integration, embracing as it does physical, intellectual, emotional, moral and social aspects of development."[1]

The physical aims of the program include development of physical vigor, neuro-muscular coordination, strength, agility, balance, endurance and skills in rhythm and sports. Subsidiary aims are the ability to resist fatigue, increase of cardiovascular efficiency, improved reaction time, and development of form. The intellectual aim is to impart knowledge about human physiology and hygiene, disease, safety, and nutrition, and to develop the strategy and tactics involved in games and in tests of grace, strength, endurance, and physical skill. Opportunities for imagination, initiative, and resourcefulness in solving problems are presented. The mental-health aspects of the physical-

---

[1] *Physical Education, Course of Study, Grades 9–12* (Cincinnati: Cincinnati Board of Education, Curriculum Bulletin 215, 1952), p. 3.

education program constitute the basis of the emotional aim. A dynamic program of exercise, games, sports, and recreational activities has a great impact on the emotional health of adolescents.

The moral aim pervades much of the program.

> Character education is not the special province of any department. The play life of the child has always been considered a powerful moral force, and physical education offers countless opportunities for the practice of civic and moral virtues. Working with others, leading, following, taking turns, playing fairly, winning graciously, losing generously, behaving courteously, are but a few of the concomitant activities that physical education emphasizes to contribute to the development of boys and girls.[2]

Finally, physical education has a social aim. The ideals of sportsmanship, teamwork, cooperation, and the responsibilities of leadership and followership are developed in organized group games and sports. Students are assisted in developing self-confidence, sociability, and a feeling of belonging. Recreational habits requiring physical activity are developed by exposing students to a wide variety of activities, by increasing their knowledge about these activities, and by building attitudes of enjoyment and appreciation in connection with physical activities.

Health and Safety

Most high-school curricula provide a combination of physical activity and academic study for each level. Typically the subject is divided into six areas: mental health, physical health, appearance, diseases, medical information, and safety. Mental health includes such topics as mental disorders, behavior, and relations between the sexes. Under physical fitness the student learns elements of nutrition and diet, care of teeth and eyes, and so on. Appearance information includes a study of skin, nails, hair, posture, and clothing. General health information about such topics as communicable diseases, constitutional diseases, narcotics, tobacco, and alcohol, misleading advertising and self-medication, and over-exposure to radiation are usually provided in the health curriculum (and occasionally in science and social studies). Discussion of the work of local, national, and international agencies, and obtaining medical services often is included

[2] *Ibid.*, p. 3.

under the same topic. Safety and first aid, including prevention of automobile accidents, safety at home, in school, at work, and in recreation are usually required units of study.

Some high schools offer health and safety in a single course, often called *hygiene*. Others combine the hygiene part of the course with the health and physical-education program on a one-day-a-week basis. Still others integrate it in other ways.

Physical Education

The high-school program in physical education may be divided into class, intramural, extramural and interscholastic activities. It is recommended that each girl and boy in grades 9–12 spend one standard class period each day in physical education under instruction by a qualified teacher in classes not exceeding thirty-five students. Adequate facilities include a gymnasium, dressing rooms, swimming pool, showers, toilets, and both outdoor and indoor facilities. Classroom instruction includes physical fitness on an individualized basis, group and individual sports and games, rhythmic and apparatus activities, tumbling and stunts, swimming, track and field, and physical testing.

The intramural program provides informal tournaments, games, and contests in which boys and girls are pitted against their equals within the school. Sports, such as golf, tennis, and volleyball offer opportunities for co-educational social experience. Usually the extramural program is primarily for girls and includes field hockey, volleyball, softball, informal field days, and weekend camping. The latter may be planned by several schools together and may include instruction in conservation, safety, aquatics, and outdoor living.

Usually, the interscholastic program provides opportunity for highly skilled boys to compete under careful supervision in individual and team sports—football, basketball, track and field, swimming, baseball, tennis, and so on. The intense rivalries that develop in football and basketball, the pressure to win, the disproportionate amount of time spent in training, the financial aspects of interscholastic sports, and other tangential but concomitant problems have given rise to serious questions about the overall educational merit of these sports. They are, of course, an indigenous aspect of American secondary education. Wise administration will seek to maximize the attainment of desirable goals through the interscholastic program and to minimize the evils.

The Curriculum

Physical Fitness.   The Presidents' Council on Youth Fitness makes the following recommendations:

> 1. Pupils who have a low level of muscular strength, agility, and flexibility should be identified by a screening test as part of the health appraisal. Pupils so identified should be required to participate in a program of developmental exercises and activities designed to raise their physical performance to desirable levels. 2. Objective valid tests of physical achievement should be used to determine pupil status, measure progress, and motivate pupils to achieve increasingly higher levels of physical fitness. 3. At least fifteen minutes of vigorous exercises and developmental activities should be included in the daily physical education period. 4. While giving priority to the three basic recommendations above, the school should strive to provide a comprehensive program of health education and physical education for all pupils.[3]

Elements of a physical-fitness program include body measurement, body conditioning exercises and figure control, posture corrective exercises, apparatus, tumbling, and stunts. There is disagreement as to the physical value of the latter; many experts maintain that tumbling and stunts contribute little to physical fitness and constitute hazardous activity for most high-school girls and boys.

Rhythmic Activities.   These include rhythms, beginning and advanced folk, square, and social dancing, modern creative dance, character dancing, and clog and tap dancing. It is often possible to plan folk, square, and social dancing as co-educational activities. The development of poise and social graces may contribute to the greater success of the Friday or Saturday night dances in the school gymnasium and to the end-of-year school proms.

Sports and Games.   These include individual, dual, and team games. The elements of a sport should be taught in the physical-education class before intramural competition is attempted. The

---

[3] *Youth Physical Fitness: Suggested Elements of a School-Centered Program* (Concepts and Foundations: President's Council on Youth Fitness, Washington, D.C.: United States Government Printing Office, 1961), Part I.

program can be developed on a continuous basis, according to teacher competencies, student interests, local mores, and seasonal conditions. For example, basketball, handball, and table tennis may be taught in the winter, while tennis, golf, or archery should be planned for the late spring.

It is important to plan the program so that boys and girls do not find themselves learning the elements of volleyball in grade 10, again in grade 11, and again in grade 12. This often happens in schools where physical education is programmed last and where students are fitted into classes regardless of grade. Under such conditions it is impossible for a department to plan a continuous and sequential program for students from grades 9 through 12.

A good, varied program of games, sports, and athletics will include individual activities, such as archery, golf, track and field events, and bowling; dual activities, such as tennis, badminton, wrestling, and fencing; and team games, such as basketball, hockey and softball. Provision should be made for each student to participate in swimming, water safety, diving, boating, canoeing, and sailing. Where possible this should be extended in camping and outdoor activities to include hiking, cook-outs, cycling, horseback riding, skating, and skiing.

Adapted Physical Education.   The handicapped include the blind or those with partial sight, the deaf or hard of hearing, those with crippling defects, those in poor health, the epileptic, and the mentally retarded. A good physical education program makes every effort to provide for the integration of the handicapped into the regular program insofar as possible. Since their need is greater, a good program may yield worthwhile results for the handicapped, including improved physical functioning, psychological adjustment, social adjustment, acquisition of sports skills, greater self-confidence, and increased security.[4] The physical education staff, in coordination with a physician, should be in a position to provide a complete range of services of physical education for each student.

Limited Facilities.   When a school has limited or no facilities, physical education teachers may:

1. Conduct classroom discussions of physical-education goals,

[4] Arthur S. Daniels, *Adapted Physical Education* (New York: Harper, 1954).

pupil self-evaluation; use audio-visual aids in teaching the rules and team play of various sports to help both boys and girls be intelligent participants in and spectators of our sports.

2. Use modified physical-fitness and motor-ability tests in classrooms (movable furniture and mats are a necessity).
3. Develop a strong physical-fitness exercise program.
4. Teach the dance: square, folk, social, creative, modern.
5. Teach social, party, and recreational games.
6. Prepare students for recreational leadership with children on playgrounds, beaches, and so on.
7. Use basement, hallways, and stages for teaching such activities as shuffleboard and table tennis (portable equipment).
8. Plan programs of outdoor activities for the school or parks.
9. Plan for camping exercises, skiing weekends, and similar outdoor activities.
10. Use community pools, bowling alleys, and recreation buildings.[5]

CORRELATION WITH OTHER AREAS OF THE CURRICULUM

The high-school health and physical-education program correlates with many other areas of the curriculum, especially science, social studies, the arts, and guidance. The health program is so closely related to biology that there should be close cooperation and possibly joint effort in organizing the courses. Elements of science are included also in safety, camping, and apparatus work.

Correlation with social studies is even more extensive. Games and sports, dancing, social-recreational activities (picnicking, social activities of the girls' athletic association, skating parties, mixed sports activities), camping, and other outdoor activities include elements of social education. Planning, leadership, group participation, team play, experimentation, evaluation, and self-reliance are among the qualities developed both in physical education and in social studies.

[5] This dynamic approach is proposed in *Physical Education Grades 7–12*, Hartford: Connecticut State Department of Education, Curriculum Bulletin Series No. XI, 1958. It is, of course, not to be regarded as a substitute for a program based on adequate facilities.

Home economics and other phases of industrial arts are related to health and physical education. Activities in home economics and in industrial arts may reinforce units in the health and safety programs. School pageants, operettas, or displays involve dance, dramatics, languages and other areas of a school's work. The department of health and physical education is in a particularly strategic position for guidance work. In the gymnasium and the swimming pool, during physical examinations, and in recreational activities and sports, the teacher is in close contact with his students, and the opportunities for guidance are numerous. A teacher who relates well to adolescent boys and girls will be consulted about personal health, dress, studies, and vocations. The opportunities and the responsibilities are great. The teachers of health and physical education should be particularly sensitive to student needs and problems and should make themselves available to the boy or girl in need.

The identification and development of leadership qualities has long been a phase of the high-school physical-education program. Student leaders play an important part in the program itself. The students should participate in the selection of their own leaders in accordance with well-defined criteria, including performance in a variety of activities. The boys' leaders club and the girls' athletic association, where a small percentage of outstanding boys and girls are selected to assist in the conduct and administration of the instructional program, serve in many ways to make the school program more effective. From an educational point of view, the fundamental value of the leaders' programs are in fostering democratic qualities of leadership—initiative, concern for others, resourcefulness, and so on.

PHYSICAL EDUCATION TEACHERS

The teacher of physical education is required to hold an undergraduate degree, and in many states, to complete a fifth year of preparation. His preparation lies in three major areas: liberal studies, general professional education, and specialized professional education. The last two include physical activities, program planning and development, administration, specialized science work, and study in health, safety, and recreation. Since the physical educator often teaches a wide variety of activities, he must develop competence in team games, individual and dual sports, dance and rhythmic activities, gymnastics, conditioning activities, swimming and water sports, body dynamics, and corrective and adaptive activities.[6] The professional association of health-education teachers is the American Association for Health, Physical Education, and Recreation, an affiliate of the NEA.

On the job the teacher will be expected to serve in many capacities in and out of the classroom and the school. About 90 percent of male physical-education teachers coach at least one interscholastic sport. In general the teacher is expected to perform many of the following services: improving community health, giving first aid, administering and grading tests, keeping records, officiating at games, conducting intramural contests, staging and publicizing exhibitions, prescribing exercises, promoting recreation among the faculty and in the community, directing athletic associations, managing finances, preparing budgets, purchasing equipment, and organizing health and safety campaigns. The primary responsibility for the instructional program includes teaching classes, guidance, and arranging indoor and outdoor games, dances, and recreational events.

His colleagues look on the teacher of physical education as a valuable source of information and will ask his advice about camping trips, schools and camps for children, athletic equipment, tickets for games, health and recreational associations, and so on. It is obvious that a well-qualified physical education teacher can make an outstanding contribution to the students, faculty, and community in fitness, health, safety, and recreation.

EVALUATION

Although a successful school program can be measured only by its long-term results, it is essential that day-to-day physical-education progress be measured through the medium of valid testing. Did each student develop habits of vigorous exercises and play, a zest for participation in individual and group games, and competence in leadership and followership? Has the student attained worthwhile knowledge, skills, and attitudes about mental and physical health, safety habits, good practices in nutrition, insight into self, and wholesome direc-

[6] Clyde Knapp and Ann S. Jewett, *Physical Education: Student and Beginning Teacher.* (New York: McGraw-Hill, 1957).

tion toward self-realization? To these and many other facets of an adolescent's growth, the school's program in health and physical education should make a major contribution.

Trends

Most pronounced of the recent trends in physical education is the broader preparation and the wide variety of competencies expected of the teacher. Today's teacher of health and physical education is expected to be a cultured person with a strong background in science and social studies.

Although attempts to de-emphasize interscholastic competition thus far has received little more than lip service, there is a strong tendency to emphasize individual or dual recreational sports such as tennis, golf, swimming, table tennis, fencing, and casting. Along with this has come a trend toward better facilities and equipment. New buildings and equipment make extensive provision for fitness, health and safety programs, and for games and sports. Maintenance of accurate health records, referral to physicians, nurses, and psychologists, recognition of the importance of adapted physical education, emphasis on safety and prevention, instruction in home, family, and social relationships, and correlation with other studies are all aspects of the modern program.

The concern of the entire physical and health-education program is the development of habits and attitudes that will continue throughout life and make healthy and happy citizens. The school is only one agency in a complex society, but the influence of a good physical-education program can be felt in improving the life of the community in its attack on disease, its concern with physical fitness and with mental and physical health, in habits and recreation, and in worthy use of leisure time.

FOR DELIBERATION and DISCUSSION

1. "Large group instruction is no more appropriate in physical education than it is in any other high-school subject." What is your evaluation of this statement?
2. Compare the health- and physical-education program appropriate to an urban high school with that designed for a rural high school. Which aspects are common to both? Which require different emphases?

3. "The physical-education curriculum presents many opportunities for the development of critical thinking." Give illustrations to support this statement.
4. The teacher of physical education enjoys unique opportunities for influencing the character development of his students. Explain.
5. How is the curriculum in health and physical education related to outdoor education programs which are gaining momentum in Michigan, Texas, California, and elsewhere?

FOR ADDITIONAL READING

DANIELS, ARTHUR S. *Adapted Physical Education.* New York: Harper, 1954. Comprehensive treatment of all aspects of physical education for the handicapped.

FAIT, HOLLIS F. *Health and Fitness for Modern Living.* Boston: Allyn and Bacon, 1961. A good modern high-school textbook illustrating the program in effect in many secondary schools.

HUNSICKER, PAUL. *Physical Fitness.* Washington, D.C.: NEA, 1963. Summarizes recent literature, and suggests areas for research. Also lists seventeen tests of physical fitness.

KNAPP, CLYDE and JEWETT, ANN S. *Physical Education: Student and Beginning Teacher.* New York: McGraw-Hill, 1957. Problems of the student teacher and beginning teacher of physical education examined in detail.

Physical Education (Girls) Grades 9–12. Cincinnati: Cincinnati Public Schools, 1952, Bulletin 215. One of the more comprehensive bulletins in the field.

Physical Education Grades 7–12. Hartford: Connecticut State Department of Education, 1958, Curriculum Bulletin Series No. XI. Another excellent curriculum bulletin in secondary physical education.

15 The Core Program

THE CORE PROGRAM

Development

Core programs have at least two common features: (1) the class stays together for a minimum of two periods each day and (2) two or more subjects are studied together. The term *core* signifies that there is a common core of learning, which is the basis of the curriculum of this group. In recent years the term has fallen into disfavor, so that the title *core curriculum* is now avoided in favor of *common learnings, unified studies, humanities, general education, fused curriculum, correlated studies, life experience curriculum,* and other similar names.

Three sources of unified studies in the high school may be distinguished. The natural partnership of English and social studies—for example, American literature and American Civilization or World History and World Literature—gave rise to correlated classes in which the teachers of social studies and of English planned their work together. Classes were programmed so that from time to time one teacher or the other met the group for a double period. Additional impetus for this type of correlation came from college courses in "Contemporary Civilization." It was an obvious step to program a high-school class for a double period in fused English–social studies with one teacher.

A second pressure for this type of programming came from the retarded or slow-learner group, whose numbers in the high school were large enough to constitute a serious problem and for whom the traditional academic curriculum was patently unsuited. Placing these students in small groups programmed for a block of time (two or more periods each day) with a good teacher and with freedom to make rather than to follow a prescribed curriculum helped develop methods and materials suitable for these students.

Finally, the revolution which progressive education had wrought in the elementary school, where the "activity program" had demonstrated amazing power for motivating pupils to plan and execute projects and to learn basic skills in an entirely new context, challenged the secondary school to adjust its practices to the newer psychology of learning. Thus, on both practical and on theoretical grounds, the secondary school had a warrant if not a mandate for the core curriculum.

It is possible to distinguish several distinct types of programs. At one extreme, in the junior high school and with non-academic students, the freest type of development is possible. Teacher and class are encouraged to plan courses of study with little regard for existing curricular prescriptions. The curriculum is built on actual "life experiences" of the children, and this term is used to describe the program. Units of study in such programs range from a few days to several weeks and are directed to "Vocational Opportunities," "The Cold War," "Getting Along in the Family," "Religions in the Community," "History of Our Community," "How to Study," and the like.

At the other extreme are the course-of-study-dominated curricula, where teacher and class must operate within a restricted, prescribed content area. Generally this is true of unified studies for the eleventh and twelfth years, particularly for the average or better students, many of whom are college-bound.

Between these extremes are a variety of types with correlated or fused content and with varying degrees of freedom on the part of teacher and class to depart from traditional subject matter and to emphasize experiences, group processes, and self-directed activities.

Core Combinations

The most common combination of subjects in core consists of English and social studies. The instruction includes human relations, and occasionally the teacher is responsible for guidance. Other subject combinations, though not as common, have been taught successfully by competent teachers. Thus, in some junior high schools, a core program may consist of English, social studies, and science. Attempts to unite science and mathematics in a core approach have encountered great difficulty since the logical and psychological development of each of these subjects, particularly the latter, is not readily amenable to readjustment. Hence, in practice, there must be either a sacrifice of one subject or a discrete treatment in accordance with the traditional separate-subject curriculum.

In some large high schools core and traditional programs operate side-by-side. Thus part of the staff and student body may be involved in an English–social studies or other type of core curriculum while the other part follows the traditional type of program. This has several obvious advantages. Teachers and students are relatively free to select the program which is best adapted to their needs, interests, and abilities. The friendly competition engendered by the presence of different curricula for the same subject stimulates initiative and effort. Finally, there is some basis for evaluation inherent in the simultaneous education of similar groups by different methods.

Aims in Core Programs

The following statement embodies most of the general aims of core programs in the secondary school. The core program aims to promote pupil growth in:

- —Acquiring and using subject matter learnings in finding answers to meaningful problems.
- —Acquiring skills; applying them in various situations.
- —Locating and using sources of information; making use of community resources.
- —Using critical judgment in regard to the selection and use of materials, resources, and processes.
- —Using the scientific method in the solution of problems.
- —Identifying and appreciating the interrelatedness of subject areas; applying concepts from many areas in various situations.
- —Understanding the importance of the contributions of all people and appreciating the need for better understanding among nations.
- —Expressing ideas and emotions—orally, in writing, and through

the media of fine and graphic arts; receiving ideas through various media.

—Working well with others in small and large groups; respecting majority decisions and minority opinions.

—Accepting responsibility; assuming leadership and exercising initiative; evaluating oneself and others fairly and objectively.

—Seeing the problems of the present in relation to the past and to the future.[1]

In the core curriculum the teacher has among her objectives the following:

—Identifying pupils' capabilities, interests and needs.

—Motivating pupils to understand and accept preparation for citizenship.

—Furthering the intellectual, emotional, and social growth of each child through individual and group guidance.

—Furthering cooperative goals and a sharing of responsibility among pupils.

—Experimenting with content, materials, and methodology in a growing program.

—Adapting curriculum to meet the needs of a specific class.

—Evaluating all phases of pupil growth—intellectual, social, and emotional.

—Evaluating the effectiveness of planned procedures on short and long term bases.[2]

A core program developed by one of the authors for twelfth year in English–social studies specified the following objectives:

1. To deepen students' insights into and quicken their understanding of the drama of American history.

2. To bring students to an appreciation of good literature about American history.

3. To foster and expand students' interests in reading and to improve their reading skills.

4. To cultivate a love for good books and to develop the habit of selecting, buying, and owning books.

5. To promote discussion, criticism, and oral presentation.

6. To develop skill in cooperation and group activities.

[1] *Developing a Core Program in the Junior High School Grades*, New York: (New York City Board of Education, Bulletin, 1957–58 Series, No. 12), pp. 4–5.
[2] *Ibid.*

7. To stimulate initiative in selecting problems and seeking solutions.
8. To integrate the intimately related areas of language, literature, and social studies in educational practice.
9. To encourage creative expression in writing, speaking, dramatizing, and criticizing.
10. To enable a close relationship of respect, understanding, and affection to develop among pupils and teachers.

ASPECTS OF THE CORE PROGRAM

Student-Teacher Planning

Although the methods and materials of good core programs in most instances are applicable to the traditional high-school program, certain practices distinguish core work and it is necessary to discuss them separately. For example, student-teacher planning is an illustration of a procedure found to a far greater extent in core programs than in traditional programs. The core teacher makes it a practice to involve the class in planning wherever possible. If the curriculum *requires* that the class study the geography of Europe, however, the teacher cannot pretend that the children are free to choose something else, though they are free to decide when and how this shall be done.

There are various situations which call for teacher-class planning. For instance, teacher and class may decide which of several novels or plays will be studied in the next unit, or they may blueprint the order of work for the next few days or weeks. (This plan may be placed on the chalkboard as a timetable for teacher and class.) Occasionally it may be necessary to choose between two courses of action, only one of which is possible. For example, should *War and Peace* or *A Tale of Two Cities* be studied in the next unit? Finally, numerous opportunities for choice may be afforded each student as he is encouraged to express preference in reading, in committee participation, in volunteer activities, and in other activities.

Individualizing Instruction

One of the major advantages of the unified-studies program is that teacher and students get to know each other better. Since the class stays together for two periods or more each day, the teacher meets half the usual number of students and thus gets to know each individual child very well. Too, the informality of the unified-studies approach—group planning, committee work, guidance emphasis—lends itself to greater attention to individual students. The teacher becomes acquainted with the intellectual, emotional, and physical characteristics of each child. Assignments can be differentiated to challenge each student on his own level.

Committee work is so closely identified with core that it requires special comment. There is no single correct use of the committee technique. For example, if the problem of securing permission to visit a museum during school hours arises, the teacher may appoint a committee to talk with the principal and another to visit the museum curator. If the origin of Jiu-jitsu is in question, a committee may be designated to do research and report to the class. This is not the typical committee of core work, but it is committee work nonetheless. More typical in core is breaking up a large task into components, each of which is investigated by one committee. For example, if the class is to study medieval Europe, one committee can make a special study of feudalism, another the Crusades, a third social customs, a fourth the Renaissance, and a fifth the medieval church. The size of committees will usually vary from three to about seven members with five being a good size. Students who learn to work well in committees become skilled in democratic processes and are able to act effectively both as leaders and as associates in a variety of undertakings.

The following outline shows one technique for guiding students in committee work and for helping student and teacher know each other's responsibility and be able to evaluate the work.

PLAN SHEET FOR A REPORT OF THE COMMITTEE ON _____

Name _____   *Class* _____
Date _____   *Teacher* _____

  1. My class is working on the subject _____
  2. In order to understand this subject better, my class has been
      organized into the following committees: _____

  _____

  3. I am a member of the _____ committee.

4. The chairman of my committee is _____

5. The secretary of my committee is _____

6. In order to complete our work, each member of the committee has undertaken a specific responsibility as follows:

Name of Member	*Responsibility*
_____	_____
_____	_____
_____	_____
_____	_____
_____	_____

7. To complete my job, I shall have to do the following: _____
    _____

8. In order to keep the other committee members informed on my work, I will _____
    _____

9. My committee will report to the class in the following ways (project, play, oral report, radio or television production, project, etc.): _____
    _____

10. Our report is due on the following date: _____

11. Teacher's Comment: _____
    _____

In committee work it often is possible to have the bright work with the less able and help them learn good work habits and research techniques. In reading it is possible to vary the assignments so that the retarded read on their own level while the more able read more and difficult books. In projects, one student may do no more than arrange a bulletin board while another writes an original script for TV. The teacher's task is to individualize the work so that while he keeps the class together, he also stimulates the growth of each student.

Since reading is a fundamental aspect of general education as well as a specialized task, the reading program in core is essential. The core teacher may need to do remedial reading work with some students during or outside regular class periods.

For those reading above grade, he will need to provide appropriate material. In short, the best reading program for a heterogeneous group is a diversified and individualized one. Of course, common class activities are necessary to develop group consciousness, so that group work may be completed. Hence some books should be read by the entire class and others by individuals.

A good device for dramatizing reading for the group and for the individual is the posting of a "reading progress chart," with the names of the students listed alphabetically in a vertical row at the left and blanks to be filled across the chart by the students as they complete a book. No stigma should be attached to the slow reader. The chart is simply a record for class and teacher to see who has read what books as the year moves along.

Guidance

Many of the aspects of good core programs also are aspects of good guidance. Indeed, a core teacher must be guidance-oriented if he is to succeed. A familiarity with standardized tests of intelligence, aptitude, and achievement, a transcript of the basic educational information for each student, an anecdotal record for each, individual conferences, and class assignments related to vocational, emotional, and social factors constitute some of the guidance aspects of core teaching.

In some schools core classes are programmed for additional guidance time, and the core teacher is the guidance counselor. In others, the students look to their core teacher for guidance merely because he is the teacher who knows them best. In any case, the core teacher is in a position to exert a strategic influence on his students because of the greater intimacy with them.

At the beginning of the year it is customary for the teacher to ask each child to list on a card information about his hobbies, spare-time activities, work, ambitions, accomplishments, favorite people, and so on. This, coupled with academic and health records, gives the teacher a good start. Generally at least one conference is held with parents during the first six weeks of the year, and if possible, one with each student. If time is limited, conferences with those presenting problems are essential. These may be supplemented with informal contacts in class as the teacher circulates around the room during committee work, during supervised study, or when students come to the desk for consultation or questions.

Not the least of the teacher's guidance activities is actual class work. Every piece of written work, each oral presentation, every comment by the teacher, contains either a signal to the teacher about the student or a guidance suggestion to the class from the teacher. Of course, some assignments can be designed specifically for guidance purposes—for example, compositions such as "My Career" or "What I Fear." High-school students especially enjoy debating or writing about controversial matters pertaining to themselves and learn much in the process. Favorite topics include the following: Should There Be a Curfew for Teen-agers? Should There Be an Age Limit on Driving? Should Students Work While in School? Should High-School Girls and Boys Go Steady? What Is Proper Student Attire for School?

Human Relations

While teaching human relations is not a monopoly of core, it is much more frequently included in core curricula than in traditional social studies, language arts, or other subject curricula. Students may study *about* human relations when a unit on "good family relations" is under consideration, or when a composition on the topic "Why I Like Mr. X" is being written and analyzed. Or they study human relations by *participation* when democratic classroom procedures are being developed, when committees are learning to function, or when the class is working out the strategy for making a request of the principal.

Appreciation of differences in race, religion, social class, economic attitudes, and national origins need to be learned. Learning to live with these differences with mutual understanding without either abandoning one's own heritage or denying equal consideration to others is a major objective of the general education program. For this reason, units on human relations are generally included in core programs, and the self-evaluation aspects of core help each student examine his own progress in this important learning.[3]

As in all good teaching, fundamentals (reading, spelling

---

[3] See Rosalind M. Zapf, *Democratic Practices in the Secondary Classroom* (Englewood Cliffs: Prentice-Hall, 1959).

and other skills) are taught well in core programs, but they are taught in context and after an atmosphere of cooperation and mutual respect has been developed. This atmosphere is easily discerned in a classroom, for it is dramatically different from the autocratic, or the *laissez-faire*.

The art of teaching is nowhere better demonstrated than in the establishment of a democratic, permissive classroom atmosphere. If the teacher truly respects each student and is genuinely concerned with his progress, this feeling is communicated to the students, who react similarly to one another and to the teacher. In this free atmosphere, the teacher renounces none of his responsibilities as an experienced, qualified, adult leader, but at the same time he recognizes that each child is an individual with emotions, aspirations, and a unique contribution to make.

In an atmosphere of mutual respect, democratic processes are learned through actual practice. The attributes of responsible leadership and enlightened followership, the methods of orderly change, the expression of unpopular points of view, recognition of the rights of minorities, acceptance of majority rule, distinction between relevant and spurious values—these and many other aspects of the democratic process are taught in a classroom in which the atmosphere is congenial. They cannot be taught in either the autocratic or the *laissez-faire* classroom, and they are at least as important as the prescribed subject matter with which many classrooms are exclusively preoccupied.

Teaching Fundamental Skills

Core teaching does not ignore all formal instruction or drill. Spelling, punctuation, sentence structure, outlining, note-taking, chemical formulas, and mathematical processes may all be taught as formally as necessary in a core class. Ideally, the request for drill or formal instruction should come from the class. Or if the teacher realizes that the class needs it, he should "sell" the drill lessons rather than force them on the class. Fundamental skills can be taught better in the natural setting and in the receptive atmosphere of a core class than in traditional classrooms, for the motivation is sounder. There is no theoretical or practical reason for neglecting these skills in the unified studies arrangement.

Special Core Methods and Materials

The core classroom generally is a beehive of activity, a minia-ture museum, and a library. The accumulation of books, pam-phlets, charts, and other educational materials follows naturally from a program in which the students help decide what learning activities will be undertaken. Since these activities often have contemporary significance, or at least current implications, it is common to have frequent reports from resource persons—stu-dents, teachers, experts, and visitors. A further step is to permit the class, or part of it, to study any outside facilities which may expand their vision of the unit. They may visit a park, museum, movie, play, government agency, legislature in action, historic site, industrial plant, newspaper, laboratory, college, library, or other institution. Thus the outside world becomes an extension of the classroom.

The outside world also is represented in the class by se-lected films, filmstrips, tape recordings, or other audio-visual aids. Of course, these are accepted as part of the instruction of traditional programs, but they are equally, if not more, con-genial to the common-core-of-learning curriculum.

Unified Studies in the Eleventh and Twelfth Year

Experience with core classes consisting of average high-school students in the eleventh and twelfth year have shown possibilities for curriculum development involving a variety of new methods and materials suited to the needs and interests of today's high-school student. A very effective innovation is the in-troduction of imaginative literature—historical fiction, drama, poetry, biography—taught from specially prepared "study guides." The study guide illustrated below is the guide to *Anne Frank: The Diary of a Young Girl.*

SAMPLE STUDY GUIDE FOR CORE PROGRAMS

Study Guide to *Anne Frank: The Diary of a Young Girl*

Anne Frank's diary opens with an entry on Sunday, June 14, 1942, two days after her thirteenth birthday, and closes with the entry of August 4, 1944, three days before the Nazi secret police raided the "Secret Annexe" and sent all occupants (except Anne's father) to their death in concentration camps.

About Anne: 1. Describe Anne's life from the time of her

birth in Germany to the time she goes into hiding in Holland. 2. In what respect is she an average thirteen-year-old girl? How is she different? 3. Use as many adjectives as you can to describe Anne, e.g., talkative, moody, quarrelsome, pretty, intelligent, etc. Prove each. 4. Describe Anne's education: a) before going into hiding; b) during her two years in hiding. 5. What are her hobbies? What does she plan to do after the war? Do you think she would have been a success? Why? 6. Does she have a sense of humor? Prove.

About the Other "Guests" of the "Secret Annexe": 1. Write brief character sketches of each of the other seven occupants of the Annexe. 2. Which one is the most interesting character? Why? Which is your favorite? Why?

About Life in the Annexe: 1. What difficulties do the occupants endure—food, sleeping, lack of privacy, toilet facilities, silence, imprisonment, etc.? 2. What makes it possible for them to endure these hardships (hope for liberty, faith in God, help of others, no other choice, remembrance of the past—what)?

About the Protectors: 1. Write brief character sketches of each of the protectors—Mr. Kraler, Koopius, Miep, and Elli. 2. Why do they risk liberty and life to help their Jewish friends? 3. In what ways do they help the occupants of the Annexe?

Human Relations in the Annexe: 1. What is Anne's relationship with her mother? What is wrong? Who is at fault? Was it too late to do anything about it? What could have been done? 2. What is Anne's relationship with her father? Is it all it should be? 3. With her sister? 4. Describe the changing relationship with Peter. Is the relationship normal? Is Anne at fault? Is Peter at fault? Why doesn't their love continue to grow? 5. Is Anne fair to Mrs. Van Daan? To Mr. Dussell? 6. Do the Franks get along better than the Van Daans? Why?

About the Outside World: 1. In the Spring of 1941, the Nazis occupied Holland. What effect did this have on the Jewish people? Why? 2. How were the Dutch people affected by the occupation?—Give illustrations of extreme suffering, of resistance, of life continuing as usual, of collaboration with the Nazis. 3. How did the occupants of the Annexe keep informed about the progress of the war? When did they think it would end? 4. What hopeful events occur in 1942? 1943? 1944? 5. What references are made to Churchill and the British? To Eisenhower? To the Russians? To Zionism? To the Nazis? Is Anne interested in politics? Why?

Special Aspects of the Diary: 1. Nature—What role does nature play in Anne's young life? Is this normal? 2. Sayings and Proverbs—Anne seems especially philosophical at times in her use of adages, e.g., p. 124, "The young always follow a bad example" or p. 152, "Whoever is happy will make others happy too." Select five other sayings from the diary. Comment on each. 3. Vocabulary—Add 10 words from this book to your own vocabulary list, e.g., p. 35, hostages and sabotage, p. 45, rendezvous and ingenuity, p. 66 reassuring, etc.

Things To Do: If you would like to read (and report on) another famous diary, try a volume of the Diary of Samuel Pepys or one of the diaries of James Boswell. 2. Keep a diary for a week and be prepared to read it (or parts of it) in class. 3. Write the script for one scene for a movie, radio, or TV dramatization adapted from the book.

Critique: 1. Is this a good choice for a class book? Why? 2. Have you ever kept a diary? How does it compare with Anne's? 3. If Anne had survived the Nazis, would her diary have been as famous as it is now? Why?[4]

Paperback books have increased the opportunities for wide reading and studying by teachers and students. Today every student can have his own diversified library at a small cost. Study guides, such as the one illustrated above can be used with the student's own books to teach traditional aspects (life of the author, the story, matters of literary structure and style, vocabulary, analysis of character, conflict, ethical problems, and human relations) and the related cultural aspects of social studies, the arts and other learnings.

EVALUATION

Just as planning is a cooperative venture involving both teacher and student, so evaluation in the core program properly involves the student. The teacher's responsibility for grading is still present, but the student is taught to evaluate his own work, the work of his colleagues, and the work of the class.

Many core teachers construct self-evaluation sheets on which students grade themselves at each marking period. The teacher examines the student's self-evaluation, pointing out agreements and disagreements, and giving his reasons for these. Similarly, the class gives its rating of a student's or a commit-

[4] Originally published by Pocket Books, Inc.

tee's work. The teacher provides his evaluation and discusses the bases for his judgment with the class. Finally, the work of the class, including the choice of content, the relative merit of activities, the order of procedure, the method used, and any other aspects of the work, is evaluated by the class. Thus the unilateral method of grading characteristic of autocratic processes is replaced by responsible evaluation in which students are involved, and before whom the teacher's process of judgment is laid bare.

There is much heat and comparatively little light about the professional evaluation of the core program itself. Proponents cite the studies of Aiken, Faunce, Ohio State University, Reiner Schwartz, H. H. Giles, S. P. McCutchen, A. N. Zechiel, and others to prove the success of the program. Opponents like Bestor, Flesch, Rickover, and others are violent in their denunciation, attributing any and all school failures to innovations such as core.

It is possible to make objective studies of comparative results on standardized tests. Where these have been made the core student has shown himself the equal of those taught by traditional curricula despite the fact that tests are designed to test for items emphasized in traditional curricula, rather than for attitudes, values, and processes stressed in the democratic, permissive atmosphere of the core class.[5] Tests for these results of core programs, *per se,* have not been designed.

Reviewing the status of core programs, Jennings states:

1. Core classes are increasing.
2. There is a trend from mere block-of-time classes toward a true core program.
3. More teacher-training institutions than ever are preparing teachers specifically for core teaching.
4. More is being written about core.
5. More core conferences are being held, and more people are attending them.
6. Studies show that core is an effective way of teaching.
7. The opinions of educators working with the program are strongly in its favor.[6]

---

[5] Margaret Willis, *The Guinea Pigs After Twenty Years* (Columbus: Ohio State U. Press, 1961). See also Wilford M. Aiken, *The Story of the Eight-Year Study* (New York: Harper, 1942).

[6] Wayne Jennings, "The Status of the Core Program" in the *Bulletin,* National Association of Secondary School Principals, 46, No. 272 (March, 1962): 55–57.

SELECTION AND TRAINING OF CORE PERSONNEL

Few teacher-education programs provide for the preparation of core teachers, and few states recognize core teaching as a special category in their certification regulations. As a result, superintendents and principals starting a core program must establish their own criteria for the selection of personnel and their own programs for in-service training. This discussion will merely sketch some of the basic attributes of a good core teacher.

The teacher in the general-studies program should be a well-rounded person with broad interests and extensive human experience. He should be particularly competent in the areas —generally English and social studies—of the core. He should be flexible in his teaching methods so that he is able and willing to experiment. He should be sympathetic to the core approach and to the permissive type of teaching. He must be a person who is still developing and growing as a teacher. He should be conversant with the current professional development, research, and experimentation in education.

The success of the core program, like that of any instructional program, hinges on the competence of the teacher. The core teacher is required to have academic competence in two or more subjects. In the past, teachers with college majors in only one subject who taught core programs sometimes tended to emphasize the subject of their competence and to neglect the other. Administrators therefore have avoided core assignments even when they valued core procedures unless teachers with academic competence in the subjects were available. Preparation of core teachers in college programs and in-service re-training of teachers are two approaches to meeting the problem of the lack of competent personnel for teaching core classes.

It is a serious mistake to draft an unwilling traditional teacher into core work. Nor is it advisable to accept a volunteer who has been unsuccessful in another department or who does not have excellent personal relations with colleagues, administrators, and students. Core requires teachers who are extremely sympathetic to the needs and problems of individual students.

A core program should be instituted only by an administration that is knowledgeable about and committed to this approach, by teachers who share this philosophy, and with community support. The parents of children going into core classes should be thoroughly informed and sympathetic, and from time to time they should be invited to special meetings, teas, or demonstrations and kept informed through statements emanating from responsible school officials.

As the core program in a school develops, the core teachers need to meet regularly as a curriculum development committee. They should be encouraged to take course work, to attend lectures and conventions, and to visit classes and schools where original work is in progress. Their own work may be publicized in curriculum bulletins, articles in learned journals, and possibly in authorized newspaper releases or feature stories.

Undoubtedly a scholarly, competent traditional teacher is far superior to a dull, weak, core teacher. But where the administration understands the philosophy of the general-education approach, seeks and finds qualified personnel to teach in the program, educates the community honestly and intelligently in what is being attempted, and supports the program in action, there is every reason for the attainment of results that will compare favorably with those of the traditional, subject-dominated secondary-school program.

FOR DELIBERATION and DISCUSSION

1. Show how a variety of learnings from various high-school subject areas may result from work on a specific core project. What special background and preparation should core teachers have?
2. What functions does a study guide serve for the students and for the teacher? Examine the study guide in the text. What teaching opportunities does it offer?
3. What problems are involved in the introduction of democratic practices and procedures in the classroom? How would you resolve them?
4. Attempts to fuse mathematics and science in a core program have generally met with less success than similar attempts in English and social studies. Why?
5. What advantages does a large block of time offer students and teacher? What are the disadvantages of core?
6. Would you prefer to teach core or a traditional program? Why?

FOR ADDITIONAL READING

AIKEN, WILFRED M. *The Story of the Eight-Year Study*. New York: Harper, 1942. Extensive study of graduates of "progressive" high schools compared with graduates of traditional high schools.

FAUNCE, ROLAND C. and CLUTE, MORREL J. *Teaching and Learning in the Junior High School.* San Francisco: Wadsworth, 1961. Contains much favorable material about core programs.

FAUNCE, ROLAND C. and BOSSING, NELSON L. *Developing the Core Curriculum.* Englewood Cliffs: Prentice-Hall, 1958. A basic text for the study of secondary-school core philosophy, organization, procedures, and outcomes.

FRENCH, WILL, *et al. Behavioral Goals of General Education in the High School.* New York: Russell Sage Foundation, 1957. An important study developing major objectives of the high-school program and their related behavioral outcomes.

HOCK, LOUISE E. and HILL, THOMAS J. *The General Education Class in the Secondary School.* New York: Holt, Rinehart, and Winston, 1960. A significant contribution to method in secondary education; theory and practice of core teaching brought up-to-date.

LAND, W. A. "Some Aspects of the Core Program," *The Core Teacher.* Philadelphia: Teachers College, Temple U., 1959, Vol. 9.

LURRY, LUCILE L. and ALBERTY, ELSIE J. *Developing a High School Core Program.* New York: Macmillan, 1957. Describes core programs used in a high-school classroom.

MITCHUM, P. M. and ISSACKSEN, ROY O. "How Effective is the Core Curriculum in the Junior High School?" *Bulletin,* Association of Secondary School Principals, 40 (April 1956).

NOALL, MATTHEW F. and BELL, TARRAL H. "Core Curriculum at Weber County, Utah," *Bulletin,* Association of Secondary School Principals (January, 1960).

The Core Teacher. Published twice each semester by College of Education, Temple University, Philadelphia. Contains articles describing core theory and practice.

TOOPS, MYRTLE DEWEY. *Working in the Core Program in Burris Laboratory School.* Muncie: Ball State Teachers College, 1955. Describes aspects of core teaching and teacher preparation.

VAN TIL, WILLIAM, VARS, GORDON F., and LOUNSBURY, JOHN H. *Modern Education for the Junior High School Years.* Indianapolis: Bobbs-Merrill, 1961. Chapters 9–12 devoted to a comprehensive description of core programs.

ZAPF, ROSALIND. *Democratic Processes in the Secondary Classroom.* Englewood Cliffs: Prentice-Hall, 1959. Describes practices in core program at Denby High School, Detroit. The objectives emphasize development of attitudes and skills in democratic human relations. An extreme core program with extremely interesting outcomes.

16 Vocational Education

CONCEPTS OF VOCATIONAL EDUCATION

Attitudes toward vocational education have a wide range. Dewey said:

> Occupation is a concrete term for continuity. It includes the development of artistic capacity of any kind, of special scientific ability, of effective citizenship, as well as professional and business occupations, to say nothing of mechanical labor or engagements in gainful pursuits . . . Nothing could be more absurd than to educate individuals with an eye to only one line of activity.[1]

The statement, "all education is vocational education," heard frequently in discussions of vocational education is understood to mean that practically everything learned has some marketable or saleable value. The statement is even more cogent when applied to the broad concept of "vocation" which includes every continuing and purposeful activity in which an individual engages, whether it is economically gainful or not.

The other concept of the term is that education is for a specific occupation so that "vocational education" is taken to mean those courses designed to prepare the student to make a living in a specific way—bookkeeper, dressmaker, electrician, and so on. Normally, the term would be used to apply only to those occupational pursuits we call "jobs" as distinguished from those we call "professions." It will be seen that, even when narrowly

---

[1] John Dewey, *Democracy and Education* (New York: Macmillan, 1915), p. 359.

262

defined, vocational education cannot properly be limited to any one phase of the curriculum since the individual's saleable potential will be enhanced by every useful skill and competency he develops.

In our discussion the high-school program will be examined on the basis of its contribution to the vocational education of girls and boys, taking the term in its narrower sense of preparation for employment but recognizing that many aspects of the curriculum which do not have vocational objectives may contribute significantly toward vocational ends.

VOCATIONAL EDUCATION AND THE HIGH SCHOOL

Three types of high schools concerned with vocational education may be distinguished—the specialized academic high school, the comprehensive high school, and the vocational high school. The first is vocational in the sense that its curriculum is directing students toward college and the professions. This, of course, is clearly a vocational objective, and the only question is the extent to which the school meets the challenge. The school for talented youngsters which offers them opportunities for creative work in library and laboratory through guided independent study, research, and experimentation with a varied and exciting industrial-arts program is certainly meeting the vocational needs of these youngsters. The experience of students in winning a large number and variety of scholarships, in gaining admittance to the best colleges, in making distinguished records at these colleges, and in attaining ultimate professional objectives in research, engineering, medicine, teaching, law, business, and industry constitutes a powerful motivating factor for each succeeding class.

The comprehensive high school is challenged to provide a suitable vocational program for its varied student body—the 15 percent or more of talented, the large middle group of average students, most of whom are college-bound, and the 15 percent of slow and retarded. This challenge is met in a variety of ways. Ideally the school provides for its talented students a program similar to that of the specialized high school. For the large average group, specialized vocational education is provided in one or more of the following areas: commercial and business education, agricultural education, work-study program (including distributive education), the industrial arts program, placement, and follow-up.

The vocational high school, usually found only in the large cities, provides its students with both a general education and specialized training for a specific vocational area—machine and metal trades, fashion, aviation, food trades, printing, and the like.

Purposes of Vocational High Schools

The purposes of the vocational high school frequently have been confused. Although it is supposed to offer specialized education for people who know their vocational objectives and to prepare them for these vocations during their high-school years, the vocational school too often serves as a terminal educational institution for the retarded or academically deficient. The result has been a failure to capitalize on the possibilities inherent in a well-equipped and well-staffed urban high school, where proximity to every industrial and commercial facility can be combined with a well-planned educational program to meet the special needs of many city girls and boys.

A report on one large city's vocational educational program made by an independent research organization constitutes a serious indictment.[2] It was noted that despite the fact that per pupil cost in the vocational high school was $931.24 a year compared with $605.39 in academic high schools, the dropout rate in the former was twice that in the latter; that vocational schools offered obsolete training; that the unemployment rate ran to 20 percent; that graduates of vocational schools spent three to five years in apprenticeship because unions refused to credit their training fully; and that there was no orderly transition to employment or adequate attempt at breakthrough by either the schools or the unions.

If this indictment is accurate, it raises very serious questions about the effectiveness of our vocational education. This becomes particularly alarming in the light of Conant's finding in *Slums and Suburbs:*

> In some slum neighborhoods I have no doubt that over half of the boys between sixteen and twenty-one are out of school

[2] "Youth and Work in New York City" prepared under the direction of Mrs. Mary Conway Kohler for the Tacomic Foundation, reported in the *New York Times,* March 12, 1962.

and out of work. Leaving aside human tragedies, I submit that a continuation of this situation is a menace to the social and political health of the large cities.[3]

It is this kind of social dynamite that leads again and again to repetitions of "West Side Story."

To assign sole or even primary responsibility to the school is obviously unrealistic. Unemployment, poverty, slum conditions, social injustice, discrimination, and despair are too much a part of our social fabric to be resolved even by a good high-school program. Nevertheless, if the dropout rate in the vocational high school is twice that in the academic high, the explanation offered by one school official that "students drop out for a number of reasons—financial, too-tough courses, a job opportunity, and the like" cannot be accepted. Rather, it should be noted that students are well aware that their high-school course is or is not leading to a reasonable promise of vocational opportunity. The best motivation for the adolescent girl or boy in high school is an exciting program consonant with his needs and interest and known to lead to opportunities for attainment of his goals. Where, as in the report cited above, there is poor correlation between job opportunities and training, it is only reasonable to expect students to be lethargic about their school work and to drop out at the first opportunity.

This is not to imply that the vocational school should prepare each student for a specific job. Even if this were possible, it would be contrary to the best interests of the individual and of society to limit him to the narrow confines of one vocational outlet. Rather, the school should open for each student the widest vocational vista, and at the same time give him a grounding in as broad as possible a job category—that is, segment of vocational competence. In today's world this is the only possible approach. Obsolescence and automation are proceeding so rapidly that it is estimated that "workers now entering the labor force must calmly envisage the necessity of being trained for three or four different jobs, each requiring a different set of skills, in the course of their work lives."[4]

[3] Conant, *Slums and Suburbs*, p. 2.
[4] Reported by Dr. Daniel Schreiber, Director of the NEA Drop-out Project, at the annual convention of the American Association of School Administration in Atlantic City, February 20, 1962.

Vocational Education, Business, and Labor

Progressive vocational schools are meeting the challenge of modern society by maintaining intimate relations with the industry or industries for which they are preparing employees. This requires a staff alert to changes and aware of trends, who constantly upgrade their own practical and theoretical preparation, and who are in a position to counsel students effectively to assist them in finding suitable placement. On the part of industry, meeting this challenge requires a well-organized program of continuous in-service education and training to anticipate change and to minimize the shock of extensive retraining.

Vocational-school personnel also must maintain good relations with labor unions. The effect of involving unions in the school program is acceptance of the program by the union and assurance of union approval of school training in meeting apprenticeship requirements.

The Scope of Vocational Education

Often vocational education in both comprehensive and specialized high schools has been regarded as a program for the below-average student. This has doomed programs from the outset, since it has stigmatized students, restricted the potential scope of instruction and utilization of facilities, and sometimes made the vocational program a repository for the mentally retarded and emotionally disturbed. A disproportionate amount of time and energy in vocational education has gone into "discipline" or into a curriculum restricted to safety education. While vocational education must teach boys and girls to protect themselves, their co-workers, and their machines, it is only with average and above-average students that it results in technical competence, specialized skills, and creative contributions.

Preparation for agricultural education and commercial or business education is more extensive than the preparation for occupations such as motors, metals and crafts, with which the term "vocational education" is generally associated. Indeed, under the Smith-Hughes Act of 1917, and its extension by the George-Barden Act of 1946, the largest share of federal support for vocational education has gone to agriculture, with trade and industrial education next, and home economics close behind. Commercial education, except for distributive education, has not been a beneficiary of federal support. Yet it is rare to find a comprehensive high school in which a substantial percentage of the students, generally girls, are not pursuing one or more of the so-called commercial courses—stenography, typewriting, bookkeeping, office machines, or office practice.

The high school has been less successful in developing marketable secretarial skills than it has been in industrial education. Rarely, despite the relatively high degree of standardization in office practice, does a high school turn out more than a small number of competent secretaries. The required skills and competencies are developed either in post-graduate secretarial schools or in on-the-job training. Secretarial competence demands a high degree of intelligence and preparation, but the ingenuity and imagination required to develop a more effective high-school program appears not yet to have been fully applied.

GUIDANCE AND COUNSELING IN VOCATIONAL EDUCATION

Junior- and senior-high-school personnel have a heavy guidance responsibility with respect to vocational education. Typically, the junior high school offers each student an opportunity to explore a variety of industrial-arts and vocational areas— planning and drafting, power machinery, and the like. Insofar as the student receives some vocational orientation without being required to make a vocational commitment, these experiences are educationally sound. The decision to specialize in a vocational course is often the subject of inquiry and counseling in the junior high school particularly in the ninth year. Testing, evaluation of a student's potential, insight into motivation, knowledge of industrial opportunities and trends, and other factors must be used to discover the best vocational choice. And, of course, avenues for reorientation should be kept open all along the line.

In the high school the student should be encouraged to pursue as complete an academic program as possible along with his vocational studies. He should have an opportunity to gain some actual experience in the vocational field of his choice, but the field should not be too narrow even at the end of the high-school course. Counseling reinforced by interviews, records, and tests, should be continuous throughout the student's schooling.

Conant makes a sound proposal to the effect that "guidance officers, especially in the large cities, ought to be given the responsibility for following the post-high-school careers of youth from the time they leave school until they are twenty-one years of age."[5]

Ultimately the choice of a vocational pursuit is made by the individual, of course, but it is the responsibility of the high-school counselor to help him and his parents make the most intelligent decision possible. If the counselor helps the student understand his aptitudes, interests and goals; advises him about the range and character of available occupations; informs him about all aspects of the school program and the relationship of each aspect to possible careers; and indicates opportunities for further education and training, he will facilitate the making of the best possible decision and thus serve the interests of the student, the school, and the community.

Guidance personnel and vocational staff members should work closely with the school placement office in securing the most advantageous and appropriate part-time or full-time placement for students or graduates. In some states an extensive state employment program makes possible the assignment of a full-time state placement officer to a school or school system and brings the resources and opportunities of the state into the school's vocational program.

WORK-STUDY PROGRAMS

The practice of placing students in part-time jobs as part of their vocational education is not new. Although in many schools the entire program is based on this design, in too many schools this practice is overlooked. Often, high-school students are permitted, even encouraged, to seek part-time employment on their own. As a result, girls and boys work after school, weekends, and summers at jobs unrelated to their vocational objectives, at locations far removed from the school, with hours, working conditions, and supervision at odds with the best interests of their educational and vocational progress.

Under a well-planned work-study program, the school acts as liaison between student and employers. The school adviser

[5] Conant, *Slums and Suburbs,* p. 41.

is in touch with employers in the community, arranges the conditions of employment, and supervises the student on the job. A nominal beginning salary may be adjusted after the student-worker gains some skill and experience and becomes more valuable. Thus exploitation of students is avoided. Frequently some school credit is attached to the out-of-school work. After graduation the student is in a position to take a full-time position, sometimes with the same employer and possibly at a higher salary.

Often local labor unions cooperate to arrange "diversified occupation" programs, in which a high-school boy begins part-time work at a specialized vocation during his junior or senior year in school. Under similar arrangements, students entering the field of merchandising are placed in appropriate part-time positions.

The advantages of this type of education more than compensate for its added cost: (1) Students are placed in employment on the basis of aptitude and interest. (2) School work is related to their occupational goals. (3) Students are supervised on the job by a teacher in the vocational-education department. (4) Work experience and schooling are considered to be, and in fact are, a single educational enterprise. In these programs there is a natural transition from part-time to full-time employment after graduation. In addition further study is encouraged and its value given recognition.

The work-study program must guard against certain dangers which are inherent to some extent in all vocational-education programs. The education of the student must not be limited or restricted to serve the selfish interests of employers. Both the vocational and the academic programs of the student must remain sufficiently broad and flexible to ensure that the student's marketable skills will be applicable to several avenues of employment and acceptable for further education, including college, if this is warranted by the student's interests and aptitudes.

TRENDS IN VOCATIONAL EDUCATION

Several well-defined trends are emerging in vocational education. At the junior-high-school level the tendency is to give the student a broad, basic, industrial and technical orientation. Here the industrial arts and vocational education are one. Experiences are grouped under four major categories: (1) *power,* including automotive, diesel, and atomic; (2) *electronics,* including electricity, computers, and TV; (3) *fabrication,* including metals, plastics, synthetics and woods; and (4) *design,* including planning, drafting, and drawing. Student experiences and accomplishments are supplemented by extensive aptitude testing and guidance in making choices about further education.

Another junior-high-school development is the unified arts program in which home economics, industrial arts, fine arts, and arts and crafts are housed in one area. A block of students is assigned to the entire area and works under a flexible program with maximum opportunity for exploration and experimentation.

In the high school the student will find continued opportunity for vocational education. The comprehensive high school offers a broad base of academic work and varied programs in agriculture, home economics, commercial education, industrial arts, distributive education, and other work-study programs. The specialized vocational school may offer concentration in a specific vocational area—aviation, machine, metal, fashion industries—with the day divided equally between study and work and with the former again divided equally between general education and vocational studies.

In the comprehensive high school the academic course has many vocational aspects. The social-studies program contains vast material of a vocational nature, including a study of the local and national industrial picture, career opportunities and conditions, laws and regulations pertaining to employment (including social security, taxation, and general economics), personal and family finance, interview techniques, and visits to local commercial and industrial plants. The vocational aspects of the high-school English, modern-languages, science, and mathematics programs are equally extensive. In short, there is no easy dividing line between what may properly be called vocational education and what is called academic. An effective vocational course retains a base in liberal education both in its association with other curriculum areas and in its stimulation of initiative, imagination, and creativity.

Both in vocational education and in industrial arts, there is a trend toward encouraging students to select their own projects. Often several will work together or assist one another in a long-range undertaking. When students are at work on a school project, such as stage design and construction for a school play or other performance, or even on a community project, such as modernization of certain recreational facilities in a park, the motivation will be high and the results educationally sound.

Guidance is assuming a more structured role in secondary education generally and in vocational education particularly. As the number of trained professionals in this area increases and as the student load is reduced, the counselor will take an increasingly active part in vocational programs in aptitude testing, arranging for resource persons and career days, planning visits to neighboring plants for specific purposes, securing and distributing literature, and providing expert counseling to students, colleagues, and parents. Electronic data processing is opening up an avenue for statistical studies through cumulative and follow-up records which may provide experimental and research evidence of great value to guidance and administrative personnel.

Finally, there is an increasing expansion of facilities for continued education in the junior-college program, the two-or-three-year trade and technical institutes, private commercial, trade, and technical schools, and evening adult-education programs. These vocational-training offerings are supplemented by vast training programs for upgrading its members socially and culturally carried on within industries and by labor unions on an in-service basis.

A good high-school vocational-education program is varied and flexible. It has a strong base in general education. It is sensitive to the needs, aptitudes, and interests of its students and to the opportunities and employment trends in the community state, and nation. It operates through a well-qualified staff, skilled guidance department, and sympathetic administration. Each student is respected as a person, is given every possible assistance in selecting and preparing for appropriate gainful occupation and is assured of the school's interest in him, both during school and after graduation.

FOR DELIBERATION and DISCUSSION

1. Comment on the statement "Every high school is a vocational school." What responsibility does this place on the staff? The guidance department? The administration?
2. Distinguish between industrial-arts and vocational education. Is industrial arts a proper field of study for the academically talented boy or girl? Explain.
3. To what extent is the high school responsible for the vocational preparation of its students? How is the high school discharging this responsibility?
4. Few high schools have follow-up procedures for keeping post-graduate records. Why? Is this desirable? Explain.
5. What is the relationship between junior- and senior-high-school vocational guidance and the secondary-school curriculum?

FOR ADDITIONAL READING

Adapting the Secondary School to the Needs of Youth. Chicago: U. of Chicago Press, 1959, Part II. (Fifty-second Yearbook of the National Society for the Study of Education.) Curriculum revision with vocational orientation in several of the chapters.

DEWEY, JOHN. *Democracy and Education.* New York: Macmillan, 1915. Chapter 23 on "Vocational Aspects of Education" is still one of the best statements on the subject.

EDUCATIONAL POLICIES COMMISSION. *Education and Manpower.* Washington, D.C.: NEA, 1956. Considers the prospects of national vocational needs in developing industrial society and the place of the school in helping to meet the needs.

HUNT, DEWITT. *Industrial Arts in the Junior High School.* Washington, D.C.: United States Office of Education, 1959, Circular 433. Describes objectives of curriculum and evaluation of vocational education in relation to industrial arts.

Work Experience Education Programs in American Secondary Schools. Washington, D.C.: United States Office of Education, 1957, Bulletin 1957, No. 5. Six types of work-experience programs are described.

STEPHENSON, R. M. "Occupational Plans for 443 Ninth Graders," *Journal of Educational Research,* 49 (September 1955). Important aspects especially pertaining to vocational-education responsibility of the schools in relation to student plans and desires.

VAN TIL, WILLIAM, VARS, GORDON F., and LOUNSBURY, JOHN L. *Modern Education for the Junior High School Years.* Indianapolis: Bobbs-Merrill, 1961. Chapter 15 devoted to certain aspects of vocational education.

17 Audio-Visual Methods
and Materials

PRINCIPLES OF TEACHING WITH AUDIO-VISUALS

Definition of Audio-Visual

The teacher has always attempted to communicate with the
learner either through speech or through a visual impression.
Although the lecture or discussion and the textbook still constitute the major avenues of instruction in secondary schools,
new media and devices in great abundance are altering the entire area of instruction. Greater understanding of the teaching
and learning processes have made audio-visual materials indispensable in secondary-school theory and practice.

Included among audio-visual materials which receive extensive use in secondary-school practice are the chalkboard,
various printed materials, maps and charts, globes and models,
films, recordings, radio, television, overhead transparencies, programmed materials and teaching machines, and a variety of
demonstration devices, such as actual specimens, dramatization,
and bulletin-board displays.

Purposes of Audio-Visual Aids

The large and growing number of devices and materials
available to the teacher presents him with new opportunities
for originality as he prepares to teach a lesson or unit. It con-
fronts him also with a new responsibility, for he must select from
the available material and methods those best suited for his instructional purpose. If he is preparing to teach *Julius Caesar*, for

example, it may or may not be appropriate to play in class one or more scenes from the Encyclopædia Britannica recordings by the Dublin Gate Theatre or have the class see the film with Marlon Brando, James Mason, Deborah Kerr, and Greer Garson. If he is to teach a lesson on life in colonial Williamsburg, it may or may not be appropriate to show one or more of the Modern Learning Aids filmstrips on this subject. If the lesson is to be the classification of vertebrates, a display in class of a commercially prepared chart may or may not be called for. In each instance, the teacher must decide if a particular audio-visual method or material will help him teach the required lesson more completely or more competently.

Audio-visual material is not designed to take the place of the teacher. Rather it is a part of making his teaching more effective. This means that the audio-visual material must be previewed or preaudited by the teacher, that it must be introduced at a specific point for a specific purpose—such as introducing a lesson or unit; supplementing, reinforcing or dramatizing printed material; summarizing or completing a concept; or for some other well-defined purpose—and that it must be planned like any other lesson. Typically, a film, filmstrip, radio, or television lesson includes an introduction by the teacher in order to prepare the students for what is to come, instructions to the students about specific tasks to accomplish during and after the lesson—things to look for, questions to answer, notes or outlines to prepare—and a follow-up discussion and evaluation.

The teacher will find that learnings are enriched and reinforced by use of multiple audio-visual media. For example, in working with equations the teacher's discussion and the textbook presentation can be supplemented by chalkboard demonstration, handling of concrete materials, visual presentation of charts, showing of a filmstrip, and so forth. The physical-education teacher can reinforce the teaching of basketball by diagrams, films, recordings of talks with famous players, visits to professional games, reading about basketball in textbooks, reference books, and fiction, and so on. Every secondary-school subject can be taught more effectively through appropriate use of audio-visuals, but the teacher must know the material and the medium, must use them as an integral part of the work, and must contrive to have the various media reinforce the concepts, skills, and attitudes he is attempting to teach.

AUDIO-VISUAL AIDS IN THE CLASSROOM

Printed Matter

The *primary* visual material available to the classroom teacher is the printed page—textbook, workbook, pamphlet, newspaper, magazine, or brochure. Sometimes the textbook is written specifically to help shape the course of study for which teacher and class are responsible. More often the textbook becomes a substitute or replacement for the course of study. Sometimes the textbook is *the* course of study. The obligation and responsibility of the teacher is to use the textbook as a tool, to assign only appropriate sections, to teach students to examine the contents critically, to require that other sources be consulted for comparison, and to instruct in reading, skimming, summarizing, and analyzing.

Workbooks serve a proper function when they are used in review and in reinforcement to help student and teacher evaluate the degree of mastery attained. If the workbook is used in class it gives the teacher an opportunity to move about and give individual instruction. The use of workbooks as a "busy work" device is never justifiable.

The use of magazines and newspapers as aids to instruction requires preparation, as does any lesson. They present teacher and class with material which informs and challenges as live issues are considered, discussed, and debated. Special newspapers, commercially prepared for classroom use, are used appropriately in the social studies, English, and science classroom only when each issue is examined by the teacher prior to distribution, and when lessons based on the printed material are prepared with definite curricular objectives in mind.

The Chalkboard

A classroom device almost as common as the textbook is the chalkboard. (The term is used in preference to "blackboard" because the latter has been improved upon by a green variety which is not shiny like slate, does not permit the chalk to scratch, and is a partial absorbent of chalk dust.) Chalk is virtually a symbol of the teaching profession: every teacher of every subject uses it to some extent. The uses of the chalkboard are extremely varied, but a few of the more common may be noted here. In teaching it often helps the class if a new word is written on the board as the teacher says it. For example, as the French teacher teaches the "Marseillaise" she writes *"Allons enfants de la patrie"* on the front board, or the English teacher places the new word "transition" on the board for all to see. Some teachers develop the habit of "talk and chalk" as they teach. If it does not distract the class, this practice may be very helpful to students and to the teacher.

The chalkboard is also a convenient and effective place to write assignments and quizzes. Occasionally a teacher may place a quiz on the board and cover it with a roll-down map or chart, which is rolled up at the proper time. Often the board is used to record the main points of the lesson in outline form. Another technique is to have a student at the chalkboard summarize what is being discussed. Others are to have teacher or student demonstrate the solution to a problem, write the answer to a homework question, or solve a problem being worked simultaneously by the class. Some teachers send half a dozen or more students at a time to work at the chalkboard. Others make elaborate drawings, diagrams, graphs, and so forth on the board before or during the lesson.

The Overhead Projector

Teachers whose classrooms are equipped with an overhead projector and slanted screen find that this device has uses similar to that of the chalkboard and that it is in some ways superior to the latter. The teacher's writing appears at once on the screen but the teacher continues to face the class as he talks and writes. Moreover, he can prepare frames in advance—maps, charts, diagrams, pictures, or other graphic material—and have them flashed on the screen by the overhead projector at the appropriate point in the lesson. The overhead projector has the additional advantages of permitting overlays to be prepared with any frame so that, for example, a frame may show the extent of the United States in 1783, then an overlay may be applied to show the United States in 1803, another in 1846, and so forth. All this can be done in color and the teacher need not leave his place in front of the class.

Room Decorations

The modern secondary-school teacher takes pride in a room attractive and alive with student work. Walls, bulletin boards, tables, and available shelves display students' essays, cartoons, posters, mobiles, dioramas, constructs, and models. Commercial posters, clippings from periodicals, and other graphic items illustrating the work of the class may be on display. A few of these may be permanent parts of the classroom decor, but most will be displayed for a day, a week, or a month. Often student committees select and arrange the items, applying the tests of quality and appropriateness and making the displays orderly and attractive.

Folding maps and charts and roll-up maps serve their functions without taking up precious space. Globes, balanced aquaria, pictures or photographs of famous people and events, or reprints of great documents may be used as permanent displays.

Demonstrations

The classroom demonstration is a time-honored audio-visual method which can be a very effective teaching device. The demonstration of an experiment in science helps students see and hear the process of discovery. The demonstration may be carried out by students or by the teacher. Sociodramas in which students enact situations extemporaneously—an interview, a debate in the halls of Congress, a scene in a supermarket or on a bus—or role-playing, in which one individual assumes the part of another, are other types of demonstrations from which much may be learned. Students may make and use puppets for similar demonstration purposes.

Resource persons may be invited to class to give a lecture and demonstration in their special areas of competence. For example, a staff member or adult in the community may give an illustrated talk on the culture of ancient China, on United States commemorative stamps, on the operation of the stock exchange, or on the art of Kandinsky.

Films, Slides, and Filmstrips

Films, moving or still, and slides with and without sound, have become a major resource in secondary-school teaching. The thousands of educational films and filmstrips being produced annually indicate that there is a vast market for this aid to teaching. Classroom teachers have found that these media can be utilized in various ways—to motivate, to provide a change of pace,

to show actual scenes from history, to illustrate expert performance, to sharpen critical skill in viewing and listening.

Most common of the three devices—film, slide, and filmstrip—is the last, because it is relatively inexpensive and easy
to use. Commercially prepared strips often are accompanied
by a teacher's manual in which each frame is pictured and explained by a descriptive discussion, thus allowing the teacher to
prepare a lesson without projecting the strip. The projector is
relatively inexpensive and easy to operate. The filmstrip has
many instructional advantages. The teacher can keep any frame
in view as long as necessary and ask questions along with the
demonstration; he can skip some frames and build his lesson
around a few important ones; he can back up and repeat
frames as often as necessary. Strips come in black and white or
in color. Sound filmstrips and three-dimensional slides are used
less frequently in the secondary classroom. In the former the
filmstrip is accompanied by a synchronized recording which
contains a narrative description of each frame. Generally the
sound is on tape.

Slides, either 2-by-2 or $3\frac{1}{4}$-by-4 inch, may be purchased commercially or can be made by teacher or students. They are easy
to project and generally serve the same purposes as does the filmstrip. A commercial set of slides can form the basis of a lesson:
on an artist or a special period in art, a period in history, the
culture of a foreign country, the life and times of Shakespeare,
or wild life in Kenya.

Motion pictures are the most expensive of the three aids
discussed here, particularly if the film is in color. Obviously,
this is the audio-visual medium with which the students are
likely to be most familiar, and they probably will associate a motion picture with entertainment. A lesson based on a film must
be carefully planned, with specific learning tasks assigned to the
class in advance. Many commercial films have high educational
value. When one of these is being shown locally at a time when
the subject of the film is being studied, an arrangement for the
class to go to the theatre or for a number of students to see the
film and report on it may be made.

Records and Tapes

Commercially produced records and tapes constitute another valuable instructional resource. (Tapes produced in

school will be discussed later.) They are used to reproduce the voice of a famous statesman or political leader, a narrative account of an event, a story, a natural sound, such as that of birds, animals or insects, native speech in a foreign language, the reading of poetry by a distinguished actor, and other auditory learning experiences the teacher may wish the class to have. Most secondary schools have the equipment—record players, tape recorders, earphones—necessary for appropriate use of these media. Their judicious use can enrich instruction in every subject.

Extra-Class Audio-Visuals

In addition to the use of audio-visual materials in the classroom, the teacher will find many ways of utilizing audio-visual appeal outside the classroom. The school library, for example, with its reference sources, supplementary reading materials, pictures, and special displays, is an excellent resource. The efforts of the librarian to assemble special exhibits for holidays, anniversaries, and new developments deserve the support of classroom teachers. Such displays can be made part of their instructional program. Display cases and bulletin boards throughout the school as well as in the library offer opportunities for instruction. The school audio-visual center may itself constitute an appropriate resource for one or more lessons.

Assembly programs are actually audio-visual instruction periods for large segments of the student body. Programs in dramatics, science, physical education, music, and so on make an audio-visual appeal which may constitute the basis for further instruction in the smaller classroom group.

Commercial community resources, such as radio and television lessons, offer almost unlimited educational possibilities for instructional purposes. Many commercial stations carry public service broadcasts of interest to schools—for example, the "Standard School Broadcasts" sponsored by the Standard Oil Company of California. A number of school systems own their own stations—for example, Atlanta (WABE), Chicago (WBEZ), Cleveland (WBOE), New York (WNYE), and St. Louis (KSLH). These stations broadcast special instructional programs and prepare manuals to aid in classroom instruction based on the broadcasts.

An examination of newspaper listings of commercial radio station programs will reveal a number of scheduled broadcasts which have distinct possibilities for classroom instruction. Students should be told what to listen for, how to make notes, and how to prepare for the classroom lesson. Of course, the assignment of a radio broadcast, whether from an educational or commercial outlet, should be based on the curriculum. The program "lesson" should embody specific teacher and student aims and should be developed along lines designed to achieve these objectives.

The trip, field-trip, or visit to museums, historic sites, industrial establishments, lectures, plays, and films are perhaps the most common extra-class audio-visual educational experiences. These outings, planned in advance, are selected because they implement the curriculum, and are followed by coordinated classroom work. An exception to the requirement of specific curriculum derivation is the trip taken by the senior class as part of its senior year experience. This is a school venture of great educational worth, though it is not immediately derived from the work of any one subject or class. These trips to distant places —Washington, D.C., Bermuda, the Grand Canyon—taken during Christmas or Easter recess may be one of the most enriching experiences of a high-school student's school life.

CREATING AUDIO-VISUALS

We have been discussing the use of audio-visual materials created for classroom use by outside sources. Students and teachers can and do prepare many of their own audio-visuals. Bulletin boards should contain as much or more student material as it does commercial. Students and teachers can tape discussions or debates conducted in the classroom for later playback and analysis. Oratorical contests, special assembly programs, and selected lessons often are recorded on tape and played over the local radio as a public service. Students use the microphone in the classroom and in the assembly, make announcements over the loudspeaker system, edit and write school newspapers, magazines, and yearbooks, and write, produce and act in shows sometimes almost as gracefully and effectively as do professionals.

On special projects students often prepare audio-visual material of high caliber. Posters and cartoons connected with election campaigns and school drives, bas-reliefs or tridimensional models of historic events, biological specimens, and illustrations of mathematical concepts are typical student products in the modern secondary school.

Teacher-Made Aids

Teachers create many audio-visual materials for their teaching. Outlines, pamphlets, and books can be duplicated and distributed to students as course aids. Charts, tapes, slides, overhead transparencies, and assignment sheets, prepared by teachers, often are used by students in independent study. Many teachers make tapes explaining difficult concepts, breaking the subject down into simple steps, and these tapes then are played outside of class by students who need individual help. The tapes can be replayed as often as necessary, and can include questions to which students write answers as they listen. Thus the teacher is able to extend his instructional influence for the benefit of individual students.

TELEVISION

Television is destined to have a great impact on education because this medium is most like the actual classroom in all respects but one—direct contact between teacher and student. This one difference rules out the likelihood that the television teacher will ever replace the classroom teacher, but the former can help the latter in countless ways.

Since the television lesson can be taught simultaneously to thousands or even millions of students, it is feasible for the teacher to spend a week selecting and preparing illustrative material, doing research, and rehearsing the lesson. The performance is done in a studio, recorded on video tape, and scheduled for several television showings so that groups may hear and see it at times best suited to their own schedules. Teachers selected for television teaching should be expert in the subject, skilled in teaching, photogenic, poised, and outgoing.

Educational TV stations present a series of weekly broadcasts for special subjects—literature, geography, economics, chemistry, foreign language, music, and so forth. Each lesson is designed for a specific grade level and tailored to meet the curriculum requirements of a specific course and each is taught by a talented teacher equipped with resources possible only under the special conditions of television broadcasting. Educational television stations in Houston, Pittsburgh, St. Louis, Boston, Philadelphia, New York, and other cities reach schools within a 100-mile radius of each center with lessons in all curriculum areas. School districts which subscribe to the programs receive descriptive literature including summaries of the programs, questions for discussion, suggested sources for additional reading and research, and other aids to teaching and learning.

Open-circuit commercial broadcasts comprise one of the richest extra-class resources available to teachers. By examining TV schedules in newspapers and magazines, teachers can make judicious selection of programs for assignment as regular curriculum undertakings.

Closed-circuit television has effective intra-school use. For example, a program in the assembly can be picked up simultaneously on half a dozen sets throughout the building so that an entire student body, which cannot be accommodated in the assembly at one time, can hear and see a special program—speaker, musical performance, demonstration, debate, and so forth. It is also used to broadcast from a school to homes in the neighborhood and from a central studio to schools in a district.

The development of ultra-high-frequency channels in large numbers will permit assignment of channels to school systems so that they can develop their own closed-circuit television and produce programs suited to their needs. This may be the solution to the problem of scheduling which has prevented television from realizing its potential in secondary education. Since schedules for high-school subjects are relatively inflexible, it has been necessary to choose between upsetting a school's schedule and not seeing a program.

Educational television has developed in recognition of the fact that we are facing a serious shortage of qualified teachers and that television may offer a partial solution to this problem. Unless, however, the television teacher is really superior, the lesson appropriate to the curriculum, the physical conditions of transmission and reception satisfactory, the cost reasonable, and the actual learning results superior to those attained by traditional methods, television may remain just one more audio-visual resource which has a place in education but which does not alter the traditional classroom situation appreciably.

PROGRAMMED LEARNING

Another innovation which has had a significant effect on educational practice is the teaching machine and its derivative, the teaching program. The principle of both is the same, but since the program is relatively inexpensive it has forged ahead, while the teaching machine has tended to disappear.

The principles of programming are based on the principles of learning enunciated by Thorndike at Columbia and revived at Harvard by Skinner, the father of the teaching machine. In printed form, programming consists of a page more or less of text followed immediately by a question (often in multiple choice form), which the student answers before turning the page to see whether he is correct. If correct, he is complimented and permitted to go ahead. If wrong, he is required to go back, re-study the text, and try again. Thus programmed material is a self-instruction device with built-in controls. Teachers are learning to write programs, to select them from commercial offerings, to utilize them in instruction, and to evaluate them. Students are learning to work with programmed material and to react to them as teaching devices. Program-makers maintain that anything that can be verbalized can be presented in a program.

The preparation of programmed material may have important implications for educational practice. In writing an effective program the teacher needs to be very specific with respect to objectives. He must break the subject down into small, comprehensible pieces of information, skill, or attitude and present the pieces in proper psychological order. He needs to devise appropriate tests of mastery. All this forces him to examine the processes of teaching and learning very carefully, more carefully perhaps than ever before.

Programmed instruction is impersonal, even mechanistic, and as such it emphasizes only intellectual aspects of education. One serious drawback to programming, therefore, is its inability to meet social and emotional needs. Even more serious is the problem of whether or not programming can develop critical thinking. Learning bits of information step-by-step may not add up to learning to think, to analyze, to judge, and to create. But since programming has shown amazing vitality and versatility and may have undiscovered possibilities, teachers cannot afford to neglect it as a valuable resource.

THE LANGUAGE LABORATORY

Since 1958, when the National Defense Education Act authorized Federal support for their construction, language laboratories have become widespread. The language laboratory is valuable in the development of skill in foreign-language listening comprehension and in speech production. Tapes, prepared in advance by native speakers, may be listened to by students at any time—both during and apart from regular class periods. Students also record and listen to their own speech. Teachers can use the laboratory to help students analyze and criticize their speech. Material is graded according to difficulty, and any part of a tape may be played back as often as necessary.

A recent study challenges the supposed superiority of language-laboratory instruction over the traditional non-laboratory system.[1] A large experimental group is now making additional evaluation studies to determine the most effective uses of the language laboratory.

SPECIAL USES OF AUDIO-VISUALS

Among the many educational uses of audio-visual media, that of self-instruction holds a special place. We have already discussed the importance of programmed material in self-instruction. Textbooks and other printed material have always been self-instructional devices, at least in part. Instruction in reading, in the use of the library, and in research techniques has been designed to increase the effectiveness of printed material in self-instruction. Microfilm, pictures, records and tapes have been added to library collections as their use in self-instruction has been recognized. In the modern high school it is not uncommon to find students studying at carrels in the library, operating a microfilm projector, listening to tapes in a language laboratory, reviewing a film or filmstrip, examining a collection of pictures, and studying specimens or performing

---

[1] Raymond Keating, "Preliminary Evaluation of the Effectiveness of Language Laboratories as Used in the Metropolitan School Study Council," Institute of Administrative Research (in press) (New York: Teachers College, Columbia U. 1963).

an experiment in a science laboratory on their own. Often the student's purpose is to review (re-view) a learning experience which he did not fully master when it was taught. Sometimes he wishes to go ahead on his own and pursue an interest beyond what was taught in class or in new directions not part of the prescribed course of study. Often it is to study material taken up in class during the student's absence.

Audio-visuals also are a boon to the handicapped—audios for the blind, and visuals for the deaf or hard of hearing. The homebound now are receiving much of their instruction via television, radio, tapes, and other media. The diagnosis of difficulties in speech and in performance is greatly facilitated for teacher and student through the use of tape recordings or by examination of moving pictures in slow motion.

ADMINISTRATION OF AUDIO-VISUAL AIDS

The effective utilization of audio-visual techniques and materials depends to a large extent on administrative details. No matter how carefully a teacher plans an audio-visual lesson, he cannot teach it successfully if the projector, player, or other instrument on which the lesson depends is not delivered at the proper time and place, if it is defective or breaks down, or if the operator is inept or untutored. Unfortunately these happenings are not infrequent and valuable class time can be lost. Proper administration can obviate these difficulties.

Teachers and supervisors need to examine and report on many tapes, films, and other materials before one is purchased. Organized procedures for recommending purchases need to be set up. Purchases of audio-visual supplies and materials need to be made part of an overall budgetary plan. A long-term program, into which specific selections are fitted, needs to be adopted and followed. All audio-visual materials in a school or school system need to be catalogued and the catalogs made available to all members of the staff, so that they may make intelligent selections for their teaching. There should be procedures by which recommendations for purchases are solicited from staff members. Storing, distributing, collecting, and maintaining resources pose administrative problems that can materially affect the quality of the audio-visual program.

Many schools find it desirable to have a student audio-visual squad under the direction of a faculty member. These boys and girls learn to operate and maintain audio-visual equipment which is kept in a centrally located room to which members of the squad report during specific free periods each day or several times a week. Squad members help keep records, repair equipment, deliver it to and recover it from classrooms, and assist in its operation. They are responsible to the faculty member and are rated on the manner in which they discharge their responsibilities. This group of students makes an important contribution to the instructional program of the school and at the same time acquires worthwhile knowledge, skills, and habits.

Selection of Audio-Visuals

The selection of audio-visual materials deserves special attention. Any good work on audio-visual instruction will direct the reader to sources. For example, Wittich and Schuller contains seventeen pages of names and addresses of manufacturers and publishers of audio-visuals.[2] Teachers and supervisors should write for catalogs and descriptive materials to each of the organizations which produce items in their areas. The literature should be carefully examined; recommendations for purchases should be made after group discussion; items should be examined as soon as received, and retained or returned after consultation.

As far as possible, teachers should be involved in the process of selection of materials, since they are the ones who will be using them in instruction. This, of course, requires much time and effort spent in examining catalogs, comparing offerings, previewing, and writing evaluations and recommendations.

A vast amount of free or inexpensive audio-visual material is available. However, many of these items are produced by industries and organizations seeking to influence the viewer and/ or listener either through subtle propaganda contained in the material or through outright advertising which precedes and follows the content material. It is incumbent on teacher and administrator to examine each item from the point of view of its propaganda message and to decide whether it may be used appropriately. The fact that an item contains a special propaganda

[2] Walter A. Wittich and Charles F. Schuller, *Audio Visual Materials* (3rd ed.; New York: Harper, 1962), pp. 477–494.

message does not automatically rule it out: indeed, the message itself may be used as a focus for instruction. But teacher and supervisor must be conscious of this aspect and make their judgments with this in mind.

Many items may be obtained on loan or rental basis from audio-visual centers. The teacher and curriculum specialist should secure loan and rental catalogs from United States Government sources, state and local audio-visual centers, professional associations, universities, trade associations, private industry, travel bureaus, and foreign-government information services. These agencies often produce items of very high caliber containing a minimum of advertising or propaganda. Borrowing or renting material is no strain on even a modest budget. In addition, the expense of storing and cataloging the item is saved and obsolescence is avoided. While every school should have a basic collection of materials commonly used, the practice of supplementing these with loans and rentals should be encouraged.

Teacher Preparation

Most institutions which prepare secondary-school teachers offer one or more courses in audio-visual education. Generally such courses are electives, since certification requirements for teaching in the secondary school ordinarily do not include preparation in creating and using audio-visual material. But most certifying agencies will accept an audio-visual course as an elective or alternative course toward certification. If a course is not available, a unit on audio-visual education should be included in the general- or special-methods course. Students should acquire some skill in operating the more common devices—film and filmstrip projectors, tape recorders, overhead projectors, and so on—and become familiar with the materials available in their special subject fields. The care and repair of audio-visual equipment is an important part of this knowledge.

College courses in communication can give the teacher insight into the teaching advantages of radio and television. During the period of preparation the teacher should begin to build a file of sources of materials and of actual materials for teaching his own and related subjects.

Teachers who have a special interest in audio-visuals would

do well to elect all available courses in this field or to take summer work at a university offering advanced courses in audio-visual education. There are many opportunities in education for professional personnel who wish to make careers in audio-visual education. Many school systems delegate responsibility for the audio-visual program to a director of audio-visual education. Others have curriculum-materials centers in which the audio-visual resources are housed under the supervision of a curriculum-materials director. There are specialists in educational television, television teachers, tape teaching specialists, and audio-visual consultants in many school systems today. Opportunities as authors, inventors, and specialists in the area of audio-visual education are virtually unlimited.

THE FUTURE OF AUDIO-VISUALS

Educational television and programmed instruction are constantly being explored both in the direction of technical improvement and in the educational uses to which they are applied. Other new processes and techniques are constantly being introduced. Motion-picture machines which do not require that the room be darkened, filmstrips with accompanying sound tracks, devices for copying a printed page exactly, reproduction of any page on overhead transparencies, and extensive use of microfilm for reproducing and storing information are examples of developments which have greatly increased the instructional effectiveness of audio-visuals. Experiments with automation and data-processing promise to open opportunities for teaching and learning and for positions of responsibility in the development and application of these devices. New computers are able to store and reproduce amazing amounts of data and information. Centralized library processing devices are being developed which will enable students to do library research in their own schools or homes through special information-retrieving apparatus. Some of these machines are so intricate that they approximate man's thinking processes. In time we will not only learn to use them as we do any other new invention, but we may gain from their use new insights into the processes of thinking, teaching, and learning. They may, in fact, immeasurably enhance the human capacity for problem solving.

Audio-visuals are bound to influence traditional school

patterns in organization and in teaching. Large-group instruction, for example, is a natural outcome of the use of such media as film projectors and tape recorders. Self-instruction, especially outside the classroom, is greatly facilitated by programming and by tapes. The preparation of teachers now requires new emphases on technological and educational developments resulting from the progress in audio-visual materials. The nature of the teacher's work, both in and out of the classroom, has been altered by the need to consider audio-visuals in planning for instruction, in utilizing available resources, and in the preparation of audio-visual materials. The continuing revolution in the production and use of audio-visual methods and materials is an important phase of the current revolution in secondary education.

FOR DELIBERATION and DISCUSSION

1. To what extent are audio-visual instructional processes synonymous with the entire teaching-learning experience? How may they be distinguished?
2. Which of the audio-visuals seems best adapted for instruction in your special subject area? Which least? Explain.
3. Prepare an audio-visual resource unit for teaching a unit of the secondary curriculum in your subject.
4. How has the development of audio-visuals influenced teacher education? Have teacher education and certification adequately met teacher needs in this area? Have the uses of audio-visuals been "oversold"?
5. Explore the instructional uses of one audio-visual medium. What, if anything, is lost by a skillful teacher who does not utilize this medium in teaching?
6. What are some of the problems involved in developing an effective audio-visual program in a secondary school? What part can the individual teacher play in helping solve them?

FOR ADDITIONAL READING

A-V Communication Review, II, No. 3 (May-June 1963). Published bimonthly by the Department of Audio-Visual Instruction, NEA. Contains articles on programming, television, and presentations of statistical material. Book reviews and research abstracts are included.

BROWN, JAMES W., LEWIS, RICHARD B., and HARCLEROAD, FRED F. *A-V Instruction Materials and Methods.* New York: McGraw-Hill, 1959. A careful, well-illustrated compilation of information on A-V matters. Useful reference sections and subject-field reference guide.

CROSS, A. J. FOY and CYPHER, IRENE F. *Audio-Visual Education.* New York: Crowell, 1961. Comprehensive treatment. Extensive bibliography and directory of sources.

DETERLINE, WILLIAM A. *An Introduction to Programmed Instruction.* Englewood Cliffs: Prentice-Hall, 1962. Includes a bibliography and a program on tests and test interpretation. Combines description of various types of programming with theoretical discussion of learning and of the rationale for programmed learning.

FREEDMAN, FLORENCE B. and BERG, ESTHER L. *Classroom Teacher's Guide to Audio-Visual Material.* Philadelphia: Chilton, 1961. Contains many ideas for the classroom teacher who wishes to use audio-visual aids.

Journal of Programmed Instruction, II, No. 1 (Spring, 1963): 57–67. Published quarterly by the Center for Programmed Instruction.

KINDER, JAMES S. *Audio-Visual Materials and Techniques.* 2nd ed.; New York: American Book, 1959. Long recognized as the standard text in audio-visual instruction, with special relevance for the classroom.

Programs, '62: A Guide to Programmed Instructional Materials Available to Educators by September 1962. Washington, D.C. United States Government Printing Office, 1962. Prepared by the Center for Programmed Instruction in cooperation with the United States Office of Education. Three-hundred sixty-seven pages of sources and actual illustrations of program items.

SUTTLER, P. H. and HARTLEY, W. H. *Educator's Guide to Free Social Studies Material.* 2nd ed.; Randolph: Educator's Progress Service, 1962. Based on the cross-media approach. Lists and classifies films, filmstrips, tapes, books and other materials.

THOMAS, R. MURRAY and SWARTOUT, SHERWIN G. *Integrated Teaching Materials: How to Choose.* New York: McKay, 1963. Detailed instructions with appropriate illustrations for working with audio-visual materials.

WITTICH, WALTER ARNO and SCHULLER, CHARLES FRANCIS. *Audio Visual Materials: Their Nature and Use.* 3rd ed.; New York: Harper, 1962. One of the best resources for the classroom teacher and for the supervisor.

PART III: ADMINISTRATION AND
SCHOOL-COMMUNITY RELATIONS

18 The Teacher and Administrative Relations

THE BOARD OF EDUCATION

Teachers perform their professional services within the policy boundaries established by the board of education of a school district. If policy development is examined carefully, it is found generally that teachers have been involved in establishing policy at some point. Of course, involvement will vary according to the degree of authoritarian-democratic administrative atmosphere prevailing.

Each teacher in a district is expected to know and follow the prescribed policies of the board. In fact, most boards of education reproduce personnel policy manuals for their staff. As examples of the areas covered in these manuals, portions from representative school-board policy manuals are cited.

Portland, Oregon Public Schools

In this school system the board of education publishes *Rules and Regulations,* a policy handbook covering both broad and specific regulations which are the responsibility of the administration. The manual outlines the duties of the administrative officials of the school system and its expectations for its teachers.

DUTIES AND RESPONSIBILITIES OF TEACHERS

1. All teachers shall register in person at their respective buildings at least 15 minutes before the beginning period in the morning. Teachers shall remain in their respective classrooms at

least 15 minutes after the close of each school day to be available for conferences with parents and pupils. The principal may permit a teacher to leave earlier when such teacher's presence is required elsewhere for school purposes or due to a personal emergency.

2. Teachers who find it necessary to be absent shall notify the office of the superintendent as soon after 7:30 A.M. as possible. Notice must also be sent to the respective principal at the school. An absent teacher shall give the office of the superintendent and his principal notice of his intention to resume school work. If the absent teacher reports for duty without giving such notice, the substitute teacher shall receive pay for one-half day and such time shall be charged to the absent teacher in accordance with the rules pertaining to salary deductions for absences. When the substitute becomes aware of his forthcoming release, he shall immediately inform the office of the superintendent.

3. Teachers shall keep all records required and shall report to the principal's office, at the time and in the manner prescribed, all absences and all failures to obtain satisfactory excuses for absences of pupils.

4. Teachers shall administer any marking system or other means of evaluating pupils' achievement that may be prescribed for the school and report to parents the progress of their children as directed by the principal.

5. Teachers may inflict corporal punishment only in extreme cases when other means fail to obtain obedience. Except in the event of forcible and physical resistance to the teacher's authority, corporal punishment shall be administered only after the teacher has procured in advance the approval of the principal. Such punishment shall be administered in the presence of the principal.

6. Teachers shall be responsible for the care, discipline, and instruction of pupils in their charge and for any or all pupils of the school outside class hours as assigned by the principal of the school; they shall enforce all rules governing the conduct of pupils, as such rules may be prescribed by the principal, the Superintendent, or the Board; they shall maintain hygienic conditions and practices in their classrooms, and shall report promptly to the principal any serious accident or illness affecting pupils in their charge.

7. Before granting permission for pupils to leave school, at the request of or in the company of any person not a school officer, teachers shall obtain the approval of the principal.

8. No person, not an employee of the school district engaged upon his official duties, shall be permitted to interview a pupil unless said interview has been authorized by the principal; the principal shall prescribe the conditions under which such an interview may take place.

9. No teacher shall accept any compensation for private instruction given pupils enrolled in his respective building; and no member of the instructional corps shall be permitted to give instruction of any nature in a school building where a charge is made for such instruction during the regular school year.

10. All teachers and others are expected to abide by both the letter and the spirit of the state law.

Oregon Law.   Chapter 336.430 ORS

"No person shall solicit, receive or permit to be solicited or received from pupils enrolled in the public schools, on any public school premises any subscription, donation of money or other thing of value for presentation of testimonials to school officials or for any purpose except such as are authorized by the district school board."

The only exceptions authorized by the Board of Directors must be those of educational value to the pupils such as those stated below:

(a) Gifts to the school. Educational values will be fully realized in gifts to the school as in gifts to the individual.
(b) Floral pieces for funerals.
(c) Gifts for illness.

11. Teachers shall cooperate with their principals when requested to supervise any of the various student activities.

12. During the three-day period Wednesday, Thursday, and Friday of the week preceding the beginning of each new school year, newly elected teachers may confer with their respective principals, supervisors, and directors of their respective offices; during this same period all teachers who have been transferred from one school to another may confer with the principal of the school to which they have been assigned.

13. It shall be the duty of all employees to notify the office of the superintendent in writing of changes in name, and the Superintendent shall then notify the business office, office of the school clerk, the Teachers' Retirement Fund Association, and the Public Employees' Retirement System.

14. In-service training credits shall be earned by work at an accredited college or university, the Northwestern College of Law, and such other institutions as may be designated by the

Board from time to time, attendance at business, art, music, or other classes directly related to the teacher's field of teaching approved by the Superintendent, work at workshops or classes conducted by the district, teaching in workshops or classes conducted by the district after regular hours, or work on curriculum committees set up by the school district.[1]

Seattle, Washington Public Schools

A significant area of school administration relating to the life of the teacher is the adopted salary schedule. Establishment of salary policies is the legal responsibility of the board of education. In addition to decisions of basic salary determination, the board may adopt other salary policies which affect teachers. In the Seattle schools, for example, the following policies are in effect:

EXPERIENCE CREDIT

Outside experience credit is allowed as follows: teachers who entered the corps prior to September, 1960, are granted experience credit at $100 per year up to 5 years; teachers who entered the corps on or after September, 1960, are granted up to 6 years; and teachers entering the corps on or after September, 1961, may be granted outside experience credit at $100 per year up to 8 years, but not to exceed the maximum in any group.

MAXIMA

The maxima for the groups requiring a B.A. and a B.A. plus 22½ quarter hours, for teachers who entered the corps prior to September, 1959, will be $6,200 and $6,600, respectively. For teachers entering the corps September, 1959, or thereafter, the maxima will be $5,600 and $5,800.

Teachers in the corps during the school year 1958–59 with less than a B.A. may be continued in that group to a maximum of $5,800. For teachers with less than a B.A. entering the corps in 1959–60 or thereafter, the maximum will be $5,200.

M.A AND PH.D.

For an M.A. or approved Doctorate, add $200 to each scheduled salary. An earned Ph.D. or a Doctor of Education, from an accredited institution, will be accepted without further evaluation. Other doctoral degrees must be brought to the Credits Committee for special consideration.

[1] *Rules and Regulations* (Portland: Board of Education, 1962), pp. 10–11.

PROFESSIONAL GROWTH REQUIREMENTS

Beginning with the 1962–63 school year, automatic salary increases based upon years of experience, and automatic retention of maximums, will be replaced with a professional study program requiring the satisfactory completion of stipulated courses in predetermined areas of work.

Appropriate committees will be designated early in the 1961–62 school year to recommend ways of implementing the professional growth features of the salary schedule. To be eligible for increment increases or to retain the maximums in 1962–63, certificated personnel must submit evidence of three-quarter hours of college or professional course study. This will be a start toward a more comprehensive plan.

UNSATISFACTORY RATINGS

Teachers receiving unsatisfactory ratings in 1961–62 and thereafter will be ineligible for salary increments.

EXTRA-CURRICULAR ACTIVITY SALARIES: HIGH SCHOOL

Position	Amount
Football Head	$660
Football Assistant	380
Basketball Head	600
Basketball Assistant	330
Baseball Head	400
Baseball Assistant	220
Track Head	400
Track Assistant	220
Golf	160
Tennis	180
Intramural	420
Yearbook Advisor	300
Class Advisor	430
Debate	230
Drama	500
Music	500
Financial Manager	550
Newspaper	400
Scholastic Advisor	150
Activity Coordinator	400
Stockroom	400[2]

[2] *Supplement to the Teachers' Handbook of Personnel Policies* (Seattle: Board of Education, 1961), pp. 2–5.

East Hartford, Connecticut Public Schools

The East Hartford Board of Education publishes a detailed administrative policy manual outlining function and responsibility not only for all school employees but for the Board members. In order to provide the beginning secondary-school teacher an opportunity to study the many facets of school administrative policy which is the province of the board of education, the following section of this manual is presented here:

ARTICLE IX—TEACHERS

1. *Connecticut Education Association—Code of Ethics*

The educational system of our country must bear a great responsibility in shaping the principles of dignity, equality, and mutual understanding, if democracy and international cooperation are to succeed. To this end the teachers strive to rid youth of prejudice and inculcate a desire for effective, democratic citizenship and human good. In order that the teacher may retain a high standard of conduct in professional relations, may be a worthy example of that which he teaches, and may promote his profession, the Connecticut Education Association has adopted this Code of Ethics. The term "teacher" used in this code shall include all persons directly engaged in educational work, whether in teaching, or administrative, or supervisory capacity.

   a. *Relations to Pupils and the Home*
   The teacher is just, firm, and kind in his relationships to pupils.
   The teacher refrains from accepting remunerations for the tutoring during the school year of pupils who are in his class.
   The teacher refrains from disclosing confidential information concerning his pupils, unless it is for the best interest of the child and the public. The teacher seeks to establish cooperation between home and school.

   b. *Relations to the Community and the Nation*
   The teacher supports the Constitution of the United States and of the State of Connecticut, obeying their laws while recognizing the principle of legal change.
   The teacher strives to inculcate in his pupils an appreciation of American democracy.
   The teacher, in the presentation of controversial matters, seeks to present objectively the issues involved.

The teacher exercises his rights, responsibilities, and duties of citizenship.

c. *Relations to the Profession*

The teacher dignifies his calling and upholds the importance of his service to society.

The teacher encourages individuals of high moral standards and scholastic attainment to enter the teaching profession.

The teacher tries to maintain professional competence by study, travel, and other appropriate means.

The teacher is an active member of his professional organizations.

The teacher seeks to secure and maintain salary schedules commensurate with professional qualifications, obligations and attainments.

The teacher works for improved school facilities and professional salaries no matter what other civic position he may hold in addition to that of teacher.

The teacher does not apply for a position currently held by another teacher.

The teacher considers professional qualifications and attainments as the primary factor in appointment or promotion.

In recommendations the teacher is truthful, inclusive, and confidential.

The teacher neither accepts nor offers a position at a salary other than that called for in effect for other teachers in the system.

The teacher faithfully discharges the terms of his contract until it is dissolved by mutual consent or by due process of law.

The teacher observes the professional courtesy of transacting official business with the properly designated authority.

The teacher avoids disseminating unfavorable criticism or injurious hearsay concerning his associates.

The teacher avoids interference between another teacher and a pupil except in performance of duty.

The teacher avoids accepting gratuities either directly or indirectly resulting from transactions involving school supplies and services.

As a member of a democratic group, the teacher accepts such responsibilities as the group shall place upon him.

The teacher refrains from exerting undue influence upon his colleagues because of being placed in a position of authority.

2. *General Duties*

It shall be the duty of teachers to study the needs, problems and interests of the children under their direction, to try to give them guidance so that the maximum development of each child may be achieved, to know and to cooperate with the parents, to encourage parents to visit school not only on visiting days but at other times so that school and home problems related to education may be fully discussed, to visit their homes as occasions arise, to discuss problems related to the education of their children, to attend parent-teacher meetings, to attend meetings called by supervisors, the principals or the Superintendent, to take courses by extension, to serve on permanent and special committees, to build courses of study, and to perform such other duties as may be prescribed by the Rules and Regulations of the Board of Education, by the Superintendent, and by State law.

3. *Responsibility*

The Board of Education is responsible for the adoption of policies while the Superintendent is responsible for putting the policies into operation. The relationship of the teacher to the Board of Education, is, therefore, indirect and although she is responsible to the Superintendent such responsibility comes largely through the building principal. The Board of Education and the Superintendent seek through the Teachers' Council the advice of teachers regarding matters of policy and execution of such matters. Any plans that an individual teacher or group of teachers may have looking toward the improvement of the schools should be discussed with the principal before being presented to the Superintendent, and any far-reaching plan that the principal has to propose to the Superintendent should first be discussed with the teachers.

The teachers are responsible for teaching their pupils in accordance with the courses of study adopted by the Board of Education. They should look to the supervisors and principals for advice in improving their teaching methods.

4. *Arrival—Tardiness*

Elementary teachers shall be in their classrooms at least 20 minutes before the opening of school. High school teachers shall be in their rooms by 8:00 each morning of school. Any case of persistent tardiness shall be reported to the Superintendent.

5. *Departure*

Elementary teachers shall remain in the building a reasonable length of time (usually 30 minutes) after the close of school until the duties of the day have been completed. Arrangements may be made with the principal for early departure one afternoon a week. High school teachers are expected to devote a regular helping period after the close of regular classes until 3:10 each day. In case of faculty meeting, committee meeting, or other assigned school duty, the teacher shall be expected to give precedence to said meeting or other duty. Teachers must never leave the room for the day when pupils are still in the classroom, and shall be present when a special teacher is instructing his or her class. At fire drills and at the close of school the teacher shall be the last person to leave the room. (A coffee break not in excess of 15 minutes may be allowed to each employee each day, provided that if it is necessary for the teacher to leave the classroom, another teacher or the principal should cover.)

6. *Absences*

Teachers who expect to be absent on a certain day, or in returning after absence, shall call the person designated by the Superintendent either the evening before said day between 6:30 and 7 P.M. or on the morning of said day between 7 and 7:30 A.M.

7. *Half-Sessions*

Teachers of classes on half-sessions (either a four-hour morning or afternoon session) are required in addition to their regular duties, to give such assignments of $1\frac{1}{2}$ hours each day as the Superintendent or principal may require.

8. *Care of Property*

Teachers shall see that the textbooks and all other school property committed to their charge are properly cared for.

9. *Money*

Teachers are advised not to leave money or valuables in their desk or elsewhere in the room.

10. *School Property*

Property of the Board of Education shall not be taken from any school building or office for private use, or for loan to any employee or other individual or to any outside organization except with the approval of the principal.

11. *Telephones*

Telephones are installed in the school for use by principals, teachers and pupils. However, neither teachers nor pupils are to be called from their classrooms during school hours to answer a telephone call unless it is a matter of extreme urgency. All out-of-town calls made are to be recorded on a form provided for the purpose and are to be paid for unless authorized by the Superintendent, and then only on school business. Principals shall enforce this regulation. Public booths, where available, shall be used for toll calls.

12. *Sales and Drives*

a. No person shall be allowed to sell or offer for sale within the schools or Board offices any articles or services to employees or pupils, or to solicit contributions or signatures of such persons; provided, however, that this rule shall not be construed as restricting or prohibiting any school activity, the solicitation and collection of Community Chest contributions, the solicitation of Red Cross memberships, or the sale of Defense Bonds and stamps or other drives approved by the Board of Education.

b. Magazines, etc.—The schools shall not be used for the the purpose of selling magazines, newspapers, seeds, pictures, lottery tickets, or other sales promotion schemes. Any variation of this rule would need Board approval. This also shall include the distribution of hand bills.

c. Beverages—Children should be educated to drink plain milk and discouraged from bringing other beverages to school for lunch or parties.

d. Candy—It is desirable that no candy, except that made by pupils be sold in the schools.

e. Supplies—Educational supplies are furnished free by the Board. Teachers shall not require pupils to pay for books, pencils, pens or paper. Pupils who wish to purchase additional books may do so through the building principal. Teachers may permit their pupils, however, to subscribe for newspapers and magazines with the approval of the principal, such as Current Events and Readers Digest, and to purchase their own fountain pens.

13. *Health and Safety*

Teachers shall regulate radiators and window ventilators so that room temperature shall stay between 68 and 72 degrees. It is desirable that children be seated so that there is no glare from windows or wall and that they do not face the light. Teachers shall report all cases of accident or serious injury to the principal. The principal shall promptly report accident facts to the Superintendent on blanks furnished for that purpose.

14. *Outside Employment*

During days that school is in session it is desirable that no full-time employee undertake any paid employment aside from school work. During national emergencies or under certain cases of necessity approved by the administration, school employees should devote no more than four hours per school day to any out-side employment except on Fridays provided that it does not conflict with school responsibility.

No member of the professional staff shall receive compensation for services offered during the school year to pupils or patrons of the school with whom he is in any way directly associated in a professional way.

He shall not promote in the schools or in the community any activity or project from which he is likely to receive compensation or remuneration other than his salary as an employee of the Board of Education without the knowledge of the Superintendent of Schools.

15. *Physical Examinations*

All school employees are encouraged to have annual physical examinations.

When an employee requests a leave for ill health, the results of an examination revealing the necessity for such leave shall be filed with the Superintendent.

When an employee wishes to return after a leave granted because of illness, he shall file a statement from his physician which states that the employee is physically able to carry on his normal assignment. The employee shall not be allowed to return until the approval of the school's medical advisor has been secured.[3]

Board of education policies affecting teachers in the school districts cited are not much different in school systems across the country. It is important for the student in education to recognize that every board of education has adopted regulations which affect the teacher, his work, and his relations with the administration in a great many ways. A quick re-examination of personnel policies from these representative school system policy manuals will indicate that the board of education exercises control over teachers and their work in the following areas:

Requirement of medical reports attesting physical fitness of the teacher.

[3] *Rules and Regulations for All Personnel* (East Hartford: Board of Education, 1959), pp. 32–37.

Specification of the time for reporting for work and for leaving the school building.

Requirement of certain procedures of record-keeping.

Specification of pupil marking systems and pupil reporting systems to parents.

Approval of disciplinary measures for pupil control.

Procedures for reporting pupil accidents.

Regulations for tutoring of pupils for pay.

Control over employment outside of school hours.

Rules over receipt of gifts from pupils and parents.

Policies concerning salary, credit for experience outside the school system, and in-service education credits applicable for pay increases.

Policies concerning extracurricular assignment and relation to pay.

Policies concerning teacher-pupil and teacher-parent relations.

Regulations about the use and care of school property.

Rules concerning the use of school telephones.

Policies over sales and drives allowed in the school system.

An easy generalization might be that the larger the district, the more authoritarian the policy, but there are some smaller districts which are as rigid in personnel policies as the larger. Not all aspects of board of education policy will affect you as a secondary-school teacher, but the relationship of teacher and administration operates broadly within the area of these stated policies. The teacher, of course, has little direct relationship with the members of the board of education except in unusual cases, such as those of a legal nature where, for example, a tenure employee is dismissed and litigation follows. The teacher's relations with administration are thus affected at the central school system office level and at the level of the principal's office.

RELATIONSHIPS OF TEACHER AND THE CENTRAL ADMINISTRATION

The Superintendent of Schools

In small school systems, the teacher's official relationship with the superintendent of schools may be close. The superintendent probably does the recruiting and interviewing, and provides the initial orientation to the position, the school system, and the community. He sets the salary (within the board of education policy) at which the teacher will begin. He may conduct faculty meetings, work directly with teachers and parents in PTA affairs, and he may conduct his work directly from an office in the high-school building. In such districts the teacher may feel that the superintendent maintains a substantial responsibility for direct supervision and observance of his work, and indeed, this is true. Instead of doing business with intermediate offices, teachers may go directly to the office of the superintendent for personal advice, for evaluation of their work, for requests of a special nature, occasionally "to bargain" for remuneration, and for other purposes.

By contrast, in the large school system, the teacher may never see the superintendent or the assistant superintendent even when he is interviewed for a position. Usually teacher personnel offices are maintained for handling necessary relationships at the central office level. Teacher applicants are interviewed by an official from this office, and in many cases the candidate is employed as a teacher without regard for individual school placement. The candidate is told he will be notified about his specific grade level and school building assignment sometime before the opening of school.

Students who are more discriminating in their choice of teaching assignments may desire employment in a medium-sized district, where delegation for interview and recommendation for appointment are given to the individual principal in whose school the vacancy exists. In these situations the student is afforded immediate opportunity to meet the person who will have more to say about the evaluation of his work than any other administrator. More often than not he will be invited to visit the school, to meet with the department head, and to have an opportunity to examine available instructional facilities. In most cases this kind of procedure is more satisfactory, and it sets the stage for initiating closer personal relationships between teacher and administration than the rather impersonal practices in the largest school systems.

It is a fairly accurate assumption that, as the size of the school system increases, the personal relationships of teacher to superintendent of schools decrease.

The Central Office Staff

In most school systems teachers have many more contacts with other central office administrators than with the superintendent of schools. Pupil personnel officials deal with admission of pupils, psychological testing and evaluation, and guidance services, all of which embrace pupil responsibilities of teachers. Teachers are involved with central office staff for individual pupil testing and reporting, for dealing with atypical children, and for cooperative decisions for psychological treatment of students.

A second board of education office which is directly related to the teacher is that of curriculum. In fact, teachers probably have more contacts with this central administrative channel than with all others combined. They may work with a director of instruction or with the head of secondary education from the board of education office on textbook selection committees, on course revision or construction, or perhaps on a committee to select new achievement tests in a department. Teacher committees often have to do evaluative work on courses of study, select professional books and instructional materials, and appraise audio-visual materials for purchase by the school system. Since the central curriculum office is generally charged with responsibility for development of instructional materials, teachers construct teaching units for system-wide use, and try out experimental techniques and procedures of teaching—team teaching, use of programmed instruction, teaching machines, programs for talented students, advanced college-preparatory courses, and the like.

Curriculum committee planning and implementation of new programs are generally assumed by teachers in addition to their teaching loads, though in some cases central office administrators will grant released time for this work. The central office curriculum staff will encourage teacher participation. Even though such involvement is professionally rewarding, teachers must remember that their job of classroom instruction must be given priority. If a teacher feels that the central office curriculum staff expects so much work that classroom teaching is suffering, a request for less involvement should be made. Administrators must be made aware of unrealistic expectations. Sensitivity to this problem is important, along with the ability to say "No" until the teacher is confident of being able to manage outside-class responsibilities for the school system and at the same time perform successfully in his own classroom.

The Personnel Office

Teachers occasionally have professional relations with the assistant superintendent for personnel, whose office deals with teachers' committees for salary and personnel policies. More tension in teacher-administrative relationships is generated by salary and working conditions than by any other problem.

Whenever remuneration, teaching conditions, and teaching load are concerned, the relationship between teachers and central-office administration can easily become quite strained. Local teachers' organizations and committees very often involve individuals—both administrators and teachers—in unfortunate personal attacks on one another. When this happens, relationships between teacher and administrator are negatively affected. These wounds take a long time to heal. In most cases the rifts come into the open during teacher negotiations with central offices for personnel.

An understanding of some of the contributing factors is very important. On the administrative side there is usually the problem of a rapidly increasing student enrollment and mounting school costs of every kind, from school building construction and maintenance to increasing demands by teachers for higher salaries and lower teacher-pupil ratio. Coupled with this is mounting taxpayer resistance to greater spending on education —at both local and state levels—so that the school administrator is "caught in a trap"—a trap from which the school official cannot extricate himself until society at large views education of children and youth more favorably.

The teacher's problem is just as grave. "The typical salary schedule in the largest school districts provides $4,700 for beginning teachers with B.A. degrees and a maximum of $8,500 with advanced training. The corresponding range in selected wealthy suburban districts is $4,800 to $9,200."[4] In the smaller districts, the typical salary begins at $4,400 with a maximum of $7,400. With the cost of living index in the United States at its highest

[4] NEA *Research Bulletin,* 40, No. 4 (December, 1962): 126.

level in history, the expenses of continued university preparation increasing greatly with each succeeding year, and the higher
rates of income tax, the teacher finds it extremely difficult to
make his monthly pay check cover his financial responsibilities.
When the teacher's financial plight is set down beside facts of increasing class size, increasing half-day sessions,[5] a burgeoning
number of high-school dropouts, more pupil discipline problems, and a smaller percentage of school budgets each year spent
for school equipment and instructional supplies, the teacher's
problems are multiplied. Conditions on both sides thus militate
against a positive, harmonious solution to problems of teacher-
administrative relationships, especially at the central office level.

Teacher-Principal Relationships

The secondary-school principal occupies a position in the
middle of the school administration hierarchy: he is neither at
the top nor at the bottom in administrative policy decisions.
He must abide by established board of education policy, just as
teachers must. But there is one significant difference between
principal and teacher—the principal is charged with responsibility for seeing that board of education policy is carried out. For
example, if board regulations indicate that teachers are to remain in the building for thirty minutes after school is dismissed,
central administrative officials hold the principal responsible
for seeing that the rule is carried out no matter how unpopular
it may be with the staff.

Although a principal may not always think a policy good,
he cannot say to his teachers: "This is a very poor policy, so
please don't blame me for it." He must accept the policy and do
his best to carry it out. In the writers' opinion teachers generally
ascribe more authority to the principal than he really has, and
they are prone to rely too greatly on his office for solution of personnel policy questions.

<hr>

[5] Thirty-four percent of our nation's classrooms in districts of 6,000 or less and
94 percent in districts of 100,000 or more enroll more than 30 pupils each; half
of our largest cities report half-day sessions for some pupils. In March, 1962,
more than 250,000 elementary pupils were on half-day sessions in the United
States. The Detroit school system, for example, had nearly 30 percent of its
pupils on half-day sessions during 1963–64; all first, fourth, and seventh-grade
students were placed on half-day sessions beginning in September, 1963.

The teacher must understand from the start of his career that almost every principal will have both strengths and weaknesses. He may have an excellent grasp of the secondary-school curriculum and yet rely too much on special activities, such as music or athletics, in the school's public-relations program. He may work hard at school-community relations and spend time in service club work but neglect the development of a positive climate in the school. Or he may spend so much time on his office work with the door closed that teachers feel they must make an appointment well in advance to see him about a problem. Rarely will a principal carry out his responsibilities in such a manner that all teachers are satisfied with him. He will make mistakes in judgments and decisions, and he will have administrative strengths and weaknesses. The teacher should be realistic in his expectations of the principal's ability to be "all things to all people."

Teacher Expectations

What can the teacher expect from the principal? First, he should expect that the principal will establish the kind of educational climate that makes it possible for teachers to carry out effective instruction in their classes. It is not possible to teach successfully when continual student misbehavior is tolerated and when there are no sharply drawn policies for dealing with individual students who disrupt classes. The final authority for student problems of a disciplinary nature is the principal. Of course, this does not lessen the teacher's responsibility for understanding individual differences, for drawing on his own knowledge and ability for dealing with pupil behavior problems, and for evaluating his own methods and personality as causal factors of student discipline patterns in his classes. But the principal's office should provide procedural policies for taking care of unusual needs in this area. The lack of written or well-understood student personnel policies or failure to implement such policy statements are causes of failure in teacher-principal relationships.

The teacher has a right to expect objective appraisal of his teaching and general recommendations for improving techniques of instruction and student relationships from his principal. This is especially important for the beginning teacher.

Probably the most important recommendations of the principal will concern personality traits, and these recommendations may be the most difficult ones for the teacher to understand and accept. Yet if these suggestions have validity, they are most helpful. Teachers should look on suggestions of the principal as one means to more successful teaching.

The principal can be expected to deal fairly with faculty members in teaching load, in size of classes, and in extracurricular assignments. Most principals will try to do what they can to alleviate extra heavy loads and assignments to the beginning teachers, knowing that the major portion of their time must be spent in gaining confidence and success in classroom teaching.

The relationship between teacher and principal must be highly professional. The principal can be expected to keep matters of a personal nature confidential, to be friendly and behave in a socially acceptable way toward teachers, and to uphold the professional stature of his position. Of course, these are standards which run in both directions: it is expected that the teacher, too, will behave in a professional and ethical manner in relationships with the principal.

Failure in human relations constitutes the most important single reason given for resignation or dismissal from the profession. By no means is this always the teacher's fault. Countless teachers, by transferring to another school, have turned unhappy and apparently unsuccessful teaching into effective and gratifying successes. Many boards of education have discovered that a secondary school operates more smoothly and accomplishes its purposes better with a change in principals. Of course, it is well for the teacher to do everything possible to get along with his principal, for it is more often the teacher rather than the principal who will transfer.

Successful teacher-administrative relationships are important if the school is to achieve its goal of meeting the educational needs of youth and of taking its rightful place as a positive agency of society. Failures in relationships may occur on either the administrative or the teaching level. Thus all employees of the school district and the members of the board of education must cooperate to analyze problems as they develop and to work together for their solution.

FOR DELIBERATION and DISCUSSION

1. Examine the code of ethics in this chapter. Should this code be applicable to school administrators? What changes, if any, would you suggest in applying it to administrative personnel?
2. Most school systems pay a differential salary to teachers with a master's degree. Is this a fair administrative policy? Can you think of situations in which a more appropriate extra-pay policy would be justified? For example, would a year's study in a foreign country for the art- or the foreign-language teacher be an acceptable substitute for additional college courses? Discuss.
3. The board of education in your school district has a policy prohibiting the acceptance of gifts from pupils. Your homeroom class presents you with a valuable gift at the end of school. What should you do?
4. The high-school football coach is paid $500 above the regular salary schedule for his coaching responsibilities, the yearbook advisor $300, and the debate coach $100. Evaluate this policy.
5. The school district in which you accept employment prohibits teachers from tutoring their students for compensation. Is this a justifiable policy? Discuss.
6. The National School Boards Association (NSBA) recently adopted the following policy: "School boards . . . shall refrain from compromise agreements based on negotiation or collective bargaining and shall not resort to mediation or arbitration nor yield to threats of reprisal on all matters affecting public schools."[6] How do such policy statements affect teacher-administrative relationships?
7. What suggestions would you have for revising the list of teacher expectations of principals discussed in this chapter?

FOR ADDITIONAL READING

AMERICAN ASSOCIATION OF SCHOOL ADMINISTRATORS. *In-Service Education for School Administration*. Washington, D.C.: The Association, 1963. This yearbook gives the reader an overview of problems and trends in the preparation of school administrators. Has general interest for teachers considering administration as a career.

ANDERSON, VIVIENNE and DAVIES, DANIEL R. *Patterns of Educational Leadership*. Englewood Cliffs: Prentice-Hall, 1956. Interestingly written. Contains many concrete illustrations involving classroom teachers.

ASSOCIATION FOR SUPERVISION AND CURRICULUM DEVELOPMENT. *Leadership for Improving Instruction*. Washington, D.C.: The Association, 1960. Valuable for teachers in understanding

[6] "U.S. Teachers Caught in Turmoil," *The Detroit News*, September 4, 1963.

expectations connected with roles in administration and supervision.

AUSTIN, DAVID B., FRENCH, WILL, and HULL, J. DAN. *American High School Administration*. 3rd ed.; New York: Holt, 1962. A survey of the entire field of high-school administration with focus on the principal. Part III discusses aspects of special interest to the teacher.

CAMPBELL, CLYDE M. *Practical Applications of Democratic Administration*. New York: Harper, 1952. An anthology centering on the dynamics of school administration.

FRANSETH, JANE. *Supervision As Leadership*. Row, Peterson, 1961. Excellent treatment of administrator-teacher relationships particularly those with central office personnel.

HICKS, WILLIAM V. and JAMESON, MARSHALL C. *The Elementary School Principal at Work*. Englewood Cliffs; Prentice-Hall, 1957. Although this book was written for elementary-school administration, principles of teacher-administrative relationships are presented so that they are applicable also to the secondary school. See especially chapters 2, 4, and 5.

HUGGETT, ALBERT J. and STINNETT, T. M. *Professional Problems of Teachers*. New York: Macmillan, 1956. Part II views the teacher in relation to professional policies. See Chapter 12 in Part III for an excellent discussion of the role of the teacher in relation to the administration.

WOODRING, PAUL and SCANLON, JOHN (eds.). *American Education Today*. New York: McGraw-Hill, 1963. Articles by well-known writers in the field of education. Provides the positive aspects as well as the critical in the profession of teaching. See Part III on merit pay and teacher responsibility.

19 Improving
School-Community
Relations

The public schools belong to the people, and school employees are agents of the people. Without community support no school and no professional staff can function effectively. And unless the community is well-informed about the work of the school, it cannot be expected to extend its support. Hence informing the public and winning community support is more than desirable; it is absolutely essential for the operation of the school.

A failure to gain and retain public support bodes ill for the future of the school. More than once a disaffected public has forced the removal of a principal or teacher or even the closing of a school, and many school superintendents do not have their contracts renewed. Although sometimes the educators involved would rather step down than yield on a point of principle, in many instances poor community relations have been responsible, at least in part, for the difficulty.

What then are the goals of good community relations? What are the sources of tensions in school-community relations? What part should the teacher play in the process? How can a good school-community relations program be developed?

GOALS OF GOOD SCHOOL-COMMUNITY RELATIONS

Although the study was made two decades ago, the results of John Hickey's examination of eighty-three communities and school districts still constitute one of the most important sets of objectives in school-community relations.

1. To inform the public as to the work of the school.
2. To establish confidence in the schools.
3. To rally support for proper maintenance of the educational program.
4. To develop awareness of the importance of education in a democracy.
5. To improve the partnership concept by uniting parents and teachers in meeting the educational needs of the children.
6. To integrate the home, the school, and the community in improving the educational opportunities for all children.
7. To evaluate the offerings of the schools in meeting the needs of the children of the community.
8. To correct misunderstandings as to the aims and activities of the school.[1]

An analysis of these goals reveals that three are designed to inform the public and three are aimed at an effective cooperation between school and community in developing the best possible educational program for the children. The two fundamental goals are "to establish confidence in the schools" and "to rally support for proper maintenance of the educational program." When these goals are met, the relations between school and community may be said to be at their optimum and the potential of the school for educating children effectively released.

SOURCES OF TENSION IN SCHOOL-COMMUNITY RELATIONS

Factors Affecting the Climate of Opinion

No school district is without a climate of opinion about the schools, and no climate of opinion can be made or unmade overnight. Rarely is the climate so bad and the forces at work against

[1] John M. Hickey, *The Direction of Public Relations in the Cities of the United States*. (Unpublished doctoral dissertation, U. of Pittsburgh, 1945), in *School Public Relations*, James J. Jones and Irving V. Stout (eds.) (New York: Putnam, 1960), p. 11.

the schools so sinister that the skillful conduct of public relations will not avail. In general, there are currents both for and against the public schools in any district, and school personnel can channel the forces for positive opinions by an effective public-relations program. This will require a correct evaluation of the existing climate and the factors affecting it.

A tremendous amount of propaganda, much of it adverse, about the public schools is spread by books, magazines and newspaper articles. Writers like Martin Mayer, Hyman Rickover, Rudolph Flesch, and Arthur E. Bestor find a ready audience in many American homes. Their steady criticism does much to undermine public confidence in the schools. Rumors about what the schools are or are not doing also tend to find a sympathetic ear with segments of the public. Reports that the public schools are "godless," "undisciplined," "socialistic," or even "un-American," no matter how unfounded they may be, can help create a damaging climate of opinion.

Who are the people that are willing to believe these patently false statements? Unfortunately, there are people in every community who look with suspicion at the public schools. Many recall unhappy school experiences of their youth—they were "left back," "failed," "expelled," harshly punished, or ridiculed. Many of them find reinforcement of their predisposition in current practices. Schools still "fail" children. Chronological age is still an absolute for admission to kindergarten. Others are adversely affected by the schools as a result of poor PTA meetings and pressure on parents to participate in school activities.

In addition to the suspicious public, there is a public which completely opposes schools. Some who have no school-age children oppose what they regard as excessive taxation for schools. Some whose children attend private or parochial schools oppose expenditure for the public schools. In short, there are many reasons why the climate of opinion, at least in a segment of the community, is adverse.

Issues That Divide the Community

Among the many issues that may divide the community are controversies between the school board and the superintendent about the use of school facilities, about the curriculum, about experimental practices, such as team teaching or the ungraded school. Federal aid to education, the composition of the school board, local sources of revenue to support the schools, selection of personnel, school construction, and any number of similar issues can be sources of friction. Often such conflicts are based on political, socio-economic, religious, or personal differences. For example, there are frequent controversies about the religious nature of a school Christmas program or a charge that a school is failing to obey the desegregation laws. On other occasions the battle lines may be drawn on the basis of political affiliation, or on the basis of support of or opposition to a strong personality in the community.

Whenever schools get caught in such battles they are damaged. It is therefore incumbent on those who work in the schools to anticipate, wherever possible, the onset of conflict and to ameliorate the issue—a feat more easily undertaken than accomplished.

Irrational Accusations

Among the most difficult and damaging problems in school-community relations are those which arise as a result of irrational and irresponsible charges, such as statements that school administrators and many teachers are subversive; that some textbooks and courses of study are un-American; that modern educational practices are linked with communism; and that public schools are the breeding ground of left-wing totalitarianism.[2]

A segment of the community is always receptive to such charges. In our society people are not always able to take a relaxed, logical view of these matters. Anxiety, rivalry, competition, strife, international anarchy, and general uncertainty all contribute to making the public receptive to irrational charges about the schools.

If a critic of the schools makes a serious accusation publicly, it is almost certain to be reported in the local newspapers and become a divisive issue in the community. At this point it is too late for the board of education to take effective action. Unless a successful program of school-community relations has succeeded in informing the public of what the schools are doing and in enlisting overwhelming public support, the irrational

---

[2] Adapted from J. W. Menge and Roland C. Faunce, *Working Together for Better Schools.* (New York: American Book, 1953), p. 11.

criticism will succeed in arousing irrational public response, and the schools will be severely damaged. Only the public can defend the schools. It is the function of a good program of school-community relations to insure public support not only in emergency situations but at all times.

An illustration may be cited here. In May, 1961, as a result of a series of attacks on the public schools of Fullerton, California, an investigation was made by the Personnel Standards Commission of the California Teachers Association and the National Commission for the Defense of Democracy Through Education of the National Education Association.

The report stated in part:

SCHOOL-COMMUNITY RELATIONS

Findings and Conclusions. A study of published statements and reports by the John Birch Society and other organizations representing the extreme right wing of political and social thought would make it apparent that such groups are active in Fullerton and Orange County. Many people in the community are confident that the separate attacks made on the schools and school personnel have been part of an organized campaign by these groups to discredit the schools. . . .

Recommendations. Extraordinary cooperative efforts by board, administration, teachers, other school employees, and all citizens who believe in public education are needed for a clear understanding of the schools' objectives, achievements, problems, and needs throughout the community.

A program to accomplish this objective might advisedly include (1) publication of a district newsletter as a means of reporting to the residents and keeping them informed about their schools; (2) an attempt to assist local newspapers to present more comprehensive school news accurately and fairly; (3) establishment of citizen committees to study various facets of the school program and serve as communicators between the schools and the community; (4) encouragement of greater parent and teacher participation in the Parent-Teacher Association to foster better understanding of the schools and to increase the PTA's effectiveness as one channel through which the community's desires can be made known to the board and staff.

It is especially important that the school districts and/or civic groups secure the guidance of experts in community relations and communications. Through understanding of the principles and techniques of effective communication between the public and its schools is not the common possession of educators or most citizens. Unplanned efforts in this field can waste time and public funds on projects of dubious value. Planned but unskilled efforts can be similarly wasteful and may produce results more negative than positive.

In developing a school-community relations program, the experts in community relations and communication should involve the community—through broad representation—in resolving differences in opinion about the role of the public school in relation to the community's total educational climate. The board and staff then can adjust the course offerings and course content to the community's goals with wisdom and confidence.

It should be noted that an effective public relations program should not be directed toward merely "informing" or "selling" the public about schools. The community relations program which the panel recommends should contribute toward a community dedicated to good schools serving goals the community itself defines and to a school personnel devoted to the community's aspirations for its schools. These in turn would enrich and upgrade the instructional program for Fullerton youth. To do less is to jeopardize the educational welfare of the students and the future of the community itself.

In this report, the panel has discussed some of the activities and policies of the school board, the school staff, the newspapers, and certain people in the community who have contributed to the dissension, misunderstanding, and fear which have damaged the the effectiveness of the school program in Fullerton.

While the tendency is to blame individuals or organizations, actual responsibility for conditions in the school system rests upon the community as a whole. It is the obligation of the total citizenry to assure that:

Enough citizens are interested in the development and maintenance of a superior school system to guarantee its achievement by becoming informed about their schools and providing adequate financial support.

Malicious gossip, ignorant rumors, and deceptive letters to the editor will not be circulated without challenge and correction.

Newspapers will be convinced of public desires for objective school news reporting, free from slanting or editorial comment which destroys confidence in and support for quality schools.

The community will not permit its resources and energy to be dissipated in conflicts created by groups striving to advance alien ideologies, narrow biases, or special interests.

Faith in democratic traditions and processes will be maintained.

The alternative to fulfillment of this responsibility would be quarreling neighbors, impotent schools with cowed teachers, and children who have been deprived of the fundamental knowledge and new skills needed to meet the challenges of an increasingly complex civilization.[3]

DEVELOPING A PROGRAM OF SCHOOL-COMMUNITY RELATIONS

Agencies

A favorable climate of opinion toward the local public schools can be created through the combined work of many groups, national and local. The National Education Association with its membership of almost a million and its vast research and publications program, can be very effective. Through its affiliate, the National School Public Relations Association, which publishes a newsletter, *Trends,* a digest, *The School Bell,* and a weekly report, *Education U.S.A.,* and maintains regional offices in every section of the country, it can disseminate information to the public about the schools.

The public needs to be kept informed, for example, about the reasons for rising school costs—the great increase in enrollment, the longer school year, the decline in the purchasing power of the dollar, the vastly enriched curriculum and its implications, the revolution in instructional methods and materials, the improvement in school architecture, and the rising standards of teacher preparation and accreditation. Each of these factors is reflected in every school budget and needs to be brought home to every member of the public.

An organization such as the National Citizens Commission

[3] California Teachers Association and NEA National Commission for the Defense of Democracy through Education, *Report of an Investigation* (Fullerton: 1961), pp. 24–26.

for the Public Schools which had a ten-year, high-level program to inform the public about its schools can be extremely effective.[4] The National Congress of Parents and Teachers, through its monthly journal, the *National Parent-Teacher,* reaches over a million readers. Magazines like the *Readers Digest, Life, Look,* and the *Ladies Home Journal* may reach twenty times that many, and it is imperative that these national media carry information favorable to the public schools. The National Committee for Support of the Public Schools, founded in 1962, by Mrs. Agnes Meyer of Washington includes among its active members Harold Taylor, James B. Conant, General Omar Bradley, John Hersey, and John K. Norton. It may fill the gap left by the National Citizens Commission.

On the community level there are many groups through which a public-relations program may be developed. These include the Chamber of Commerce, the real estate board, labor unions, the League of Women Voters, veterans' associations, such civic and fraternal groups as Rotary, Kiwanis, Lions, and Elks, the local chapters of the American Association of University Women and of the United Nations Association. Each of these groups is interested in better schools and will prove an asset if properly involved.

Principles of School-Community Relations

Before we examine the part that the individual teacher can play in school-community relations, there are some general principles to be considered.

1. The work of the public schools is a joint effort of the public and professional educators. Originally, school people regarded laymen as outsiders whose only function was to pay for the schools. Later came the necessary step of "selling" the school program to the public. Finally, we have the mature and workable relationship of involving the public directly and willingly in the work of the schools through advisory groups, study groups, school visits, joint undertakings, such as community sponsorship of special

---

[4] The Commission which was founded in 1949 by Roy E. Larson of *Time Magazine,* Alvin C. Eurich of The Ford Foundation, and James B. Conant of Harvard, became the National Citizens Council for Better Schools in 1955 and disbanded at the end of 1959.

school activities, public meetings, and a variety of school-community contacts. The community will leave professional decisions of curriculum and method to educators not because they are compelled to but because they recognize the wisdom of the procedure.

2. The school administrator should be familiar with the patterns of community thinking and with the individuals and organizations that influence thought and action in the community.

3. The teacher should be recognized as an important agent of school-community relations, and should be encouraged to build good relations with parents and public. The attitude of parents to the school will depend in large measure on understanding and approval of what the teacher is doing.

4. "Sound public relations must be *honest* in intent and execution, *intrinsic* in the school program, *continuous* in application, *positive* in approach, *comprehensive* in character, *sensitive* to the public concerned, and *simple* in meaning and conception."[5]

In summary: tell the facts; use simple language; reach all the people; keep at it all the time.[6]

THE SECONDARY-SCHOOL TEACHER AND COMMUNITY RELATIONS

Teacher-Student Relations

Even if he never has direct contact with any adult in the community, the classroom teacher is an important agent in school-community relations. If every secondary-school teacher had the ability and the inclination to do an outstanding professional job, it would be almost impossible to undermine community support for the school. There are many teachers whose devotion to boys and girls, to their subject, and to teaching is so great that they leave a permanent mark on every student. These are the teachers who build the school's status in the community.

---

[5] *Public Relations for America's Schools* (Washington, D.C.: NEA, 1950), p. 17, in J. W. Menge and Roland C. Faunce, *Working Together for Better Schools* (New York: American Book, 1953), p. 65.

[6] *Ibid.*, pp. 65–71.

For example, homework is nothing more than an extension of classroom teaching. If the latter is good, there is no reason why the former should not be accepted, even welcomed. If students feel a connection between homework and class they will enjoy doing work outside the class. If, however, the work in class is drudgery, uninspired "memorization and recitation," more of the same in the form of homework will be regarded as busy work and will be disliked by students—and, properly, criticized by parents. Homework also has its public-relations aspects. A good teacher will gear both the classroom work and the homework to the ability level of the student, challenging him steadily but never overwhelming him or defeating him. Teachers who delight in "failing" students whom they describe as too "stupid" or "lazy" or "disinterested" to learn their lessons are poor teachers and poor public-relations agents.

The devoted teacher is often a friend—warm, understanding, sympathetic, and realistic. These are the teachers whom girls and boys seek for guidance and advice in educational, vocational, and personal matters. These are the people who hear students' worries, thoughts, doubts, hopes, and aspirations. Parents whose relationship with their children is not easy or intimate often welcome the guidance that their children get from sympathetic teachers. Often a friendly teacher can help a student find a job or attain some other worthy objective. What these fine teachers see as nothing but performance of duty, the community may well regard as dedicated service.

Many of the personal contacts between students and teachers are made in the informal atmosphere of the school's extracurricular program. The teachers who volunteer for those services, who remain after school to work with small groups or with individuals, who accept each child for what he is and try to help him become a better person, are good public-relations agents as well as good teachers. Indeed, if one is the former, he is almost certain to be the latter.

Teacher-Parent Relations

The most common teacher-parent contact on the high-school level is the periodic report card which the parent is required to sign. High schools are adopting report cards on which the teacher enters both a grade and a descriptive statement, with the latter assuming greater importance, particularly if the grade is expressed as a letter (A, B, C, D, F) or as merely "Pass," "Fail," or "Doubtful." The report card also is a device to help parents and students evaluate progress intelligently and with the teacher's help to make the best use of the school program.

The teacher who finds it necessary to fail half or more of the class should examine his procedures. They are not only bad public relations but probably are educationally unsound as well. Some teachers always fail large numbers at the first marking period as a matter of "principle." Others seem to feel that the number of failures is an indication of "standards." There seems to be a relation between those who are "tough" teachers, who "pile on" the homework, who give "difficult" examinations, and who "fail" large numbers of students. Undoubtedly, as Kilpatrick pointed out, their students are learning to dislike both the subject they are "teaching" and school, even if they are learning nothing else. Some parents may consider this good teaching, but today most know better.

Direct contact between teacher and parent may be made through a letter, a telephone call, or a visit. Courtesy and consideration should be practiced on every occasion. Even when a parent seems misinformed or unreasonable, as is sometimes the case, the teacher should seek every means to avoid friction. There will be an opportunity to resolve the misunderstanding, unless precipitous action causes irreparable damage.

In any situation which is not directly related to the child's welfare, a letter, phone call, or visit should be handled through the office by personnel not directly involved. Administrators are generally more experienced than teachers in handling difficult situations involving parents. Of course, if a teacher has social contacts with a student's family, through having taught other members of the family or through mutual friends, he is in an excellent position to be a good public-relations ambassador for the school.

The most frequent source of direct contact with parents is a visit of the parent to school at a PTA meeting, at open-school night, during American Education Week, or at some other school activity. Parents may also act as chaperons at dances, trips, or school affairs. The nature of these functions offers excellent opportunities for building good school-community relations. Even the more formal teacher-parent conference presents a good opportunity for the teacher to remove suspicions, explain the school program, and win allies among the public. Self-confidence, honesty, and tact on the part of the teacher will leave even the most skeptical parent with a feeling of respect for teacher and school.

Teacher-Community Relations

The teacher is in contact with members of the community in a variety of ways. If he resides in the community, he meets and gets to know people in social, religious, civic, and business relationships. A reputation as an honest, conscientious, decent citizen will help build good school-community relations.

Teachers have perhaps overlooked the importance of working at this task. In the average community approximately one person in every hundred works for the public schools in one capacity or another. If all were aware of public relations, there would be a mighty force for translating the work of the schools into public understanding and appreciation.

Even the teacher who does not live in the community in which he teaches has public-relations opportunities and responsibilities. He can help the school public-relations program as a citizen in his own community. In the community in which he teaches, he can make opportunities to appear as a speaker or resource person at community functions. He can also bring members of the community into his classroom. Undoubtedly he can enrich his class work by arranging various trips and visits to places in the community which offer opportunities for supplementing and enriching his school program.

The secondary-school teacher may have pursued a college course involving general education, special subject concentration and professional work, completed an internship in student teaching, served as a regular teacher for many years and undergone in-service education—all without ever understanding his public-relations responsibilities. The intent of this chapter has been to emphasize for the prospective teacher significant goals and principles inherent in the development of optimum relations with the public, and to point out some important factors describing the role of the teacher in this effort.

FOR DELIBERATION and DISCUSSION

1. Is school-community relations a proper topic for study by prospective teachers? Discuss.
2. During public discussion of school matters, groups in the community have been known to hire professional public-relations firms to conduct their campaigns for public support. Do you approve of this practice? Why or why not?
3. By what process of reasoning do professional educators accept the involvement of laymen in formulating the educational program of the schools?
4. "Since the success of the football team is more important in building good community relations than the success of the instructional program, the former should receive more attention from the professional staff than the latter." Comment on this statement.
5. Should the school district employ a public-relations official at public expense? Give the pros and cons of this question.
6. Does it make any difference to a classroom teacher whether the principal is skillful or inept in the conduct of public relations? Explain.
7. How do each of the following affect school-community relations: (a) the board of education budget, (b) the hiring of teachers and administrators, (c) the length of the school year, (d) the curriculum of the school, (e) the introduction of new organization or methods (team teaching, educational television), (f) the school's winning the state interscholastic basketball championship, and (g) the school's winning the largest number of college scholarships in the state?

FOR ADDITIONAL READING

HYMES, JAMES L. JR., *Effective Home-School Relations*. Englewood Cliffs: Prentice-Hall, 1953. A practical discussion of all aspects of school public relations. The author talks to the reader in simple common-sense terms.

JONES, JAMES J. and STOUT, IRVING W. *School Public Relations: Issues and Cases*. New York: Putnams, 1960. In eight chapters the authors discuss each of the following issues and present specific cases illustrating various positions on these issues: school boards, finance and budget preparation, school plant, personnel policies, curriculum, instruction, and community groups. In the concluding chapter the authors state and explain forty-two guiding principles for good public relations.

MENGE, J. W. and FAUNCE, ROLAND C. *Working Together for Better Schools*. New York: American Book, 1953. Testing the premise that "democracy is based on participation," this book develops the thesis that the widest possible public participation in all phases of the school program will encourage good public relations and good schools.

MOEHLMAN, ARTHUR B. and VAN ZWOLL, JAMES A. *School Public Relations.* New York: Appleton-Century-Crofts. 1959. A comprehensive treatment of the entire field based on Moehlman's *Social Interpretation.* Gives philosophic bases and concrete illustrations of school public-relations practices. A basic book in the field.

NATIONAL ASSOCIATION OF MANUFACTURERS. *Our Teachers: Their Importance to Our Children and Our Community.* New York: The Association, 1958. A pamphlet by a very influential organization describing the importance of teachers and advocating higher salaries.

NELSON, JACK and ROBERTS, GENE, JR. *The Censors and the Schools.* Boston: Little, Brown, 1963. Describes in detail recent controversies involving textbook censorship, the individuals and associations who provide the leadership in the censoring of textbooks, and the methods they employ.

RAYWID, MARY ANNE. *Ax-Grinders.* New York: Macmillan, 1962. Identifies individuals and organizations whose purpose is to attack the public schools. Discusses their motives and methods and indicated procedures for minimizing the damages they do to public education. Originally a doctoral study at the University of Illinois.

STOUT, DORMAN G. *School-Community Leadership.* Dubuque: Wm. C. Brown, 1956. A thoughtful, logical, comprehensive presentation of problems in school-community relations by a sociologist. Contains much original material on both goals and techniques. Excellent end-of-chapter material.

PART IV: THE FUTURE OF SECONDARY EDUCATION

20 Unresolved Issues in Secondary Education

FINANCING SECONDARY-SCHOOL EDUCATION

Mounting Costs

The cost of educating a secondary-school student has mounted steadily during the twentieth century, and there is no reason to believe the trend will not continue. Three major reasons for the increase are: (1) increasing costs of commodities and services because of inflation; (2) increasing responsibilities assumed by the secondary school; and (3) introduction of methods, materials, and practices involving large capital outlays.

The momentum of the inflationary trend resulting from the wars and military preparations of the twentieth century needs no documentation here. "Expenditures for public elementary and secondary schools, excluding capital outlay and interest totaled $12.9 billion, or $390 per pupil in average daily attendance (1959–1960). In 1930, current expenditures totaled $1.8 billion or $86.70 per pupil in average daily attendance."[1] With rising costs of buildings, equipment, supplies, transportation, and salaries, school boards are hard pressed to meet their responsibilities in providing necessary educational services without adopting budgets that appear outlandish.

A second source of rising per capita costs of secondary-

---

[1] NEA *Research Bulletin*, 39, No. 1 (February, 1961): 26.

school education is the steady addition of services to the school program. To the traditional curriculum and cocurriculum of the high school have been added health services (physicians, nurses, psychologists and psychiatrists), education of the exceptional child (mentally retarded, physically handicapped, emotionally disturbed, and the gifted), cafeteria services, transportation, guidance, adult education, the all-year school, trips, and the like.

Third, the schools have attempted to incorporate technological developments into their work. The latest architectural advances—soundproofing, campus-type schools, flexible classrooms, more durable materials—coupled with such teaching aids as television, moving pictures, tape recordings, teaching machines, and language laboratories have increased costs considerably. These facts are not cited as criticism of the adoption of these devices but merely to indicate a trend leading to one of the unresolved issues in education.

Finally, the total cost of secondary-school education has increased steadily during this century because of the increase in the number of students. This increase has been twofold. Mounting native population figures have been augmented by waves of immigrants—the Puerto Rican being the most recent—adding steadily to our school population. But the largest factor has been the increase in secondary-school attendance relative to all-school attendance. Thus while in 1900 only about one in every ten in the age group from fourteen to seventeen attended high school, today the number is close to nine in every ten.

Taxpayer Resistance

With these facts in mind it is possible to understand both the magnitude of the problem of financing secondary-school education and the resistance which school budgets have been meeting during the past decade. The number of school districts which have defeated proposed budgets has increased at an alarming rate during the years since the end of World War II. This period parallels inflation and rising costs, a great increase in the relative and absolute number of secondary-school students, a virtual revolution in methods and materials resulting from the introduction of technology into education, and a sharp increase in the number of students attending private and parochial schools which has resulted in lessened support of the public schools.[2]

While the cost of educating a secondary-school student has increased steadily, we are spending proportionately less on the education of our boys and girls today than we did twenty-five years ago. If we consider the phenomenal rise in the price level and the multiplication of the gross national product during the past quarter-century, the cost of education, despite the added burdens, represents a smaller proportion of G.N.P. than it did twenty-five years ago. In fact, if taxpayers were to spend as much on education annually as they do on automobiles, our schools would be in a position to help each new generation in ways we know about but find impossible to implement under current budgetary allotments.

Substandard Education

By any reasonable evaluation a very large percentage of America's children are getting substandard education, and many are getting very little education. During World War II almost three million men (about one-sixth of those called up for induction) were rejected by the armed services for inability to meet the minimum military standard of literacy and health. While educational levels have been raised during the past two decades, we are still, as a nation, far below our potential level of attainment.

The factors contributing to low educational standards include: (1) a school year too short for the attainment of minimal education goals; (2) failure to enforce school attendance laws; (3) a part-time school day; (4) uncertified teachers; (5) dual educational standards based on racial and other differences; (6) a high percentage of dropouts; and (7) unsatisfactory curricula. Let us examine each of these factors briefly. In doing so, it will become clear that the financial factor is the key to the establishment and maintenance of suitable standards for all of America's children.

In thirty-nine of the fifty states the minimum number of school days required by law is less than half the calendar days in the year. In fourteen states the number is set by law at one

[2] James B. Conant, *Education and Liberty: The Role of the School in a Modern Democracy*. (Cambridge: Harvard U. Press, 1956), pp. 79–84.

hundred fifty or less. In many states farm children are exempted from the compulsory school attendance laws during the fall harvest and spring planting. Even more serious than the lax attendance laws is the failure to enforce existing laws. In many communities there is no machinery at all for enforcement of the attendance laws other than resort to the courts, and this is seldom taken. In larger communities the number of attendance personnel is often inadequate. In addition to the fact that truancy often leads to or is accompanied by delinquency, it certainly promotes illiteracy. Often non-attendance is abetted, encouraged, or even instigated by parents who seek the income of children through need or avarice. Others see the school as a state agency which they regard with suspicion.

Unfortunately the number of children on part-time school schedules is on the increase. School construction at the secondary-school level has not kept pace with the increase in school population during the past two decades. The solutions adopted have been large classes, double and triple sessions, or both. The effect on the education of the adolescent is often disastrous. Even the best teachers fail to reach the individual under these conditions. Many fall by the wayside, and standards are lowered.

Coupled with these factors is the specter of the uncertified and the incompetent teacher. The two are not necessarily synonymous, of course, but there is no denying the implication of the fact that over 70,000 of the 500,000 secondary-school teachers do not hold teaching certificates. Add to this an equal number who were certified more than thirty-five years ago, and approximately 50,000 who for physical, mental or emotional reasons should be classified as substandard, and we can begin to realize the difficulties of maintaining acceptable standards of achievement in our schools.

A more subtle but very significant factor in substandard education is the dual standard. The most obvious and best-known illustration of this is the "separate but equal" Southern schools which segregate white and Negro children. Most standardized tests of achievement have found the Negro child performing well below the white. The traditional explanation that the Negro is inferior in native ability has been refuted repeatedly in studies by reputable anthropologists, psychologists, and sociologists. As a result of the Supreme Court decision the practice of segregation will end eventually, but the basis of the difficulty resides in group attitudes and in economic power.[3]

School dropouts add appreciably to the number of semi-literate and illiterate people in the population. While the percentage of dropouts has been declining, it is still large enough to warrant concern, since one in every three ninth-graders fails to finish high school.[4] The problem of dropouts arises from many factors. In school, the factors are (1) intelligence (or scholastic aptitude), (2) reading ability, (3) failure to engage in extracurricular activities, and (4) lack of rapport with teachers.[5] This raises the question of unsatisfactory curricula. Too many schools are still using curricula designed fifty or more years ago with content and organization not suited to today's average secondary-school student. The doctrine that "if children don't like what they are being taught or the way they are being taught, so much the worse for them" can result only in resistance to education, premature dropouts, and to a defeat of the purposes of mass education in our democracy. If we are to succeed in having each person continue his formal education as long as he is able to benefit from it, it is incumbent on us to consider the backgrounds, motives, interests, and potentials of our students in formulating curricula.

FEDERAL AID TO EDUCATION

Most people seriously concerned with the future of American public education are agreed that federal aid is essential to the fulfillment of the task of educating all American youth to reasonable standards of excellence.

During the 1950's Congress repeatedly wrestled with proposals to provide federal aid to education. Despite urgent requests from school boards, from the American Association of School Administrators, from several departments of the NEA, and from many citizens deeply committed to the public schools, the best Congress was able to do was to enact the National Defense Education Act of 1958, which appropriated some $300 mil-

[3] *Brown, et al.* v. *Board of Education of Topeka, Kansas, et al.,* 347, U.S. 483 (1954).
[4] "High School Drop-Outs," NEA, *Research Bulletin,* 38, No. 1 (February 1960): 11–14.
[5] NEA, Research Division, *High School Drop-Outs* (rev.; September, 1959).

lion for scholarships, language teaching, television, and student loans. The money went to both public and non-public schools, but it did little or nothing for school construction or teachers' salaries.

Major opposition to federal aid to public schools comes from four sources: (1) Southern Democrats, (2) conservative Republicans, (3) the Catholic church, and (4) critics of the public schools. The arguments against federal aid to public education are that it would lead to federal control, discriminate against private and parochial schools, and increase the power of the professional educator.

In 1963, President Kennedy asked Congress for $5.6 billion for a four-year period of aid to the public schools. The bill specifically called for support both for school construction and for teachers' salaries. It provided formulas for appropriations based on need, so that standards in underprivileged areas might be raised to approximate the national level. Opposition has been stated by all of the four groups mentioned above, and Congress has not yet committed itself to enactment of the bill.

MORAL AND SPIRITUAL VALUES

Two Views

During the nineteenth and early twentieth centuries, the public schools ministered to the educational needs of American youth with varying emphasis on the moral and spiritual. The school was not yet regarded as the agency for doing whatever society was failing to do. The home and the church were conceived to be the proper realm for instruction in moral and spiritual values. The school was not, however, denied a partnership in this sphere. Instruction in manners and morals, building character, and development of a system of values were regarded as proper school goals. Bible reading, the singing of hymns, and the recitation of the Lord's Prayer were practiced and approved in most public schools. At Christmas, Easter, and Thanksgiving, plays, pageants, and other semi-religious ceremonies were enacted in the schools. The curriculum also included historical studies of religious developments, such as the origins of Christianity, the Crusades, the Reformation, and the foundation of various religious sects.

In recent years the controversy over religion in public schools has taken on a tone of acerbity, with recriminations that bear examination. Opponents of the public schools have denounced them as godless. The methods of John Dewey have been represented as inimical to religion. Requests that children be released from public schools for religious instruction have been adjudicated. In some districts, the singing of hymns in school is mandatory. The words "under God" have been added by Congress to the pledge of allegiance to the flag. Instruction in "moral and spiritual values" is required by some school systems. Indeed, the entire question of the function of the public school with respect to these values has become a no-man's land.

In 1962 the United States Supreme Court ruled in *Engel* v. *Vitale* that the recitation of a prayer composed by the State Regents in the public schools of New York was a violation of the Constitution. The following year in *Murray* v. *Curlett* (Baltimore, Maryland) and *Abington Township* v. *Schempp* (Pennsylvania), the Court was asked to answer the question: Are readings from the Holy Bible and recitation of the Lord's Prayer, conducted by school authorities as part of the opening daily exercises in the public schools essentially religious services, thus constituting an "establishment of religion" in violation of the United States Constitution? It answered in the affirmative.

Obviously the court restricts itself to the church-state aspects of the controversy and apparently feels constrained to rule that any mandating of religious practices in the public schools may not be permitted. Those who disagree argue that these decisions constitute a reversal of our traditional public-school practice and are a denial of the fundamentally religious traditions of our heritage.

As with other basic conflicts, it becomes necessary to step away, gain perspective, and examine the question as fundamentally as possible and that means a return to philosophy. Taking each of the terms "moral" and "spiritual" separately, we will find two basic philosophic positions at odds in defining them.

With respect to "morals" there is the position which sees them as a development of "mores," etymologically and culturally. Thus the matter of right conduct is seen as man-made and man-oriented. Man himself examines his morals, considers their consequences, contrasts them with the morals of other peoples, and confirms, alters, or rejects them on the basis of his own best judgment. The school is the agency for examining and constructively criticizing. Obviously, the morals of our society are not to be lightly altered or discarded. Hence the school will teach appreciation of and adherence to our codes because they are the work of man's wisdom and the result of man's experience. With changing mores, there may come changing moral patterns. Therefore our morals are regarded as subject to scrutiny and possibly to revision or rejection.

A second view regards morals as having their origin in the natural law and God. In this view the moral law is found in part through revelation, in part through conscience, and in part through reason. The moral code, therefore, is something sacred to be learned from earliest childhood, practiced faithfully, and revised, if at all, only when it appears certain that human error has occurred.

The first view may be called the humanistic. It is inherent in the philosophy of John Dewey and has a wide following among Americans, teachers and laymen, though few can describe their philosophic position precisely. The second view is the theistic. It is the philosophy of lay and ecclesiastical religionists. It too has a wide following among Americans.

Traditionally morals have been taught by each home and church according to its beliefs and by each school only as a peripheral learning. If the schools are to teach morals it becomes important whether morals are regarded as man-made or based on divine law.

With respect to spiritual values, the issue is more clearly drawn and not so vexing. There are those who insist that no education can be worthy of the name if it fails to minister to the child's spiritual nature and needs. The term *spiritual* is used in the sense of relation to the divine. Indeed, many believe that this is the heart of education and send their children to religious schools. Others either deny the validity of the term spiritual or take it in a naturalistic sense—that is, man is regarded as a product of nature and his inspiration is at one with nature. Still others accept the divine origin of man, regard spiritual instruction as important, but insist that this is not at all the function of the school but rather of the home and of the church.

Moral and Spiritual Values in the Schools

The nature of the dilemma is clear. The school cannot satisfy both those who regard the spiritual as non-existent and those who regard it as the center of education. Nor can it undertake to satisfy the religious dogma of any one group. The only answer is to find a common denominator that will take into account the pressing demands for recognition of the spiritual without alienating any group.

Similarly, with respect to the moral, the school cannot approach the question from a humanistic position without alienating those who regard morals as religiously based. Nor can it take the latter view if it is to retain the support of those whose outlook is humanistic. To take a religion-oriented position would open a Pandora's box of sectarian controversy and conflict. The issue remains unresolved.

INTEGRATION

Segregation in the South

The issue of desegregation of our public schools hit the nation with explosive force as a result of the Supreme Court decision in 1954 in *Brown v. the Board of Education* (Topeka). It had been apparent to thoughtful people that legal segregation was bound to be swept away sooner or later. Segregation is contrary to every tenet of the American dream and of the professions of democracy in our great national charters—the Declaration of Independence and the Constitution—and in most of our state constitutions.

Segregation had been practiced in public education in the South since 1876, and had been sanctioned, at least implicitly, by the Supreme Court since the 1896 decision of *Plessy v. Ferguson.*[6]

Even the NAACP, which has taken the leadership in bringing segregation cases into court, recognizes the difficulties of attempting immediate integration. A school population of over 6 million would have to be reassigned. Some 12,000 schools, both Negro and white, would have to be desegregated. In some pre-

[6] 163 U.S., 537 (1896).

dominantly white or overwhelmingly Negro communities, integration would necessitate unusual steps in redistricting.

Would the political leaders of the South bow to the inevitable and set in motion the wheels of integration "with all deliberate speed"? Would the advocates of integration adopt a moderate position and support gradualism? Would each side act in good faith? Enough time has elapsed to know that the answers to all these questions are both "yes" and "no." Where the answer has been "yes," desegregation has proceeded without incident, and schools formerly all white or all Negro, such as those in Lexington, Kentucky, or Washington, D.C., have brought both races together for common education and common welfare. But where, as in Little Rock, Arkansas, Prince Edward County, Virginia, and the states of Alabama, Georgia, Mississippi, and Louisiana, there has been a clash of wills, public education has suffered. In some places violence and intimidation have kept Negroes out of "white" schools. In others, state and local authorities have closed schools rather than integrate them. In still others, legal devices, such as establishing schools as private corporations, have been used. Sometimes whites have abandoned the public schools and sent their children to private schools.

By 1963 the mood of the Negro community had become sullen, hostile, and aggressive in the face of dilatory tactics of segregationists and apathy of large segments of the white community. Attempts to desegregate the University of Mississippi and the University of Alabama, mass picketing, sit-downs, demonstrations, boycotts, freedom rides, and a "Freedom March" by 200,000 people have dramatized before America and the world the determination of Negro and white integrationists to achieve equality of educational opportunity. The movement for equality in educational opportunity has been extended to housing, employment, and civil rights in general.

Segregation in the North

One of the by-products of the Supreme Court decision outlawing segregation in education was the disclosure of widespread segregation in Northern schools despite the fact that the law has prohibited segregation in these cities and states for more than a century. The Negro community with the assistance of many whites has pressed adamantly for absolute equality in education. This will necessitate widespread revision of existing practices in both North and South. The principle of "racial balance," adopted by Negro leadership, holds that a school is segregated if 51 percent of the student population is Negro. By this criterion perhaps more than a thousand Northern school districts will have to be desegregated or face heavy pressure from the community.

The Price of Segregation

The cost of segregation has been and is great. First, the basis of the decision in *Brown* v. *Board of Education* (Topeka) was properly psychological. The effect of separating Negro and white was not only to mark the Negro as different but to mark him as inferior. No attempt to pretend that this is not true can alter the facts. The perpetuation of segregation in public schools deepened this stigma, and these effects are not restricted to the Negro alone. The effect on sensitive white citizens who feel guilty because of the injustices meted out to the Negro is also destructive. On psychological grounds alone, therefore, the price of segregation is extremely high.

In actual dollars and cents, the maintenance of two school systems ("separate but equal") instead of one places a heavy burden on the taxpayer. Economists and educators in general are in agreement that the small school and the small school district are wasteful and educationally unsound. In rural districts where there are few children scattered over a wide area, the one-room schoolhouse and the one-school district is perhaps partially justifiable. But the multiplication of small districts and one-room schools because of enforced segregation is both costly and indefensible.

Finally, a realistic evaluation of the "separate but equal" doctrine shows it to be a fiction. The education of Negroes in the South, by and large, has never been "equal" to that of whites. The entire educational experience with its psychological concomitant and the inequality of opportunity in economic life has given the Negro child an almost impossible handicap. The economic cost to the nation of deliberately keeping 18 million people far below their production potential is incalculable.

The Future

Clearly, equal opportunity will not be possible until the first step of integration of all our public schools everywhere is taken. Any minority group—Negro, Puerto Rican, Mexican, Indian, or other—which is kept apart in separate schools or in separate classes within the same school, will receive an inferior education. And, though the struggle to achieve integration continues, large numbers of Negro children and children of other minorities are educated in separate schools or classes. A large percentage, perhaps even a majority, of white Americans, Northern and Southern, look with disfavor on sending their children to schools where there is a large Negro, or other racial minority, attendance. Enrollment in private schools and in religious schools is growing rapidly. In part, this represents an attempt by white parents to evade integration.

Equal opportunity may mean many things, but currently it means equality of opportunity for the Negro. Closely allied to this are the low educational standards of some states as compared with others. The adoption of a comprehensive program of federal aid to public education probably would speed up both equalization of educational opportunities among the states and among the races. At this time, however, the issue remains unresolved.

SALARIES

The Secondary-School Teacher's Standard of Living

The steady rise in teachers' salaries during the past half-century must be measured against the rising cost of living and the rise in wages and salaries of those in other occupations, if there is to be a proper evaluation of any change in the teacher's standard of living. Additional factors, such as length of school day and school year, teachers' college preparation, graduate school, and in-service education, and fringe benefits need to be considered to complete the picture.

In late 1959 in New York City, for example, a teacher in the first salary bracket earned $4,500 a year. Women accounting clerks (senior) averaged $4,576 a year, private secretaries $4,758, and tabulating machine operators $5,044; and they had no papers to correct, no lessons to plan, and no summer in-service courses to take—and pay for out of their own pockets. Also, their work week was down to thirty-six hours, pretty close to the in-school job-time of many teachers.[7]

A chart labeled "Change in Purchasing Power since 1904" accompanying the above article shows graphically that the purchasing power of workers in manufacturing industries rose 187 percent in the fifty-five year period (1904–1959), that of teachers in small city elementary schools rose 136 percent, that of teachers in small city high schools rose only 61 percent, and that of professors in large universities only 24 percent. In the same article the writer says ". . . No one can fail to see why there is still a shortage of well-trained teachers after a fifteen-year postwar campaign for better salaries." (The relative advantage in the salary of the elementary-school teacher over that of the high-school teacher is due to the much lower base from which the elementary-school teacher started in 1904, and the tendency of school districts during the past fifteen years to adopt single salary schedules.)

A recent NEA report indicates:

> . . . various studies have shown that the average earnings of professional workers are substantially higher than those of workers in general, and that teachers' salaries are far below the earnings of other professional groups. Until some real acceleration occurs in the relative rate of increase in teachers' salaries, large urban school districts will continue to be handicapped in staffing their schools.[8]

However, the trend of salary schedules during the decade 1950–1960 was in favor of the teacher. A report issued by the NEA describes the situation as follows:

> Average salaries of members of the instructional staff gained steadily in the past 10 years at an average annual rate of 5.6 percent. The average salary in 1960–61 is estimated at $5,389, greater than the salary in 1950–51 by $2,263, or 72.4 percent.
>
> The real gain in purchasing power of the salary is reduced by increases in the cost of living as measured by the Consumer Price Index of the U.S. Department of Labor. In September 1960, the Index, based on prices in 1947–49 as 100.0, stood at

[7] Sidney G. Tickton, *Saturday Review, Education Supplement,* Nov. 19, 1960, p. 66.
[8] NEA, *Research Bulletin,* 39, No. 2 (May 1961): 54.

126.8. In terms of 1947–49 prices the purchasing power of the average salary of the instructional staff member was $2,876 in 1950–51 and had advanced to $4,250 in September 1960.

Insofar as the Consumer Price Index is an accurate measure of increases in the cost of living for instructional staff members throughout the country, the real gain in purchasing power of the average salary amounted to $1,374, or 48 percent, in the 10 years since 1950.[9]

When such matters as length of school day, length of school year, and fringe benefits are added to the picture, the position of the secondary-school teacher relative to other occupations and professions has been growing worse during the past quarter-century. The school day will continue to lengthen as a result of the pressures for increasing the academic load of talented high-school students, and there is a trend toward a longer school year with many districts exploring the twelve-month year and Saturday studies. Fringe benefits vary considerably, but teachers are probably falling behind despite sabbatical leaves, fellowships, exchanges, bonuses, and similar opportunities. The majority of the instructional staff seldom participates in these benefits.[10]

The Single Salary Schedule

From the statistics quoted above the elementary-school teacher obviously has fared far better economically than the secondary-school teacher. Moreover, the tendency to close the salary gap between the two divisions is continuing. The National Education Association reports

> For 1960–61 the average salary of classroom teachers is estimated at $5,215, or 97 percent of the figure for the entire instructional staff. The estimated average salary of elementary-school teachers in 1960–61 is $5,034; and of secondary-school teachers, $5,500. Although the average salary of elementary-school teachers is lower than that of secondary-school teachers, over the past years the difference appears to have been growing smaller. In 1950–51 the average annual salary of elementary-school teachers was 81.9 percent of the corresponding figure for secondary-school teachers; by 1960–61 the average salary of elementary-school teachers increased to 91.5 percent of the salary estimated for

[9] NEA, *Research Bulletin,* 39, No. 1 (February 1961): 5.
[10] J. H. Kleinman, *Fringe Benefits for Public School Personnel* (New York: Bureau of Publications, Teachers College, Columbia U., 1962).

secondary-school teachers. Many factors may account for this decrease in the difference between the two average salaries: increased preparation of elementary-school teachers, more acute shortages of elementary-school teachers in the past 10 years, longer periods of service, and improved status of the position of the elementary-school teachers. Adoption of the single salary schedule for classroom teachers has facilitated the relatively faster advance of salaries of elementary-school classroom teachers.[11]

Traditionally boards of education adopted different salary schedules for elementary teachers and high-school teachers, with the latter receiving about 25 percent higher salaries. With the appearance of the junior high school some districts adopted intermediate salary schedules for the staff of the new institution while others placed all secondary teachers on the secondary schedule. During the past quarter-century, however, as a college degree became the standard requirement for certification to teach in the elementary school, the practice of a single salary schedule for all teachers having similar preparation was adopted. This is now standard practice throughout the country with differential for teachers based on preparation (bachelor's degree, master's degree, thirty semester hours beyond the master's, and doctorate) and not on the division or department for which the teacher is certified and to which he is assigned.

The single salary schedule has had a tremendous upgrading effect on the elementary-school teacher and, to a lesser extent, on the junior-high-school teacher. In Europe, where the secondary school corresponds roughly to a combination of our preparatory school and junior college, the teachers of the *gymnasium* or *lycée* are a class entirely apart economically, socially, and professionally from the teachers in the lower schools. In this country, while the gap was never so wide, it did exist. During the past quarter-century, as more and more schools adopted the single salary schedule, the status gap has narrowed.

Merit Pay

Most people, both inside and outside of education, who are concerned with the welfare of the profession are agreed that there is a much greater difference in the quality of performance of classroom teachers within each grade and level than

---

[11] NEA, *Research Bulletin,* 39, No. 1, (February, 1961): 5.

there is between the various grades and levels. Thus teachers will agree that a master kindergarten teacher is worth much more than an incompetent high-school physics teacher, no matter how much they might disagree as to the relative value of each were they equally competent. There is further agreement that in the typical group of one hundred secondary-school teachers, for example, there will be several highly qualified and several incompetents. Yet in most systems college training and years of service are the only criteria for salary rates. This obvious injustice is in sharp contrast with the incentives offered for superior achievement in business and industry. Furthermore, it may act to inhibit or at least to limit teachers' best efforts. Even if a teacher is devoted or dedicated, he may find it necessary to supplement his income by taking part-time employment afternoons, evenings, weekends, or summers. If the teacher is a master teacher or potential master teacher, this extra time and energy could be saved for the school, if it recognized his merit and paid him a differential on this basis.

Theoretically merit ratings and merit pay are the obvious solution to this problem. In practice, however, merit ratings have serious weaknesses. For example, in 1938–1939, 20.4 percent of school districts reported a "superior service maximum," but in 1961 only 6.2 percent had such provisions. In studying the causes of thirty school districts' dropping merit plans, the NEA discovered the following reasons: unsatisfactory evaluation, dissension created, ratings not based on merit, sense of injustice created, opposition by teacher organizations, quota system restrictive, burden on raters, partial financing cause of resentment, discontinuance recommended by a survey, and poor inauguration of the plan.[12]

Another interesting NEA study found that "management experts are divided on the desirability of merit ratings." The report states:

> No evidence supports the popular assumption that business and industry universally and successfully use merit rating to fix salaries. In fact:
> Merit rating as a basis of fixing pay is used by considerably less than half of the business and industrial firms.

[12] NEA, *Research Bulletin*, 39, No. 2 (May 1961): 61–62.

The firms that use merit ratings are most likely to use them for manual workers; fewer use them for clerical workers; and still fewer for administrative and professional workers.

Studies of the use of merit rating in industry show relatively low measures of reliability and validity.

Problems of merit rating in business and industry closely resemble the problems of merit rating in the public schools.

Many business and industrial firms are now emphasizing merit rating as an instrument for supervision rather than as an instrument for determining salary.[13]

Seemingly, attempts to institute procedures for identifying and rewarding superior merit in classroom teaching have not met with success.

Satisfactory Procedures for the Recognition of Excellence in Teaching

Satisfactory inducements for the attraction and retention of excellent teachers need to be developed. We do not imply that excellent teachers are not now attracted and retained in large numbers, only that their numbers might be larger if satisfactory procedures for the recognition of excellence were developed and applied. A number of steps are now being taken toward this end.

Team Teaching.   In Lexington (Massachusetts), Norwalk (Connecticut), and elsewhere, instructional programs for large groups of children are being developed and implemented by groups of teachers, assistant teachers, and teacher aides. The team leader is an experienced master teacher who receives special recognition and compensation for this excellence. One or more of the team teachers may also be compensated above the regular maximum for special contributions and excellence in teaching. Assistant teachers, trainees, and teacher aides are employed at lesser salaries to free the masters for creative teaching tasks.

Television Teaching.   Increasingly, lessons are being taught in all subject areas and on all school levels by expert teachers to large numbers of students by way of open- and closed-circuit television. Some of these lessons are recorded on tapes for playback. The expertness required, the preparation, and the strain

[13] NEA, *Research Bulletin,* 39, No. 1 (February 1961): 16.

are no less for the teacher than that for a commercial television performer. Paul Woodring points out that those television teachers who survive the pressure and competition of the medium will merit and will receive larger financial rewards and recognition as master teachers.

Recordings.   Language laboratories, teaching machines, educational records and films, and electronic teaching devices need expert teachers whose work will reach large numbers of students and whose compensation and recognition should be in accord with the contributions they make.

Professional Payment Plan.   Dr. N. L. Englehardt, Jr., in a report to the Greenwich (Connecticut) Public Schools, suggests this plan as an alternative to rigid salary schedules on the one hand and merit pay on the other.

> Every teacher participates in an in-service training program oriented to meet the professional needs *of the district,* not individual ambitions. This training includes such items as updating curriculums, visitation, research, revision of courses, and individual study of value to the district." Under this plan, a full-time "director of growth and development" with a staff of co-ordinators (superior teachers selected by the district and rewarded with a stipend) establishes standards for hiring teachers, sets up personnel policies, develops a system of evaluation, and creates an in-service training curriculum and a work schedule for teachers. Under the 1961 schedule in Greenwich the maximum was $10,350 with a Ph.D. in sixteen steps. Only two of some five hundred teachers were on this maximum, with the mode (thirty-six teachers) at $9,600 (maximum of M.A. plus one year in fifteen steps). Under the Englehardt plan the maximum of $12,250 in ten steps would be attained by one hundred eighty-seven teachers. They would be "expected to work at their jobs, as full-time professionals, twelve months a year and as many hours a day as it takes to get the job done.[14]

Other plans designating "career teachers," "experienced teachers," and "master teachers" are variations of the merit pay plans. They, in common with the plans discussed above, designate a minority of teachers as leaders in professional competence. The basic question of adequate salaries for the rank and file member of the teaching profession is unanswered.

[14] "A Break-Through in Teacher Pay," *School Management* (July 1961): 38–41.

SUPERVISION AND PROFESSIONALISM

Traditional Supervision and Administration

Traditionally the organizational structure in education is hierarchical. At the top is a policy-making board of education, which relies for the execution of policy on a chief administrator or superintendent of schools. Depending on the size of the system, there may be assistant superintendents, principals, heads of departments, and so on. Duties overlap, but some of the intermediate administrative staff are charged directly with the supervision of instruction.

Teachers' salaries, teaching assignments, promotions, transfers, leaves of absence, ratings, selection of textbooks, special assignments, rooms, schedules, and many other matters are often determined in part by the administrative and supervisory personnel. For example, a teacher may be required to submit written lesson plans to a principal. These may be criticized, rated and returned. Or a supervisor may be required to visit a teacher at work and make a written report on the teaching. The principal is presumed to be an expert whose criticism will improve instruction.

Conflict With Professionalism

In no other profession are such procedures followed. In law, medicine, dentistry, engineering, or accounting, once a professional is certified, he is assumed to be competent. His self-respect and professional stature are not demeaned by having another member of the profession examine, criticize, and perhaps reject his work. Of course, the teacher, unlike most other professionals, is a public employee. The question is: Is the best interest of the public served by denying the teacher professional status?

It may be argued that a beginning teacher needs supervision and direction. Indeed, most beginners crave sympathetic guidance and help from experienced members of the staff. But to continue the practice of supervision throughout a teacher's career and to deny him any participation in professional decisions about textbooks, courses, schedules, experiments, and teaching procedures is to attack the very basis of his professional status. Many, if not most, school systems provide machinery by which the professionalism of the staff is recognized and protected. Yet many do not, and virtually all reserve the right to treat teachers with less than professional status.

Although participation in professional bodies, such as the NEA and its affiliates, may give individual teachers some status in the profession and does give them opportunities for influencing trends, policies, and decisions, it is not a substitute for actual professionalism in their own jobs.

The American Federation of Teachers devotes itself largely to matters of salary, working conditions, contractual rights, collective bargaining, and similar labor-oriented matters. But, though these factors are important, they do not go to the heart of professionalism. There is, in fact, no organized movement among teachers to secure representation in policy-making in such professional matters as the revision of curricula, the scheduling of students, teachers, and courses, the adoption of methods, the use of materials, and educational experimentation. The question of true professionalism remains unanswered.

FOR DELIBERATION and DISCUSSION

1. What are the arguments for and against federal aid to the public schools? What are the arguments for and against federal aid to *all* schools–public, private and parochial?
2. Would federal aid to denominational schools basically alter the structure of American education? Explain.
3. What issues must be faced by a board of education which attempts to draw up policy regulation about moral and spiritual values in the public schools?
4. What are the arguments for and against salary differentials based on merit rating of teachers? Which groups tend to favor these plans? Which are opposed? Why? What is your position on merit rating? Defend it.
5. It is implied in the last paragraph of this chapter that teachers should participate as a matter of right in the revision of curricula, scheduling, and so on. Do you agree?
6. Which of the issues discussed in this chapter do you think will be the first to be resolved? Which the last? Why?

FOR ADDITIONAL READING

BLAKEMAN, EDWARD W. *Spiritual Values in Public Education: A Selected Bibliography*. Berkley: 1959, mimeographed by the author. Several hundred appropriate references to books, pamphlets, and magazine articles.
BRICKMAN, WILLIAM W. and LEHRER, STANLEY. *Countdown on Segre-*

gated Education. New York: Society for the Advancement of Education, 1960. Ten chapters on segregation—historical and contemporary, national and international. Includes a chronology 1619–1962.

_____. *Religion, Government, and Education.* New York: Society for the Advancement of Education, 1962. Contains articles on controversial state-church issues in education representing various points of view.

DEWEY, JOHN. *Moral Principles in Education.* New York: Philosophical Library, 1954. A good introduction to Dewey's mode of thinking about problems in philosophy of education. Develops the concepts of "moral" as a social phenomenon.

EHLERS, HENRY and LEE, GORDON C. *Crucial Issues in Education.* rev. ed.; New York: Holt, 1959. Selected statements representing various positions on crucial issues in education including academic freedom, religion, segregation, and curriculum design.

"Federal Aid to Church Related Schools," *NEA Journal* (May, 1962): 26–28. States the legal position as seen by the Department of Health, Education and Welfare and by the National Catholic Welfare Conference.

FELLMAN, DAVID (ed.). *The Supreme Court and Education.* New York: Bureau of Publications, Teachers College, Columbia U., 1960. Excerpts from leading cases on education decided by the Supreme Court since 1925.

GORDON, ROBERT, GORMAN, WILLIAM, JOHNSON, F. ERNEST, and LAKACHMAN, ROBERT. *Religion and the Schools.* New York. Fund for the Republic. 1959. Presents various viewpoints on the relations between public education and religion.

INSTITUTE OF HUMAN RELATIONS OF THE AMERICAN JEWISH COMMITTEE. *Church, State, and the Public Schools.* New York: The Institute, 1963. A pamphlet tracing historically the church-state issue in the United States and quoting authorities in support of complete separation.

KLEINMAN, JACK H. *Fringe Benefits for Public School Personnel.* New York: Bureau of Publications, Teachers College, Columbia U., 1962.

MADDEN, WARD. *Religious Values in Education.* New York: Harper, 1951. A thoughtful, original examination of the part education may play in developing common religious values in our culture.

Moral and Spiritual Values in the Public Schools. Washington, D.C.: NEA Educational Policies Commission, 1951. An enlightened discussion of a difficult subject from many angles. Contains examples of classroom situations and recommendations.

MUSE, BENJAMIN. *Virginia's Massive Resistance.* Bloomington: Indiana U. Press, 1961. Scholarly discussion and analysis of the desegregation issue in Virginia, especially since 1954, by a Virginia writer and human-relations worker.

NEA Research Bulletin. Published by the Research Division of NEA four times a year (February, May, October, and December). Research reports on a variety of matters of professional interest.

New York Times. The Sunday education page, has reports by Fred M. Hechinger and others on contemporary developments and issues in education. (Similar reports are found in the North American Newspaper Alliance stories by Benjamin Fine written in interesting popular style, containing factual and editorial reports in member newspapers throughout the United States and Canada.)

O'NEILL, J. M. *Religion and Education Under the Constitution.* New York: Harper, 1949. Analysis of speeches, documents, court cases, and other important aspects of American history from a Catholic point of view on education.

PELTASON, J. W. *Fifty-Eight Lonely Men: Southern Federal Judges and School Segregation.* New York: Harcourt, Brace and World, 1961. The task (and personalities) of the federal district judges in the South faced with the task of implementing the desegration decision of the Supreme Court.

Saturday Review, Education Supplement. One issue of this weekly each month contains a section on education—editorials, articles, letters to the editor, biographical sketches, book notices and book reviews. Sponsored jointly by SR and the Fund for the Advancement of Education.

SHOEMAKER, DON (ed.). *With All Deliberate Speed.* New York: Harper, 1958. A record of accomplishment and frustration in attempts to desegregate the schools of the South during the first three years following the Supreme Court decision of 1954. Factual articles by a dozen writers.

School and Society. Published bi-weekly (except in July and August) by the Society for the Advancement of Education, Inc., William W. Brickman (ed.). Articles, book reviews and critical commentary on the contemporary scene in education.

THAYER, V. T. *The Attack Upon the American Secular School.* Boston: Beacon, 1951. A long-time student of public education analyzes the issues and forces, particularly of organized religion, opposing the secular school.

21 Design for the Future

The following description of the schools of the future is based on a number of factors, some sufficiently developed to be called trends, others only straws in the wind and still others proposals and recommendations as yet found only in the literature of secondary education. All are probabilities which the authors believe to be on the way to realization in secondary-school practice. Obviously only time can tell which of the innovations discussed in this chapter will become fully instituted in secondary-school practice and which, either because of changing conditions, or inherent weaknesses, or some unforeseen contingency, will fall by the wayside.

THE CURRICULUM

Flexible Scheduling

The traditional secondary-school schedule calls for a day of six or more periods of about forty to fifty-five minutes. A shorter home room period at the beginning of the day and occasional shortening of periods to provide for a special occasion, such as an assembly period, constitute the only variations in most schedules. In the secondary school of the future, flexible time scheduling will replace this rigid pattern.[1] Large blocks of time, running in some instances to half a day, in others from one to two

[1] J. Lloyd Trump, *Images of the Future, A New Approach to the Secondary School* (Urbana: Commission on the Experimental Study of the Utilization of the Staff of the Secondary School, 1959).

hours, will be allotted for activities requiring these arrangements. For example, science lecture, demonstration, and laboratory sessions will be scheduled in a large block of time. Long periods for independent study and research may be found necessary. Large blocks of time will be provided for audio-visual lessons—television, movies, tape recordings, and machine teaching.

The organization recommended by William H. Kilpatrick, in which a common-learnings program is combined with specialized instruction, calls for approximately a half day spent in the common-learnings class during the seventh and eighth grade, gradually decreasing to perhaps a fourth in the twelfth. In this plan students and one teacher are together for a large part of the day. The remaining time is spent in special work in mathematics, science, languages, and arts with teacher-specialists in those areas.

Time for independent study, research, special projects, lectures, and demonstrations may be provided in the late afternoon and on Saturdays, for the secondary school of the future will be an all-day, all-year school. The variation in time scheduling also will include periods shorter than the present standard forty- to fifty-five minute unit. Brief teaching sessions, group meetings, guidance periods, tutoring, and other purposes may be served by bringing teacher and students together for periods running from twenty to thirty minutes at various times during the week.

The attention span of most adolescents is limited to short periods, and teachers even in the traditional school have found it necessary to break up a forty-five-minute period on this principle. The secondary school of the future will schedule periods for sessions appropriate to this arrangement. Further experiments in the psychology of learning and in the learning process will help provide the basis for variety in time scheduling.

Flexible Grouping

The rigid grouping of thirty or forty students in each class in the traditional school has broken down and will be replaced in the future by large groups, small groups, and individual instruction according to the demands of each situation. A television lesson, a lecture, a lesson based on a film or filmstrip, or a talk and demonstration given by a visitor or resource person can be scheduled for a large group, perhaps of several hundred students. Seminars and special instruction will take place with small groups of ten and fifteen. Tutoring, counseling, remedial work, consultation, and other types of special instruction can be arranged for individual student-teacher meetings.

In some classes, the grouping will be heterogeneous, in others homogeneous. Instruction in the general-studies program, with its emphasis on citizenship, democratic practices, and human relations, may require heterogeneous grouping. The home-room, lunch room, and possibly health-education groupings will be heterogeneous. Other activities demand homogeneous groupings. The secondary school of the future will have un-graded classes of highly gifted students in science, mathematics, languages, leadership, humanities, and social sciences—small groups which can proceed at their own pace under the leadership of specially trained, talented teachers. Homogeneous grouping of talented, retarded, and handicapped students has proven its value in the school of today. It will be continued and expanded in the secondary school of the future. The school will program each child for a block of time in a heterogeneous common-learnings class and will regroup the children into homogeneous groups by talent in special electives—academic, commercial, vocational or other—the rest of the school day.

Undoubtedly, the secondary school of the future will have extensive facilities for guidance. The ideal of a sound mind in a healthy body will continue to be the concern of the school, but in addition each student will receive expert help in finding and preparing for a suitable vocation and be directed toward a junior or senior college with a program of studies and extra-class activities for the attainment of his objective.

Longer School Day, Week, and Year

The typical secondary school of the 1950's was in session some five to six hours a day, five days a week, for a total of about 180 days a year. The secondary school of the 1960's and 1970's will move toward an all-year program, with a longer school day, week, and year. The normal school day may well run to seven hours, with many students remaining another hour or more for extra-class activities. Some students will return for school work on Saturday; others will take special work on a nearby college campus on Saturdays or in the afternoon.

The school day will be extended because students will be taking more subjects, and because they will be conducting experiments alone or in groups, pursuing independent study and projects of their own choosing, or completing individual library and laboratory research. Many will be taking work for advanced standing, special progress, or supplemental requirements, available by arrangement with neighboring colleges. The traditional extracurricular school program will be vastly expanded and enriched as a result of the upgrading of the teaching staff into the category of career professionals. The school will be open at least half a day on Saturday for extra-class activities. Saturday will also be the time for many of the special courses for students on college campuses.

The secondary school of the future will be organized on a twelve-month basis. Some will adopt the trimester plan now in use in an increasing number of colleges. Instead of a school year of some thirty-eight weeks with fourteen weeks of holiday time, the school year will run forty-eight weeks, with four weeks vacation. In some cases, this will mean three trimesters of sixteen weeks each, with a few days between trimesters. In other cases, the two-semester plan will be continued with a full-scale summer session each year for all students. At the moment the Fairfield (Conn.) schools are offering summer courses in advanced English classes in speed-reading, grammar, and creative writing; special mathematics courses in calculus and analytic geometry; laboratories for independent science experimentation under the guidance of the ablest teachers; intensive three-hour sessions in modern languages (a kind of scheduling that the normal school day rarely permits); and a number of special seminars in foreign relations, art, and music.[2] This type of solid, all-year high-school program will result in wholesale acceleration, so that the average student can be graduated from the junior college at approximately eighteen and/or from the senior college at twenty. The talented student will complete the work a year earlier. Since most professions today require at least several years of graduate training, there will be some alleviation of the

---

[2] Grace Hechinger and Fred M. Hechinger, "Should School Keep All Year Round?" *New York Times Magazine*, January 24, 1960. The Michigan public school systems of Jackson, Pontiac, and Saginaw have maintained comprehensive programs for several years during the summer.

situation by which many do not begin to be financially self-supporting until their thirties.

Summer sessions will see an increasing number of secondary-school students, particularly in the upper grades, taking work at the colleges by special arrangement between college and high-school staffs.

Integration With the Junior High and the Junior College

The senior-high-school staff—teaching, guidance, administrative, special services—will be in close touch with the staffs of both the junior high school and the junior college. Most communities will have junior colleges either directly under the board of education or closely affiliated with it. The staffs of the three institutions will plan curricula jointly. The senior-high-school staff will be in a key position for historical and practical reasons. As the oldest of the three institutions, its traditions and stability will carry weight. As the receiver and transmitter of students, its middle position will give it importance. Senior-high-school staffs, also will contribute a high percentage of the staff members of the community colleges. Thus a secondary-school staff of strong professional caliber will wield great influence in shaping the programs of the junior high school and the junior college into compatible patterns.

The object of this integration, of course, will be to coordinate the work of the three institutions so that no one is dominant. The senior-high-school staff will need to realize that the relative newness of the other institutions is in one sense their greatest strength. Since they are bound by no curriculum or other traditions, they will be free to experiment, and they will be anxious to do so. The work of each will proceed more effectively if integration between the programs of junior high school, senior high school, and community college are worked out. This is demanded for the stability if not for the very survival of the high school. It is safe to predict that integration of curricula will be a growing concern of the high school of the future.

Concern for the Individual Student

A greater concern for the individual will mark the work of the secondary school of the future. For a time, class sizes of forty to fifty with strict departmental programming placed so heavy a burden on the teacher that he lost sight of the individual student. The secondary school today is embarrassed by its former neglect of the gifted, its failure to solve the problem of the retarded reader, its inability to provide adequate instruction in written English, and its high dropout rate. Each of these problems is now under attack, and there is promise of significant progress all along the line.

The key to success in these and other problems of the secondary school—delinquency, lack of interest, improper programming, and so on—is the individual student. The school of the future will attempt to reach the individual from many directions. Homogeneous grouping, individual programming, expanded guidance services, provision for acceleration and advanced standing, small groupings, extra-class activities, early identification of special talents, expanded scholarship opportunities, well-compensated professional teachers, special studies of the social mores of the adolescent, renewed attack on the learning process—these and other developments indicate that each secondary-school student of the future will be an important individual.

"The largest single block to excellence in our schools," says Frank Brown, "is the lockstep grade sequence. The practice of advancing pupils arbitrarily grade-by-grade began a century ago, and it has been imprisoning talent and blunting intellect ever since."[3] A promising approach to the problem, is the increasing reliance on independent study in the high school. For example, at Blackwell, Oklahoma, the new senior high school makes independent study of all kinds the central feature of its design.

"Where and how does a student study on his own? Since most study halls are simply cavernous rooms lined with rows of seats or equipped only with chairs, tables, and spitballs, it is the library, or something very much like a library, that is the most logical setting for real independent study."[4] At the Brien McMahon High School in Norwalk (Connecticut) cubicles are being installed in the library to provide facilities for an increasing number of students found to be sufficiently mature (not necessarily talented) to undertake independent study.

[3] Frank Brown, "The Ungraded High School," *Overview* (May, 1961): 61.
[4] *High Schools—1962* (New York: Educational Facilities Laboratories, 1961), p. 38.

INSTRUCTIONAL STAFF

Types of Personnel

The instructional staff of the secondary school of the future will include several categories of professional and semiprofessional personnel. At the top of the salary schedule will be the professional teacher, variously described as career teacher, teacher specialist, team leader, master teacher, or expert teacher. The assistant teacher, an aspirant to this position, will perhaps lack only experience, training, or skill. He will have less responsibility in planning, leadership, difficult instructional tasks, and experimental procedures. He will teach for a lower salary, but his position will not be terminal, since additional experience and training may qualify him for leadership.

Lower in the schedule will be the teacher intern or trainee, who will be apprenticed to the experienced teacher while he pursues graduate work. Hopefully, the intern will have the ability and drive to move along with additional experience and responsibility to the category of career teacher. Some of the career teachers will become specialists in the general-education program, others in teaching in an academic subject area.

Another category will be the semiprofessional teacher aide, who will have less preparation for and less responsibility in teaching. The function of the aide will be to relieve the career teacher of routine aspects of "teaching." The teacher-aide will supervise lunch rooms or study halls, patrol corridors, keep attendance and other records, collect money, check homework, proctor examinations, and do all other clerical tasks connected with teaching. While each of these functions may have educational importance, they are not on the same level as curriculum planning, organizing and coordinating instruction, presentation and development of concepts, motivating individual and group effort, directing study, experimentation and research, analyzing and correcting difficulties, inspiring individual and group projects and, in general, doing the things associated with the work of the experienced teacher.

The secondary school of the future will make maximum use of still another category of professional—resource persons. These will include both full-time and part-time specialists or consultants. On the permanent staff, experts in health, guidance, research, and the education of the exceptional child will work with the experienced teacher. Community consultants, by occasional, prearranged visits, or with the more formal status of part-time instructor, will give lectures, demonstrations, or series of lessons in such special areas as science, literature, the arts, agriculture, business, language, and geography.

An inventory of the personnel resources of the community will be conducted by the school district, with a view to integrating community resources and the school program. Community specialists—for example, specialists in advanced mathematics, nuclear physics, biochemistry, creative writing, practical politics, human relations, and mental health—will join the high-school staff on a permanent basis to teach one or two special classes daily. In short, the instructional staff of the future will be far less monolithic in rank and assignment than that of the traditional secondary school.

Team Teaching

Because of the variety of categories of teaching personnel and the differences in function based on training and experience, it will be desirable to organize teams of teachers, with each team including one or more teachers from each of the categories described above. The team leader will be an experienced teacher able to assume responsibility for directing curriculum and lesson planning, organizing instruction, welding a team of teachers and students into a strong instructional unit, and providing motivation and direction for a variety of educational activities. Each team will include assistant teachers, teacher interns, teacher aides, teacher specialists, and resource persons. It will be responsible for the education of a large group of students for a long period, generally a year. Team teaching as described by Arthur D. Morse in *Schools of Tomorrow—Today* is already a reality.[5] It will be further developed and refined and become a common method of organization in the high school of the future.

Team teaching involves joint planning, specialization of function and contribution, and exposure of more students to master teachers and specialists. The half dozen or more staff

[5] Arthur D. Morse, *Schools of Tomorrow—Today* (Albany: U. of the State of New York, 1960).

members of the team will discuss aims, methods, and evaluation techniques. Each staff member will know the plan and will have participated in its preparation. This is a far cry from today's curriculum, in which each department is a law unto itself, rarely consulting others for joint curriculum planning and often working at cross purposes with other departments.

In the traditional secondary school, both career teacher and beginning teacher have approximately the same assignment, so that the former, like the latter, spends most of his time and energy on work that might be done almost as well—and, sometimes better—by a teacher aide. The team-teaching idea is designed to utilize the skill and art of the career teacher to the fullest extent and to make him available to a larger number of students and colleagues.

Salaries and Professionalism

The professional teacher and the staff expert will be dedicated people working full time at their jobs on a twelve-month basis, free from traditional supervision. They will hold advanced degrees, be recognized specialists in subject matter, methods, or both, be engaged constantly in curriculum revision and construction, experimentation, and research, participate in public discussion, publication, and conference reporting and, in general, play an active part in advancing education as a profession.

As dedicated professional members whose status is recognized within and outside the profession, teachers will be obligated to examine or to establish and to maintain suitable standards of admission, assignment, advancement, and tenure in the profession. They will be active in associations for accreditation of secondary schools and teacher-education institutions. Tenure will no longer be a shield protecting incompetent or unethical teachers and administrators. The body of professionals will protect students and the profession by putting into practice legal procedures for expulsion, and for implementing them without fear or favor whenever necessary.

Salaries of secondary-school staff members who are experienced teachers will range from $15,000 to $20,000 (in today's buying power). Those of assistant teachers will be in the $10,000 to $15,000 range. The funds necessary to pay such salaries will be supplemented increasingly from federal and state sources, and by foundations and private aid. Generally, foundation aid is given for experimentation and research, while private aid is for scholarships, libraries, equipment, and sometimes building and construction. Thus boards of education will find financial resources to compensate professional staff members at a level with their training and experience and adequate to command their full time and energy.

Teacher Education

The secondary-school teacher of the future will have a broad liberal arts education. Work in professional education (taken in addition to the liberal arts program) will consist of an approximately equal balance between course work and internship. In undergraduate teacher-education programs some full-time internship experience will start during the junior year or even before and become more concentrated during fourth and fifth years. A large proportion, if not an overwhelming majority, of secondary-school teachers will be graduates of liberal arts colleges. They will receive most of their professional education during fifth- and sixth-year programs.

The internship will give the trainee an opportunity to work with one or more experienced teachers, perhaps in a team, and to receive remuneration while learning. The intern will assume definite responsibility for educational tasks—teaching, tutoring, marking papers, going on trips, assisting in library or laboratory, and attending teacher meetings, conferences on planning, and school functions. Teacher education, particularly the internship phase, will be a joint undertaking of the college and the public-school district. The latter will pay the trainee a salary commensurate with his or her assignment and will arrange, in cooperation with the college representative, professional experiences and responsibilities as described in the preceding paragraph. The college will provide some field supervision but will be responsible primarily for conducting classes and seminars of a theoretical nature designed to give the intern a critical orientation to the history, philosophy, and rationale of curriculum and method.

Some of the theoretical course work at the college and most of the practical demonstrations in the field will be conducted by experienced teachers, supervisors, and administrators of co-operating schools. Many of these professionals will be pursuing work toward advanced degrees at the cooperating college. Studies leading toward the doctoral degree will be organized chiefly around action research projects, using the curriculum, students, and facilities of the school. These research projects may be conducted jointly by the faculties of the college and the cooperating school. Many of them will be supported by public grants—from the United States Office of Education or from state education departments—or from private foundations, such as the Fund for the Advancement of Education, the Carnegie Corporation, the Rockefeller Foundation, or the Ford Foundation.

The professional education of teachers will be a continuing process, beginning in college, continuing in graduate school, and progressing to experimentation and research in-service. Obviously, not all staff members will be able or willing to undertake work of this nature. Those who do will be the senior professional teachers in the highest salary bracket.

EDUCATIONAL FACILITIES

Architecture and School Plant Design[6]

Architecturally the secondary school of the future will bear less and less resemblance to the standardized beehive, with identical "rooms." Variations in size, construction, and content of rooms based on utilization of function will be the rule. There will be a number of large rooms of lecture-hall size, designed to accommodate several hundred students and equipped with television, motion picture projectors, and other audio-visual properties. These facilities will be in constant use, since large-group scheduling will be common.

There will also be a large number of small conference rooms designed for seminars, small-group teaching, committee work, and similar activities. These too will contain special equipment depending on the use for which they are designed. Classrooms of various size will contain library facilities, audio-visual aids, science equipment, and other learning aids. Students' desks will have built-in automation, including provision for radio, TV, tape recording, and two-way communication sets.

[6] See *High Schools—1962.*

The self-contained desk, as well as the self-contained classroom, will be common in a school situation where independent study will be the rule.

Equipment for Teaching

Many of the more advanced materials and devices formerly restricted to industry will be used in the secondary school of the future. Telemation will describe the kind of television and telephonics that will be used in teaching. Not only will these devices and materials be used by teachers but students will learn something of the nature and potential of automation in all areas of human endeavor.

The paperback revolution will affect every student. Textbooks provided by the school will become the property of the student. Each room or team area will have its own library of special volumes supplementing that of the school library.

One or more demonstration classrooms designed with one-way visibility will be used for teacher education and for experimental purposes. Teaching machines, language laboratories, well-equipped shops, and the most modern design for work areas will be found in all departments. Many of these developments are now appearing, and many more are on the drawing board.

Special School Equipment

Several aspects of the secondary school will be completely altered by developments now in progress. The school cafeteria of the future, for example, will be completely automatic, with a variety of hot lunches served, dishes collected and washed, money collected and counted, and the entire room stocked, cleaned, and conditioned, with a minimum of human participation. Automatic data-processing equipment will replace the tedious, time-consuming, inaccurate record-keeping practices of the past. Student programming, attendance, report cards, permanent records, health reports, guidance files, and other necessary information will be processed by automatic devices. The teacher time and administrator time saved by this equipment will revolutionize the organization of the school. Staff records —attendance, assignments, payroll, and the like—also will be processed through automation. Microfilming and other recording developments will do for spacesaving what data processing will do for the saving of time and energy.

Educational television (ETV) is already on the scene, and we may expect far-reaching developments in the use of both open- and closed-circuit instruction. The Educational Television Act, appropriating $32 million to expand facilities throughout the country is a signal for things to come in the expanded and varied use of this powerful medium.

A vast increase in the use of programmed teaching material may also be anticipated. Better programming, and educationally sound utilization of this method will free the teacher from drill and mechanical teaching, and place the student in appropriate learning situations.

The school library will be a branch of a vast network of resources united electronically, so that anyone can be in touch at once with the resources of all the others through a few major centers. Thus research workers will be saved countless hours of searching, waiting, and copying. Many schools will be equipped with a planetarium, a mechanical brain, an atomic reactor, and similar scientific developments, which at present are too costly to be included in the budget of the average senior high school.

Through trips and visits, through resource persons, and through the devices described above, the student of the future will be in intimate contact with the latest developments in all fields—industry, agriculture, the arts, and politics. The educational facilities of the future secondary school will be enriching beyond belief.

NEW EMPHASES

Teaching and Learning, Aims and Methods

Lest it appear from the foregoing discussion that the teacher in the high school of tomorrow will be merely a button-pusher, it is necessary to note the increasing reliance that will be placed on teaching as a science and as an art. The emphasis in teaching and learning will not be on the accumulation of facts but on the ability to study, to think analytically and critically, to initiate projects, and to solve problems. Teachers will be concerned with the learning process, with how concepts are formulated, with speed of learning, readiness, and similar problems.[7] Emphasis will be on the individual—his creativity, motivation, progress, and prospects. Student-initiated projects will be highly valued, independent study and research fostered, and a flexible curriculum followed. In this type of educational climate, teachers of exceptional ability and experience will be needed.

There is some evidence to support the theory that programmed material can greatly assist in individualizing instruction. With material appropriate for programming, it will be possible to permit each student to proceed at his own pace and to go as far as he can without the limitations inherent in group instruction. Of course, the mechanical process is not the only nor the most effective for individualizing instruction.

Research and evaluation studies will be carried on intensively and extensively to determine the relative merits of traditional and experimental procedures. In many instances, these studies will be cooperative ventures financed by federal, state, and local governments, by foundations, by private research bodies, and by educational groups, such as the NEA and the National Association of Secondary School Principals. In order to make this research more effective, it will be necessary to define the goals of secondary education specifically and, what is perhaps even more difficult, to devise new instruments for evaluating the outcomes of instruction on the basis of these goals.

Content

Of necessity, the curriculum of the secondary school will emphasize different content. Internationalism will be felt in all parts of the curriculum because the proximity of all nations in our "one world" will necessitate a better understanding of the history, language, and customs of other peoples. The United Nations will have an important part in secondary-school social studies. Language studies will be vital and important. Student exchange and travel also will have an impact on the school curriculum.

Developments in science will continue to force constant reexamination of secondary-school curricula. Advances in energy and space knowledge lead to emphasis on special units in earth

---

[7] Jerome S. Bruner, *The Process of Education* (Cambridge: Harvard U., 1961). A report of a conference of some thirty scientists and educators who met under the auspices of the National Academy of Sciences in 1959.

science, physics, and mathematics. The biological sciences, as well as the social sciences, will undergo far-reaching revision as research in medicine and in human relations progresses.

Guidance will have a much greater role in the work of the school. Each school will operate the equivalent of a career clinic in order to direct students along a path best designed to utilize their talents and interests. Mental health will be an important content area in the curriculum, since the findings of psychiatry and psychology can probably be translated into action most effectively in the secondary school.

Finally, the secondary school will be the strategic arena in which the findings of the behavioral and the social sciences will be taught and practiced in a growing content area called "human relations." Clearly, then, new teaching devices will be merely an aid, not a replacement, for the vital work of the teacher-artist in the future.

CONFLICTING TRENDS

At this point it may be well to reconsider and to reconcile, if possible, future trends which may be or which seem to be in conflict.

Homogeneous Grouping *vs.* Democratization

A great amount of homogeneous grouping will be found in the secondary school. Democratic processes will also be further developed in student-student and student-teacher (and teacher-teacher and teacher-supervisor) relations. Each group—the slow, the average, and the talented—will function democratically and study democratic practice. The false notion that grouping students according to ability is undemocratic leads to the doctrine that homogeneous grouping should be abolished. It is a violation of the democratic rights of each child to place him either in a group with which he cannot cope or in which he is prevented from moving forward at his best pace. There is no inherent conflict between homogeneous grouping and democratic practices.

Large Classes *vs.* Independent Study

Each of these tendencies will be much in evidence in the work of the secondary school. For part of the day or week a student will find himself in an assembly hall listening to a lecture, taking notes, or watching a demonstration, film, or television lesson. For another part of the day or week, he will be working independently—reading, pursuing research, carrying on an experiment, taking notes on his work, organizing his findings, writing reports, listening to recordings, viewing slides or microfilm, or doing one of many things that can be best carried on in individual study. Not only is there no conflict between the two, but it is necessary to schedule both kinds of activities if the resources of the school and the talents of the student are to be exploited effectively.

Mass Education vs. Individualism

This is another way of looking at the apparent conflict discussed in the two items immediately above. As the number of secondary-school students continues to mount, as large-group teaching and team organization become standard, the question "What about the individual?" will be raised with increasing urgency. All we can say at this time is that there are sufficient contrary forces at work—guidance, grouping, extra-class activities, and high caliber professional staff—to insure even greater concern for the individual than we have heretofore known. There is no reason why we cannot perfect the techniques of mass education while providing every facility for the optimum development of the individual. It is a challenge of which the secondary school of the future will be aware and for which it will be prepared.

Professionalism vs. Staff Categories

If we use medicine as a parallel, there is no reason to suppose that the existence of teaching categories—professional, assistant, intern, aide, specialist, resource person—will militate against professionalism. In teaching, as in medicine and in other professions, those most highly trained and most experienced will receive the highest recognition both in status and in remuneration. Theirs will be the responsibility for setting the standards of the profession. No weakening, but rather a strengthening of professionalism in education should be the result.

In surveying the prospects of the secondary school of the future, it is obvious that an exciting revolution in almost every aspect of its work is in progress. It is equally obvious that those concerned with the work of the secondary school—teachers, administrators, parents, students—are displaying the will and the resourcefulness to develop a school of the future that will meet its responsibilities to the individual and to society.

FOR DELIBERATION and DISCUSSION

1. Which of the developments discussed in this chapter seem to you to offer most promise for improving secondary-school education? Which the least? Discuss.
2. Many of the statements in this chapter predicting change are based on informed guesses. List the predictions in which you think the authors may be wrong and indicate why you think so. List some innovations in the American secondary school not mentioned in this chapter.
3. Some educators contend that the current transformation of the secondary school is largely a matter of "catching up" with the elementary school. To what extent is this true? To what extent do developments in the secondary school mark advances over past educational practice?
4. Compare the discussion of professionalism in this chapter with the discussion in the chapter on "The Secondary School Teacher." Are they consistent? Explain. How may team teaching be considered an alternative to merit rating?
5. Paul Woodring predicts that the television teacher of the future will be compensated more nearly like the star television performer than like the average experienced teacher. Do you agree? Why?
6. Will automation increase or diminish the professional status of the teacher? Discuss.
7. The trend in industry is toward a shorter work day and week. Can this be reconciled with the trend in education toward longer hours? How? What effect will this have on teaching as a profession?

FOR ADDITIONAL READING

BRICKELL, HENRY M. *Commissioner's 1961 Catalog of Educational Change.* Albany: New York State Education Department, 1961. Describes new programs of instruction. Advanced placement, team teaching, ETV, language laboratories, SMSG, large- and small-group instruction, use of laymen to assist teachers, teaching of foreign languages in the elementary school, and instruction during evening, weekend, and summer.

BRUNER, JEROME S. *The Process of Education.* Cambridge: Harvard U. Press, 1961. A fresh look at the learning process resulting from a conference of leading scholars, scientists, and educators. Analyzes structure, readiness, intuition, and motives. Recognizes areas where knowledge is lacking and formulates problems for significant research.

Bulletin, National Association of Secondary School Principals, 46, No. 270 (January 1962). Contains a number of articles on team teaching in secondary schools throughout the country.

"Changing Secondary Schools," *Bulletin,* National Association of Secondary School Principals, 47, No. 283 (May 1963). Contains articles on team teaching, the non-graded school, flexible scheduling, instructional technology, and curricular innovations.

COCHRAN, J. R. "Grouping Students in the Junior High School," *Educational Leadership,* 18 (April 1961): 414–419.

The Contemporary Challenge to American Education. Washington, D.C.: Educational Policies Commission, NEA, 1958. Makes basic recommendations in a number of areas including education of the gifted, guidance, improvement of teaching, and public relations.

DUNGAN, R. H. "A Junior High Summer Reading Program," *Bulletin,* National Association of Secondary School Principals. 42 (October 1958): 97–98.

GRUHN, WILLIAM T. "What is New in Junior High School Education?" *Bulletin,* National Association of Secondary School Principals, 44 (February 1960): 6–12.

High Schools—1962: A Status Report on Educational Change and Architectural Consequences. New York: Educational Facilities Laboratories. Detailed description of ten new senior high schools—some not yet completed—and the educational revolution they are designed to serve. Other EFL publications (obtainable on request) including *Design for ETV, Schools for Team Teaching, Profiles of Significant Schools* (a continuing series of which *High Schools—1962* is one) and *Case Studies of Educational Facilities* (a continuing series).

MILLS, ANNICE L. (ed.). *Programmed Learning and the Educational Process.* New York: Thomas Alva Edison Foundation, 1961. Summary of a 1960 conference at the Center for Advanced Study in the Behavioral Sciences. A careful statement about the potential of programmed instruction.

MORSE, ARTHUR D. *Schools of Tomorrow—Today.* Albany: U. of State of New York, 1960. Study of the most promising innovations in education, discusses team teaching, the ungraded school, teacher aides, educational television, and the master-of-arts-in-teaching programs.

The New High School by Editors of *Overview.* Architectural proposals for the high school of the future. Layout provides for programmed learning base, teacher offices, conference, seminar, large-group area, workshop, reference center, and house coordinator.

NOALL, MATTHEW F. and JENSEN LAWRELL. "Team Teaching at Roosevelt Junior High School," *Bulletin,* National Association of Secondary School Principals, 44 (January 1960): 156–163.

Planning for Schools with Television. New York: Educational Facilities Laboratories, 1960. Considers all aspects—technical, physical, educational—of EVT. Beautifully illustrated.

"Senior High School: Issues and Prospects," *Educational Leadership,* 18, No. 4 (January 1961). Stimulating articles on innovations in senior-high-school practice and theory.

STODDARD, ALEXANDER. *Schools for Tomorrow: An Educator's Blueprint.* New York: Fund for the Advancement of Education, 1957. An early discussion of the possibilities of ETV and the problems that must be overcome in its implementation.

STOLURNOW, LAWRENCE M. *Teaching by Machines.* Washington, D.C.: United States Department of Health, Education and Welfare, 1961, Research Monograph #6.

"Teaching Methods and Devices," *Educational Leadership,* 18, No. 5 (February 1961). Contains articles on teaching machines, foreign-language laboratories, and other aspects of educational technology.

TRUMP, J. LLOYD. *Images of the Future: A New Approach to the Secondary School.* Washington, D.C.: National Association of Secondary School Principals, 1959. A first report of the Commission on the Experimental Study of the Utilization of the Staff in the Secondary School. Contains many original suggestions on organization, methods, and so on, a number of which are already becoming common practice.

———. *New Directions to Quality Education: The Secondary School Tomorrow.* Washington, D.C.: National Association of Secondary School Principals, 1960. Sets forth eleven areas for improvement—needs of students, needs of teachers, grouping for instruction, flexible schedules, staff patterns, team teaching, organization of curriculum, educational facilities, guidance of students, improvement of staff, and utilization of funds—with suggested changes, suggested means of accomplishment, and questions to evaluate results under each of the eleven areas.

———. *New Horizons for Secondary School Teachers.* Urbana: Commission on the Experimental Study of the Utilization of the Staff in Secondary Schools, 1957. Considers ways of meeting the problem of staffing the secondary schools and of effective utilization of staff personnel.

TRUMP, J. LLOYD and BOYNHAM, DORSEY. *Focus on Change: Guide to Better Schools*. Chicago: Rand McNally, 1961. One of the most complete blueprints for change in the secondary school of the future by experts close to developments. *Study Guide* including bibliographical suggestions available.

VAN TIL, WILLIAM, and LOUNSBURY, JOHN L. *Modern Education for the Junior High School Years*. Indianapolis: Bobbs-Merrill, 1961. Chapter 22 discusses future school plant, staff, scheduling, general education, meeting personal-social needs of students, block-time programs, curriculum and elective courses.

Year Round School. Washington, D.C.: American Association of School Administrators, 1960. Considers four plans for keeping schools in operation throughout the year. Bibliographies.

Index